AF355996

Advances in Difference Equations

Advances in Difference Equations

Editors

Azhar Ali Zafar
Nehad Ali Shah

Basel • Beijing • Wuhan • Barcelona • Belgrade • Novi Sad • Cluj • Manchester

Editors
Azhar Ali Zafar
Government College
University
Lahore
Pakistan

Nehad Ali Shah
Sejong University
Seoul
Republic of Korea

Editorial Office
MDPI AG
Grosspeteranlage 5
4052 Basel, Switzerland

This is a reprint of articles from the Special Issue published online in the open access journal *Axioms* (ISSN 2075-1680) (available at: https://www.mdpi.com/journal/axioms/special_issues/Q347A8Q4L2).

For citation purposes, cite each article independently as indicated on the article page online and as indicated below:

Lastname, A.A.; Lastname, B.B. Article Title. *Journal Name* **Year**, *Volume Number*, Page Range.

ISBN 978-3-7258-2359-8 (Hbk)
ISBN 978-3-7258-2360-4 (PDF)
doi.org/10.3390/books978-3-7258-2360-4

Contents

About the Editors

Azhar Ali Zafar

Azhar Ali Zafar is an Associate Professor at the Department of Mathematics at GC University Lahore, Pakistan. He holds a PhD from the Abdus Salam School of Mathematical Sciences, Government College University Lahore, and completed his postdoctoral fellowship at Lodz University of Technology, Poland. His primary research interests lie in the areas of dynamical systems and fractional partial differential equations. He has contributed significantly to the field of applied mathematics, particularly in understanding complex dynamical systems and the use of differential equations in scientific modeling.

Nehad Ali Shah

Nehad Ali Shah is a researcher in the field of mechanical engineering. He is currently affiliated with Sejong University in Seoul, Republic of Korea. His areas of research expertise include heat transfer, fluid dynamics, and thermodynamics. He has served as a guest editor for a number of scientific journals. He was listed as one of the top 2% of researchers globally based on a study published by Stanford University in 2020.

Editorial

Advances in Difference Equations

Azhar Ali Zafar

Department of Mathematics, Government College University, Lahore 54000, Pakistan; azharalizafar@gcu.edu.pk

1. Introduction

This editorial concerns the Special Issue of *Axioms* entitled "Advances in Difference Equations". It is well known that difference equations provide an extreme and yet widely recognized representation of complex dynamical systems. The kernel of non-integer order derivative operators holds significant relevance as an empirical explanation for these complex phenomena. In recent years, the theory of non-integer order derivative operators has been successfully applied to the study of anomalous behaviors in both social and physical sciences. This Special Issue thus highlights high-quality research papers featuring novel findings, with a focus on the theory and applications of differential and difference equations, particularly in the fields of science and engineering.

2. An Overview of the Published Papers

This Special Issue includes 10 papers that were accepted for publication following a thorough and rigorous review process.

In the first contribution, several new types of partial fractional derivatives in both continuous and discrete settings are introduced. Moreover, some classes of the abstract fractional differential equations and the abstract fractional difference equations depending on several variables are investigated.

The second contribution presents new nonlinear delayed integral inequalities which can be utilized to study the existence, stability, boundedness, uniqueness, and asymptotic behavior of solutions of nonlinear delayed integro-differential equations. These inequalities can be used in the symmetrical properties of functions and also generalize several well-known inequalities in the literature.

In the third contribution to this Special Issue, a class of nonlinear ordinary differential equations with impulses at variable times is considered. The existence and uniqueness of the solution are given. Simultaneously, the classical definitions of continuous dependence and Gâteaux differentiability are modified. The results provide a foundation to study optimal control problems of systems governed by differential equations with impulses at variable times.

The fourth contribution deals with the oscillatory behavior of solutions of a new class of second-order nonlinear differential equations. Some new criteria, that guarantee the oscillation of all solutions of the dynamical model without additional restrictions, are introduced. This new approach improves the standard integral averaging technique to obtain simpler oscillation theorems for new classes of nonlinear differential equations.

The Special Issue's fifth contribution aims to describe the dynamics of a discrete fractional-order reaction–diffusion FitzHugh–Nagumo model. Acceptable requirements for the local asymptotic stability of the system's unique equilibrium are established. Moreover, it is established that the constant equilibrium solution is globally asymptotically stable.

In the sixth contribution, the problem of synchronization-control in a fractional discrete nonlinear biological model is investigated using the Caputo h-difference operator and an L1 finite difference scheme. Furthermore, this research revealed that the L1 finite difference scheme and the second-order central difference scheme may successfully retain the properties of the related continuous system.

Citation: Zafar, A.A. Advances in Difference Equations. *Axioms* **2024**, *13*, 651. https://doi.org/10.3390/axioms13090651

Received: 19 September 2024
Accepted: 20 September 2024
Published: 22 September 2024

In the seventh contribution to this Special Issue, topological degree and fixed point theorems are applied to investigate the existence, uniqueness, and multiplicity of solutions for a boundary value problem associated with a fractional-order difference equation. The results are validated by the provision of appropriate examples.

In eighth contribution, the qualitative properties of solutions to a general difference equation are investigated. Necessary and sufficient conditions for the existence of prime period-two and period-three solutions are provided. Furthermore, the boundedness and global stability of the solutions is investigated.

The ninth contribution forwards a neural network approach based on Lie series in Lie groups of differential equations to solve Burgers–Huxley nonlinear partial differential equations, where initial or boundary value terms in loss functions are investigated. The proposed technique yields closed analytic solutions that possess excellent generalization properties. Moreover, a thorough comparison with its exact solution is carried out to validate the practicality and effectiveness of the proposed method, using vivid graphics and detailed analysis.

Finally, the tenth contribution to this Issue offers novel adequate conditions for difference equations with forcing, positive, and negative terms to ensure non-oscillatory solutions. To help establish the main results, an analogous representation for the main equation, called a Volterra-type summation equation, is constructed. Two numerical examples are provided to demonstrate the validity of the theoretical findings.

Conflicts of Interest: The author declares no conflicts of interest.

List of Contributions:

1. Kostić, M. Multidimensional Fractional Calculus: Theory and Applications. *Axioms* **2024**, *13*, 623. https://doi.org/10.3390/axioms13090623
2. Samar, M.; Zhu, X.; Shakoor, A.; Osman, M. New Nonlinear Retarded Integral Inequalities and Their Applications to Nonlinear Retarded Integro-Differential Equations. *Axioms* **2024**, *13*, 356. https://doi.org/10.3390/axioms13060356
3. Xia, H.; Peng, Y.; Zhang, P. Existence and Properties of the Solution of Nonlinear Differential Equations with Impulses at Variable Times. *Axioms* **2024**, *13*, 126. https://doi.org/10.3390/axioms13020126
4. Al-Jaser, A.; Qaraad, B.; Ramos, H.; Serra-Capizzano, S. New Conditions for Testing the Oscillation of Solutions of Second-Order Nonlinear Differential Equations with Damped Term. *Axioms* **2024**, *13*, 105. https://doi.org/10.3390/axioms13020105
5. Hamadneh, T.; Hioual, A.; Alsayyed, O.; Al-Khassawneh, Y.A.; Al-Husban, A.; Ouannas, A. The FitzHugh–Nagumo Model Described by Fractional Difference Equations: Stability and Numerical Simulation. *Axioms* **2023**, *12*, 806. https://doi.org/10.3390/axioms12090806
6. Abu Falahah, I.; Hioual, A.; Al-Qadri, M.O.; AL-Khassawneh, Y.A.; Al-Husban, A.; Hamadneh, T.; Ouannas, A. Synchronization of Fractional Partial Difference Equations via Linear Methods. *Axioms* **2023**, *12*, 728. https://doi.org/10.3390/axioms12080728
7. Lv, Z.; Wu, C.; O'Regan, D.; Xu, J. Solvability of a Boundary Value Problem Involving Fractional Difference Equations. *Axioms* **2023**, *12*, 650. https://doi.org/10.3390/axioms12070650
8. Moaaz, O.; Altuwaijri, A.A. The Dynamics of a General Model of the Nonlinear Difference Equation and Its Applications. *Axioms* **2023**, *12*, 598. https://doi.org/10.3390/axioms12060598
9. Wen, Y.; Chaolu, T. Study of Burgers–Huxley Equation Using Neural Network Method. *Axioms* **2023**, *12*, 429. https://doi.org/10.3390/axioms12050429
10. Alzabut, J.; Grace, S.R.; Jonnalagadda, J.M.; Santra, S.S.; Abdalla, B. Higher-Order Nabla Difference Equations of Arbitrary Order with Forcing, Positive and Negative Terms: Non-Oscillatory Solutions. *Axioms* **2023**, *12*, 325. https://doi.org/10.3390/axioms12040325

Article

Multidimensional Fractional Calculus: Theory and Applications

Marko Kostić

Faculty of Technical Sciences, University of Novi Sad, Trg D. Obradovića 6, 21125 Novi Sad, Serbia; marco.s@verat.net

Abstract: In this paper, we introduce several new types of partial fractional derivatives in the continuous setting and the discrete setting. We analyze some classes of the abstract fractional differential equations and the abstract fractional difference equations depending on several variables, providing a great number of structural results, useful remarks and illustrative examples. Concerning some specific applications, we would like to mention here our investigation of the fractional partial differential inclusions with Riemann–Liouville and Caputo derivatives. We also establish the complex characterization theorem for the multidimensional vector-valued Laplace transform and provide certain applications.

Keywords: multidimensional fractional calculus; multidimensional discrete fractional calculus; multidimensional generalized Weyl fractional calculus; abstract partial fractional differential equations; abstract partial fractional difference equations; multidimensional vector-valued Laplace transform; multivalued linear operators

MSC: 26A33; 39A14; 45D05; 39A99; 47D99

Citation: Kostić, M. Multidimensional Fractional Calculus: Theory and Applications. *Axioms* **2024**, *13*, 623. https://doi.org/10.3390/axioms13090623

Academic Editors: Azhar Ali Zafar and Nehad Ali Shah

Received: 28 July 2024
Revised: 29 August 2024
Accepted: 10 September 2024
Published: 12 September 2024

1. Introduction and Preliminaries

Fractional calculus is an important field of theoretical and applied mathematics which generalizes the classical differential and integral calculus with the operations of integration and differentiation of noninteger order. Fractional calculus and fractional differential equations have earned considerable popularity and importance in the past few decades in various fields of applied science; for further information in this direction, see [1–8] and the references quoted therein. We will only mention here that fractional differential equations are invaluable and important in modeling of various phenomena appearing in mathematical physics, viscoelasticity, optics, acoustics, rheology, bioengineering, control theory, electrical and mechanical engineering and so on.

Discrete fractional calculus is also a rapidly developing branch of mathematics. The first serious study of discrete fractional differences can be attributed to F. Atici and P. Eloe ([9], 2009); for more details about this topic, we refer the reader to the research monograph [10] by C. Goodrich and A. C. Peterson, and the references quoted therein. Fractional difference equations are extremely useful in modeling discrete phenomena in different fields such as economics, physics, engineering and biology, and undoubtedly, there is a vast literature on them; for example, T. Zhang and Y. Li [11] recently analyzed the global exponential stability of discrete-time almost automorphic Caputo–Fabrizio BAM fuzzy neural networks (it would be very difficult to summarize and quote here all relevant references concerning discrete fractional calculus and its applications). The stability, boundedness, periodicity and asymptotic behavior of solutions for various classes of the fractional difference equations are very well explored by now. Concerning the existence and uniqueness of almost periodic solutions to the abstract fractional difference equations and the abstract Volterra difference equations, we refer the reader to the research monograph [12] and the list of references quoted therein.

The partial fractional derivatives of functions have not attracted as much attention of the authors working in the field of fractional calculus to date. With the exception of the structural theory developed in Chapter 5 of the fundamental research monograph [7] by S. G. Samko, A. A. Kilbas and O. I. Marichev and some structural results about the partial fractional differential equations given in Chapter 7 in the fundamental research monograph [4] by A. A. Kilbas, M. Srivastava and J. J. Trujillo, we can freely say that almost all established results about partial fractional derivatives of functions and partial fractional differential equations given to date are rather fragmentary and concern some very special kinds of functions and partial fractional differential equations. In this research study, we tried to overcome the shortcomings of existing research by investigating many interesting topics that have not attracted the attention of authors working in the field of fractional calculus yet; for example, we initiated the study of the abstract partial fractional differential-difference inclusions with multivalued linear operators here (the multidimensional Laplace transform of functions with values in complex Banach spaces is also a very unexplored chapter of the theory of integral transforms).

For example, H. M. Srivastava, R. C. Singh Chandel and P. K. Vishwakarma analyzed, in [13], the partial fractional derivatives of certain generalized hypergeometric functions of several variables (see also [14]); the partial fractional differential equations with Riesz space fractional derivatives of positive real order (see [7] (Section 25, p. 357) for the notion and more details) were analyzed by H. Jiang et al. in [15] (see also [16]). It is also worth mentioning the recent research article [17] by V. Pilipauskaitė and D. Surgailis, where the authors analyzed certain fractional operators and fractionally integrated random fields on $\mathbb{Z}^n$. Further on, M. O. Mamchuev [18] and A. V. Pshku [19] considered the systems of multidimensional fractional partial differential equations containing the terms of form $D_{x_j}^{\alpha_j} u(x_1, ..., x_n)$ with just one index $j \in \mathbb{N}_n$ and not the general forms of partial fractional derivatives introduced in this paper. More precisely, A. V. Pshku considered, in [19], the well-posedness of the following multidimensional fractional partial differential equation:

$$\sum_{k=1}^{n} a_k \frac{\partial^{\sigma_k}}{\partial x_k^{\sigma_k}} u(x) + \lambda u(x) = f(x), \quad x \in [0, \infty)^n, \tag{1}$$

where $(\partial^{\sigma_k} / \partial x_k^{\sigma_k} u)$ denotes the fractional partial derivative of order σ_k with respect to the variable x_k with origin $x_k = 0$ (in the sense of the Riemann–Liouville, Caputo or Dzhrbashyan–Nersesyan approach); here $a_k > 0$ for $1 \le k \le n$, $\lambda \in \mathbb{R}$ and $f(\cdot)$ is a locally integrable function. We also refer the reader to the works mentioned in [7] (pp. 623–624) and some recent results about nonlinear fractional partial differential equations obtained in [20–25].

The structure and main ideas of this paper can be briefly summarized as follows. First of all, we explain the notation and terminology used throughout the paper and recall the basic facts about the generalized Hilfer fractional derivatives and differences (cf. Section 1.1). Section 2 examines the multidimensional generalized Hilfer fractional derivatives and differences. We first introduce the notion of a multidimensional generalized Hilfer fractional derivative $\mathbb{D}_{\mathbf{a,b}}^{\alpha} u$ for a class of locally integrable functions $u : [0, \infty)^n \to X$; here and hereafter, $(X, \| \cdot \|)$ denotes a complex Banach space. After that, we introduce the multidimensional generalized Hilfer fractional discrete derivative $\mathbb{D}_{\mathbf{a,b}}^{\alpha} u$, for any sequence $u : \mathbb{N}_0^n \to X$. It seems that the notion introduced in this section is not considered elsewhere in the existing literature, even for the Riemann–Liouville or Caputo fractional derivatives.

Section 3, which is broken down into two subsections, examines the multidimensional generalized Weyl fractional derivatives and differences. The first subsection investigates the generalized Weyl fractional derivatives and differences in the one-dimensional setting. In Definition 3, we introduce the notion of a generalized Weyl fractional derivative $D_W^{\alpha, a} u$ of function $u(\cdot)$. After that, we examine the basic structural properties of the introduced fractional derivatives. If $a : \mathbb{N}_0 \to \mathbb{C}$ and $f : \mathbb{Z} \to X$ are given sequences, then we define the Weyl fractional difference operator $\Delta_{W,a,m} f$. We show that the approach of R. Hilfer [3] is meaningless for the definitions of Weyl fractional derivatives and differences.

The second subsection investigates the generalized Weyl fractional derivatives and differences in the multidimensional setting (concerning some predecessors of this work, we would like to mention here the research articles [26] by V. B. L. Chaurasia and R. S. Dubey, [27] by S. P. Goyal and Trilok Mathur, [28] by B. B. Jaimini and H. Nagar and [29] by R. K. Raina; see also the lists of references quoted therein). We first introduce the notion of a generalized Weyl $(\alpha, \mathbf{a})$-fractional derivative $\mathbb{D}_W^{\alpha,\mathbf{a}} u$; a very special case of the partial fractional derivative $\mathbb{D}_W^{\alpha,\mathbf{a}} u$ is the generalized Weyl $(\alpha, \mathbf{a})$-fractional derivative $\mathbb{D}_W^{\alpha} u$. After that, if the sequences $a_j : \mathbb{N}_0 \to \mathbb{C}$ and $u : \mathbb{Z}^n \to X$ are given and $m_j \in \mathbb{N}$ is a given integer $(1 \le j \le n)$, then we introduce the multidimensional Weyl fractional difference operator $\mathbb{D}_{W,\mathbf{a},\mathbf{m}} u$. We investigate the law of exponents for generalized Weyl derivatives and integrals and provide an interesting open problem about the generation of C-regularized solution operator families by the Weyl fractional differential operators with constant coefficients. Furthermore, we reconsider the well-known Clairaut's theorem on equality of mixed partial derivatives (sometimes also called Schwartz's theorem or Young's theorem) in the fractional setting and prove that it is not valid for the Riemann–Liouville and Caputo fractional derivatives (see [7], p. 342) for the first results established in this direction) as well as that it is valid for the Weyl fractional derivatives under certain reasonable assumptions.

In Section 4, we introduce and analyze the partial fractional derivatives of functions defined on some special regions in $\mathbb{R}^n$ and the partial fractional differences of sequences defined on some special subsets of $\mathbb{Z}^n$ (we tried to furnish an illustrative example for each partial fractional derivative introduced in this paper; unfortunately, in the present situation, we cannot precisely explain the physical meaning for each partial fractional derivative introduced here). Further on, the investigation of two-dimensional scalar-valued Laplace transform starts probably with the works of D. L. Bernstein [30,31] and J. C. Jaeger [32] (1939–1941); for more details about the multidimensional scalar-valued Laplace transform and its applications to (fractional) partial integro-differential equations, we refer the reader to the research articles [33–38] and the doctoral dissertations [39–41]. For the purpose of our investigations of the partial fractional integro-differential inclusions, we provide the basic details and results about the multidimensional vector-valued Laplace transform in Section 5 (we will systematically analyze multidimensional vector-valued Laplace transform elsewhere). Our main structural result established in this section is Theorem 1, where we clarify the complex inversion theorem for the multidimensional vector-valued Laplace transform.

The fractional partial differential inclusions with Riemann–Liouville and Caputo derivatives are investigated in Section 6.1, whose main results are Theorems 2 and 3 (cf. also Remarks 3 and 4); Section 6.2, whose main result is Theorem 4, investigates the abstract multiterm fractional partial differential equations with Riemann–Liouville and Caputo derivatives, while Section 6.3 investigates the fractional partial difference equations with generalized Weyl derivatives. Many other types of fractional partial differential-difference equations will be considered in [12].

We introduce many new types of partial fractional derivatives in this paper. Before fixing the notation and explaining some preliminaries, we would like to emphasize that it is our duty to say that the motivation behind our innovations is still not sufficiently explained as well as that future research studies should shed a light on these new concepts.

Notation and terminology. In the sequel, we will always assume that m, $n \in \mathbb{N}$, $(X, \|\cdot\|)$ is a complex Banach space, $L(X)$ is the Banach space of all bounded linear operators on X and $C \in L(X)$; $\mathbb{N}_n := \{1, ..., n\}$, $\mathbb{N}_0^n := \{0, 1, ..., n\}$ and $\lceil s \rceil := \inf\{k \in \mathbb{Z} : s \le k\}$ $(n \in \mathbb{N}; s \in \mathbb{R})$. If A is a closed linear operator on X, then $[D(A)]$ denotes the Banach space $D(A)$ equipped with the graph norm. The finite convolution product $*_0$ of the Lebesgue measurable functions $a(\cdot)$ and $b(\cdot)$ defined on $[0, \infty)$ is given by $(a *_0 b)(t) := \int_0^t a(t-s)b(s)\,ds$, $t \ge 0$; if the sequences $(a_k)_{k \in \mathbb{N}_0}$ and $(b_k)_{k \in \mathbb{N}_0}$ are given, then we define $(a *_0 b)(\cdot)$ by $(a *_0 b)(k) := \sum_{j=0}^k a_{k-j} b_j$, $k \in \mathbb{N}_0$. If A and B are non-empty sets, then we define $B^A := \{f \,|\, f : A \to B\}$. By $\Gamma(\cdot)$ we denote the Euler Gamma function; we set $g_\alpha(t) := t^{\alpha-1}/\Gamma(\alpha)$, $t > 0$ and $g_0(t) := \delta(t)$, the Dirac δ-distribution. If $\alpha \in (0, \pi]$, then we define $\Sigma_\alpha := \{z \in \mathbb{C} \setminus \{0\} : |\arg(z)| < \alpha\}$; further on, if $\varnothing \neq \Omega \subseteq \mathbb{R}^n$ is a Lebesgue measurable set, then $L^1_{loc}(\Omega)$ denotes the space of all locally integrable complex-valued functions defined on Ω. For more details about the multivalued linear operators, we refer the reader to [5]; we will use the same terminology as in this monograph.

If $u \in L^1_{loc}([0,\infty)^n)$, $j \in \mathbb{N}_n$ and $\alpha_j > 0$, then we define

$$J^{\alpha_j}_{t_j} u(x_1,...,x_{j-1},x_j,x_{j+1},...,x_n) := \int_0^{x_j} g_{\alpha_j}(x_j - s) u(x_1,...,x_{j-1},s,x_{j+1},...,x_n)\,ds,$$

$$\mathbf{x} = (x_1,...,x_{j-1},x_j,x_{j+1},...,x_n) \in [0,\infty)^n.$$

If $\alpha > 0$, then the Cesàro sequence $(k^\alpha(v))_{v \in \mathbb{N}_0}$ is defined by

$$k^\alpha(v) := \frac{\Gamma(v+\alpha)}{\Gamma(\alpha)v!}.$$

It is well-known that for every $\alpha > 0$ and $\beta > 0$, we have $k^\alpha *_0 k^\beta \equiv k^{\alpha+\beta}$. Define $k^0(0) := 1$ and $k^0(v) := 0$, $v \in \mathbb{N}$; then $k^\alpha *_0 k^\beta \equiv k^{\alpha+\beta}$ for all α, $\beta \geq 0$.

If (u_k) is a one-dimensional sequence in X, then the Euler forward difference operator Δ is defined by $\Delta u_k := u_{k+1} - u_k$. The operator Δ^m is defined inductively; then, for every integer $m \geq 1$, we have

$$\Delta^m u_k = \sum_{j=0}^m (-1)^{m-i} \binom{m}{j} u_{k+j}.$$

If A and B are non-empty sets, then we define $B^A := \{f \mid f : A \to B\}$.

If $j = (j_1,...,j_n) \in \mathbb{N}_0^n$ and $k = (k_1,...,k_n) \in \mathbb{N}_0^n$, then we write $j \leq k$ if and only if $j_m \leq k_m$ for all $1 \leq m \leq n$. If the sequences $(a_k)_{k \in \mathbb{N}_0^n}$ and $(b_k)_{k \in \mathbb{N}_0^n}$ are given, then we define $(a *_0 b)(\cdot)$ by

$$(a *_0 b)(\mathbf{k}) := \sum_{j \in \mathbb{N}_0^n; j \leq k} a_{k-j} b_j, \quad \mathbf{k} \in \mathbb{N}_0^n;$$

and it can be simply proved that the convolution product $*_0$ is commutative and associative. If the sequences $(a_k)_{k \in \mathbb{N}_0^n}$ and $(b_k)_{k \in \mathbb{Z}^n}$ are given, then we define the Weyl convolution product $(a \circ b)(\cdot)$ by

$$(a \circ b)(\mathbf{v}) := \sum_{l \in \mathbb{Z}^n; l \leq v} a(\mathbf{v}-l)b(l), \quad \mathbf{v} \in \mathbb{Z}^n,$$

whenever the last series is absolutely convergent.

Finally, if $a(\cdot)$ is a given sequence in X which depends on the variables $v_1,...,v_n$, then we define

$$\Delta_{v_i} a(v_1,...,v_i,...,v_n) := a(v_1,...,v_i+1,...,v_n) - a(v_1,...,v_i,...,v_n).$$

After that, we set $\Delta^2_{v_i v_j} a := \Delta_{v_i} \Delta_{v_j} a$ and $\Delta^2_{v_i v_i} a := \Delta_{v_i} \Delta_{v_i} a$; the terms

$$\Delta^m_{v_{i_1}...v_{i_m}} a \text{ and } \Delta^{|\alpha|}_{v_1^{\alpha_1} \cdot...\cdot v_n^{\alpha_n}} a$$

are defined recursively, as for the partial derivatives of functions ($\alpha_i \in \mathbb{N}_0$; $|\alpha| = \alpha_1 + ... + \alpha_n$). It is worth noting that for every permutation $\sigma : \mathbb{N}_n \to \mathbb{N}_n$, we have

$$\Delta^{|\alpha|}_{v_1^{\alpha_1} \cdot...\cdot v_n^{\alpha_n}} a = \Delta^{|\alpha|}_{v_{\sigma(1)}^{\alpha_{\sigma(1)}} \cdot...\cdot v_{\sigma(n)}^{\alpha_{\sigma(n)}}} a, \tag{2}$$

as easily proved. Many other important results of mathematical analysis, like Green's formula in the plane and the Grönwall inequality, have analogues for the difference operators; see [42] (pp. 23–25, 43–44) for more details in this direction.

1.1. Generalized Hilfer Fractional Derivatives and Differences

If $\delta(t)$ denotes the Dirac delta distribution, then we accept the formal convention $\int_0^t \delta(t-s)f(s)\,ds \equiv f(t)$. Suppose now that $u : [0,\infty) \to X$ is locally integrable, $\alpha > 0$, $m = \lceil \alpha \rceil$, $a \in L^1_{loc}([0,\infty))$ or $a(t) = \delta(t)$, and $b \in L^1_{loc}([0,\infty))$ or $b(t) = \delta(t)$. Set

$$v_a(t) := \int_0^t a(t-s)u(s)\,ds, \quad t \geq 0.$$

The following extension of the usual Hilfer fractional derivative $D_t^{\alpha,\beta}u(t)$, when $a(t) = g_{(1-\beta)(m-\alpha)}(t)$ and $b(t) = g_{\beta(m-\alpha)}(t)$ for some $\beta \in [0,1]$, was recently introduced in [43] (for $\beta = 0$, resp. $\beta = 1$, we obtain the usual Riemann–Liouville fractional derivative $D_R^\alpha u$ of order α, resp., the Caputo fractional derivative $\mathbf{D}_C^\alpha u$ of order α).

Definition 1. *The generalized Hilfer (a,b,α)-fractional derivative of function $u(\cdot)$, denoted shortly by $D^\alpha_{a,b}u$, is defined for any locally integrable function $u(\cdot)$ such that the function $v_a^{(m-1)}(t)$ is locally absolutely continuous for $t \geq 0$, by*

$$D^\alpha_{a,b}u(t) := \left(b *_0 v_a^{(m)}\right)(t) = \left(b *_0 \left(a *_0 u\right)^{(m)}\right)(t), \quad a.e.\ t \geq 0. \tag{3}$$

Suppose now that $u : \mathbb{N}_0 \to X$, $\alpha > 0$, $m = \lceil \alpha \rceil$, $a : \mathbb{N}_0 \to \mathbb{C}$ and $b : \mathbb{N}_0 \to \mathbb{C}$. The following is a discrete version of the notion considered above (cf. [44] (Definition 3.1)).

Definition 2. *The generalized Hilfer (a,b,α)-fractional derivative of sequence $u(\cdot)$, denoted shortly by $D^\alpha_{a,b}u$, is defined by*

$$D^\alpha_{a,b}u(v) := \left(b *_0 \Delta^m \left(a *_0 u\right)\right)(v), \quad v \in \mathbb{N}_0.$$

If $0 \leq \beta \leq 1$, then the usual Hilfer fractional derivative $D^{\alpha,\beta}u$ of order α and type β is defined as the generalized Hilfer (a,b,α)-fractional derivative of $u(\cdot)$, with $a(v) = k^{(1-\beta)(m-\alpha)}(v)$ and $b(v) = k^{\beta(1-\alpha)}(v)$.

In both cases, the continuous one and the discrete one, we define

$$D^0_{a,b}u := a *_0 b *_0 u.$$

2. Multidimensional Generalized Hilfer Fractional Derivatives and Differences

Suppose that $0 < T_j < +\infty$ and $I_j = [0,T_j)$, $I_j = [0,T_j]$ or $I_j = [0,+\infty)$ for $1 \leq j \leq n$. Set $I := I_1 \times I_2 \times \dots \times I_n$. Suppose that $u : I \to X$ is a locally integrable function, and for every $j \in \mathbb{N}_n$, $a_j \in L^1_{loc}(I_j)$ or $a_j(t) = \delta(t)$, and $b_j \in L^1_{loc}(I_j)$ or $b_j(t) = \delta(t)$. Suppose further that $\alpha_j \geq 0$ for all $j \in \mathbb{N}_n$. Define $\alpha := (\alpha_1, ..., \alpha_n)$ and

$$\mathbb{D}^\alpha_{\mathbf{a},\mathbf{b}}u(x_1, ..., x_n) := \left[D^{\alpha_1}_{a_1,b_1}\left(D^{\alpha_2}_{a_2,b_2}\left(...\left(D^{\alpha_n}_{a_n,b_n}u(\cdot, ..., \cdot)\right)...\right)\right)\right](x_1, ..., x_n), \tag{4}$$

for a.e. $(x_1, ..., x_n) \in I$, provided that the right-hand side of (4) is well-defined. Here, we assume that the variables $x_1, x_2, ..., x_{n-1}$ are fixed in the computation of the term $D^{\alpha_n}_{a_n,b_n}u(x_1, ..., x_n)$, ..., as well as that the variables $x_2, x_3, ..., x_n$ are fixed in the computation of the final term on the right-hand side of (4). We call $\mathbb{D}^\alpha_{\mathbf{a},\mathbf{b}}u$ the multidimensional generalized Hilfer $(\mathbf{a}, \mathbf{b}, \alpha)$-fractional derivative of the function $u(\cdot)$. If for each $j \in \mathbb{N}_n$, we have $D^{\alpha_j}_{a_j,b_j} = D^{\alpha_j}_R$, resp., for each $j \in \mathbb{N}_n$ we have $D^{\alpha_j}_{a_j,b_j} = \mathbf{D}^{\alpha_j}_C$, then the corresponding partial fractional derivative $\mathbb{D}^{\alpha}_{\mathbf{a},\mathbf{b}}$ is called the multidimensional Riemann–Liouville fractional operator (cf. also [7] (pp. 340–342)), resp., the multidimensional Caputo fractional operator, and it is denoted by $\mathbb{D}^{\alpha}_{\mathbf{a},\mathbf{b}} = \mathbb{D}^{\alpha}_R$, resp. $\mathbb{D}^{\alpha}_{\mathbf{a},\mathbf{b}} = \mathbb{D}^{\alpha}_C$.

In the discrete setting, we assume that $u : \mathbb{N}_0^n \to X$, $a_j : \mathbb{N}_0 \to \mathbb{C}$ and $b_j : \mathbb{N}_0 \to \mathbb{C}$ are given sequences $(1 \leq j \leq n)$. We define

$$\mathbb{D}^{\alpha}_{\mathbf{a},\mathbf{b}} u(v_1, ..., v_n) := \left[D^{\alpha_1}_{a_1,b_1} \left(D^{\alpha_2}_{a_2,b_2} \left(\cdots \left(D^{\alpha_n}_{a_n,b_n} u(\cdot, ..., \cdot) \right) \cdots \right) \right) \right] (v_1, ..., v_n), \qquad (5)$$

for any $(v_1, ..., v_n) \in \mathbb{N}_0^n$; note that the right-hand side of (5) is always well-defined. We call $\mathbb{D}^{\alpha}_{\mathbf{a},\mathbf{b}} u$ the multidimensional generalized Hilfer $(\mathbf{a}, \mathbf{b}, \alpha)$-fractional derivative of the sequence $u(\cdot)$; the multidimensional Riemann–Liouville fractional difference operator $\mathbb{D}^{\alpha}_R$ and the multidimensional Caputo fractional difference operator $\mathbb{D}^{\alpha}_C$ are defined similarly.

We continue by providing certain illustrative examples.

Example 1.

(i)   *Suppose that $\varnothing \neq D \subseteq [0, +\infty)^n$ is a finite set, $c_\beta \in \mathbb{C}$ for all $\beta = (\beta_1, ..., \beta_n) \in D$ and*

$$u(x_1, ..., x_n) := \sum_{\beta \in D} c_\beta g_{\beta_1}(x_1) \cdot ... \cdot g_{\beta_n}(x_n), \quad x_1 \geq 0, \ ..., \ x_n \geq 0.$$

Suppose further that $\alpha_j \geq 0$, $a_j(t) = g_{\gamma_j}(t)$ and $b_j(t) = g_{\delta_j}(t)$ for some non-negative numbers $\gamma_j \geq 0$ and $\delta_j \geq 0$ such that $\gamma_j + \beta_j \geq m_j$ $(1 \leq j \leq n)$. Set $f_j(t) := g_{\delta_j + \gamma_j + \beta_j - m_j}(t)$, $t > 0$, if $\gamma_j + \beta_j > m_j$ and $f_j(t) := 0$, $t \geq 0$, if $\gamma_j + \beta_j = m_j$. Then we have

$$\mathbb{D}^{\alpha}_{\mathbf{a},\mathbf{b}} u(x_1, ..., x_n) = \sum_{\beta \in D} c_\beta f_1(x_1) \cdot ... \cdot f_n(x_n), \quad x_1 \geq 0, \ ..., \ x_n \geq 0.$$

This formula enables one to clarify a great number of various partial fractional differential equations which do have the function $u(x_1, ..., x_n)$ as its solution; for example, we have

$$\mathbb{D}^{\alpha}_{\mathbf{a},\mathbf{b}} u(x_1, ..., x_n)$$
$$= \left[\sum_{\beta \in D} c_\beta \frac{x_1^{\delta_1 + \gamma_1 - m_1}}{\Gamma(\delta_1 + \beta_1 + \gamma_1 - m_1)} \cdot ..... \cdot \frac{x_n^{\delta_n + \gamma_n - m_n}}{\Gamma(\delta_n + \beta_n + \gamma_n - m_n)} \right] \cdot u(x_1, ..., x_n),$$

for any $x_1 \geq 0$, ..., $x_n \geq 0$, provided that $\delta_j + \gamma_j > m_j$ for $1 \leq j \leq n$.

(ii)   *Suppose that $\varnothing \neq D \subseteq [0, +\infty)^n$ is a finite set, $c_\beta \in \mathbb{C}$ for all $\beta = (\beta_1, ..., \beta_n) \in D$ and*

$$u(v_1, ..., v_n) := \sum_{\beta \in D} c_\beta k^{\beta_1}(v_1) \cdot ... \cdot k^{\beta_n}(v_n), \quad v_1 \in \mathbb{N}_0, \ ..., \ v_n \in \mathbb{N}_0.$$

Suppose further that $\alpha_j \geq 0$, $a_j(v) = k^{\gamma_j}(v)$ and $b_j(v) = k^{\delta_j}(v)$ for some non-negative numbers $\gamma_j \geq 0$ and $\delta_j \geq 0$ such that $\gamma_j + \beta_j \geq m_j$ $(1 \leq j \leq n)$. Set

$$f_j(v) := k^{\delta_j + \gamma_j + \beta_j - m_j}(v + m_j) - \sum_{l=v+1}^{v+m_j} k^{\gamma_j + \beta_j - m_j}(v + m_j - l) k^{\delta_j}(l), \quad v \in \mathbb{N}_0.$$

We know that (see [45] (Example 3)):

$$\Delta^{\alpha} k^{\beta}(\cdot) = k^{\beta - \alpha}(\cdot + \lceil \alpha \rceil), \quad \beta \geq \alpha > 0.$$

This simply implies

$$\mathbb{D}^{\alpha}_{\mathbf{a},\mathbf{b}} u(v_1, ..., v_n) = \sum_{\beta \in D} c_\beta f_1(v_1) \cdot ... \cdot f_n(v_n), \quad v_1 \in \mathbb{N}_0, \; ..., \; v_n \in \mathbb{N}_0.$$

Remark 1.

(i)   *Instead of the generalized Hilfer fractional derivatives and differences, we can consider here any other type of fractional derivatives of functions defined on the segment of the non-negative real axis ([46]). In such a way, we can extend the notion considered in this section and obtain much more general forms of the partial fractional derivatives.*

(ii)   *It is well-known that the composition of the Riemann–Liouville (Caputo) fractional derivatives of orders $\alpha > 0$ and $\beta > 0$ is not the Riemann–Liouville (Caputo) fractional derivative of order $\alpha + \beta$; see [6] (Sections 2.3.5 and 2.3.6) for more details. We can further extend the notion of fractional derivative $\mathbb{D}^{\alpha}_{\mathbf{a},\mathbf{b}} u$ by replacing some terms $D^{\alpha_j}_{a_j,b_j}$ in its definition by the finite compositions $D^{\alpha_{j_1}}_{a_{j_1},b_{j_1}} D^{\alpha_{j_2}}_{a_{j_2},b_{j_2}} \cdot ... \cdot D^{\alpha_{j_s}}_{a_{j_s},b_{j_s}}$ of terms with respect to the variable x_j $(1 \leq j \leq n)$.*

Let us recall that Clairaut's theorem on equality of mixed partial derivatives states that if a function $u : \Omega \to \mathbb{R}$ defined on a non-empty set $\Omega \subseteq \mathbb{R}^n$ is given, as well as that $x \in \mathbb{R}^n$ is a point such that some neighborhood $O(x)$ of it belongs to Ω, and $u(\cdot, \cdot)$ has continuous second partial derivatives on $O(x)$, then we have

$$\frac{\partial^2 u}{\partial x_i \partial x_j}(x) = \frac{\partial^2 u}{\partial x_j \partial x_i}(x).$$

This equality cannot be so easily interpreted for the generalized Hilfer partial fractional derivatives, because the equality

$$\left[D^{\alpha_1}_{a_1,b_1} \left(D^{\alpha_2}_{a_2,b_2} u \right) \right](x_1, x_2) = \left[D^{\alpha_2}_{a_2,b_2} \left(D^{\alpha_1}_{a_1,b_1} u \right) \right](x_1, x_2), \tag{6}$$

is not true, in general (of course, it is true in the case that $b = d$, $a = c$ and $m_1 = m_2$, at least almost everywhere). The Formula (6) does not hold even for the Riemann–Liouville fractional derivatives and the Caputo fractional derivatives, as the following simple counterexample shows.

Example 2. *Suppose that $0 < \alpha_1 < 1, 0 < \alpha_2 < 1$ and $\alpha_1 \neq \alpha_2$. Let us consider the Caputo approach, in which $a_1(t) = a_2(t) = \delta(t)$, $b_1(t) = g_{1-\alpha_1}(t)$, $b_2(t) = g_{1-\alpha_2}(t)$ and $m_1 = m_2 = 1$. Then a simple computation shows that the equality (6) is equivalent with*

$$\int_0^{x_1} g_{1-\alpha_2}(x_1 - r) \frac{d}{dr} \int_0^{x_2} g_{1-\alpha_1}(x_2 - l) \frac{\partial u}{\partial l} u(r, l) \, dl \, dr$$

$$= \int_0^{x_1} g_{1-\alpha_1}(x_1 - r) \frac{d}{dr} \int_0^{x_2} g_{1-\alpha_2}(x_2 - l) \frac{\partial u}{\partial l} u(r, l) \, dl \, dr. \tag{7}$$

Take now $u(x_1, x_2) := x_1 x_2$ for $x_1 \geq 0$ and $x_2 \geq 0$. Then (7) is equivalent with

$$g_{2-\alpha_2}(x_1) \cdot g_{2-\alpha_1}(x_2) = g_{2-\alpha_1}(x_1) \cdot g_{2-\alpha_2}(x_2),$$

which is wrong. In the discrete setting, we cannot expect the validity of nontrivial fractional analogues of Equation (2).

We continue with the observation that the formulae [1] (1.13, 1.21) can be straightforwardly extended to the multidimensional setting. For example, if $u \in L^1_{loc}([0,\infty)^n)$ and $\alpha_j \geq 0$ for all $j \in \mathbb{N}_n$, then we have

$$D_R^{\alpha_1} D_R^{\alpha_2} \cdot ... \cdot D_R^{\alpha_n} J_{t_n}^{\alpha_n} \cdot ... \cdot J_{t_2}^{\alpha_2} J_{t_1}^{\alpha_1} u = u$$

and

$$\mathbf{D}_C^{\alpha_1} \mathbf{D}_C^{\alpha_2} \cdot ... \cdot \mathbf{D}_C^{\alpha_n} J_{t_n}^{\alpha_n} \cdot ... \cdot J_{t_2}^{\alpha_2} J_{t_1}^{\alpha_1} u = u,$$

with the meaning clear. The situation is a little bit complicated if we consider the second formulae in Equations (1.13) and (1.21) from [1]; for example, in the two-dimensional setting, we have

$$J_{t_2}^{\alpha_2} J_{t_1}^{\alpha_1} D_R^{\alpha_1} D_R^{\alpha_2} u (x_1, x_2)$$

$$= u(x_1, x_2) - \sum_{k=0}^{m_2-1} \frac{\partial^k}{\partial x_2^k} \left[J_{t_2}^{m_2-\alpha_2} *_0 u \right](x_1, 0) \cdot g_{\alpha_2+k+1-m_2}(x_2)$$

$$- \sum_{k=0}^{m_1-1} \left\{ \int_0^{x_2} g_{\alpha_2}(x_2 - s) \left[\frac{\partial^k}{\partial x_1^k} \left[J_{t_1}^{m_1-\alpha_1} *_0 D_R^{\alpha_2} u \right](x_1, x_2) \right]_{x_1=0, x_2=s} ds \right\} \cdot g_{\alpha_1+k+1-m_1}(x_1), \tag{8}$$

for any $(x_1, x_2) \in [0,\infty)^2$, provided that $u \in L^1_{loc}([0,\infty)^2)$, $m_1 = \lceil \alpha_1 \rceil$, $m_2 = \lceil \alpha_2 \rceil$, for each $x_2 \geq 0$ the function $x_1 \mapsto D_R^{\alpha_2} u(x_1, x_2)$, $x_1 > 0$ is locally integrable and satisfies $J_{t_1}^{m_1-\alpha_1} *_0$ $D_R^{\alpha_2} u \in W^{m_1,1}_{loc}([0,\infty) : X)$, and for each $x_1 \geq 0$ we have $J_{t_2}^{m_2-\alpha_2} *_0 (\partial^{m_2-1}/\partial x_2^{m_2-1}) u \in W^{m_2,1}_{loc}([0,\infty) : X)$, as well as

$$J_{t_2}^{\alpha_2} J_{t_1}^{\alpha_1} \mathbf{D}_C^{\alpha_1} \mathbf{D}_C^{\alpha_2} u(x_1, x_2) = u(x_1, x_2) - \sum_{k=0}^{m_2-1} \left[\frac{\partial^k}{\partial x_2^k} u(x_1, 0) \right] \cdot g_{k+1}(x_2)$$

$$- \sum_{k=0}^{m_1-1} \left[\int_0^{x_2} g_{\alpha_2}(x_2 - s) \left[\frac{\partial^k}{\partial x_1^k} \mathbf{D}_C^{\alpha_2} u(x_1, x_2) \right]_{x_1=0, x_2=s} ds \right] \cdot g_{k+1}(x_1), \tag{9}$$

for any $(x_1, x_2) \in [0,\infty)^2$, provided that $m_1 = \lceil \alpha_1 \rceil$, $m_2 = \lceil \alpha_2 \rceil$, $u \in L^1_{loc}([0,\infty)^2)$, for each $x_2 \geq 0$ the function $x_1 \mapsto f(x_1) := (\partial^{m_1-1}/\partial x_1^{m_1-1}) \mathbf{D}_C^{\alpha_2} u(x_1, x_2)$, $x_1 \geq 0$ is continuous, $g_{m_1-\alpha_1} *_0 f \in W^{m_1,1}_{loc}([0,\infty) : X)$, for each $x_1 \geq 0$ the function $x_2 \mapsto g(x_2) := (\partial^{m_2-1}/\partial x_2^{m_2-1}) u(x_1, x_2)$, $x_2 \geq 0$ is continuous and $g_{m_2-\alpha_2} *_0 g \in W^{m_2,1}_{loc}([0,\infty) : X)$. Here, $W^{m_1,1}_{loc}([0,\infty) : X)$ and $W^{m_2,1}_{loc}([0,\infty) : X)$ denote the usual Sobolev spaces; cf. [1] for the notation used.

3. Multidimensional Generalized Weyl Fractional Derivatives and Differences

In this section, which consists of two separate subsections, we investigate the multidimensional generalized Weyl fractional derivatives and differences.

3.1. Generalized Weyl Fractional Derivatives and Differences

If $u : \mathbb{R} \to X$ is a locally integrable function, $\alpha \geq 0$ and $m = \lceil \alpha \rceil$, then the Weyl fractional derivative $D_W^\alpha u$ of function $u(\cdot)$ of order α is well-defined if the mapping $x \mapsto \int_{-\infty}^x g_{m-\alpha}(x - s) u(s) \, ds$, $x \in \mathbb{R}$ is well-defined and m-times continuously differentiable, by

$$\left[D_W^\alpha u \right](x) := \frac{d^m}{dx^m} \int_{-\infty}^x g_{m-\alpha}(x - s) u(s) \, ds, \quad x \in \mathbb{R};$$

cf. [47] for more details. Now we would like to propose the following notion.

Definition 3. *Suppose that $a \in L^1_{loc}([0, \infty))$, $u : \mathbb{R} \to X$ is a locally integrable function, $\alpha \geq 0$ and $m = \lceil \alpha \rceil$. The generalized Weyl fractional derivative $D^{\alpha,a}_W u$ of function $u(\cdot)$ is well-defined if the mapping $x \mapsto \int_{-\infty}^{x} a(x - s)u(s)\,ds$, $x \in \mathbb{R}$ is well-defined and m-times continuously differentiable, by*

$$\left[D^{\alpha,a}_W u \right](x) := \frac{d^m}{dx^m} \int_{-\infty}^{x} a(x - s)u(s)\,ds, \quad x \in \mathbb{R}.$$

We call the function $x \mapsto I_{W,a}(x) := \int_{-\infty}^{x} a(x - s)u(s)\,ds$, $x \in \mathbb{R}$, if it is well-defined, the generalized Weyl a-integral of function $u(\cdot)$. If $a(t) = g_\zeta(t)$ for some $\zeta \in (0,1)$, then the class of functions for which the above integral absolutely converges and behaves nicely was considered for the first time by M. J. Lighthill in [48], where it was called the class of "good functions". In the general case, we have

$$\int_{-\infty}^{x} a(x - s)u(s)\,ds = \int_{0}^{+\infty} a(s)u(x - s)\,ds, \quad x \in \mathbb{R}$$

and the dominated convergence theorem implies

$$\frac{d}{dx^n} \int_{-\infty}^{x} a(x - s)u(s)\,ds = \int_{0}^{+\infty} a(s)u^{(n)}(x - s)\,ds, \quad x \in \mathbb{R}, \; n \in \mathbb{N},$$

provided that there exists $m \in \mathbb{N}$ such that $\int_{0}^{+\infty} |a(s)|(1 + s)^{-m}\,ds < +\infty$, and the function $u(\cdot)$ and all its derivatives are differentiable almost everywhere and for each $n \in \mathbb{N}$ and $\alpha \in \mathbb{N}_0$ there exists a finite real number $M_{n,\alpha} \geq 1$ such that $\|u^{(\alpha)}(x)\| \leq M_{n,\alpha}(1 + |x|)^{-n}$, $x \in \mathbb{R}$; we call such functions "vector-valued good functions" and denote the corresponding class by $\mathbf{S}(X)$. If (G) holds, where

(G) There exists an integer $m \in \mathbb{N}$ such that $\int_{0}^{+\infty} |a(s)|(1 + s)^{-m}\,ds < +\infty$ and $\int_{0}^{+\infty} |b(s)|(1 + s)^{-m}\,ds < +\infty$,

then we can repeat verbatim the argumentation from [47] (Section 3, pp. 239–240) in order to see that the law of exponents for generalized Weyl integrals holds true:

$$I_{W,a} I_{w,b} u = I_{W,a *_0 b} u, \quad u \in \mathbf{S}(X); \tag{10}$$

Here, we we will only note that the Dirichlet integral formula given on [47] (p. 239, l.-7–l.-4) in our new framework takes the form

$$\int_{t}^{w} a(x - t)\left[\int_{x}^{w} b(s - x)f(s)\,ds \right] dx = \int_{t}^{w} \left(a *_0 b \right)(s - t)f(s)\,ds,$$

which follows from an elementary change of variables in the double integral. Furthermore, if (G) holds, then we can repeat verbatim the argumentation from [47] (Section 4, pp. 240–244) in order to see that the law of exponents for generalized Weyl derivatives holds true:

$$D^{\alpha,a}_W D^{\beta,b}_W u = D^{\lceil \alpha \rceil + \lceil \beta \rceil, a *_0 b}_W u, \quad u \in \mathbf{S}(X). \tag{11}$$

In connection with the above issue, we would like to note that the approach of R. Hilfer is insignificant for the definitions of Weyl fractional derivatives introduced above. Without going into full detail, we will only note here that the following formula holds true:

$$\int_{-\infty}^{x} b(x - s)\frac{d^m}{ds^m} \int_{-\infty}^{s} a(s - r)u(r)\,dr\,ds = \frac{d^m}{dx^m} \int_{-\infty}^{x} \left(a *_0 b \right)(x - s)u(s)\,ds, \; x \in \mathbb{R}, \tag{12}$$

provided that $u \in \mathbf{S}(X)$ and (G) holds; furthermore, the assumption $u \in \mathbf{S}(X)$ can be slightly relaxed and all abovementioned statements can be slightly generalized keeping in mind the concrete value of integer $m \in \mathbb{N}$ satisfying (G); details can be left to interested readers.

Suppose now that $a : \mathbb{N}_0 \to \mathbb{C}$ and $f : \mathbb{Z} \to X$ are given sequences. If the series $\sum_{s=0}^{+\infty} a(s)f(v-s)$ is absolutely convergent for all $v \in \mathbb{Z}$, then we define

$$\left(\Delta_{W,a}f\right)(v) := \sum_{s=-\infty}^{v} a(v-s)f(s) = \sum_{s=0}^{+\infty} a(s)f(v-s), \quad v \in \mathbb{Z}. \tag{13}$$

Assume that the sequence $\Delta_{W,a}f : \mathbb{Z} \to X$ is well-defined and $m \in \mathbb{N}$. Then we put

$$\left(\Delta_{W,a,m}f\right)(v) := \left(\Delta^m \Delta_{W,a}f\right)(v), \quad v \in \mathbb{Z}.$$

It is worth noting that if $m = \lceil \alpha \rceil$ and $a \equiv k^{m-\alpha}$ for some $\alpha > 0$, then the operator $\Delta_{a,m}$ reduces to the Weyl fractional derivative $D_W^\alpha f$ of sequence $f(\cdot)$ of order α; cf. [49] (Definition 2.3). Because of that, we will call the sequence $\Delta_{W,a,m}f$ the generalized Weyl (a, m)-fractional derivative of sequence $f(\cdot)$.

Concerning the discrete counterpart of Formula (12), let us first define ($0 \le \beta \le 1$; $b : \mathbb{N}_0 \to \mathbb{C}$)

$$\Delta_W^{\alpha,\beta} f := \Delta^{\beta(m-\alpha)} \Delta^m \Delta^{(1-\beta)(m-\alpha)} f \quad \text{and} \quad \Delta_{a,b}f := \Delta_a \Delta^m \Delta_b f.$$

Then, under certain logical assumptions, we have the following (the multidimensional analogues of these formulae can be also achieved):

$$\Delta_W^{\alpha,\beta} f = D_W^\alpha f \quad \text{and} \quad \Delta_{a,b}f = \Delta_{a *_0 b}f. \tag{14}$$

Both formulae can be proved in the same manner, with the help of the discrete Fubini theorem and the result established in [50] (Theorem 3.12(ii), (iii)). For the sake of brevity, we will prove here the first formula in (14) only, extending thus the result established in [49] (Remark 2.4):

$$\left[\Delta_W^{\alpha,\beta} f\right](v) = \sum_{s=-\infty}^{v} k^{\beta(m-\alpha)}(v-s)\left[\Delta^m \Delta^{(1-\beta)(m-\alpha)} f\right](s)$$

$$= \sum_{s=-\infty}^{v} k^{\beta(m-\alpha)}(v-s)\sum_{i=0}^{m}(-1)^{m-i}\binom{m}{i}\left[\Delta^{(1-\beta)(m-\alpha)} f\right](s+i)$$

$$= \sum_{i=0}^{m}(-1)^{m-i}\binom{m}{i}\sum_{s=-\infty}^{v+i} k^{\beta(m-\alpha)}(v+i-s)\left[\Delta^{(1-\beta)(m-\alpha)} f\right](s)$$

$$= \sum_{i=0}^{m}(-1)^{m-i}\binom{m}{i}\sum_{s=-\infty}^{v+i} k^{\beta(m-\alpha)}(v+i-s)\sum_{l=-\infty}^{s} k^{(1-\beta)(m-\alpha)}(s-l)f(l)$$

$$= \sum_{i=0}^{m}(-1)^{m-i}\binom{m}{i}\sum_{s=-\infty}^{v+i} k^{m-\alpha}(v+i-s)f(s) = \left[D_W^\alpha f\right](v), \quad v \in \mathbb{Z}.$$

3.2. Continuation: Multidimensional Generalized Weyl Fractional Calculus

Suppose now that $a_j \in L^1_{loc}([0,\infty))$ for all $j \in \mathbb{N}_n$, $u : \mathbb{R}^n \to X$ is a locally integrable function and $\alpha_j \ge 0$ for all $j \in \mathbb{N}_n$. Define $\alpha := (\alpha_1, ..., \alpha_n)$ and

$$\mathbb{D}_W^{\alpha,\mathbf{a}} u(x_1, ..., x_n) := \left[D_W^{\alpha_1,a_1}\left(D_W^{\alpha_2,a_2}\left(...\left(D_W^{\alpha_n,a_n} u(\cdot, ..., \cdot)\right)...\right)\right)\right](x_1, ..., x_n), \tag{15}$$

for a.e. $(x_1, ..., x_n) \in \mathbb{R}^n$, provided that the right-hand side of (15) is well-defined. Here, we assume that the variables $x_1, x_2, ..., x_{n-1}$ are fixed in the computation of the term $D_W^{\alpha_n,a_n} u(x_1, ..., x_n)$, ..., as well as that the variables $x_2, x_3, ..., x_n$ are fixed in the computation of the final term on the right-hand side of (15). We call $\mathbb{D}_W^{\alpha,\mathbf{a}} u$ the multidimensional generalized Weyl $(\alpha, \mathbf{a})$-fractional derivative of the function $u(\cdot)$. If $a_j \equiv g_{m_j-\alpha_j}$, where

$m_j = \lceil \alpha_j \rceil$ for all $j \in \mathbb{N}_n$, then we call $\mathbb{D}_W^\alpha u := \mathbb{D}_W^{\alpha,\mathbf{a}} u$ the multidimensional generalized Weyl α-fractional derivative of function $u(\cdot)$; cf. also [7] (p. 343) for the scalar-valued version of this notion. We call the function

$$\mathbf{x} \mapsto I_{W,\mathbf{a}}(\mathbf{x}) := \int_{-\infty}^{x_1} \int_{-\infty}^{x_2} \cdot \ldots \cdot \int_{-\infty}^{x_n} a_1(x_1 - s_1) a_2(x_2 - s_2) \cdot \ldots \cdot a_n(x_n - s_n)$$
$$\times\, u(s_1, s_2, ..., s_n)\, ds_1\, ds_2 \cdot \ldots \cdot ds_n, \quad \mathbf{x} = (x_1, x_2, ..., x_n) \in \mathbb{R}^n,$$

if it is well-defined, the generalized Weyl $\mathbf{a}$-integral of function $u(\cdot)$.

Suppose now that $u : \mathbb{Z}^n \to X$, $a_j : \mathbb{N}_0 \to \mathbb{C}$ are given sequences and $m_j \in \mathbb{N}$ are given integers ($1 \leq j \leq n$). Then we introduce the following multidimensional fractional difference operator

$$\mathbb{D}_{W,\mathbf{a},\mathbf{m}} u(v_1, ..., v_n)$$
$$:= \left[\Delta_{W,a_1,m_1} \left(\Delta_{W,a_2,m_2} \left(... \left(\Delta_{W,a_n,m_n} u(\cdot, ..., \cdot) \right) ... \right) \right) \right] (v_1, ..., v_n), \quad (16)$$

for any $(v_1, ..., v_n) \in \mathbb{Z}^n$, provided that the right-hand side of (16) is well-defined. We call $\mathbb{D}_{W,\mathbf{a},\mathbf{m}} u$ the generalized multidimensional Weyl $(\mathbf{a}, \mathbf{m})$-fractional derivative of $u(\cdot)$. If $m_j = \lceil \alpha_j \rceil$ and $a_j \equiv k^{m_j - \alpha_j}$ for $1 \leq j \leq n$, then we call $\mathbb{D}_{W,\mathbf{a},\mathbf{m}} u$ the generalized multidimensional Weyl α-fractional derivative of $u(\cdot)$, where $\alpha = (\alpha_1, ..., \alpha_n)$.

Remark 2. *It is clear that in place of the generalized Weyl fractional derivatives and differences, we can consider here any other type of fractional derivatives of functions defined on the whole real axis (see, e.g., [7] (Chapter 5) and [46,51]).*

The formulae [47] ((7.4), (7.6), (7.10), (7.12), (7.13)) can be simply formulated in the multidimensional setting. For example, we have

$$D_W^{\alpha_1} D_W^{\alpha_2} ... D_W^{\alpha_n} e^{a_1 x_1 + a_2 x_2 + ... + a_n x_n} = a_1^{\alpha_1} a_2^{\alpha_2} \cdot \ldots \cdot a_n^{\alpha_n} e^{a_1 x_1 + a_2 x_2 + ... + a_n x_n}, \quad (17)$$

provided that $a_j > 0$ and $\alpha_j > 0$ for $1 \leq j \leq n$, with the meaning clear.

If all partial derivatives of a function $u : \mathbb{R}^n \to X$ are continuous almost everywhere and for each $m \in \mathbb{N}$ and $\alpha \in \mathbb{N}_0^n$ there exists a finite real number $M_{m,\alpha} \geq 1$ such that $\|u^{(\alpha)}(x)\| \leq M_{m,\alpha}(1 + |x|)^{-n}$, $x \in \mathbb{R}^n$, then we say that $u(\cdot)$ is a vector-valued good function of several variables; the corresponding class of vector-valued good functions will be denoted by $\mathbf{S}_n(X)$ henceforth. If $u \in \mathbf{S}_n(X)$, then the function $I_{W,\mathbf{a}}(\cdot)$ is infinitely differentiable and for each $\alpha \in \mathbb{N}_0^n$ and $\mathbf{x} \in \mathbb{R}^n$ we have

$$I_{W,\mathbf{a}}^{(\alpha)}(\mathbf{x}) = \int_{[0,+\infty)^n} a_1(s_1) a_2(s_2) \cdot \ldots \cdot a_n(s_n) \frac{\partial^\alpha u}{\partial x_1^{\alpha_1} \cdot \ldots \cdot \partial x_n^{\alpha_n}} (\mathbf{x} - \mathbf{s})\, d\mathbf{s}.$$

Furthermore, if the following condition holds:

(G1) There exists an integer $m \in \mathbb{N}$ such that $\int_0^{+\infty} |a_j(s)|(1+s)^{-m}\, ds < +\infty$ and $\int_0^{+\infty} |b_j(s)|(1+s)^{-m}\, ds < +\infty$ for all $j \in \mathbb{N}_n$,

then we can apply the Fubini theorem and (10) in order to see that the law of exponents for generalized multidimensional Weyl integrals holds true:

$$I_{W,\mathbf{a}} I_{w,\mathbf{b}} u = I_{W,\mathbf{a} *_0 \mathbf{b}} u, \quad u \in \mathbf{S}_n(X), \quad (18)$$

where $\mathbf{a} *_0 \mathbf{b} := (a_1 *_0 b_1, ..., a_n *_0 b_n)$. If (G1) is valid, then the following multidimensional analogue of (11) holds:

$$\mathbb{D}_W^{\alpha,\mathbf{a}} \mathbb{D}_W^{\beta,\mathbf{b}} u = \mathbb{D}_W^{\lceil \alpha \rceil + \lceil \beta \rceil, \mathbf{a} *_0 \mathbf{b}} u, \quad u \in \mathbf{S}_n(X), \quad (19)$$

where $\lceil \alpha \rceil + \lceil \beta \rceil := (\lceil \alpha_1 \rceil + \lceil \beta_1 \rceil, ..., \lceil \alpha_n \rceil + \lceil \beta_n \rceil)$; in particular, we can clarify Clairaut's theorem on equality of mixed partial Weyl fractional derivatives of type (6).

The generation of C-regularized solution operator families in $L^p(\mathbb{R}^n)$ by the Weyl fractional differential operators of the form

$$A = \sum_{\alpha \in D} c_\alpha \mathbb{D}_W^\alpha u,$$

where D is a non-empty subset of $\mathbb{N}_0^n$ and $c_\alpha \in \mathbb{C}$ for all $\alpha \in D$, is a rather nontrivial problem. We will consider this issue elsewhere.

4. Multidimensional Fractional Calculus on Some Special Regions of $\mathbb{R}^n$

Keeping in mind the notion introduced in the previous two sections, we have an open door to consider the partial fractional derivatives of functions defined on the subsets $I \subseteq \mathbb{R}^n$ which have the form $I = I_1 \times I_2 \times ... \times I_n$, where $I_j = [0, T_j)$, $I_j = [0, T_j]$, $I_j = [0, +\infty)$ or $I_j = \mathbb{R}$ for $1 \leq j \leq n$; for example, in the two-dimensional setting, we can consider functions defined on the half-space $I = [0, \infty) \times \mathbb{R}$ or the closed rectangle $[0, T] \times \mathbb{R}$, where $T > 0$.

Suppose that $f : I \to X$ and I has the above form. Suppose, further, that $\alpha_j \geq 0$ for all $j \in \mathbb{N}_n$ and $\alpha = (\alpha_1, ..., \alpha_n)$. We define

$$\mathbb{D}^\alpha u(x_1, ..., x_n) := \left[D^{\alpha_1} \left(D^{\alpha_2} \left(... \left(D^{\alpha_n} u(\cdot, ..., \cdot) \right) ... \right) \right) \right] (x_1, ..., x_n), \tag{20}$$

for a.e. $(x_1, ..., x_n) \in I$, provided that the right-hand side of (20) is well-defined, where $D^{\alpha_j} = D_{a_j, b_j}^{\alpha_j}$ for some $a_j \in L_{loc}^1(I_j)$ or $a_j(t) = \delta(t)$, and $b_j \in L_{loc}^1(I_j)$ or $b_j(t) = \delta(t)$, provided that $I_j = [0, T_j)$, $I_j = [0, T_j]$ or $I_j = [0, +\infty)$, and $D^{\alpha_j} = D_W^{\alpha, a_j}$ with some $a_j \in L_{loc}^1([0, \infty))$, if $I_j = \mathbb{R}$. We will not consider here the partial fractional derivatives of functions defined on some other regions of $\mathbb{R}^n$; for example, it could be interesting to consider the partial fractional derivatives of functions defined on convex polyhedrals in $\mathbb{R}^n$.

In the discrete setting, we will only consider the sets $I \subseteq \mathbb{Z}^n$ which have the form $I = I_1 \times I_2 \times ... \times I_n$, where $I_j = \mathbb{N}_0$ or $I_j = \mathbb{Z}$ for $1 \leq j \leq n$. If I has such a form and $u : I \to X$, then we define the partial fractional derivative $\mathbb{D}^\alpha u(v_1, ..., v_n)$ similar to the continuous setting; for example, in the two-dimensional setting, we can consider sequences defined on the set $I = \mathbb{N}_0 \times \mathbb{Z}$ or $I = \mathbb{Z} \times \mathbb{N}_0$.

We continue by providing the following illustrative example.

Example 3. *Suppose that $n \geq 2$, $\varnothing \neq D \subseteq [0, +\infty)^n$ is a finite set, $c_\beta \in \mathbb{C}$ for all $\beta = (\beta_1, ..., \beta_n) \in D$, $\beta_n > 0$ and*

$$u(x_1, ..., x_n) := \sum_{\beta \in D} c_\beta g_{\beta_1}(x_1) \cdot ... \cdot g_{\beta_{n-1}}(x_{n-1}) e^{\beta_n x_n}, \; x_1 \geq 0, \; ..., \; x_{n-1} \geq 0, \; x_n \in \mathbb{R}.$$

Suppose further that $\alpha_j \geq 0$, $a_j(t) = g_{\gamma_j}(t)$ and $b_j(t) = g_{\delta_j}(t)$ for some non-negative numbers $\gamma_j \geq 0$ and $\delta_j \geq 0$ such that $\gamma_j + \beta_j \geq m_j$ $(1 \leq j \leq n-1)$. Let $D^{\alpha_j} u = D_{a_j, b_j}^{\alpha_j} u$ for $1 \leq j \leq n-1$, and let $D^{\alpha_n} u = D_W^{\alpha_n}$. If we define the functions $f_j(\cdot)$, for $1 \leq j \leq n-1$, as in Example 1(i), then we have

$$\mathbb{D}^\alpha u(x_1, ..., x_n) = \sum_{\beta \in D} c_\beta \beta_n^{\alpha_n} f_1(x_1) \cdot ... \cdot f_{n-1}(x_{n-1}) e^{\beta_n x_n},$$

for any $x_1 \geq 0$, ..., $x_{n-1} \geq 0$ and $x_n \in \mathbb{R}$; cf. also (17).

As in Example 1(i), we can construct a great number of various partial fractional differential equations having the function $u(x_1, ..., x_n)$ as their solution; for example, we have

$$\mathbb{D}_{\mathbf{a,b}}^{\alpha} u(x_1, ..., x_n)$$

$$= \left[\sum_{\beta \in D} c_\beta \beta_n^{\alpha_n} \frac{x_1^{\delta_1 + \gamma_1 - m_1}}{\Gamma(\delta_1 + \beta_1 + \gamma_1 - m_1)} \cdot \; ..... \; \cdot \frac{x_{n-1}^{\delta_{n-1} + \gamma_{n-1} - m_{n-1}}}{\Gamma(\delta_{n-1} + \beta_{n-1} + \gamma_{n-1} - m_{n-1})} \right] \cdot u(x_1, ..., x_n),$$

for any $x_1 \geq 0$, ..., $x_{n-1} \geq 0$ and $x_n \in \mathbb{R}$, provided that $\delta_j + \gamma_j > m_j$ for $1 \leq j \leq n - 1$.

5. Multidimensional Vector-Valued Laplace Transform

The multidimensional vector-valued Laplace transform has not attracted as much attention of the authors to date. Suppose that $f : [0, +\infty)^n \to X$ is a locally integrable function. Then the multidimensional vector-valued Laplace transform of $f(\cdot)$, denoted by $F(\cdot) = \tilde{f} = \mathcal{L}f$, is defined through

$$F(\lambda_1, ..., \lambda_n) := \int_0^{+\infty} ... \int_0^{+\infty} e^{-\lambda_1 t_1 - ... - \lambda_n t_n} f(t_1, ..., t_n) \, dt_1 ... dt_n, \tag{21}$$

if it is well-defined. We say that $f(\cdot)$ is Laplace transformable if and only if there exist real constants $\omega_1 \in \mathbb{R}$, ..., $\omega_n \in \mathbb{R}$ such that $F(\lambda_1, ..., \lambda_n)$ is well-defined for $\Re \lambda_1 > \omega_1$, ..., $\Re \lambda_n > \omega_n$. This is always the case if there exist finite real constants $M \geq 1$ and $\omega_1 \in \mathbb{R}$, ..., $\omega_n \in \mathbb{R}$ such that $\|f(t_1, ..., t_n)\| \leq M \exp(\omega_1 t_1 + ... + \omega_n t_n)$ for a.e. $t_1 \geq 0$, ..., $t_n \geq 0$, when we say that $f(\cdot)$ is exponentially bounded; then $F(\lambda_1, ..., \lambda_n)$ is well-defined for $\Re \lambda_1 > \omega_1$, ..., $\Re \lambda_n > \omega_n$ and $F(\cdot)$ is analytic in this region of $\mathbb{C}^n$ (see L. Hörmander [52] for the basic introduction to the theory of analytic functions of several complex variables). The uniqueness theorem for Laplace transform holds in the multidimensional framework.

The numerical inversion of a multidimensional vector-valued Laplace transform has been considered in many research articles to date (these papers can be easily located online and we will not quote them here). On the other hand, it seems that the complex inversion theorem for the multidimensional Laplace transform in both the scalar-valued setting and the vector-valued setting has not been properly formulated by now. Concerning this issue, we will state and prove the following extension of [53] (Theorem 2.5.1):

Theorem 1. *Suppose that $M > 0$, $\omega_1 \geq 0$, ..., $\omega_n \geq 0$, $\epsilon_1 > 0$, ..., $\epsilon_n > 0$ and $F : \{\lambda \in \mathbb{C} : \Re \lambda > \omega_1\} \times ... \times \{\lambda \in \mathbb{C} : \Re \lambda > \omega_n\} \to X$ is an analytic function such that*

$$\left\| F(\lambda_1, ..., \lambda_n) \right\| \leq M |\lambda_1|^{-1-\epsilon_1} \cdot \; ... \; \cdot |\lambda_n|^{-1-\epsilon_n}, \quad \Re \lambda_j > \omega_j \; (1 \leq j \leq n). \tag{22}$$

Then there exist a real number $M_1 > 0$ and a continuous function $f : [0, +\infty)^n \to X$ such that

$$\left\| f(t_1, ..., t_n) \right\| \leq M_1 [t_1^{\epsilon_1} e^{\omega_1 t_1} \cdot \; ... \; \cdot t_n^{\epsilon_n} e^{\omega_n t_n}] \text{ for all } t_1 \geq 0, \; ..., \; t_n \geq 0 \tag{23}$$

and $F(\lambda_1, ..., \lambda_n) = (\mathcal{L}f)(\lambda_1, ..., \lambda_n)$ for $\Re \lambda_j > \omega_j$ $(1 \leq j \leq n)$.

Proof. We present the main details of the proof only. Let $a_j > \omega_j$ be pairwisely distinct numbers $(1 \leq j \leq n)$, and let

$$f(t_1, ..., t_n) := \frac{1}{(2\pi i)^n} \int_{a_1 - i\infty}^{a_1 + i\infty} ... \int_{a_n - i\infty}^{a_n + i\infty} e^{\lambda_1 t_1 + ... + \lambda_n t_n} F(\lambda_1, ..., \lambda_n) \, d\lambda_1 ... d\lambda_n, \tag{24}$$

for any $t_1 \geq 0$, ..., $t_n \geq 0$; it can be easily shown that the integral appearing in (24) is absolutely convergent so that $f(\cdot)$ is well-defined. The dominated convergence theorem implies that $f(\cdot)$ is continuous; moreover, we can use the Fubini theorem, the growth rate of $F(\cdot)$ and the computation carried out in the proof of the last mentioned theorem in order to see that there exists a constant $M_1 > 0$, independent of $a_1, \dots, a_n$, such that

$$\|f(t_1, \dots, t_n)\| \leq M_1[t_1^{\epsilon_1} e^{a_1 t_1} \cdot \dots \cdot t_n^{\epsilon_n} e^{a_n t_n}] \text{ for all } t_1 \geq 0, \ \dots, \ t_n \geq 0.$$

On the other hand, an elementary contour argument shows that the definition of function $f(\cdot)$ does not depend on the choice of numbers $a_1 > \omega_1, \dots, a_n > \omega_n$. In actual fact, we can fix the numbers $a_1 > \omega_1, \dots, a_{n-1} > \omega_{n-1}$ and prove first that the definition of function $f(\cdot)$ does not depend on the choice of number $a_n > \omega_n$; after that, we can repeat this procedure $(n-1)$ times. Using this fact and letting $a_j \to \omega_j+$ for $1 \leq j \leq n$, we obtain (23). It remains to be proved that $F(\lambda_1, \dots, \lambda_n) = (\mathcal{L}f)(\lambda_1, \dots, \lambda_n)$ for $\Re \lambda_j > \omega_j$ $(1 \leq j \leq n)$. Let the numbers $\lambda_1, \dots, \lambda_n$ enjoy the above properties and let $\omega_j < a_j < \Re \lambda_j$ for $1 \leq j \leq n$. Then the Fubini theorem and an elementary argumentation shows that

$$(\mathcal{L}f)(\lambda_1, \dots, \lambda_n) = \frac{1}{(2\pi i)^n} \int_{a_1-i\infty}^{a_1+i\infty} \dots \int_{a_n-i\infty}^{a_n+i\infty} \frac{F(z_1, \dots, z_n)}{(\lambda_1 - z_1) \cdot \dots \cdot (\lambda_n - z_n)} \, dz_1 \dots dz_n.$$

Using the residue theorem and deforming the line $[a_n - i\infty, a_n + i\infty]$ into the union of the segment $[a_n - iR, a_n + iR]$ and the semi-circle $a_n + \{Re^{i\theta} : -\pi/2 \leq \theta \leq \pi/2\}$, we obtain

$$(\mathcal{L}f)(\lambda_1, \dots, \lambda_n) = \frac{1}{(2\pi i)^{n-1}}$$
$$\times \int_{a_1-i\infty}^{a_1+i\infty} \dots \int_{a_{n-1}-i\infty}^{a_{n-1}+i\infty} \frac{F(z_1, \dots, z_{n-1}, \lambda_n)}{(\lambda_1 - z_1) \cdot \dots \cdot (\lambda_{n-1} - z_{n-1})} \, dz_1 \dots dz_{n-1}.$$

Repeating this argument, we simply obtain the required equality. $\quad\square$

6. Some Classes of Fractional Partial Differential-Difference Inclusions

In this section, we investigate some classes of the fractional partial differential-difference inclusions. We will divide the material of this section into three separate subsections.

6.1. Fractional Partial Differential Inclusions with Riemann–Liouville and Caputo Derivatives

Suppose that $\alpha_1 \in [0, 2)$, $\alpha_2 \in [0, 2)$, $m_1 = \lceil \alpha_1 \rceil$, $m_2 = \lceil \alpha_2 \rceil$ and $\mathcal{A}$ is a closed MLO in X (the precise assumptions about $\mathcal{A}$ will be clarified a little bit later). In this subsection, we will provide certain results about the well-posedness of the following abstract two-dimensional Cauchy inclusions:

$$D_R^{\alpha_1} D_R^{\alpha_2} u(x_1, x_2) \in \mathcal{A}u(x_1, x_2) + f(x_1, x_2), \quad x_1 \geq 0, \ x_2 \geq 0, \tag{25}$$

subjected to the initial conditions of the form

$$\frac{\partial^k}{\partial x_2^k} \left[J_{t_2}^{m_2 - \alpha_2} *_0 u \right](x_1, 0) = f_k(x_1), \quad 0 \leq k \leq m_2 - 1; \tag{26}$$

$$\int_0^{x_2} g_{\alpha_2}(x_2 - s) \left[\frac{\partial^k}{\partial x_1^k} \left[J_{t_1}^{m_1 - \alpha_1} *_0 D_R^{\alpha_2} u \right](x_1, x_2) \right]_{x_1=0, x_2=s} ds = h_k(x_2), \tag{27}$$

for $0 \leq k \leq m_1 - 1$, and

$$\mathbf{D}_C^{\alpha_1} \mathbf{D}_C^{\alpha_2} u(x_1, x_2) \in \mathcal{A}u(x_1, x_2) + f(x_1, x_2), \quad x_1 \geq 0, \ x_2 \geq 0, \tag{28}$$

subjected to the initial conditions of the form

$$\frac{\partial^k}{\partial x_2^k} u(x_1, 0) = f_k(x_1), \quad 0 \leq k \leq m_2 - 1; \tag{29}$$

$$\int_0^{x_2} g_{\alpha_2}(x_2 - s) \left[\frac{\partial^k}{\partial x_1^k} \mathbf{D}_C^{\alpha_2} u(x_1, x_2) \right]_{x_1=0, x_2=s} ds = h_k(x_2), \quad 0 \leq k \leq m_1 - 1. \tag{30}$$

Our basic assumption will be that $f(\cdot, \cdot)$ is a Laplace transformable function.

Let us consider first the problem (28) equipped with the initial conditions (29)–(30). Assuming that $f \in L^1_{loc}([0, \infty)^2 : X)$, all conditions for applying the Formula (9) are satisfied and using the fact that for every locally integrable function $u \in L^1_{loc}([0, \infty)^2 : X)$, the assumption

$$J_{t_2}^{\alpha_2} J_{t_1}^{\alpha_1} u(x_1, x_2) = 0, \quad x_1 \geq 0, \ x_2 \geq 0$$

implies $u \equiv 0$, we obtain that the problem [(28)–(30)] is equivalent with

$$u(x_1, x_2) - \sum_{k=0}^{m_2-1} g_{k+1}(x_2) \cdot f_k(x_1) - \sum_{k=0}^{m_1-1} g_{k+1}(x_1) \cdot h_k(x_2)$$

$$\in A \int_0^{x_2} g_{\alpha_2}(x_2 - r) \int_0^{x_1} g_{\alpha_1}(x_1 - s) u(s, r) \, ds \, dr$$

$$+ \int_0^{x_2} g_{\alpha_2}(x_2 - r) \int_0^{x_1} g_{\alpha_1}(x_1 - s) f(s, r) \, ds \, dr, \quad x_1 \geq 0, \ x_2 \geq 0, \tag{31}$$

since $\mathcal{A}$ is closed. Similarly, if $f \in L^1_{loc}([0, \infty)^2 : X)$ and all conditions for applying the Formula (8) are satisfied, the problem [(25)–(27)] is equivalent with

$$u(x_1, x_2) - \sum_{k=0}^{m_2-1} g_{\alpha_2+k+1-m_2}(x_2) \cdot f_k(x_1) - \sum_{k=0}^{m_1-1} g_{\alpha_1+k+1-m_1}(x_1) \cdot h_k(x_2)$$

$$\in A \int_0^{x_2} g_{\alpha_2}(x_2 - r) \int_0^{x_1} g_{\alpha_1}(x_1 - s) u(s, r) \, ds \, dr$$

$$+ \int_0^{x_2} g_{\alpha_2}(x_2 - r) \int_0^{x_1} g_{\alpha_1}(x_1 - s) f(s, r) \, ds \, dr, \quad x_1 \geq 0, \ x_2 \geq 0. \tag{32}$$

We will use the following notion (cf. also [5] (Definition 3.1.1(i))).

Definition 4. *It is said that a locally integrable function* $u : [0, \infty)^2 \to X$ *is*

(i) *A solution of [(28)–(30)] if and only if*

$$\int_0^{x_2} g_{\alpha_2}(x_2 - r) \int_0^{x_1} g_{\alpha_1}(x_1 - s) u(s, r) \, ds \, dr \in D(\mathcal{A})$$

and (32) holds for a.e. $x_1 \geq 0$ *and* $x_2 \geq 0$.

(ii) *A strong solution of [(28)–(30)] if and only if there exists a locally integrable function* $u_{\mathcal{A}, \alpha_1, \alpha_2} : [0, \infty)^2 \to X$ *such that*

$$\int_0^{x_2} g_{\alpha_2}(x_2 - r) \int_0^{x_1} g_{\alpha_1}(x_1 - s) u_{\mathcal{A}, \alpha_1, \alpha_2}(s, r) \, ds \, dr$$

$$\in A \int_0^{x_2} g_{\alpha_2}(x_2 - r) \int_0^{x_1} g_{\alpha_1}(x_1 - s) u(s, r) \, ds \, dr \text{ for a.e. } x_1 \geq 0 \text{ and } x_2 \geq 0,$$

and

$$u(x_1, x_2) - \sum_{k=0}^{m_2-1} g_{k+1}(x_2) \cdot f_k(x_1) - \sum_{k=0}^{m_1-1} g_{k+1}(x_1) \cdot h_k(x_2)$$

$$= \int_0^{x_2} g_{\alpha_2}(x_2 - r) \int_0^{x_1} g_{\alpha_1}(x_1 - s) u_{A,\alpha_1,\alpha_2}(s,r) \, ds \, dr$$

$$+ \int_0^{x_2} g_{\alpha_2}(x_2 - r) \int_0^{x_1} g_{\alpha_1}(x_1 - s) f(s,r) \, ds \, dr \text{ for a.e. } x_1 \geq 0 \text{ and } x_2 \geq 0.$$

We similarly define the notion of a (strong) solution of problem [(25)–(27)].

It is clear that any strong solution of [(28)–(30)] ([(25)–(27)]) is likewise a solution of the same problem and that the converse statement is not true, in general.

Let us now take a closer look at the abstract Cauchy inclusions (31) and (32). Applying the two-dimensional Laplace transform and the Fubini theorem, we obtain that the problem (31) is equivalent with

$$\int_0^{+\infty} \int_0^{+\infty} e^{-zx_1 - \lambda x_2} u(x_1, x_2) \, dx_1 \, dx_2 - \sum_{k=0}^{m_2-1} \lambda^{-1-k} \int_0^{+\infty} e^{-zx_1} f_k(x_1) \, dx_1$$

$$- \sum_{k=0}^{m_1-1} z^{-1-k} \int_0^{+\infty} e^{-\lambda x_2} h_k(x_2) \, dx_2$$

$$\in \mathcal{A}\left[z^{-\alpha_1} \lambda^{-\alpha_2} \int_0^{+\infty} \int_0^{+\infty} e^{-zx_1 - \lambda x_2} u(x_1, x_2) \, dx_1 \, dx_2 \right]$$

$$+ z^{-\alpha_1} \lambda^{-\alpha_2} \int_0^{+\infty} \int_0^{+\infty} e^{-zx_1 - \lambda x_2} f(x_1, x_2) \, dx_1 \, dx_2, \tag{33}$$

for all $z \in \mathbb{C}$ with $\Re z > \omega_1$ for some $\omega_1 > 0$ and $\lambda \in \mathbb{C}$ with $\Re\lambda > \omega_2$ for some $\omega_2 > 0$, under certain logical assumptions, as well as that the problem (32) is equivalent with

$$\int_0^{+\infty} \int_0^{+\infty} e^{-zx_1 - \lambda x_2} u(x_1, x_2) \, dx_1 \, dx_2 - \sum_{k=0}^{m_2-1} \lambda^{m_2-1-k-\alpha_2} \int_0^{+\infty} e^{-zx_1} f_k(x_1) \, dx_1$$

$$- \sum_{k=0}^{m_1-1} z^{m_1-1-k-\alpha_1} \int_0^{+\infty} e^{-\lambda x_2} h_k(x_2) \, dx_2$$

$$\in \mathcal{A}\left[z^{-\alpha_1} \lambda^{-\alpha_2} \int_0^{+\infty} \int_0^{+\infty} e^{-zx_1 - \lambda x_2} u(x_1, x_2) \, dx_1 \, dx_2 \right]$$

$$+ z^{-\alpha_1} \lambda^{-\alpha_2} \int_0^{+\infty} \int_0^{+\infty} e^{-zx_1 - \lambda x_2} f(x_1, x_2) \, dx_1 \, dx_2, \tag{34}$$

for all $z \in \mathbb{C}$ with $\Re z > \omega_1$ for some $\omega_1 > 0$ and $\lambda \in \mathbb{C}$ with $\Re\lambda > \omega_2$ for some $\omega_2 > 0$, under certain logical assumptions. After setting

$$\widetilde{u}(z, \lambda) := \int_0^{+\infty} \int_0^{+\infty} e^{-zx_1 - \lambda x_2} u(x_1, x_2) \, dx_1 \, dx_2,$$

we obtain that the problem (33) is equivalent with

$$\left(z^{\alpha_1} \lambda^{\alpha_2} - \mathcal{A} \right) \widetilde{u}(z, \lambda) \ni \sum_{k=0}^{m_2-1} z^{\alpha_1} \lambda^{\alpha_2-1-k} \int_0^{+\infty} e^{-zx_1} f_k(x_1) \, dx_1$$

$$- \sum_{k=0}^{m_1-1} z^{\alpha_1-1-k} \lambda^{\alpha_2} \int_0^{+\infty} e^{-\lambda x_2} h_k(x_2) \, dx_2 + \widetilde{f}(z, \lambda), \tag{35}$$

for all $z \in \mathbb{C}$ with $\Re z > \omega_1$ and $\lambda \in \mathbb{C}$ with $\Re\lambda > \omega_2$, while the problem (34) is equivalent with

$$\left(z^{\alpha_1}\lambda^{\alpha_2} - \mathcal{A}\right)\widetilde{u}(z,\lambda) \ni \sum_{k=0}^{m_2-1} z^{\alpha_1}\lambda^{m_2-1-k}\int_0^{+\infty} e^{-zx_1}f_k(x_1)\,dx_1$$

$$-\sum_{k=0}^{m_1-1} z^{m_1-1-k}\lambda^{\alpha_2}\int_0^{+\infty} e^{-\lambda x_2}h_k(x_2)\,dx_2 + \widetilde{f}(z,\lambda), \tag{36}$$

for all $z \in \mathbb{C}$ with $\Re z > \omega_1$ and $\lambda \in \mathbb{C}$ with $\Re\lambda > \omega_2$. In the case that there exists an injective operator $C \in L(X)$ which commutes with $\mathcal{A}$ and condition (C1) clarified below holds, then the inclusion (35), resp., (36), is equivalent with:

$$\widetilde{u}(z,\lambda) = \left(z^{\alpha_1}\lambda^{\alpha_2} - \mathcal{A}\right)^{-1}C\sum_{k=0}^{m_2-1} z^{\alpha_1}\lambda^{\alpha_2-1-k}\int_0^{+\infty} e^{-zx_1}f_k(x_1)\,dx_1$$

$$-\left(z^{\alpha_1}\lambda^{\alpha_2} - \mathcal{A}\right)^{-1}C\sum_{k=0}^{m_1-1} z^{\alpha_1-1-k}\lambda^{\alpha_2}\int_0^{+\infty} e^{-\lambda x_2}h_k(x_2)\,dx_2 + \left(z^{\alpha_1}\lambda^{\alpha_2} - \mathcal{A}\right)^{-1}C\widetilde{f}(z,\lambda), \tag{37}$$

for all $z \in \mathbb{C}$ with $\Re z > \omega_1$ and $\lambda \in \mathbb{C}$ with $\Re\lambda > \omega_2$, resp.,

$$\widetilde{u}(z,\lambda) = \left(z^{\alpha_1}\lambda^{\alpha_2} - \mathcal{A}\right)^{-1}C\sum_{k=0}^{m_2-1} z^{\alpha_1}\lambda^{m_2-1-k}\int_0^{+\infty} e^{-zx_1}f_k(x_1)\,dx_1$$

$$-\left(z^{\alpha_1}\lambda^{\alpha_2} - \mathcal{A}\right)^{-1}C\sum_{k=0}^{m_1-1} z^{m_1-1-k}\lambda^{\alpha_2}\int_0^{+\infty} e^{-\lambda x_2}h_k(x_2)\,dx_2 + \left(z^{\alpha_1}\lambda^{\alpha_2} - \mathcal{A}\right)^{-1}C\widetilde{f}(z,\lambda), \tag{38}$$

for all $z \in \mathbb{C}$ with $\Re z > \omega_1$ and $\lambda \in \mathbb{C}$ with $\Re\lambda > \omega_2$.

Now we will formalize all this and state the following result by assuming some special conditions on the multivalued linear operator $\mathcal{A}$.

Theorem 2. *Suppose that $C \in L(X)$ is injective and commutes with $\mathcal{A}$, $f(\cdot;\cdot)$ is Laplace transformable and the following condition holds:*

(C1) There exist real numbers $\omega_1 > 0$ and $\omega_2 > 0$ such that $z^{\alpha_1}\lambda^{\alpha_2} \in \rho_C(\mathcal{A})$ for all $z \in \mathbb{C}$ with $\Re z > \omega_1$ and $\lambda \in \mathbb{C}$ with $\Re\lambda > \omega_2$.

Denote by D_1 the set of all indexes $k \in \mathbb{N}_{m_2-1}^0$ such that $f_k(\cdot)$ is not identically equal to the zero function and by D_2 the set of all indexes $k \in \mathbb{N}_{m_1-1}^0$ such that $h_k(\cdot)$ is not identically equal to the zero function. If the following conditions hold:

(i)   For every $k \in D_1$, there exists a Laplace transformable function $u_k^1(\cdot;\cdot)$ such that

$$\widetilde{u_k^1}(z,\lambda) = z^{\alpha_1}\lambda^{\alpha_2-1-k}\left(z^{\alpha_1}\lambda^{\alpha_2} - \mathcal{A}\right)^{-1}C\int_0^{+\infty} e^{-zx_1}f_k(x_1)\,dx_1,$$

resp.

$$\widetilde{u_k^1}(z,\lambda) = z^{\alpha_1}\lambda^{m_2-1-k}\left(z^{\alpha_1}\lambda^{\alpha_2} - \mathcal{A}\right)^{-1}C\int_0^{+\infty} e^{-zx_1}f_k(x_1)\,dx_1,$$

for $\Re z > \omega_1$ and $\Re\lambda > \omega_2$.

(ii)   For every $k \in D_2$, there exists a Laplace transformable function $u_k^2(\cdot;\cdot)$ such that

$$\widetilde{u_k^2}(z,\lambda) = z^{\alpha_1-1-k}\lambda^{\alpha_2}\left(z^{\alpha_1}\lambda^{\alpha_2} - \mathcal{A}\right)^{-1}C\int_0^{+\infty} e^{-\lambda x_2}h_k(x_2)\,dx_2,$$

resp.

$$\widetilde{u_k^2}(z,\lambda) = z^{m_1-1-k}\lambda^{\alpha_2}\left(z^{\alpha_1}\lambda^{\alpha_2} - \mathcal{A}\right)^{-1}C\int_0^{+\infty} e^{-\lambda x_2}h_k(x_2)\,dx_2,$$

for $\Re z > \omega_1$ and $\Re\lambda > \omega_2$.

(iii)   There exists a Laplace transformable function $u_k^2(\cdot;\cdot)$ such that

$$\widetilde{u_f}(z,\lambda) = \left(z^{\alpha_1}\lambda^{\alpha_2} - \mathcal{A}\right)^{-1} C\widetilde{f}(z,\lambda),$$

for $\Re z > \omega_1$ and $\Re \lambda > \omega_2$.

Then there exists a unique solution of problem $u(x_1,x_2)$ of [(28)–(30)], resp., [(25)–(27)], which is given by

$$u(x_1,x_2) = \sum_{k\in D_1} u_k^1(x_1,x_2) + \sum_{k\in D_2} u_k^2(x_1,x_2) + u_f(x_1,x_2) \text{ for a.e. } x_1 \geq 0,\ x_2 \geq 0. \tag{39}$$

Furthermore, suppose that (i)–(iii) and the following conditions hold:

(is)   For every $k \in D_1$, there exists a Laplace transformable function $u_k^1(\cdot;\cdot)$ such that

$$\widetilde{u_k^1}(z,\lambda) = z^{2\alpha_1}\lambda^{2\alpha_2-1-k}\left(z^{\alpha_1}\lambda^{\alpha_2} - \mathcal{A}\right)^{-1} C \int_0^{+\infty} e^{-zx_1} f_k(x_1)\, dx_1$$
$$- z^{\alpha_1}\lambda^{\alpha_2-1-k}\int_0^{+\infty} e^{-zx_1} f_k(x_1)\, dx_1,$$

resp.

$$\widetilde{u_k^1}(z,\lambda) = z^{2\alpha_1}\lambda^{\alpha_2+m_2-1-k}\left(z^{\alpha_1}\lambda^{\alpha_2} - \mathcal{A}\right)^{-1} C \int_0^{+\infty} e^{-zx_1} f_k(x_1)\, dx_1$$
$$- z^{\alpha_1}\lambda^{m_2-1-k}\int_0^{+\infty} e^{-zx_1} f_k(x_1)\, dx_1,$$

for $\Re z > \omega_1$ and $\Re \lambda > \omega_2$.

(iis)   For every $k \in D_2$, there exists a Laplace transformable function $u_k^2(\cdot;\cdot)$ such that

$$\widetilde{u_k^2}(z,\lambda) = z^{2\alpha_1-1-k}\lambda^{2\alpha_2}\left(z^{\alpha_1}\lambda^{\alpha_2} - \mathcal{A}\right)^{-1} C \int_0^{+\infty} e^{-\lambda x_2} h_k(x_2)\, dx_2$$
$$- z^{\alpha_1-1-k}\lambda^{\alpha_2} C \int_0^{+\infty} e^{-\lambda x_2} h_k(x_2)\, dx_2,$$

resp.

$$\widetilde{u_k^2}(z,\lambda) = z^{\alpha_1+m_1-1-k}\lambda^{2\alpha_2}\left(z^{\alpha_1}\lambda^{\alpha_2} - \mathcal{A}\right)^{-1} C \int_0^{+\infty} e^{-\lambda x_2} h_k(x_2)\, dx_2$$
$$- z^{m_1-1-k}\lambda^{\alpha_2} C \int_0^{+\infty} e^{-\lambda x_2} h_k(x_2)\, dx_2,$$

for $\Re z > \omega_1$ and $\Re \lambda > \omega_2$.

(iiis) There exists a Laplace transformable function $u_k^2(\cdot;\cdot)$ such that

$$\widetilde{u_f}(z,\lambda) = z^{\alpha_1}\lambda^{\alpha_2}\left(z^{\alpha_1}\lambda^{\alpha_2} - \mathcal{A}\right)^{-1} C\widetilde{f}(z,\lambda) - C\widetilde{f}(z,\lambda),$$

for $\Re z > \omega_1$ and $\Re \lambda > \omega_2$.

Then there exists a unique solution of problem $u(x_1,x_2)$ of [(28)–(30)], resp., [(25)–(27)], which is given by

$$u(x_1,x_2) = \sum_{k\in D_1} u_k^1(x_1,x_2) + \sum_{k\in D_2} u_k^2(x_1,x_2) + u_f(x_1,x_2) \text{ for a.e. } x_1 \geq 0,\ x_2 \geq 0. \tag{40}$$

Then the function $u(x_1,x_2)$, given by (40), is a strong solution of problem $u(x_1,x_2)$ of [(28)–(30)], resp., [(25)–(27)].

Proof. Since we assume the conditions (i)–(iii), we simply infer that the function $u(x_1, x_2)$, given by (40), satisfies (37), resp., (38). Arguing reversely, we obtain that (35), resp., (36), holds true. Applying the inverse double Laplace transform, we obtain that (33), resp., (34), holds true, which simply completes the proof of the first part of theorem. The second part of theorem follows similarly since, in this case, there exists a locally integrable function $u_{\mathcal{A},\alpha_1,\alpha_2}(\cdot;\cdot)$ such that $u_{\mathcal{A},\alpha_1,\alpha_2}(\cdot;\cdot) \in \mathcal{A}u(\cdot;\cdot)$ a.e. on $[0,+\infty)^2$, which can be proved by performing the double Laplace transform and (is)–(iiis); see also [5] (Theorem 1.2.4(i)). $\square$

The subsequent result follows immediately from Theorems 1 and 2 (we can similarly clarify the corresponding conditions ensuring the existence of a unique strong solution of problems under our consideration; we use the symbol $\tilde{\ }$ to denote both the one-dimensional and the two-dimensional Laplace transform here, which will not cause any confusion).

Theorem 3. *Suppose that $f(\cdot;\cdot)$ is Laplace transformable and the following condition holds: (C1s)(C1) holds and there exist real numbers $M > 0$ and $\beta \in (0,1]$ such that*

$$\left\|\left(z^{\alpha_1}\lambda^{\alpha_2} - \mathcal{A}\right)^{-1}C\right\| \le \frac{M}{(1 + |z|^{\alpha_1}|\lambda|^{\alpha_2})^\beta}, \quad \Re z > \omega_1,\ \Re\lambda > \omega_2. \tag{41}$$

Suppose, further, that the following conditions hold:

(i) *For every $k \in D_1$, there exist real numbers $M_{k,1} > 0$, $\epsilon_{1,1}^k > 0$ and $\epsilon_{1,2}^k > 0$ such that*

$$\left\||z|^{\alpha_1}|\lambda|^{\alpha_2-1-k}\frac{\|\widetilde{f_k}(z)\|}{(1 + |z|^{\alpha_1}|\lambda|^{\alpha_2})^\beta}\right\| \le M_{k,1}|z|^{-1-\epsilon_{1,1}^k}|\lambda|^{-1-\epsilon_{1,2}^k}, \quad \Re z > \omega_1,\ \Re\lambda > \omega_2.$$

(ii) *For every $k \in D_2$, there exist real numbers $M_{k,2} > 0$, $\epsilon_{2,1}^k > 0$ and $\epsilon_{2,2}^k > 0$ such that*

$$\left\||z|^{\alpha_1-1-k}|\lambda|^{\alpha_2}\frac{\|\widetilde{h_k}(\lambda)\|}{(1 + |z|^{\alpha_1}|\lambda|^{\alpha_2})^\beta}\right\| \le M_{k,1}|z|^{-1-\epsilon_{2,1}^k}|\lambda|^{-1-\epsilon_{2,2}^k}, \quad \Re z > \omega_1,\ \Re\lambda > \omega_2.$$

(iii) *There exist real numbers $M' > 0$, $\epsilon_1 > 0$ and $\epsilon_2 > 0$ such that*

$$\left\|\frac{\|\widetilde{f}(z,\lambda)\|}{(1 + |z|^{\alpha_1}|\lambda|^{\alpha_2})^\beta}\right\| \le M'|z|^{-1-\epsilon_1}|\lambda|^{-1-\epsilon_2}, \quad \Re z > \omega_1,\ \Re\lambda > \omega_2.$$

Then there exists a unique continuous solution $u(x_1, x_2)$ of problem [(28)–(30)], resp., [(25)–(27)], and we have

$$\left\|u(x_1, x_2)\right\| \le M''\left[\sum_{k \in D_1} x_1^{\epsilon_{1,1}} x_2^{\epsilon_{1,2}} e^{\omega_1 x_1 + \omega_2 x_2}\right.$$

$$\left. + \sum_{k \in D_2} x_1^{\epsilon_{2,1}} x_2^{\epsilon_{2,2}} e^{\omega_1 x_1 + \omega_2 x_2} + x_1^{\epsilon_1} x_2^{\epsilon_2} e^{\omega_1 x_1 + \omega_2 x_2}\right], \quad x_1 \ge 0,\ x_2 \ge 0.$$

If $0 \notin D_1 \cup D_2$, then the requirements of Theorem 3 are satisfied in many important real situations, even for the degenerate Poisson heat operator $\Delta \cdot m(x)^{-1}$; cf. [5] and references cited therein for further information in this direction.

Remark 3. *Suppose that $\alpha_1 + \alpha_2 < 2$. Then it is clear that the estimate (41) holds if $\Sigma_{(\alpha_1+\alpha_2)\pi/2} \subseteq \rho_C(\mathcal{A})$ and there exists $\beta \in (0,1]$ such that*

$$\left\|(\lambda - A)^{-1}C\right\| \le \frac{M}{(1 + |\lambda|)^\beta}, \quad \lambda \in \Sigma_{(\alpha_1+\alpha_2)\pi/2}.$$

Unfortunately, we cannot prove that (41) *holds if there exists a positive real number $a > 0$ such that $a + \Sigma_{(\alpha_1+\alpha_2)\pi/2} \subseteq \rho_C(\mathcal{A})$ and*

$$\left\| (\lambda - \mathcal{A})^{-1} C \right\| \leq \frac{M}{(1 + |\lambda|)^\beta}, \quad \lambda \in a + \Sigma_{(\alpha_1+\alpha_2)\pi/2}.$$

The main problem lies in the fact that for every real number $\omega_1 > 0$, we have

$$\lim_{x \to \pm\infty} dist\left(\{ re^{i\alpha_1} : r \geq 0 \}, (\omega_1 + ix)^{\alpha_1} \right) = 0.$$

Remark 4. *Suppose that $\alpha_1 + \alpha_2 \geq 2$. Then we can apply Theorem 3, with $C \neq I$, to a class of two-dimensional partial fractional differential equations involving the single-valued linear operators $\mathcal{A} = A$ whose C-resolvent is bounded by $(1 + |\cdot|)^{-1}$ on the set of form $\mathbb{C} \setminus K$, where K is compact; see [5] for the corresponding examples. In particular, if $\alpha_1 = \alpha_2 = 1$, then we can analyze the well-posedness of the problem*

$$\frac{\partial^2}{\partial x_1 \partial x_2} u(x_1, x_2) = Au(x_1, x_2) + f(x_1, x_2), \quad x_1 \geq 0, \ x_2 \geq 0,$$

subjected to the initial conditions $u(x_1, 0) = f_0(x_1)$, $x_1 \geq 0$ and $u(0, x_2) = u(0,0) + h_0(x_2)$, $x_2 \geq 0$.

Using the multidimensional generalizations of the Formulae (8) and (9), we can similarly analyze the well-posedness of the abstract fractional Cauchy inclusions

$$D_R^{\alpha_1} D_R^{\alpha_2} \cdot \ldots \cdot D_R^{\alpha_n} u(\mathbf{x}) \in \mathcal{A}u(\mathbf{x}) + f(\mathbf{x}), \quad \mathbf{x} = (x_1, x_2, \ldots, x_n) \in [0, +\infty)^n$$

and

$$\mathbf{D}_C^{\alpha_1} \mathbf{D}_C^{\alpha_2} \cdot \ldots \cdot \mathbf{D}_C^{\alpha_n} u(\mathbf{x}) \in \mathcal{A}u(\mathbf{x}) + f(\mathbf{x}), \quad \mathbf{x} = (x_1, x_2, \ldots, x_n) \in [0, +\infty)^n,$$

subjected to certain initial conditions (for the scalar-valued case, see also [54] (Section 3)). Details can be left to interested readers.

6.2. The Abstract Multiterm Fractional Partial Differential Equations with Riemann–Liouville and Caputo Derivatives

In this subsection, we investigate the following operator extensions of the partial fractional differential Equation (1):

$$\sum_{k=1}^{n} A_k D_R^{(0,\ldots,\alpha_k,\ldots,0)} u(x_1, \ldots, x_k, \ldots, x_n) = f(x_1, \ldots, x_n), \quad x_1 \geq 0, \ \ldots, \ x_n \geq 0, \tag{42}$$

subjected to the initial conditions

$$\left[\frac{\partial^j}{\partial x_k^j} J_{t_k}^{m_k - \alpha_k} u(x_1, \ldots, x_n) \right]_{x_k = 0} = f_{k,j}(x_1, \ldots, x_{k-1}, x_{k+1}, \ldots, x_n), \tag{43}$$

for $1 \leq k \leq n$, $0 \leq j \leq m_k - 1$, and

$$\sum_{k=1}^{n} A_k D_C^{(0,\ldots,\alpha_k,\ldots,0)} u(x_1, \ldots, x_k, \ldots, x_n) = f(x_1, \ldots, x_n), \quad x_1 \geq 0, \ \ldots, \ x_n \geq 0, \tag{44}$$

subjected to the initial conditions

$$\left[\frac{\partial^j}{\partial x_k^j} u(x_1, ..., x_n)\right]_{x_k=0} = f_{k,j}(x_1, ..., x_{k-1}, x_{k+1}, ..., x_n), \qquad (45)$$

for $1 \leq k \leq n$, $0 \leq j \leq m_k - 1$, where A_k is a closed linear operator and $\alpha_k \geq 0$ for $1 \leq k \leq n$. In order to do that, we essentially apply the multidimensional vector-valued Laplace transform.

We will use the following notion.

Definition 5.

(i)   *By a mild LT-solution $u(x_1, ..., x_n)$ of [(42) and (43)], resp. [(44) and (45)], we mean any Laplace transformable function $u(x_1, ..., x_n)$ such that the terms $D_R^{(0,...,\alpha_k,...,0)} u(x_1, ..., x_k, ..., x_n)$, resp. $D_C^{(0,...,\alpha_k,...,0)} u(x_1, ..., x_k, ..., x_n)$, are well-defined and Laplace transformable for $1 \leq k \leq n$ as well as that the terms $(\partial^j / \partial x_k^j) J_{t_k}^{m_k - \alpha_k} u(x_1, ..., x_n)$, resp. $(\partial^j / \partial x_k^j) u(x_1, ..., x_n)$, are well-defined and continuous with respect to the variable x_j for $1 \leq k \leq n, 0 \leq j \leq m_k - 1$,*

$$\sum_{k=1}^{n} A_k \left(\mathcal{L} D_R^{(0,...,\alpha_k,...,0)} u(x_1, ..., x_k, ..., x_n) \right)(\lambda_1, ..., \lambda_n) = \tilde{f}(\lambda_1, ..., \lambda_n), \qquad (46)$$

for $\Re\lambda_j > \omega_j$ $(1 \leq j \leq n)$ and some non-negative real numbers $\omega_1 \geq 0$, ..., $\omega_n \geq 0$, resp. (46) holds with the term $D_R^{(0,...,\alpha_k,...,0)} u(x_1, ..., x_k, ..., x_n)$ replaced with the term $D_C^{(0,...,\alpha_k,...,0)} u(x_1, ..., x_k, ..., x_n)$ therein, and (43), resp. (45), holds.

(ii)   *By a strong LT-solution $u(x_1, ..., x_n)$ of [(42) and (43)], resp. [(44) and (45)], we mean any mild LT-solution $u(x_1, ..., x_n)$ of this problem which additionally satisfies that the terms $A_k D_R^{(0,...,\alpha_k,...,0)} u(x_1, ..., x_k, ..., x_n)$, resp. $A_k D_C^{(0,...,\alpha_k,...,0)} u(x_1, ..., x_k, ..., x_n)$, are well-defined and Laplace transformable for $1 \leq k \leq n$.*

The uniqueness theorem for Laplace transform and the closedness of operators A_k for $1 \leq k \leq n$ show that any strong LT-solution of [(42) and (43)], resp. [(44) and (45)], satisfies that (42), resp. (44), holds for a.e. $x_1 \geq 0$, ..., $x_n \geq 0$.

Our main result concerning the well-posedness of Equations (42)–(45) reads as follows

Theorem 4. *Suppose that $C \in L(X)$ is injective, A_k is a closed linear operator commuting with C and $\alpha_k \geq 0$ for $1 \leq k \leq n$. Suppose, further, that there exist non-negative real numbers $\omega_1 \geq 0$, ..., $\omega_n \geq 0$ such that the operator $\sum_{k=1}^{n} \lambda_k^{\alpha_k} A_k$ is injective and $(\sum_{k=1}^{n} \lambda_k^{\alpha_k} A_k)^{-1} C \in L(X)$ for $\Re\lambda_1 > \omega_1$, ..., $\Re\lambda_n > \omega_n$. Let the following conditions also hold:*

(i)   *There exists a locally integrable, exponentially bounded function $h(x_1, ..., x_n)$ for $x_1 \geq 0$, ..., $x_n \geq 0$ satisfying that $D_R^{(0,...,\alpha_k,...,0)} h(x_1, ..., x_k, ..., x_n)$, resp. $D_C^{(0,...,\alpha_k,...,0)} h(x_1, ..., x_k, ..., x_n)$, is well-defined, locally integrable and exponentially bounded $(1 \leq k \leq n)$, the terms $(\partial^j / \partial x_k^j) J_{t_k}^{m_k - \alpha_k} h(x_1, ..., x_n)$, resp. $(\partial^j / \partial x_k^j) h(x_1, ..., x_n)$, are well-defined and continuous with respect to the variable x_j for $1 \leq k \leq n, 0 \leq j \leq m_k - 1$, and*

$$\tilde{h}(\lambda_1, ..., \lambda_n) = \left(\sum_{k=1}^{n} \lambda_k^{\alpha_k} A_k \right)^{-1} C \tilde{f_0}(\lambda_1, ..., \lambda_n), \quad \Re\lambda_1 > \omega_1, ..., \Re\lambda_n > \omega_n, \qquad (47)$$

where $f = C f_0$.

(ii)   *If $1 \leq k \leq n$ and $0 \leq j \leq m_k - 1$, then there exists a locally integrable, exponentially bounded function $h_{k,j}(x_1, ..., x_{k-1}, x_{k+1}, ..., x_n)$ for $x_1 \geq 0$, ..., $x_{k-1} \geq 0$, $x_{k+1} \geq 0$, ..., $x_n \geq 0$ satisfying that the terms $D_R^{(0,...,\alpha_v,...,0)} h_{k,j}(x_1, ..., x_{k-1}, x_{k+1}, ..., x_n)$, resp. $D_C^{(0,...,\alpha_v,...,0)} h_{k,j}(x_1, ..., x_{k-1}, x_{k+1}..., x_n)$, are well-defined, locally integrable and exponentially bounded for*

$1 \le v \le n$, the terms $(\partial^j / \partial x_v^j) J_{t_k}^{m_k - \alpha_k} h_{k,j}(x_1, ..., x_{k-1}, x_{k+1}, ..., x_n)$, resp. $(\partial^j / \partial x_v^j) h_{k,j}$ $(x_1, ..., x_{k-1}, x_{k+1}, ..., x_n)$ *are well-defined and continuous with respect to the variable* x_v *for* $1 \le v \le n$, *and*

$$\widetilde{h_{k,j}}(\lambda_1, ..., \lambda_{k-1}, \lambda_{k+1}, ..., \lambda_n) = \left(\sum_{k=1}^{n} \lambda_k^{\alpha_k} A_k\right)^{-1} CA_k \widetilde{f_{k,j,0}}(\lambda_1, ..., \lambda_{k-1}, \lambda_{k+1}, ..., \lambda_n), \tag{48}$$

provided that $\Re\lambda_1 > \omega_1, ..., \Re\lambda_{k-1} > \omega_{k-1}, \Re\lambda_{k+1} > \omega_{k+1}, ..., \Re\lambda_n > \omega_n$, *where* $f_{k,j} = Cf_{k,j,0}$.

Then there exists a unique mild LT-*solution* $u(x_1, ..., x_n)$ *of* [(42) *and* (43)], *resp.* [(44) *and* (45)], *and we have*

$$u(x_1, ..., x_n) = \sum_{k=1}^{n} \sum_{j=0}^{m_k - 1} h_{k,j}(x_1, ..., x_n) + h(x_1, ..., x_n), \quad x_1 \ge 0, ..., x_n \ge 0. \tag{49}$$

Furthermore, if the following conditions hold:

(is) *If* $1 \le v \le n$, *then the terms* $A_v h(x_1, ..., x_v, ..., x_n)$ *and* $D_R^{(0,...,\alpha_v,...,0)} A_v h(x_1, ..., x_v, ..., x_n)$, *resp.* $D_C^{(0,...,\alpha_v,...,0)} A_v h(x_1, ..., x_v, ..., x_n)$, *are well-defined, locally integrable and exponentially bounded;*

(iis) *If* $1 < v \le n, 1 \le k \le n$ *and* $0 \le j \le m_k - 1$, *then the terms* $A_v h_{k,j}(x_1, ..., x_{k-1}, x_{k+1}, ..., x_n)$ *and* $D_R^{(0,...,\alpha_v,...,0)} A_v h_{k,j}(x_1, ..., x_{k-1}, x_{k+1}, ..., x_n)$, *resp.* $D_C^{(0,...,\alpha_v,...,0)} A_v h_{k,j}(x_1, ..., x_{k-1}, x_{k+1}..., x_n)$, *are well-defined, locally integrable and exponentially bounded,*

then the function $u(x_1, ..., x_n)$, *given by* (49), *is a strong* LT-*solution of* [(42) *and* (43)], *resp.* [(44) *and* (45)].

Proof. Let $u(x_1, ..., x_n)$ be given by (49), and let $\Re\lambda_1 > \omega_1, ..., \Re\lambda_n > \omega_n$. Our assumptions imply that the term $D_R^{(0,...,\alpha_k,...,0)} u(x_1, ..., x_k, ..., x_n)$, resp. $D_C^{(0,...,\alpha_k,...,0)} u(x_1, ..., x_k, ..., x_n)$, is well-defined as well as that we have the following (see also Equations (1.22)–(1.23) [1] and Equation (16) [55]):

$$D_R^{(0,...,\alpha_k,...,0)} u(x_1, ..., x_k, ..., x_n) = \lambda_k^{\alpha_k} \tilde{u}(\lambda_1, ..., \lambda_n)$$
$$- \sum_{j=0}^{m_k - 1} \left[\mathcal{L}_{t_1,...,t_{k-1},t_{k+1},...,t_n} f_{k,j} \right] (\lambda_1, ..., \lambda_{k-1}, \lambda_{k+1}, ..., \lambda_n) \lambda_k^{m_k - 1 - j}, \tag{50}$$

resp.

$$D_C^{(0,...,\alpha_k,...,0)} u(x_1, ..., x_k, ..., x_n) = \lambda_k^{\alpha_k} \tilde{u}(\lambda_1, ..., \lambda_n)$$
$$- \sum_{j=0}^{m_k - 1} \left[\mathcal{L}_{t_1,...,t_{k-1},t_{k+1},...,t_n} f_{k,j} \right] (\lambda_1, ..., \lambda_{k-1}, \lambda_{k+1}, ..., \lambda_n) \lambda_k^{\alpha_k - 1 - j}, \tag{51}$$

where $\mathcal{L}_{t_1,...,t_{k-1},t_{k+1},...,t_n}$ denotes the multidimensional Laplace transform with respect to the variables $t_1, ..., t_{k-1}, t_{k+1}, ..., t_n$. Furthermore, our assumptions simply imply that

$$\tilde{u}(\lambda_1, ..., \lambda_n) = \sum_{k=1}^{n} \left(\sum_{k=1}^{n} \lambda_k^{\alpha_k} A_k\right)^{-1} CA_k \sum_{j=0}^{m_k - 1} \left[\mathcal{L}_{t_1,...,t_{k-1},t_{k+1},...,t_n} f_{k,j,0} \right]$$

$$(\lambda_1, ..., \lambda_{k-1}, \lambda_{k+1}, ..., \lambda_n) + \left(\sum_{k=1}^{n} \lambda_k^{\alpha_k} A_k\right)^{-1} C\widetilde{f_0}(\lambda_1, ..., \lambda_n).$$

This simply implies

$$\left[\sum_{k=1}^{n} \lambda_k^{\alpha_k} A_k\right] \tilde{u}(\lambda_1, \dots, \lambda_n) - \sum_{k=1}^{n} A_k$$

$$\times \sum_{j=0}^{m_k-1}\left[\mathcal{L}_{t_1,\dots,t_{k-1},t_{k+1},\dots,t_n} f_{k,j}\right](\lambda_1, \dots, \lambda_{k-1}, \lambda_{k+1}, \dots, \lambda_n)\lambda_k^{m_k-1-j} = \tilde{f}(\lambda_1, \dots, \lambda_n),$$

resp.

$$\left[\sum_{k=1}^{n} \lambda_k^{\alpha_k} A_k\right] \tilde{u}(\lambda_1, \dots, \lambda_n) - \sum_{k=1}^{n} A_k$$

$$\times \sum_{j=0}^{m_k-1}\left[\mathcal{L}_{t_1,\dots,t_{k-1},t_{k+1},\dots,t_n} f_{k,j}\right](\lambda_1, \dots, \lambda_{k-1}, \lambda_{k+1}, \dots, \lambda_n)\lambda_k^{\alpha_k-1-j} = \tilde{f}(\lambda_1, \dots, \lambda_n).$$

Keeping in mind Equations (50) and (51), it readily follows that Equation (46) and its analogue with Caputo fractional derivatives hold good. Therefore, the function $u(x_1, \dots, x_n)$ is a mild LT-solution of problem [(42) and (43)], resp. [(44) and (45)]. The uniqueness of mild LT-solutions of this problem follows from a simple argumentation involving the injectiveness of the operator $\sum_{k=1}^{n} \lambda_k^{\alpha_k} A_k$ for $\Re\lambda_1 > \omega_1, \dots, \Re\lambda_n > \omega_n$ and the uniqueness theorem for the Laplace transform. Finally, if the conditions (is) and (iis) hold, then we can simply prove that the function $A_v D_R^{(0,\dots,\alpha_v,\dots,0)} u(x_1, \dots x_n)$ is Laplace transformable and

$$\mathcal{L}\left[A_v D_R^{(0,\dots,\alpha_v,\dots,0)} u(x_1, \dots x_n)\right] = A_v\left[\mathcal{L}u(x_1, \dots x_n)\right],$$

which simply completes the proof. $\square$

Keeping in mind Theorem 1, we can apply Theorem 4 in many concrete situations, even if $\alpha_k > 2$ for some indexes $k \in \mathbb{N}_n$; cf. [5,55] for more details. Let us finally observe that we can similarly analyze some generalizations of the problems [(42)–(45)] with various types of generalized Laplace fractional derivatives, especially with the generalized Hilfer (a, b, α)-fractional derivatives [43].

6.3. Fractional Partial Difference Equations with Generalized Weyl Derivatives

In our recent research article [56], we investigated various classes of the abstract non-scalar Volterra difference equations of several variables. In order to do that, we introduced and analyzed the notion of a discrete $(k, C, B, (A_i)_{1 \leq i \leq n}, (v_i)_{1 \leq i \leq n})$-existence family (cf. [56] (Definition 2.1)); the generation of discrete $(k, C, B, (A_i)_{1 \leq i \leq n}, (v_i)_{1 \leq i \leq n})$-existence families was analyzed in [56] (Theorem 2.1) under certain very mild assumptions.

In [56], (Theorem 2.2(i)), we proved the following result:

Lemma 1. *Suppose that* $v_1 \in \mathbb{N}_0^n, \dots, v_m \in \mathbb{N}_0^n, (S(v))_{v \in \mathbb{N}_0^n} \subseteq L(X)$ *is a discrete* $(k, C, B, (A_i)_{1 \leq i \leq m}, (v_i)_{1 \leq i \leq m})$-existence family, $\sum_{v \in \mathbb{N}_0^n} \|S(v)\| < +\infty$ *and the following holds:*

(a) $f : \mathbb{Z}^n \to X$ *is a bounded sequence,* $k \in l^1(\mathbb{N}_0^n : \mathbb{C})$ *and* $\sum_{v \in \mathbb{N}_0^n} |a_i(v)| < +\infty$ *for* $1 \leq i \leq m$,
   or

(b) $f \in l^1(\mathbb{Z}^n : X), k : \mathbb{N}_0^n \to \mathbb{C}$ *is a bounded sequence and* $a_i : \mathbb{Z}^n \to \mathbb{C}$ *is a bounded sequence for* $1 \leq i \leq m$.

Define

$$u(v) := \sum_{l \in \mathbb{Z}^n; l \leq v} S(v - l)f(l), \quad v \in \mathbb{Z}^n \tag{52}$$

and

$$g(\mathrm{v}) := A_1 \left(\sum_{l \le \mathrm{v}+\mathrm{v}_1} - \sum_{l \le \mathrm{v}} \right) (a_1 *_0 S)(\mathrm{v} + \mathrm{v}_1 - l) f(l) + \dots$$

$$+ A_m \left(\sum_{l \le \mathrm{v}+\mathrm{v}_m} - \sum_{l \le \mathrm{v}} \right) (a_m *_0 S)(\mathrm{v} + \mathrm{v}_m - l) f(l), \quad v \in \mathbb{Z}^n. \tag{53}$$

Then $u(\cdot)$ is bounded if (a) *holds, $u \in l^1(\mathbb{Z}^n : X)$ if* (b) *holds, and we have*

$$Bu(\mathrm{v}) = A_1 \sum_{l \in \mathbb{Z}^n; l \le \mathrm{v}+\mathrm{v}_1} a_1(\mathrm{v} + \mathrm{v}_1 - l) u(l) + \dots$$

$$+ A_m \sum_{l \in \mathbb{Z}^n; l \le \mathrm{v}+\mathrm{v}_m} a_1(\mathrm{v} + \mathrm{v}_m - l) u(l) + g(\mathrm{v}), \; v \in \mathbb{Z}^n.$$

For some concrete applications of Lemma 1 to the fractional partial difference equations with generalized Weyl derivatives, we will particularly consider the situation in which the sequences $a_i(\cdot)$ have the following form:

$$a_i(v_1, \dots, v_n) = a_1^i(v_1) \cdot \dots \cdot a_n^i(v_n), \quad (v_1, \dots, v_n) \in \mathbb{N}_0^n \; (1 \le i \le m). \tag{54}$$

Suppose now that $\mathrm{v}_1 \in \mathbb{N}_0^n$, ..., $\mathrm{v}_m \in \mathbb{N}_0^n$, $(S(\mathrm{v}))_{\mathrm{v} \in \mathbb{N}_0^n} \subseteq L(X)$ is a discrete $(k, C, B, (A_i)_{1 \le i \le m}, (\mathrm{v}_i)_{1 \le i \le m})$-existence family, $\sum_{\mathrm{v} \in \mathbb{N}_0^n} \|S(\mathrm{v})\| < +\infty$, (54) and the following conditions hold:

(a1) $f : \mathbb{Z}^n \to X$ is a bounded sequence, $k \in l^1(\mathbb{N}_0^n : \mathbb{C})$ and $\sum_{v=0}^{+\infty} |a_j^i(v)| < +\infty$ for $1 \le j \le n$ and $1 \le i \le m$, or

(b1) $f \in l^1(\mathbb{Z}^n : X)$, $k : \mathbb{N}_0^n \to \mathbb{C}$ is a bounded sequence and $a_j^i : \mathbb{Z} \to \mathbb{C}$ is a bounded sequence for $1 \le j \le n$ and $1 \le i \le m$.

Let $\mathbf{m} = (m_1, \dots, m_n) \in \mathbb{N}^n$ be fixed, and let the sequences $u(\cdot)$ and $g(\cdot)$ be defined by (52) and (53), respectively. Then $u(\cdot)$ is bounded if (a1) holds, $u \in l^1(\mathbb{Z}^n : X)$ if (b1) holds, and a simple computation shows that we have

$$\left(\Delta_{v_1^{m_1} \cdot \dots \cdot v_n^{m_n}}^{m_1 + \dots + m_n} Bu \right)(\mathrm{v})$$

$$= A_1 \left(\Delta_{W, a_1, \mathbf{m}} u \right)(\mathrm{v} + \mathrm{v}_i) + \dots + A_m \left(\Delta_{W, a_m, \mathbf{m}} u \right)(\mathrm{v} + \mathrm{v}_m), \quad \mathrm{v} \in \mathbb{Z}^n. \tag{55}$$

Further on, if $\alpha_1 = (\alpha_1^1, \dots, \alpha_n^1) \in [0, +\infty)^n$ ..., $\alpha_m = (\alpha_1^m, \dots, \alpha_n^m) \in [0, +\infty)^n$, $m_j^i = \lceil \alpha_j^i \rceil$ for $1 \le j \le n$ and $1 \le i \le m$, $a_j^i(v_j) = k^{m_j^i - \alpha_j^i}(v_j)$ for $1 \le j \le n$, $1 \le i \le m$, and

$$m_j = m_j^1 = \dots = m_j^n, \quad 1 \le j \le n,$$

then we have

$$\left(\Delta_{v_1^{m_1} \cdot \dots \cdot v_n^{m_n}}^{m_1 + \dots + m_n} Bu \right)(\mathrm{v}) = A_1 \left(\Delta_W^{\alpha_1} u \right)(\mathrm{v} + \mathrm{v}_i) + \dots + A_m \left(\Delta_W^{\alpha_m} u \right)(\mathrm{v} + \mathrm{v}_m), \; \mathrm{v} \in \mathbb{Z}^n. \tag{56}$$

We can also analyze some other relatives of (55) and (56) as well as the existence and uniqueness of almost periodic-type solutions to (55) and (56); cf. [56] for more details.

7. Conclusions

In this paper, we introduced and analyzed several new types of partial fractional derivatives in the continuous setting and the discrete setting. We investigated the well-posedness of some classes of the abstract fractional differential equations and the abstract fractional difference equations depending on several variables, providing also many illustrative examples and useful remarks. We also provided some new applications of the multidimensional vector-valued Laplace transform.

We can also consider several new types of partial fractional derivatives using the multidimensional convolution products

$$\left(\mathbf{a} *_0 \mathbf{b}\right)(\mathbf{x}) := \int_0^{x_1} \cdots \cdot \int_0^{x_n} \mathbf{a}\left(x_1 - s_1, \ldots, x_n - s_n\right) \mathbf{b}\left(s_1, \ldots, s_n\right) ds_1 \ldots ds_n,$$

for $\mathbf{x} = \left(x_1, \ldots, x_n\right) \in [0, +\infty)^n$, where $\mathbf{a}, \mathbf{b} \in L^1_{loc}([0, +\infty)^n)$, and

$$\left(\mathbf{a} \circ \mathbf{b}\right)(\mathbf{x}) := \int_{-\infty}^{x_1} \cdots \cdot \int_{-\infty}^{x_n} \mathbf{a}\left(x_1 - s_1, \ldots, x_n - s_n\right) \mathbf{b}\left(s_1, \ldots, s_n\right) ds_1 \ldots ds_n, \tag{57}$$

for $\mathbf{x} = \left(x_1, \ldots, x_n\right) \in \mathbb{R}^n$, where $\mathbf{a} \in L^1_{loc}([0, +\infty)^n)$ and $\mathbf{b} \in L^1_{loc}(\mathbb{R}^n)$. It is clear that Equation (57) presents an extension of the generalized Weyl $\mathbf{a}$-integral; if $\mathbf{a} \in L^1_{loc}([0, +\infty)^n)$, $\mathbf{u} \in L^1_{loc}(\mathbb{R}^n)$, $\alpha_j \geq 0$ for $1 \leq j \leq n$ and $\alpha = (\alpha_1, \ldots, \alpha_n)$, then we also define

$$\mathbb{D}_W^{\alpha, \mathbf{a}, 1} \mathbf{u} := \frac{\partial^m}{\partial x_1^{m_1} \cdot \ldots \cdot \partial x_n^{m_n}} \left(\mathbf{a} \circ \mathbf{u}\right)(\mathbf{x}), \quad \mathbf{x} = \left(x_1, \ldots, x_n\right) \in \mathbb{R}^n,$$

where $m_j = \lceil \alpha_j \rceil$ for $1 \leq j \leq n$ and $m = m_1 + \ldots + m_n$. It is worth noting that the Formulae (18) and (19) continue to hold in this framework.

In the discrete framework, several new types of fractional partial difference operators can be introduced and analyzed using the multidimensional convolution products $*_0$, $\circ$ and the sequences $a : \mathbb{N}_0^n \to \mathbb{C}$ which do not have the form (54). We will consider such operators elsewhere.

Let us finally note that the multidimensional fractional calculus is still a very unexplored field of mathematics. It is our strong belief that the partial fractional differential-difference equations will receive the considerable attention of authors in the near future. Without any doubt, this will reinforce the significance of our research and greatly enhance the impact of this paper.

Funding: This research is partially supported by grant 451-03-68/2020/14/200156 of the Ministry of Science and Technological Development, Republic of Serbia.

Data Availability Statement: Data are contained within the article.

Acknowledgments: The author would like to thank Managing Editor for inviting him to publish a paper in this special issue.

Conflicts of Interest: The author declares no conflicts of interest.

References

1. Bazhlekova, E. Fractional Evolution Equations in Banach Spaces. Ph.D. Thesis, Eindhoven University of Technology, Eindhoven, The Netherlands, 2001.
2. Diethelm, K. *The Analysis of Fractional Differential Equations*; Springer: Berlin/Heidelberg, Germany, 2010.
3. Hilfer, R. *Applications of Fractional Calculus in Physics*; World Scientific: Singapore, 2000.
4. Kilbas, A.A.; Srivastava, H.M.; Trujillo, J.J. *Theory and Applications of Fractional Differential Equations*; Elsevier Science B.V.: Amsterdam, The Netherlands, 2006.
5. Kostić, M. *Abstract Degenerate Volterra Integro-Differential Equations*; Mathematical Institute SANU: Belgrade, Serbia, 2020.
6. Podlubny, I. *Fractional Differential Equations*; Academic Press: New York, NY, USA, 1999.
7. Samko, S.G.; Kilbas, A.A.; Marichev, O.I. *Fractional Integrals and Derivatives: Theory and Applications*; Nauka i Tehnika: Minsk, Belarus, 1987. (In Russian)
8. Zhou, Y. *Basic Theory of Fractional Differential Equations*; World Scientific: Singapore, 2014.
9. Atici, F.M.; Eloe, P.W. Discrete fractional calculus with the nabla operator. *Electron. J. Qual. Theory Differ. Equ.* **2009**, *3*, 1–12. [CrossRef]
10. Goodrich, C.; Peterson, A.C. *Discrete Fractional Calculus*; Springer: Berlin/Heidelberg, Germany, 2015.

11. Zhang T.; Li Y. Global exponential stability of discrete-time almost automorphic Caputo–Fabrizio BAM fuzzy neural networks via exponential Euler technique. *Knowl.-Based Syst.* **2022**, *246*, 108675. [CrossRef]
12. Kostić, M. *Almost Periodic Type Solutions to Integro-Differential-Difference Equations*; Book Manuscript: Novi Sad, Serbia, 2024.
13. Srivastava, H.M.; Singh Chandel, R.C.; Vishwakarma, P.K. Fractional derivatives of certain generalized hypergeometric functions of several variables. *J. Math. Anal. Appl.* **1994**, *184*, 560–572. [CrossRef]
14. Singh Chandel, R.C.; Vishwakarma, P.K. Multidimensional fractional derivatives of the multiple hypergeometric functions of several variables. *Jnanabha* **1994**, *24*, 19–27.
15. Jiang, H.; Liu, F.; Turner, I.; Burrage, K. Analytical solutions for the multi-term time—Space Caputo–Riesz fractional advection—Diffusion equations on a finite domain. *J. Math. Anal. Appl.* **2012**, *389*, 1117–1127. [CrossRef]
16. Li, M.; Chen, C.; Li, F.-B. On fractional powers of generators of fractional resolvent families. *J. Funct. Anal.* **2010**, *259*, 2702–2726. [CrossRef]
17. Pilipauskaitė, V.; Surgailis, D. Fractional operators and fractionally integrated random fields on $\mathbb{Z}^v$. *Fractal Fract.* **2024**, *8*, 353. . fractalfract8060353. [CrossRef]
18. Mamchuev, M.O. A boundary balue problem for a system of multidimensional fractional partial differential equations. *Vestn. Samar. Gos. Univ. Estestvennonauchn. Ser.* **2008**, *8*, 164–175.
19. Pskhu, A.V. Boundary value problem for a multidimensional fractional partial differential equation. *Differ. Equ.* **2011**, *47*, 385–395. [CrossRef]
20. Alquran, M.; Al-Khaled, K.; Chattopadhyay, J. Analytical solutions of fractional population diffusion model: Residual power series. *Nonlinear Stud.* **2015**, *22*, 31–39.
21. Burqan, A.; Saadeh, R.; Qazza, A.; Momani, S. ARA-residual power series method for solving partial fractional differential equations. *Alex. Eng. J.* **2023**, *62*, 47–62. [CrossRef]
22. Demir, A.; Bayrak, M.A. A new approach for the solution of space-time fractional order heat-like partial differential equations by residual power series method. *Commun. Math. Appl.* **2019**, *10*, 585–597. [CrossRef]
23. Gupta, R.K.; Yadav, P. Extended Lie method for mixed fractional derivatives, unconventional invariants and reduction, conservation laws and acoustic waves propagated via nonlinear dispersive equation. *Qual. Theory Dyn. Syst.* **2024**, *23*, 203. [CrossRef]
24. Ismail, G.M.; Abdl-Rahim, H.R.; Ahmad, H.; Chu, Y.M. Fractional residual power series method for the analytical and approximate studies of fractional physical phenomena. *Open Phy.* **2020**, *18*, 799–805. [CrossRef]
25. Rahman, M.M.; Habiba, U.; Salam, M.A.; Datta, M. The traveling wave solutions of space-time fractional partial differential equations by modified Kudryashov method. *J. Appl. Math. Phys.* **2020**, *8*, 2683–2690. [CrossRef]
26. Chaurasia, V.B.L.; Dubey, R.S. The n-dimensional generalized Weyl Fractional calculus containing to n-dimensional H-transforms. *Gen. Math. Notes* **2011**, *6*, 61–72.
27. Goyal, S.P.; Mathur, T. A theorem relating multidimensional generalized Weyl fractional Integral, Laplace and Varma transforms with applications. *Tamsui Oxf. J. Math. Sci.* **2003**, *19*, 41–54.
28. Jaimini, B.B.; Nagar, H. On multidimensional Weyl type fractional integral operator involving a general class of polynomials and multidimensional integral transforms. *J. Rajahstan Acad. Phy. Sci.* **2004**, *3*, 237–245.
29. Raina, R.K. A note on the multidimensional Weyl fractional operator. *Proc. Indian Acad. Sci. Math. Sci.* **1991**, *101*, 179–181. [CrossRef]
30. Bernstein, D.L. The Double Laplace Integral. Ph.D. Thesis, Brown University, Providence, RI, USA, 1939.
31. Bernstein, D.L. The double Laplace integral. *Duke Math. J.* **1941**, *8*, 460–496. [CrossRef]
32. Jaeger, J.C. The solution of boundary value problems by a double Laplace transformation. *Bull. Am. Math. Soc.* **1940**, *46*, 687–693. [CrossRef]
33. Bernstein, D.L.; Coon, G.A. Some properties of the double Laplace transformation. *Trans. Am. Math. Soc.* **1953**, *74*, 135–176.
34. Debnath, L. The double Laplace transforms and their properties with applications to functional, integral and partial differential equations. *Int. J. Appl. Comput. Math.* **2016**, *2*, 223–241. [CrossRef]
35. Debnath, J.; Dahiya, R.S. Theorems on multidimensional laplace transform for solution of boundary value problems. *Comput. Math. Appl.* **1989**, *18*, 1033–1056. [CrossRef]
36. Eltayeb, H.; Kilicman, A.; Bachar, I. On the application of multi-dimensional Laplace decomposition method for solving singular fractional pseudo-hyperbolic equations. *Fractal Fract.* **2022**, *6*, 690. [CrossRef]
37. Eltayeb, H.; Kilicman, A., Mesloub, S. Exact evaluation of infinite series using double laplace transform technique. *Abstr. Appl. Anal.* **2014**, *2014*, 327429. [CrossRef]
38. Saadeh, R.; Burqan, A. Adapting a new formula to generalize multidimensional transforms. *Math. Meth. Appl. Sci.* **2023**, *46*, 15285–15304. [CrossRef]
39. Ahmood, W.A. Extension of Laplace transform to Multi-Dimensional Fractional Integro-Differential Equations. Ph.D. Thesis, Universiti Putra Malaysia, Seri Kembangan, Malaysia, 2017.
40. Babakhani, A. Theory of Multidimensional Laplace Transforms and Boundary Value Problems. Ph.D. Thesis, Iowa State University, Ames, IA, USA, 1989.
41. Mughrabi, T.A. Multi-Dimensional Laplace Transforms and Applications. Ph.D. Thesis, Iowa State University, Ames, IA, USA, 1988.

42. Cheng, S.S. *Partial Difference Equations*; CRC Press: London, UK; New York, NY, USA, 2003.
43. Kostić, M.; Fedorov, V.E. Abstract Fractional Differential Inclusions with Generalized Laplace Derivatives. Available online: https://www.researchgate.net/publication/380665443 (accessed on 27 July 2024).
44. Kostić, M.; Koyuncuoğlu, H.C.; Katıcan, T.: Asymptotic Constancy for Solutions of Abstract Non-Linear Fractional Equations with Delay and Generalized Hilfer (a, b, α)-Derivatives. Available online: https://www.researchgate.net/publication/380940008 (accessed on 27 July 2024).
45. Kostić, M.: Abstract multi-term fractional difference equations. *arXiv* **2024**, arXiv:2403.19697v1.
46. de Oliveira, E.C.; Machado, J.A.T. A review of definitions for fractional derivatives and integral. *Math. Prob. Eng.* **2014**, *2014*, 238459. [CrossRef]
47. Miller, K.S.; Ross, B. *An Introduction to the Fractional Calculus and Fractional Differential Equations*; Wiley: New York, NY, USA, 1993.
48. Lighthill, M.J. *Introduction to Fourier Transform and Generalised Functions*; Cambridge University Press: Cambridge, UK, 1959.
49. Abadias, L.; Lizama, C. Almost automorphic mild solutions to fractional partial difference-differential equations. *Appl. Anal.* **2015**, *95*, 1347–1369. [CrossRef]
50. Keyantuo, V.; Lizama, C.; Rueda, S.; Warma, M. Asymptotic behavior of mild solutions for a class of abstract nonlinear difference equations of convolution type. *Advances Diff. Equ.* **2019**, *2019*, 251. [CrossRef]
51. Mitrović, D. On a Leibnitz type formula for fractional derivatives. *Filomat* **2013**, *27*, 1141–1146. [CrossRef]
52. Hörmander, L. *An Introduction to Complex Analysis in Several Variables*, 3rd ed.; North Holland: Amsterdam, The Netherlands, 1990.
53. Arendt, W.; Batty, C.J.K.; Hieber, M.; Neubrander, F. Vector-valued laplace transforms and cauchy problems. In *Monographs in Mathematics*; Birkhäuser: Basel, Switzerland, 2001; Volume 96.
54. Kilicman, A.; Ahmood, W.A. Solving multi-dimensional fractional integro-differential equations with the initial and boundary conditions by using multi-dimensional Laplace Transform method. *Tbilisi Math. J.* **2017**, *10*, 105–115. [CrossRef]
55. Kostić, M. *Abstract Volterra Integro-Differential Equations*; CRC Press: Boca Raton, FL, USA, 2015.
56. Kostić, M. Abstract Non-Scalar Volterra Difference Equations of Several Variables. Available online: https://www.researchgate.net/publication/379579966 (accessed on 27 July 2024).

Article

New Nonlinear Retarded Integral Inequalities and Their Applications to Nonlinear Retarded Integro-Differential Equations

Mahvish Samar [1], Xinzhong Zhu [2,*], Abdul Shakoor [3] and Mawia Osman [1]

[1]   School of Mathematical Sciences, Zhejiang Normal University, Jinhua 321004, China; mahvishsamar@hotmail.com (M.S.); mawiaosman@zjnu.edu.cn (M.O.)
[2]   School of Computer Science and Technology, Zhejiang Normal University, Jinhua 321004, China
[3]   Department of Mathematics, The Islamia University of Bahawalpur, Bahawalpur 63100, Pakistan; ashakoor313@iub.edu.pk
*   Correspondence: zxz@zjnu.edu.cn

Abstract: The purpose of this article is to present some new nonlinear retarded integral inequalities which can be utilized to study the existence, stability, boundedness, uniqueness, and asymptotic behavior of solutions of nonlinear retarded integro-differential equations, and these inequalities can be used in the symmetrical properties of functions. These inequalities also generalize some former famous inequalities in the literature. Two examples as applications will be provided to demonstrate the strength of our inequalities in estimating the boundedness and global existence of the solution to initial value problems for nonlinear integro-differential equations and differential equations which can be seen in graphs. This research work will ensure opening new opportunities for studying nonlinear dynamic inequalities on a time-scale structure of a varying nature.

Keywords: retarded integral inequality; Gronwall–Bellman inequality; nonlinear integral; differential equations

MSC: 39B72; 26D10; 34A34

Citation: Samar, M.; Zhu, X.; Shakoor, A.; Osman, M. New Nonlinear Retarded Integral Inequalities and Their Applications to Nonlinear Retarded Integro-Differential Equations. *Axioms* **2024**, *13*, 356. https://doi.org/10.3390/axioms13060356

Academic Editors: Azhar Ali Zafar, Nehad Ali Shah and Branko Malesevic

Received: 16 April 2024
Revised: 16 May 2024
Accepted: 24 May 2024
Published: 27 May 2024

1. Introduction

It is well known that there exists a class of mathematical models that are described by differential equations, and a lot of differential equations do not apply directly to analyze the global existence, boundedness, uniqueness, stability, and other properties of the solutions. On the other hand, integral inequalities occupy a very privileged position in all mathematical sciences, and they have many applications to questions of the existence, stability, boundedness, uniqueness, and asymptotic behavior of the solutions of nonlinear integro-differential equations. They can be used in various problems involving symmetry (see [1–7]). In 1919, Gronwall [8] was the first person to introduce the following inequality (which can be used to estimate the solution of a linear differential equation):

Gronwall's Inequality [8]. Suppose x to be a continuous function defined on $[\alpha, \alpha + k]$ with $\alpha, k, c,$ and d being non-negative constants. Then, inequality

$$0 \leq x(r) \leq \int_{\alpha}^{r} (c\, x(\mu) + d)d\mu, \quad \forall\, r \in [\alpha, \alpha + k], \tag{1}$$

implies

$$0 \leq x(r) \leq dk \exp(ck), \quad \forall\, r \in [\alpha, \alpha + k]. \tag{2}$$

A significant generalization of Gronwall's inequality was given by Bellman [9] in 1943, which is stated below as follows:

Gronwall–Bellman Inequality [9]. Assume x and h to be non-negative continuous functions defined on $E_1 = [0, k]$ where x_0 and k are positive constants. Then, inequality

$$x(r) \leq x_0 + \int_0^r h(\mu)x(\mu)d\mu, \quad \forall \, r \in E_1, \tag{3}$$

gives

$$x(r) \leq x_0 \exp\left(\int_0^r h(\mu)d\mu\right), \quad \forall \, r \in E_1. \tag{4}$$

A huge number of useful generalizations of (1) and (3) were given by many mathematicians and scientists after the establishment of Gronwall's inequality and the Gronwall–Bellman inequality which can be found in [4–6,10–20]. Among them, Abdeldaim and Yakout [16] in 2011 extended the inequality (3) as given below:

$$x(r) \leq x_0 + \left(\int_0^r h(\mu)x(\mu)d\mu\right)^2 + \int_0^r h(\mu)x(\mu)\left(x(\mu) + 2\int_0^\mu h(\theta)x(\theta)d\theta\right)d\mu, \tag{5}$$

where $x(r)$ and $h(r)$ are non-negative real valued continuous functions defined on $\mathbb{R}_+ = [0, \infty)$ and x_0 is a positive constant. Retarded or delayed arguments were introduced in differential and integral equations to solve real-life problems such as the involvement of a significant memory effect in a refined model. In these perspectives, retarded integral inequalities were introduced, where non-retarded argument r is modified into retarded argument $\vartheta(r)$. In 2015, the following inequality was studied in [12] in which the retarded case of inequality (5) was obtained by replacing r by a function $\vartheta(r)$:

$$x(r) \leq x_0 + \int_0^{\vartheta(r)} [h(\mu)x(\mu) + p(\mu)]d\mu + \int_0^{\vartheta(r)} h(\mu)\int_0^\mu b(\theta)x(\theta)d\theta d\mu. \tag{6}$$

In 2020, Shakoor et al. [19] improved the above results, where they generalized inequality (6) to the general form of

$$x(r) \leq q(r) + \int_0^{\vartheta(r)} \left(h(\mu)x(\mu) + p(\mu)\right)d\mu + \int_0^{\vartheta(r)} h(\mu)\int_0^\mu b(\theta)x(\theta)d\theta d\mu, \quad \forall r \in \mathbb{R}_+. \tag{7}$$

Recently, in 2023, Sun and Xu [6] established new weakly singular Volterra-type integral inequalities that include the maxima of the unknown function of two variables while in [5] the new retarded nonlinear integral inequalities with mixed powers were studied and utilized to study the property of boundedness and the global existence of solutions of the Volterra-type integral equations with delay.

Motivated by the inequalities mentioned above, we prove more general integral inequalities with an addition of a differentiable function to replace the constant outside the integral sign. In addition, the nonlinear function $\varphi(x(r))$ will be introduced to replace the linear function $x(r)$. The objective of this article is to establish some new nonlinear retarded integral inequalities that will generalize and cover the inequalities presented in [3,9,12–16]. These inequalities can be used to analyze the existence, stability, boundedness, uniqueness, and asymptotic behavior of the solutions of nonlinear integro-differential equations in the symmetrical properties of functions. Further, two examples, in terms of application, will be provided to demonstrate the strength of our inequalities in estimating the boundedness and global existence of a solution to the initial value problems of nonlinear integro-differential equations and differential equations, which can be seen in graphs. This research work will ensure the opening up of new opportunities for the studying of nonlinear dynamic inequalities on a time-scale structure of a varying nature.

The remaining parts of the article will proceed as follows: Section 2 contains a few preliminary results of new nonlinear retarded integral inequalities with the addition of a differentiable function to replace the constant outside the integral sign, and the nonlinear function $\varphi(x(r))$ will be introduced replacing the linear function $x(r)$ for the Gronwall–Bellman–Pachpatte type in Section 3. Section 4 presents applications for the purpose of demonstrating the strength of our inequalities in estimating the boundedness and existence of solutions for differential equations and integro-differential equations, which can be seen in graphs. Lastly, the conclusion of this study will be given in Section 5.

2. Preliminaries

Throughout this article, $\mathbb{R}$ presents the set of real numbers, while $\mathbb{R}_+ = [0, \infty)$ is the subset of $\mathbb{R}$ and $\prime$ represents the derivative, whereas $\mathbb{E}(\mathbb{R}_+, \mathbb{R}_+)$ and $\mathbb{E}'(\mathbb{R}_+, \mathbb{R}_+)$ stand for the sets of all non-negative continuous functions and nondecreasing continuously differentiable functions from $\mathbb{R}_+$ into $\mathbb{R}_+$, respectively. Now, we are ready to present some preliminary results.

The inequality

$$x(r) \leq x_0 + \int_0^r h(\mu)x(\mu)d\mu + \int_0^r h(\mu)\left(\int_0^\mu b(\theta)x(\theta)d\theta\right)d\mu, \quad \forall r \in \mathbb{R}_+, \tag{8}$$

was discovered by Pachpatte [13] in 1973 taking $x(r), h(r)$, and $b(r)$ to be non-negative real valued continuous functions defined on $\mathbb{R}_+$ and x_0 to be a positive constant. The inequality

$$x(r) \leq x_0 + \int_0^r \left(h(\mu)x(\mu) + p(\mu)\right)d\mu + \int_0^r h(\mu)\int_0^\mu b(\theta)x(\theta)d\theta d\mu, \quad \forall r \in \mathbb{R}_+, \tag{9}$$

was derived by Pachpatte [3] in 1998 considering $x(r)$, $h(r)$, $p(r)$, and $b(r)$ to be non-negative continuous functions defined on $\mathbb{R}_+$ and x_0 to be a non-negative constant. The inequality

$$x^{p+1}(r) \leq x_0 + \left(\int_0^r h(\mu)x^p(\mu)d\mu\right)^2 + 2\int_0^r h(\mu)x^p(\mu)\left(x(\mu) + \int_0^\mu h(\theta)x^p(\theta)d\theta\right)d\mu, \tag{10}$$

was established by Abdeldaim and Yakout [16] in 2011 with the same assumptions as given in (8) and $p \in (0, 1)$. The inequalities

$$x(r) \leq x_0 + \left(\int_0^{\vartheta(r)} h(\mu)\varphi(x(\mu))d\mu\right)^2 + \int_0^{\vartheta(r)} h(\mu)\varphi(x(\mu))\left(\varphi(x(\mu))\right.$$

$$\left. +2\int_0^\mu h(\theta)\varphi(x(\theta))d\theta\right)d\mu, \tag{11}$$

and

$$
\phi(x(r)) \;\leq\; x_0 + \left(\int_0^{\vartheta(r)} h(\mu)\varphi(x(\mu))d\mu \right)^2 + \int_0^{\vartheta(r)} h(\mu)\varphi(x(\mu)) \Bigg(x(\mu)
$$
$$
+ 2\int_0^{\mu} h(\theta)\varphi(x(\theta))d\theta \Bigg) d\mu, \tag{12}
$$

were developed by Wang [15] in 2012 assuming x, $h \in \mathbb{E}(\mathbb{R}_+, \mathbb{R}_+)$, φ, φ', $\vartheta \in \mathbb{E}'(\mathbb{R}_+, \mathbb{R}_+)$ with $\varphi'(r) \leq k, \vartheta(r) \leq r; k$, x_0 to be positive constants and x, $h \in \mathbb{E}(\mathbb{R}_+, \mathbb{R}_+)$, ϕ, φ, $\vartheta \in \mathbb{E}'(\mathbb{R}_+, \mathbb{R}_+)$ with $\phi'(r) = \varphi(r), \vartheta(r) \leq r$; and x_0 to be a positive constant. The following inequality has the same assumptions as given in (11) studied by Abdeldaim and El-Deeb [14] in 2015

$$
x(r) \leq x_0 + \int_0^{\vartheta(r)} h(\mu)\varphi(x(\mu)) \left(\varphi(x(\mu)) + \int_0^{\mu} b(\theta)\varphi(x(\theta))d\theta \right) d\mu, \quad \forall r \in \mathbb{R}_+. \tag{13}
$$

The following result was studied by Abdeldaim and El-Deeb [12] in 2015

$$
x(r) \;\leq\; x_0 + \int_0^{\vartheta(r)} \varphi(x(\mu)) \Big(h(\mu)\varphi(x(\mu)) + q(\mu) \Big) d\mu + \int_0^{\vartheta(r)} \varphi(x(\mu))h(\mu)
$$
$$
\times \left(\int_0^{\mu} b(\theta)\varphi(x(\theta))d\theta \right) d\mu, \tag{14}
$$

considering the same assumptions as given in (11).

We now introduce the following basic lemmas, which are very helpful in the proofs of our main results.

Lemma 1 ([10]). *Suppose that $a \geq 0$, $m \geq n \geq 0$, and $m \neq 0$.*

(a)   If $K > 0$, then

$$
a^{\frac{n}{m}} \leq \frac{n}{m} K^{\frac{n-m}{m}} a + \frac{m-n}{m} K^{\frac{n}{m}}.
$$

(b)   If $K = 1$, then

$$
a^{\frac{n}{m}} \leq \frac{n}{m} a + 1 - \frac{n}{m}.
$$

Lemma 2 ([11]). *Let x, $h \in \mathbb{E}(\mathbb{R}_+, \mathbb{R}_+)$, and q, φ, $\vartheta, \in \mathbb{E}'(\mathbb{R}_+, \mathbb{R}_+)$ with $\vartheta(r) \leq r, \forall r \in \mathbb{R}_+$. If*

$$
x(r) \;\leq\; q(r) + \int_0^{\vartheta(r)} h(\mu)\varphi(x(\mu))d\mu, \quad \forall r \in \mathbb{R}_+,
$$

holds, then

$$
x(r) \;\leq\; \Psi^{-1}\left(\Psi(q(r)) + \int_0^{\vartheta(r)} h(\mu)d\mu \right), \quad \forall r \in (0, R_1),
$$

where

$$\Psi(t) = \int\limits_{1}^{r} \frac{d\mu}{\varphi(\mu)}, \quad \forall t > 0,$$

Ψ^{-1} *is the inverse function of* Ψ*, and* $R_1 \in \mathbb{R}_+$ *is the largest number such that*

$$\Psi(q(R_1)) + \int\limits_{0}^{\vartheta(R_1)} h(\mu)d\mu \leq \int\limits_{1}^{\infty} \frac{d\mu}{\varphi(\mu)}.$$

3. Results on Retarded Integral Inequalities

In this section, we state and prove the following nonlinear retarded integral inequality with the addition of a differentiable function to replace the constant outside the integral sign for the inequality of the Gronwall–Bellman–Pachpatte type. These results will generalize a few important inequalities in [3,9,12,13].

Theorem 1. *Let* x, h, p, $b \in \mathbb{E}(\mathbb{R}_+, \mathbb{R}_+)$ *and* q, $\vartheta \in \mathbb{E}'(\mathbb{R}_+, \mathbb{R}_+)$ *with* $\vartheta(r) \leq r$ *on* $\mathbb{R}_+$*, and* $m \in (0, 1]$*. The inequality*

$$x(r) \leq q(r) + \int\limits_{0}^{\vartheta(r)} [h(\mu)x(\mu) + p(\mu)]^m d\mu + \int\limits_{0}^{\vartheta(r)} h(\mu) \int\limits_{0}^{\mu} b(\theta)x(\theta)d\theta d\mu, \quad \forall r \in \mathbb{R}_+, \tag{15}$$

implies

$$x(r) \leq q(r) + \int\limits_{0}^{\vartheta(r)} \left(mp(\mu) + (1 - m) \right)d\mu + \int\limits_{0}^{r} \vartheta'(\mu)f(\vartheta(\mu))\exp\left(\int\limits_{0}^{\vartheta(\mu)} (mh(\eta) + \frac{1}{m}b(\eta))d\eta \right)$$

$$\times \left(mq(0) + \int\limits_{0}^{\vartheta(\mu)} \left(mq'(\vartheta^{-1}(\theta)) + m^2 p(\theta) + m(1 - m) \right) \right)$$

$$\times \exp\left(-\int\limits_{0}^{\theta} (mh(\eta) + \frac{1}{m}b(\eta))d\eta \right)d\theta \right)d\mu, \quad \forall r \in \mathbb{R}_+. \tag{16}$$

Proof. With the help of Lemma 1 (b), from (15) we have

$$x(r) \leq q(r) + \int\limits_{0}^{\vartheta(r)} \left(m(h(\mu)x(\mu) + p(\mu)) + (1 - m) \right)d\mu + \int\limits_{0}^{\vartheta(r)} h(\mu) \int\limits_{0}^{\mu} b(\theta)x(\theta)d\theta d\mu, \tag{17}$$

for all $r \in \mathbb{R}_+$. Let $J(r)$ be the right hand side of (17) that is a non-negative and nondecreasing function on $\mathbb{R}_+$, and $J(0) = q(0)$. Thus, from (17) we have

$$x(r) \leq J(r), \ x(\vartheta(r)) \leq J(\vartheta(r)) \leq J(r), \quad \forall r \in \mathbb{R}_+. \tag{18}$$

After differentiating $J(r)$, we obtain

$$J'(r) = q'(r) + \vartheta'(r)\left(mh(\vartheta(r))x(\vartheta(r)) + mp(\vartheta(r)) + (1 - m) \right) + \vartheta'(r)h(\vartheta(r)) \int\limits_{0}^{\vartheta(r)} b(\theta)x(\theta)d\theta,$$

by utilizing (18), we have

$$J'(r) \leq q'(r) + m\vartheta'(r)p(\vartheta(r)) + \vartheta'(r)(1-m) + \vartheta'(r)h(\vartheta(r))V(r), \quad \forall r \in \mathbb{R}_+, \tag{19}$$

where

$$V(r) = mJ(r) + \int_0^{\vartheta(r)} b(\theta)J(\theta)d\theta, \quad \forall r \in \mathbb{R}_+, \tag{20}$$

is a non-negative and nondecreasing function on $\mathbb{R}_+$, and we also have $V(0) = mJ(0) = mq(0)$, $J(r) \leq \frac{1}{m}V(r)$, and $J(\vartheta(r)) \leq \frac{1}{m}V(\vartheta(r)) \leq \frac{1}{m}V(r)$. We obtain the following inequality after differentiating inequality (20) and utilizing inequality (19):

$$V'(r) \leq mq'(r) + m^2\vartheta'(r)p(\vartheta(r)) + \vartheta'(r)m(1-m) + \vartheta'(r)\left(mh(\vartheta(r)) + \frac{1}{m}b(\vartheta(r))\right)V(r),$$

which is equivalent to

$$V'(r) - \vartheta'(r)\left(mh(\vartheta(r)) + \frac{1}{m}b(\vartheta(r))\right)V(r) \leq mq'(r) + m^2\vartheta'(r)p(\vartheta(r)) + \vartheta'(r)m(1-m),$$

for all $r \in \mathbb{R}_+$. We have the following estimation for $V(r)$ after integrating the above inequality from 0 to r:

$$\begin{aligned}
V(r) \ \leq \ &\exp\left(\int_0^{\vartheta(r)} (mh(\eta) + \frac{1}{m}b(\eta))d\eta\right)\left(mq(0) + \int_0^{\vartheta(r)} \left(mq'(\vartheta^{-1}(\theta)) + m^2p(\theta) + m(1-m)\right)\right. \\
&\left. \times \exp\left(-\int_0^{\theta}(mh(\eta) + \frac{1}{m}b(\eta))d\eta\right)d\theta\right), \quad \forall r \in \mathbb{R}_+.
\end{aligned} \tag{21}$$

Putting (21) into (19), we have

$$\begin{aligned}
J'(r) \ \leq \ &q'(r) + \vartheta'(r)\left(mp(\vartheta(r)) + (1-m)\right) + \vartheta'(r)h(\vartheta(r))\exp\left(\int_0^{\vartheta(r)}(mh(\eta) + \frac{1}{m}b(\eta))d\eta\right) \\
&\times \left(mq(0) + \int_0^{\vartheta(r)} \left(mq'(\vartheta^{-1}(\theta)) + m^2p(\theta) + m(1-m)\right)\right. \\
&\left. \times \exp\left(-\int_0^{\theta}(mh(\eta) + \frac{1}{m}b(\eta))d\eta\right)d\theta\right), \quad \forall r \in \mathbb{R}_+.
\end{aligned} \tag{22}$$

Setting $r = \mu$ in (22) and integrating it from 0 to r, then substituting $J(r)$ in (18), we obtain (16). The proof is completed. $\square$

Remark 1. *It is very interesting to observe that Theorem 1 generalizes some former famous results such as the following:*

(1). If we take $q(r) = x_0$ (a constant) and $m = 1$, then Theorem 1 is converted into inequality (6) [12].

(2). When we suppose $q(r) = x_0$ (a constant), $m = 1$, and $\vartheta(r) = r$, then inequality (9) [3] becomes the corollary of Theorem 1.

(3). If we put $q(r) = x_0$ (a constant), $\vartheta(r) = r$, $b(r) = 0$, $p(r) = 0$, and $m = 1$, then we obtain the Gronwall–Bellman inequality [9] given in (3).

(4). When we put $q(r) = x_0$ (a constant), $\vartheta(r) = r$, $m = 1$, and $p(r) = 0$, then Theorem 1 is reduced to inequality (8) [13].

Generalization of the results given in [12,14–16] will be established in the upcoming new inequalities which can also be utilized to study the global existence of solutions to the generalized Liénard equation with time delay and to a retarded Rayleigh type equation:

Theorem 2. *Let x, b, p, $h \in \mathbb{E}(\mathbb{R}_+, \mathbb{R}_+)$ and q, φ, φ', $\vartheta, \in \mathbb{E}'(\mathbb{R}_+, \mathbb{R}_+)$ with $q(r) \geq 1$, $\varphi'(r) \leq k$, (a positive constant) $\varphi > 0$, $\vartheta(r) \leq r$, for all $r \in \mathbb{R}_+$ and $m \in (0, 1]$. The inequality*

$$x(r) \leq q(r) + \int_0^{\vartheta(r)} \varphi(x(\mu))[h(\mu)\varphi(x(\mu)) + p(\mu)]^m d\mu + \int_0^{\vartheta(r)} \varphi(x(\mu))h(\mu)$$

$$\times \left(\int_0^{\mu} b(\theta)\varphi(x(\theta))d\theta \right) d\mu, \quad \forall r \in \mathbb{R}_+, \tag{23}$$

gives

$$x(r) \leq \Psi^{-1}\left(\Psi(q(0)) + \int_0^{\vartheta(r)} \left(q'(\vartheta^{-1}(\mu)) + p(\mu) + (1 - m) + h(\mu)\beta(\mu) \right) d\mu \right), \tag{24}$$

for all $r \in \mathbb{R}_+$, where

$$\Psi(t) = \int_1^t \frac{dr}{\varphi(r)}, \quad t > 0, \tag{25}$$

$$\beta(r) = \frac{\exp(\int_0^{\vartheta(r)} (kp(\mu) + k(1 - m) + \frac{1}{m}b(\mu))d\mu)}{C_1 - k \int_0^{\vartheta(r)} (mq'(\vartheta^{-1}(\mu)) + h(\mu))\exp(\int_0^{\mu} (kp(\theta) + k(1 - m) + \frac{1}{m}b(\theta))d\theta)d\mu}, \tag{26}$$

for all $r \in \mathbb{R}_+$, $C_1 = m\varphi^{-1}(q(0))$, Ψ^{-1} and φ^{-1} are the inverse functions of Ψ and φ, respectively, such that

$$C_1 - k \int_0^{\vartheta(r)} (mq'(\vartheta^{-1}(\mu)) + h(\mu))\exp(\int_0^{\mu} (kp(\theta) + k(1 - m) + \frac{1}{m}b(\theta))d\theta)d\mu > 0.$$

Proof. Applying Lemma 1 (b) to inequality (23), we obtain

$$x(r) \leq q(r) + \int_0^{\vartheta(r)} \varphi(x(\mu))[m(h(\mu)\varphi(x(\mu)) + p(\mu)) + (1 - m)]d\mu + \int_0^{\vartheta(r)} \varphi(x(\mu))h(\mu)$$

$$\times \left(\int_0^{\mu} b(\theta)\varphi(x(\theta))d\theta \right) d\mu, \quad \forall r \in \mathbb{R}_+. \tag{27}$$

Assume that $J_1(r)$ is the right hand side of (27) that is a non-negative and nondecreasing function on $\mathbb{R}_+$ and $J_1(0) = q(0)$. Thus, from (27), we have

$$x(r) \leq J_1(r), \quad x(\vartheta(r)) \leq J_1(\vartheta(r)) \leq J_1(r), \quad \forall r \in \mathbb{R}_+. \tag{28}$$

Differentiation of $J_1(r)$ gives

$$J_1'(r) \;=\; q'(r) + \vartheta'(r)\varphi(x(\vartheta(r)))[m(h(\vartheta(r))\varphi(x(\vartheta(r)))) + p(\vartheta(r)) + (1-m)]$$
$$+\vartheta'(r)\varphi(x(\vartheta(r)))h(\vartheta(r)) \int_0^{\vartheta(r)} b(\mu)\varphi(x(\mu))d\mu, \quad r \in \mathbb{R}_+.$$

By utilizing (28), we have

$$J_1'(r) \le q'(r) + \vartheta'(r)\varphi(J_1(r))[p(\vartheta(r)) + (1-m)] + \vartheta'(r)\varphi(J_1(r))h(\vartheta(r))V_1(r), \tag{29}$$

where

$$V_1(r) = m\varphi(J_1(r)) + \int_0^{\vartheta(r)} b(\mu)\varphi(J_1(\mu))d\mu, \quad \forall r \in \mathbb{R}_+, \tag{30}$$

and we have $V_1(0) = m\varphi(J_1(0)) = m\varphi(q(0))$, and $\varphi(J_1(r)) \le \frac{1}{m}V_1(r)$. After differentiating (30) and using the relation $\varphi'(J_1(r)) \le k$ and (29), we obtain

$$V_1'(r) \;\le\; kmq'(r) + \vartheta'(r)\left(kp(\vartheta(r)) + k(1-m) + \frac{1}{m}b(\vartheta(r))\right)V_1(r)$$
$$+k\vartheta'(r)h(\vartheta(r))V_1^2(r), \quad \forall r \in \mathbb{R}_+.$$

As $q(r) \ge 1$, $V_1(r) \ge 1$ which gives that $\frac{q'(r)}{V_1(r)} \le q'(r)$, so dividing the above inequality by $V_1^2(r)$, we have

$$V_1^{-2}(r)V_1'(r) \;\le\; \vartheta'(r)\left(kp(\vartheta(r)) + k(1-m) + \frac{1}{m}b(\vartheta(r))\right)V_1^{-1}(r)$$
$$+kmq'(r) + k\vartheta'(r)h(\vartheta(r)), \quad \forall r \in \mathbb{R}_+. \tag{31}$$

If we let $V_1^{-1}(r) = W(r)$, $W(0) = V_1^{-1}(0) = m\varphi^{-1}(q(0))$, and $V_1^{-2}(r)V_1'(r) = -W'(r)$, then inequality (31) gives

$$W'(r) + \vartheta'(r)\left(kp(\vartheta(r)) + k(1-m) + \frac{1}{m}b(\vartheta(r))\right)W(r) \ge -k\left(mq'(r) + \vartheta'(r)h(\vartheta(r))\right),$$

for all $r \in \mathbb{R}_+$. Applying integration from 0 to r to the above inequality gives an estimation for $W(r)$ as follows:

$$W(r) \ge \frac{C_1 - k\int_0^{\vartheta(r)}\left(mq'(\vartheta^{-1}(\mu)) + h(\mu)\right)\exp\left(\int_0^{\mu}(kp(\theta) + k(1-m) + \frac{1}{m}b(\theta))d\theta\right)d\mu}{\exp\left(\int_0^{\vartheta(r)}(kp(\mu) + k(1-m) + \frac{1}{m}b(\mu))d\mu\right)},$$

for all $r \in \mathbb{R}_+$, where $C_1 = m\varphi^{-1}(q(0))$. Thus, $V_1(r) = W^{-1}(r) \le \beta(r)$, where $\beta(r)$ is defined in (26). Substituting $V_1(r) \le \beta(r)$ in (29), we obtain

$$J_1'(r) \le q'(r) + \vartheta'(r)\varphi(J_1(r))[p(\vartheta(r)) + (1-m)] + \vartheta'(r)\varphi(J_1(r))h(\vartheta(r))\beta(r). \tag{32}$$

Since $q(r) \ge 1$ and $\varphi(J_1(r)) \ge 1$, which implies that $\frac{q'(r)}{\varphi(J_1(r))} \le q'(r)$, we can write (32) as follows:

$$\frac{J_1'(r)}{\varphi(J_1(r))} \le q'(r) + \vartheta'(r)[p(\vartheta(r)) + (1-m)] + \vartheta'(r)h(\vartheta(r))\beta(r), \quad \forall r \in \mathbb{R}_+. \tag{33}$$

Setting $r = \mu$ in (33), integrating it from 0 to r, and utilizing (25), we obtain

$$J_1(r) \leq \Psi^{-1}\left(\Psi(q(0)) + \int_0^{\vartheta(r)} \left(q'(\vartheta^{-1}(\mu) + p(\mu) + (1-m) + h(\mu)\beta(\mu) \right) d\mu \right), \quad \forall r \in \mathbb{R}_+.$$

Putting the above inequality in (28), we obtain the required result of (24). The proof is completed. $\square$

Remark 2. *It is very interesting to observe that Theorem 2 generalizes former inequalities such as the following:*

(1). *If we take $q(r) = x_0$ (a constant) and $m = 1$, then we obtain inequality (14) [12].*
(2). *When we put $q(r) = x_0$ (a constant), $p(r) = 0$, and $m = 1$, then we obtain inequality (13) [14].*
(3). *It is observed that inverse Ψ^{-1} is well defined, continuous, and increasing in its corresponding domain as Ψ is strictly increasing.*

Generalization of the inequalities given in [15,16] will be established in the following new inequality:

Theorem 3. *Let x, $h \in \mathbb{E}(\mathbb{R}_+, \mathbb{R}_+)$ and q, φ, φ', ϑ, $\in \mathbb{E}'(\mathbb{R}_+, \mathbb{R}_+)$ with $q(r) \geq 1$, $\varphi'(r) \leq k$ (a positive constant), $\varphi > 0$, $\vartheta(r) \leq r$, for all $r \in \mathbb{R}_+$ and $m \in (0,1]$. The inequality*

$$
\begin{aligned}
x(r) \;\leq\; & q(r) + \left(\int_0^{\vartheta(r)} h(\mu)\varphi(x(\mu))d\mu \right)^2 + \int_0^{\vartheta(r)} h(\mu)\varphi(x(\mu)) \big[\varphi(x(\mu)) \\
& + 2\int_0^{\mu} h(\eta)\varphi(x(\eta))d\eta \big]^m d\mu, \quad \forall r \in \mathbb{R}_+,
\end{aligned}
$$
(34)

implies

$$x(r) \leq \Psi^{-1}\left(\Psi(q(0)) + \int_0^{\vartheta(r)} \left(q'(\vartheta^{-1}(\mu) + h(\mu)\beta_1(\mu) \right) d\mu \right), \quad \forall r \in \mathbb{R}_+,$$
(35)

where

$$\Psi(t) = \int_1^t \frac{dr}{\varphi(r)}, \quad t > 0,$$
(36)

$$\beta_1(r) = \frac{\exp\left(2(1 + \tfrac{1}{m}) \int_0^{\vartheta(r)} h(\mu)d\mu \right)}{(C_2)^{-1} - k \int_0^{\vartheta(r)} \left(mq'(\vartheta^{-1}(\mu)) + h(\mu) \right) \exp\left(2(1 + \tfrac{1}{m}) \int_0^{\mu} h(\theta)d\theta \right) d\mu},$$
(37)

for all $r \in \mathbb{R}_+$, $C_2 = m\varphi(q(0)) + 1 - m$, Ψ^{-1} is the inverse function of Ψ, such that

$$(C_2)^{-1} - k \int_0^{\vartheta(r)} \left(mq'(\vartheta^{-1}(\mu)) + h(\mu) \right) \exp\left(2(1 + \frac{1}{m}) \int_0^{\mu} h(\theta)d\theta \right) d\mu > 0.$$

Proof. Applying Lemma 1 (b) to inequality (34), we obtain

$$
\begin{aligned}
x(r) \;\leq\; q(r) + \left(\int_0^{\vartheta(r)} h(\mu)\varphi(x(\mu))d\mu \right)^2 + \int_0^{\vartheta(r)} h(\mu)\varphi(x(\mu))\Big(m\varphi(x(\mu)) \\
+2m \int_0^{\mu} h(\eta)\varphi(x(\eta))d\eta + (1-m) \Big) d\mu, \qquad \forall r \in \mathbb{R}_+.
\end{aligned}
\tag{38}
$$

Let $J_2(r)$ be the right hand side of (38) that is a non-negative and nondecreasing function on $\mathbb{R}_+$, and $J_2(0) = q(0)$. Thus, from (38), we have

$$
x(r) \leq J_2(r), \quad x(\vartheta(r)) \leq J_2(\vartheta(r)) \leq J_2(r), \qquad \forall r \in \mathbb{R}_+.
\tag{39}
$$

After differentiating $J_2(r)$, we obtain

$$
\begin{aligned}
J_2'(r) \;=\; q'(r) + 2\alpha'(r)h(\vartheta(r))\varphi(x(\vartheta(r))) \int_0^{\vartheta(r)} h(\mu)\varphi(x(\mu))d\mu + \vartheta'(r)h(\vartheta(r))\varphi(x(\vartheta(r))) \\
\times \left(m\varphi(x(\vartheta(r))) + 2m \int_0^{\vartheta(r)} h(\mu)\varphi(x(\mu))d\mu + (1-m) \right), \qquad \forall r \in \mathbb{R}_+.
\end{aligned}
$$

By using (39), we have

$$
J_2'(r) \leq q'(r) + \vartheta'(r)h(\vartheta(r))\varphi(J_2(r))V_2(r), \qquad \forall r \in \mathbb{R}_+,
\tag{40}
$$

where

$$
V_2(r) = m\varphi(J_2(\vartheta(r))) + 2 \int_0^{\vartheta(r)} h(\mu)\varphi(J_2(\mu))d\mu + 2m \int_0^{\vartheta(r)} h(\mu)\varphi(J_2(\mu))d\mu + (1-m),
\tag{41}
$$

is a non-negative and nondecreasing function on $\mathbb{R}_+$, and we also have $V_2(0) = m\varphi(J_2(0)) + (1-m) = m\varphi(q(0)) + (1-m)$ and $\varphi(J_2(\vartheta(r))) \leq \frac{1}{m}V_2(r)$. After differentiating (41), and using the relation $\varphi'(J_2(r)) \leq k$ and (40), we obtain

$$
V_2'(r) \leq kmq'(r) + k\vartheta'(r)h(\vartheta(r))V_2^2(r) + 2(1 + \frac{1}{m})\vartheta'(r)h(\vartheta(r))V_2(r), \quad \forall r \in \mathbb{R}_+.
$$

Since $q(r) \geq 1$ and $V_2(r) \geq 1$ which implies that $\frac{q'(r)}{V_2(r)} \leq q'(r)$, dividing the above inequality by $V_2^2(r)$, we have

$$
V_2^{-2}(r)V_2'(r) \leq kmq'(r) + k\vartheta'(r)h(\vartheta(r)) + 2(1 + \frac{1}{m})\vartheta'(r)h(\vartheta(r))V_2^{-1}(r), \quad \forall r \in \mathbb{R}_+.
\tag{42}
$$

If we let $V_2^{-1}(r) = W_1(r)$, $W_1(0) = V_2^{-1}(0) = \left(m\varphi(q(0)) + (1-m) \right)^{-1}$ and $V_2^{-2}(r)V_2'(r) = -W_1'(r)$, then inequality (42) implies

$$
W_1'(r) + 2(1 + \frac{1}{m})\vartheta'(r)h(\vartheta(r))W_1(r) \geq -k\left(mq'(r) + \vartheta'(r)h(\vartheta(r)) \right), \qquad \forall r \in \mathbb{R}_+.
$$

We have the following estimation for $W_1(r)$ after applying integration from 0 to r to the above inequality:

$$W_1(r) \geq \frac{(C_2)^{-1} - k \int_0^{\vartheta(r)} \left(mq'(\vartheta^{-1}(\mu)) + h(\mu) \right) \exp\left(2(1 + \tfrac{1}{m}) \int_0^{\mu} h(\theta)d\theta \right) d\mu}{\exp\left(2(1 + \tfrac{1}{m}) \int_0^{\vartheta(r)} h(\mu)d\mu \right)},$$

for all $r \in \mathbb{R}_+$, where $C_2 = m\varphi(q(0)) + 1 - m$. Thus, $V_2(r) = W_1^{-1}(r) \leq \beta_1(r)$, where $\beta_1(r)$ is defined in (37). Substituting $V_2(r) \leq \beta_1(r)$ in (40), we obtain

$$J_2'(r) \leq q'(r) + \vartheta'(r)h(\vartheta(r))\varphi(J_2(r))\beta_1(r), \quad \forall r \in \mathbb{R}_+.$$

Since $q(r) \geq 1$ and $\varphi(J_2(r)) \geq 1$, which implies that $\frac{q'(r)}{\varphi(J_2(r))} \leq q'(r)$, we have

$$\frac{J_2'(r)}{\varphi(J_2(r))} \leq q'(r) + \vartheta'(r)h(\vartheta(r))\beta_1(r), \quad \forall r \in \mathbb{R}_+. \tag{43}$$

Setting $r = \mu$ in (43), integrating it from 0 to r, and utilizing (36), we obtain

$$J_2(r) \leq \Psi^{-1}\left(\Psi(q(0)) + \int_0^{\vartheta(r)} \left(q'(\vartheta^{-1}(\mu)) + h(\mu)\beta_1(\mu) \right) d\mu \right), \quad \forall r \in \mathbb{R}_+.$$

Putting the above inequality in (39), we obtain the required result of (35). The proof is completed. $\square$

Remark 3. *It is very interesting to observe that Theorem 3 generalizes former results such as the following:*

(1). *If we take $q(r) = x_0$ (a constant) and $m = 1$, then we obtain inequality (11) [15].*
(2). *When we put $q(r) = x_0$ (a constant), $\vartheta(r) = r$, $\varphi(x(r)) = x(r)$, and $m = 1$, then we obtain inequality (5) [16].*

Now, we present the last inequality of this section which will generalize the inequalities in [15,16].

Theorem 4. *Let $x, h \in \mathbb{E}(\mathbb{R}_+, \mathbb{R}_+)$, and $q, \phi, \varphi, \phi', \varphi/r, \vartheta, \in \mathbb{E}'(\mathbb{R}_+, \mathbb{R}_+)$ with $q(r) \geq 1$, $\phi'(r) = \varphi(r)$, $\vartheta(r) \leq r$, for all $r \in \mathbb{R}_+$ and $m \in (0, 1]$. The inequality*

$$\phi(x(r)) \ \leq \ q(r) + \left(\int_0^{\vartheta(r)} h(\mu)\varphi(x(\mu))d\mu \right)^2 + \int_0^{\vartheta(r)} h(\mu)\varphi(x(\mu))$$

$$\times \left(x(\mu) + 2\int_0^{\mu} h(\eta)\varphi(x(\eta))d\eta \right)^m d\mu, \quad \forall r \in \mathbb{R}_+, \tag{44}$$

gives

$$x(r) \leq \exp\left(\Psi^{-1}\left(\Psi\left(C_3 + m \int_0^{\vartheta(r)} (q'(\vartheta^{-1}(\mu)) + h(\mu))d\mu \right) + 2(m+1) \int_0^{\vartheta(r)} h(\mu)d\mu \right) \right), \tag{45}$$

for all $r \in (0, R_1)$, where

$$\Psi(t) = \int_1^t \frac{\exp(r)}{\varphi(\exp(r))} dr, \quad \forall t > 0, \tag{46}$$

$C_3 = \ln(1 + m\phi^{-1}(q(0)) - m)$, Ψ^{-1} *and* ϕ^{-1} *are the inverses of* Ψ *and* ϕ, *respectively, and* $R_1 \in \mathbb{R}_+$ *is the largest number such that*

$$\Psi\left(C_3 + m \int_0^{\vartheta(R_1)} (q'(\vartheta^{-1}(\mu)) + h(\mu))d\mu\right) + 2(m+1) \int_0^{\vartheta(R_1)} h(\mu)d\mu \leq \int_1^{\infty} \frac{\exp(r)dr}{\phi(\exp(r))}. \tag{47}$$

Proof. Applying Lemma 1 (b) to inequality (44), we have

$$\phi(x(r)) \leq q(r) + \left(\int_0^{\vartheta(r)} h(\mu)\varphi(x(\mu))d\mu\right)^2 + \int_0^{\vartheta(r)} h(\mu)\varphi(x(\mu))\left(mx(\mu) + 2m\right.$$

$$\left. \times \int_0^{\mu} h(\eta)\varphi(x(\eta))d\eta + (1 - m)\right)d\mu, \quad \forall r \in \mathbb{R}_+, \tag{48}$$

Let $\phi(J_3(r))$ be the right hand side of (48) that is a non-negative and nondecreasing function on $\mathbb{R}_+$, and $J_3(0) = \phi^{-1}(q(0))$. Thus, from (48), we obtain

$$x(r) \leq J_3(r), \quad x(\vartheta(r)) \leq J_3(\vartheta(r)) \leq J_3(r) \quad \forall r \in \mathbb{R}_+. \tag{49}$$

After differentiating $\phi(J_3(r))$ and utilizing (49), we have

$$\phi'(J_3(r))J_3'(r) \leq q'(r) + 2\vartheta'(r)h(\vartheta(r))\varphi(J_3(\vartheta(r))) \int_0^{\vartheta(r)} h(\mu)\varphi(J_3(\mu))d\mu$$

$$+\vartheta'(r)h(\vartheta(r))\varphi(J_3(\vartheta(r)))\left(mJ_3(\vartheta(r)) + 2m \int_0^{\vartheta(r)} h(\mu)\varphi(J_3(\mu))d\mu\right.$$

$$\left. +(1 - m)\right), \quad \forall r \in \mathbb{R}_+.$$

Since $q(r) \geq 1$ and $\varphi(J_3(r)) \geq 1$ which implies that $\frac{q'(r)}{\varphi(J_3(r))} \leq q'(r)$, and using the relation $\phi'(J_3(r)) = \varphi(J_3(r))$, we obtain

$$J_3'(r) \leq q'(r) + \vartheta'(r)h(\vartheta(r))\left(mJ_3(r) + 2(m+1) \int_0^{\vartheta(r)} h(\mu)\varphi(J_3(\mu))d\mu + (1 - m)\right)$$

$$\leq q'(r) + \vartheta'(r)h(\vartheta(r))V_3(r), \quad \forall r \in \mathbb{R}_+, \tag{50}$$

where

$$V_3(r) = mJ_3(r) + 2(m+1) \int_0^{\vartheta(r)} h(\mu)\varphi(J_3(\mu))d\mu + (1 - m), \quad \forall r \in \mathbb{R}_+.$$

is a non-negative and nondecreasing function on $\mathbb{R}_+$, and we also have $V_3(0) = mJ_3(0) + (1 - m) = m\phi^{-1}(q(0)) + (1 - m)$, and $J_3(r) \leq V_3(r)$. After differentiating $V_3(r)$ with respect to r and utilizing (50), we obtain

$$V_3'(r) \leq mq'(r) + m\vartheta'(r)h(\vartheta(r))V_3(\vartheta(r)) + 2(m+1)\vartheta'(r)h(\vartheta(r))\varphi(V_3(\vartheta(r))), \ \forall r \in \mathbb{R}_+.$$

As $q(r) \geq 1$ and $V_3(\vartheta(r)) \geq 1$ which implies that $\frac{q'(r)}{V_3(\vartheta(t))} \leq q'(r)$, dividing the above inequality by $V_3(\vartheta(r))$, we obtain

$$\frac{V_3'(r)}{V_3(r)} \leq mq'(r) + m\vartheta'(r)h(\vartheta(r)) + 2(m+1)\vartheta'(r)h(\vartheta(r))\frac{\varphi(V_3(\vartheta(r)))}{V_3(\vartheta(r))}, \ \forall r \in \mathbb{R}_+. \tag{51}$$

Applying integration from 0 to r to (51), we obtain

$$\ln V_3(r) \ \leq \ C_3 + m \int_0^{\vartheta(r)} \left(q'(\vartheta^{-1}(\mu)) + h(\mu) \right) d\mu + 2(m+1) \int_0^{\vartheta(r)} h(\mu)\frac{\varphi(V_3(\mu))}{V_3(\mu)} d\mu$$

$$\leq \ C_3 + m \int_0^{\vartheta(r)} \left(q'(\vartheta^{-1}(\mu)) + h(\mu) \right) d\mu + 2(m+1) \int_0^{\vartheta(r)} h(\mu)\frac{\varphi(\exp(\ln V_3(\mu)))}{\exp(\ln V_3(\mu))} d\mu,$$

where $C_0 = \ln(1 + m\phi^{-1}(q(0)) - m)$. Applying Lemma 2 and utilizing (46), we have

$$\ln V_3(r) \leq \Psi^{-1}\left(\Psi\left(C_3 + m \int_0^{\vartheta(r)} \left(q'(\vartheta^{-1}(\mu)) + h(\mu) \right) d\mu \right) + 2(m+1) \int_0^{\vartheta(r)} h(\mu)d\mu \right),$$

for all $r \in (0, R_1)$. By using the relation $x(r) \leq J_3(r) \leq V_3(r)$, this gives (45). The proof is completed. $\square$

Remark 4. *It is very interesting to observe that Theorem 4 generalizes some famous results such as the following:*

(1).   If we take $q(r) = x_0$ (a constant) and $m = 1$, then we obtain inequality (12) [15].
(2).   When we put $q(r) = x_0$ (a constant), $\vartheta(r) = r$, $\varphi(x(r)) = x^p(r)$, $\phi(x(r)) = x^{p+1}(r)$, and $m = 1$, then we obtain inequality (10) [16].
(3).   It is noted that R_1 is confined by inequality (47). Particularly, (45) is valid for all $r \in (0, R_1)$ when ϕ satisfies $\int_1^{\infty} \frac{\exp(r)dr}{\phi(\exp(r))} = \infty$.

4. Existence and Boundedness of Solution

In this section, we present two examples to demonstrate the strength of our derived inequalities from Section 3 as well as to study the boundedness and existence of solutions for integro-differential equations and differential equations.

Example 1. *Consider the nonlinear integro-differential equation of the initial value problem*

$$\begin{cases} x'(r) = q'(r) + F(r, x(\vartheta(r)), \int_0^r G(\theta, x)), & \forall r \in \mathbb{R}_+, \\ x(0) = q(0), \end{cases} \tag{52}$$

where $F \in \mathbb{E}(\mathbb{R}_+^3, \mathbb{R})$, $G \in \mathbb{E}(\mathbb{R}_+^2, \mathbb{R})$, and $q(0)$ is a positive constant. Assume

$$\int_0^r |q'(\mu) + F(\mu, x(\vartheta(\mu)), H)| d\mu \;\leq\; \int_0^r \Big(q'(\mu) + \varphi(|x|)[h(\mu)\varphi(|x|) + p(\mu)]^m$$

$$+ \varphi(|x|)h(\mu)|H| \Big) d\mu, \quad \forall r \in \mathbb{R}_+, \tag{53}$$

$$H = G(r, x(r)) \leq b(r)(\varphi(|x(r)|)), \quad \forall r \in \mathbb{R}_+, \tag{54}$$

where the functions x, h, q, p, ϑ, φ, b, and m are already defined as in Theorem 2. If x is the solution of (52), then

$$x(r) = q(r) + \int_0^r F\Big(\mu, x(\vartheta(\mu)), \int_0^\mu h(\theta, x(\vartheta(\theta)))d\theta \Big) d\mu, \quad \forall r \in \mathbb{R}_+, \tag{55}$$

Utilizing (53) and (54) in (55), we obtain

$$|x(r)| \;\leq\; |q(r)| + \int_0^r \varphi(|x(\vartheta(\mu))|)[h(\mu)\varphi(|x(\vartheta(\mu))|) + p(\mu)]^m d\mu$$

$$+ \int_0^{\vartheta(r)} \varphi(|x(\vartheta(\mu))|)h(\mu)\Big(\int_0^\mu b(\theta)\varphi(|x(\vartheta(\theta))|)d\theta \Big) d\mu$$

$$\leq\; |q(r)| + \int_0^{\vartheta(r)} \frac{\varphi(|x(\mu)|)}{\vartheta'(\vartheta^{-1}(\mu))}[h(\mu)\varphi(|x(\mu)|) + p(\mu)]^m d\mu$$

$$+ \int_0^{\vartheta(r)} \frac{h(\vartheta^{-1}(\mu))}{\vartheta'(\vartheta^{-1}(\mu))} \varphi(|x(\mu)|)\Big(\int_0^\mu b(\theta)\varphi(|x(\theta)|)d\theta \Big) d\mu, \quad \forall r \in \mathbb{R}_+. \tag{56}$$

As an application of Theorem 2, the inequality (56) implies

$$x(r) \leq \Psi^{-1}\Big(\Psi(q(0)) + \int_0^{\vartheta(r)} \frac{1}{\vartheta'(\vartheta^{-1}(\mu))} \Big(q'(\vartheta^{-1}(\mu) + p(\mu) + (1-m) + h(\mu)\beta(\mu) \Big) d\mu \Big),$$

for all $r \in \mathbb{R}_+$, which gives boundedness and global existence for x, where Ψ and k are defined in Theorem 2 and

$$\beta(r) = \frac{\exp\Big(\int_0^{\vartheta(r)} \frac{\big(kp(\mu)+k(1-m)+\frac{1}{m}b(\mu)\big)}{\vartheta'(\vartheta^{-1}(\mu))} d\mu \Big)}{m\varphi^{-1}(q(0)) - k \int_0^{\vartheta(r)} \frac{(mq'(\vartheta^{-1}(\mu))+h(\mu))}{\vartheta'(\vartheta^{-1}(\mu))} \exp\big(\int_0^\mu \big(kp(\theta) + k(1-m) + \frac{1}{m}b(\theta)\big)d\theta\big)d\mu},$$

for all $r \in \mathbb{R}_+$. The estimated boundedness and existence of unknown x for $0 \leq r \leq 1$ are shown in Figure 1.

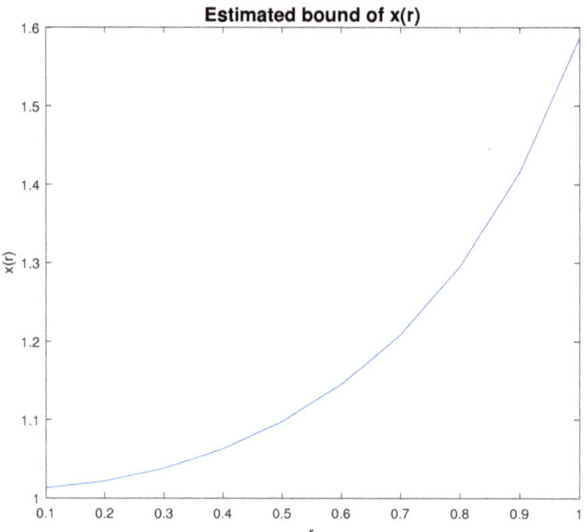

Figure 1. Estimated boundedness and existence of $x(r)$.

At the end of this section, we present another example to demonstrate the result of Theorem 3.

Example 2. *Consider the nonlinear differential equation of the initial value problem*

$$\begin{cases} x'(r) = q'(r) + F(r, x(\vartheta(r)) + H(r, x(\vartheta(t)), G(r, x(\vartheta(r))))), & \forall r \in \mathbb{R}_+, \\ x(0) = q(0), \end{cases} \tag{57}$$

where F, $G \in \mathbb{E}(\mathbb{R}_+^2, \mathbb{R})$, $H \in \mathbb{E}(\mathbb{R}_+^3, \mathbb{R})$, and $q(0)$ is a positive constant. Assume that

$$|q'(r) + F(r, x(\vartheta(r)))| \le h^2(\vartheta(r))|\varphi(x(\vartheta(r)))|^2, \tag{58}$$

$$|G(r, x(\vartheta(r)))| \le h(\vartheta(r))|\varphi(x(\vartheta(r)))|, \tag{59}$$

$$|H(r, x, G| \le |G|(\varphi|x|)^m + 2\int_0^r |G|^m d\mu, \tag{60}$$

for all $r \in \mathbb{R}_+$, where x, h, q, ϑ, φ, φ', k, and m are already defined as in Theorem 3. Taking integration from 0 to r on (57), we have

$$x(r) = q(r) + \int_0^r F(\mu, x(\vartheta(\mu)))d\mu + \int_0^r H(\mu, x(\vartheta(\mu)), G(\mu, x(\vartheta(\mu))))d\mu, \quad \forall r \in \mathbb{R}_+. \tag{61}$$

Using (58)–(60) in (61), we obtain

$$
\begin{aligned}
|x(r)| \;=\; & |q(r)| + \int_0^r h^2(\vartheta(\mu))|\varphi(x(\vartheta(\mu)))|^2 d\mu + \int_0^r h(\vartheta(\mu))|\varphi(x(\vartheta(r)))| \Big(|\varphi(x(\vartheta(\mu)))| \\[2mm]
& + 2\int_0^\mu h(\vartheta(\theta))|\varphi(x(\vartheta(\theta)))| d\theta \Big)^m d\mu \\[2mm]
\leq \;& |q(r)| + \Big(\int_0^{\vartheta(r)} \frac{h(\mu)|\varphi(x(\mu))|}{\vartheta'(\vartheta^{-1}(\mu))} d\mu \Big)^2 + \int_0^{\vartheta(r)} \frac{h(\mu)|\varphi(x(\mu))|}{\vartheta'(\vartheta^{-1}(\mu))} \Big(\varphi(|x(\vartheta(\mu))|) \\[2mm]
& + 2\int_0^\mu h(\theta)|\varphi(x(\theta))| d\theta \Big)^m d\mu, \qquad \forall r \in \mathbb{R}_+.
\end{aligned}
\tag{62}
$$

As an application of Theorem 3, the inequality (62) implies

$$
x(r) \le \Psi^{-1}\Big(\Psi(q(0)) + \int_0^{\vartheta(r)} \frac{1}{\vartheta'(\vartheta^{-1}(\mu))} \Big(q'(\vartheta^{-1}(\mu)) + h(\mu)\beta_1(\mu) \Big) d\mu \Big), \qquad \forall r \in \mathbb{R}_+,
$$

which gives boundedness and global existence for x, where Ψ *and k are defined in Theorem 3 and*

$$
\beta_1(r) = \frac{\exp\Big(2(1+\tfrac{1}{m}) \int_0^{\vartheta(r)} \frac{h(\mu)}{\vartheta'(\vartheta^{-1}(\mu))} d\mu \Big)}{\Big(m\varphi(q(0)) + 1 - m \Big)^{-1} - k \int_0^{\vartheta(r)} \frac{mq'(\vartheta^{-1}(\mu)) + h(\mu)}{\vartheta'(\vartheta^{-1}(\mu))} \exp\Big(2(1+\tfrac{1}{m}) \int_0^\mu h(\theta) d\theta \Big) d\mu},
$$

for all $r \in \mathbb{R}_+$. *The estimated boundedness and existence of unknown x for* $0 \le r \le 1$ *are shown in Figure 2.*

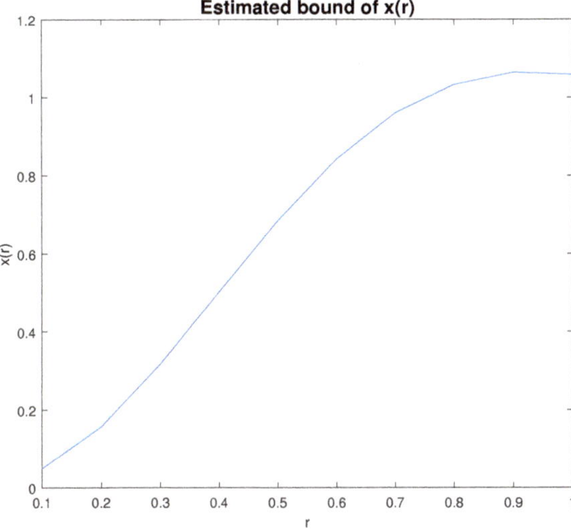

Figure 2. Estimated boundedness and existence of $x(r)$.

5. Conclusions

It is well known that there exists a class of mathematical models that are described by differential equations, and a large number of differential equations do not possess exact solutions or the existence of solutions or the boundedness of solutions. On the other hand, integral inequalities occupy a very privileged position in all mathematical sciences, and they have many applications to questions of existence, stability, boundedness, and uniqueness, and to the asymptotic behavior of the solutions of nonlinear integro-differential equations (see [1–4]). But, in certain cases, the existence and boundedness studied by the integral inequalities given in the current literature (see references) are not directly applicable, and they are not feasible for studying the stability and asymptotic behavior of the solutions of classes of more general nonlinear retarded integral, differential, and integro-differential equations. However, the inequalities established in this manuscript permit us to analyze the existence, uniqueness, stability, boundedness, and asymptotic behavior, as well as the other properties of the solutions of classes of more general retarded nonlinear differential, integro-differential, and integral equations. Many renowned and existing famous inequalities can be explored on the basis of different choices of parameters (see Remarks 1–4) from the integral inequalities of this article. The importance of these inequalities stems from the fact that it is applicable in certain situations in which other available inequalities do not apply directly. As such, these inequalities can handle the problems of nonlinear partial differential equations in applied sciences. This research work will ensure the opening up of new opportunities for the studying of nonlinear dynamic inequalities on a time-scale structure of a varying nature.

Author Contributions: Conceptualization, M.S. and X.Z.; Methodology, A.S.; Software, M.S.; Validation, M.S and A.S.; Formal analysis, X.Z. and M.O; Investigation, A.S.; Resources, X.Z.; Data curation, A.S. and M.O.; Writing—original draft, A.S. and M.S.; Supervision, X.Z.; Project administration, X.Z. All authors have read and agreed to the published version of the manuscript.

Funding: This work was supported by the Zhejiang Normal University Postdoctoral Research Fund (Grant No. ZC304022938), the Natural Science Foundation of China (project no. 61976196), the Zhejiang Provincial Natural Science Foundation of China under Grant No. LZ22F030003.

Data Availability Statement: Data are contained within the article.

Acknowledgments: The authors would like to thank the editor and the reviewers for their generous time to review and giving valuable comments/suggestions which improve the quality of this article.

Conflicts of Interest: The authors declare no conflicts of interest.

References

1. Bainov, D.; Simeonov, P. *Integral Inequalities and Applications*; Kluwer Academic: Dordrecht, The Netherlands, 1992.
2. Hardy, G.H.; Littlewood, J.E.; Polya, G. *Inequalities*, 2nd ed.; Cambridge University Press: Cambridge, UK, 1952.
3. Pachpatte, B.G. *Inequalities for Differential and Integral Equations*; Academic Press: London, UK, 1998.
4. Boichuk, A.A.; Samoilenko, A.M. *Generalized Inverse Operators and Fredholm Boundary Value Problems*, 2nd ed.; Walter de Gruyter: Berlin, Germany; Boston, MA, USA, 2016.
5. Shakoor, A.; Samar, M.; Athar, T.; Saddique, M. Results on retarded nonlinear integral inequalities with mix powers and their applications in delay integro-differential. *Ukr. Math. J.* **2023**, *75*, 478–493. [CrossRef]
6. Sun, Y.; Xu, R. Some weakly singular Volterra integral inequalities with maxima in two variables. *J. Inequal. Appl.* **2023**, *2023*, 36. [CrossRef]
7. Abuelela, W.; El-Deeb, A.A.; Baleanu, D. On Some Generalizations of Integral Inequalities in n Independent Variables and Their Applications. *Symmetry* **2022**, *14*, 2257. [CrossRef]
8. Gronwall, T.H. Note on the derivatives with respect to a parameter of the solutions of a system of differential equations. *Ann. Math.* **1919**, *20*, 292–296. [CrossRef]
9. Bellman, R. The stability of solutions of linear differential equations. *Duke Math. J.* **1943**, *10*, 643–647. [CrossRef]
10. Jiang, F.; Meng, F. Explicit bounds on some new nonlinear integral inequalities with delay. *J. Comput. Appl. Math.* **2007**, *205*, 479–486. [CrossRef]
11. Agarwal, R.P.; Deng, S.; Zheng, W. Generalization of a retarded Gronwall-like inequality and its applications. *Appl. Math. Comput.* **2005**, *165*, 599–612. [CrossRef]

12. Abdeldaim, A.; El-Deeb, A.A. On generalized of certain retarded nonlinear integral inequalities and its applications in retarded integro-differential equations. *Appl. Math. Comput.* **2015**, *256*, 375–380. [CrossRef]
13. Pachpatte, B.G. A note on Gronwall-Bellman inequality. *Math. Anal. Appl.* **1973**, *44*, 758–762. [CrossRef]
14. Abdeldaim, A.; El-Deeb, A.A. On some generalizations of certain retarded nonlinear integral inequalities with iterated integrals and an application in retarded differential equation. *J. Egypt. Math. Soc.* **2015**, *23*, 470–475. [CrossRef]
15. Wang, W.S. Some retarded nonlinear integral inequalities and their applications in retarded differential equations. *J. Inequal. Appl.* **2012**, *2012*, 75. [CrossRef]
16. Abdeldaim, A.; Yakout, M. On some new integral inequalities of Gronwall-Bellman-Pachpatte type. *Appl. Math. Comput.* **2011**, *217*, 7887–7899. [CrossRef]
17. Shakoor, A.; Ali, I.; Azam, M.; Rehman, A.; Iqbal, M.Z. Further Nonlinear Retarded Integral Inequalities for Gronwall-Bellman Type and Their Applications. *Iran. J. Sci. Technol. Trans. Sci.* **2019**, *43*, 2559–2568. [CrossRef]
18. Cheung, W.S. Some new nonlinear inequalities and applications to boundary value problems. *Nonlinear Anal.* **2006**, *64*, 2112–2128. [CrossRef]
19. Shakoor, A.; Ali, I.; Wali, S.; Rehman, A. Some Generalizations of Retarded Nonlinear Integral Inequalities and Its Applications. *J. Math. Inequal.* **2020**, *14*, 1223–1235. [CrossRef]
20. Shakoor, A.; Samar, M.; Wali, S.; Saleem, M. Retarded nonlinear integral inequalities of Gronwall-Bellman-Pachpatte type and their applications. *Honam Math. J.* **2023**, *45*, 54–70.

Article

Existence and Properties of the Solution of Nonlinear Differential Equations with Impulses at Variable Times

Huifu Xia [1,*], Yunfei Peng [1] and Peng Zhang [2]

[1]   School of Mathematics and Statistics, Guizhou University, Guiyang 550025, China; yfpeng@guess.edu.cn
[2]   Department of Mathematics, Zunyi Normal University, Zunyi 563006, China; zhangpeng@zync.edu.cn
*   Correspondence: 20120067@git.edu.cn

Abstract: In this paper, a class of nonlinear ordinary differential equations with impulses at variable times is considered. The existence and uniqueness of the solution are given. At the same time, modifying the classical definitions of continuous dependence and Gâteaux differentiability, some results on the continuous dependence and Gâteaux differentiable of the solution relative to the initial value are also presented in a new topology sense. For the autonomous impulsive system, the periodicity of the solution is given. As an application, the properties of the solution for a type of controlled nonlinear ordinary differential equation with impulses at variable times is obtained. These results are a foundation to study optimal control problems of systems governed by differential equations with impulses at variable times.

Keywords: differential equation; impulses at variable times; existence; qualitative theory; pulse phenomena

MSC: 34A37; 34A12

1. Introduction

We begin by introducing the problem studied. Let $\mathbb{R}^+ \triangleq [0, +\infty)$, $Y(t) = \{y_i(t) | i \in \Lambda \triangleq \{1, 2, \cdots, p\}\}$, $f : \mathbb{R}^+ \times \mathbb{R}^n \longrightarrow \mathbb{R}^n$, $y_i : \mathbb{R}^+ \longrightarrow \mathbb{R}^n$ and $J_i : \mathbb{R}^n \longrightarrow \mathbb{R}^n$ $(i = 1, 2, \cdots, p)$ be given maps. Consider the following differential equations with impulses at variable times

$$
\begin{cases}
\dot{x}(t) = f(t, x(t)), & \{x(t)\} \bigcap Y(t) = \varnothing, t \geq 0, \\
x(t+) = J_i(x(t)) + x(t), & \{x(t)\} \bigcap Y(t) = y_i(t), t \geq 0, \\
x(0) = x_0.
\end{cases}
\tag{1}
$$

The main purpose of this study is (i) to provide a sufficient condition for the existence and uniqueness of solution x for impulsive system (1); and (ii) to give the necessary and sufficient condition for the exact times when solution x meets set $Y(t)$; (iii) to present the properties of the solution relative to the initial value.

There are some interesting phenomena for impulsive system (1). First, it is clear that the system $\dot{x}(t) = x(t) + u(t)$ is controllable (see [1]), but the following impulsive system

$$
\begin{cases}
\dot{x}(t) = x(t) + u(t), & x(t) \neq 1, \\
x(t+) = 0, & x(t) = 1
\end{cases}
$$

is not controllable. Similarly, the system $\dot{x}(t) = -x(t)$ is stable, but the impulsive system

$$
\begin{cases}
\dot{x}(t) = -x(t), & x(t) \neq 1, \\
x(t+) = 2, & x(t) = 1
\end{cases}
$$

Citation: Xia, H.; Peng, Y.; Zhang, P. Existence and Properties of the Solution of Nonlinear Differential Equations with Impulses at Variable Times. *Axioms* **2024**, *13*, 126. https://doi.org/10.3390/axioms13020126

Academic Editor: Chris Goodrich

Received: 31 December 2023
Revised: 1 February 2024
Accepted: 13 February 2024
Published: 18 February 2024

is not stable when the initial value $x(0) \geq 1$. Let us look at the third example. Denote by $x(\cdot; 0, x_0)$ the solution of the following impulsive differential system

$$\begin{cases} \dot{x}(t) = 2t, & x(t) \neq 1, t > 0, \\ x(t+) = 0, & x(t) = 1, t \geq 0 \end{cases}$$

with the initial value $(0, x_0)$. Then, we have

$$\begin{cases} x\left(t; 0, 1 + \frac{1}{n}\right) = t^2 + 1 + \frac{1}{n}, t \geq 0, \\ x(t; 0, 1) = \begin{cases} 1, & t = 0, \\ t^2 - m, & t \in \left(\sqrt{m}, \sqrt{m+1}\right], m \in \mathbb{N}. \end{cases} \end{cases}$$

This implies that the impulsive system (1) never has any continuous solution with respect to the initial value in L^1. In addition, we can also use simple cases to show that the impulsive system (1) may not have a global solution.

The motivation for studying this problem is as follows. First of all, many physical phenomena and application models are characterized by (1). For example, integrate-and-fire models derived from a physical oscillation circuit [2,3] is widely used in neuroscience research, which is concerned with current–voltage relations at which the states can be reset once the voltage reaches a threshold level [4,5]. Again, in the application, it is crucial to choose appropriate threshold levels for making decisions to trigger or suspend an impulsive intervention: ref. [6] used glucose threshold level-guided injections of insulin; ref. [7] used the time that when an economic threshold was reached by the number of pests as the time of impulsive intervention. Second, the theory of impulsive differential equations has been an object of increasing interest because of its wide applicability in biology, medicine and more and more fields (see [8] and its references). The significant interest in the investigation of differential equations with impulse effects is explained by the development of equipment in which a significant role is played by complex systems [9–11]. In particular, the qualitative theory of impulsive system (1) has not been systematically established and it is natural to investigate it. We discuss the existence and uniqueness of a global solution and its properties for nonlinear ordinary differential equations with impulses at variable times (1) under weaker conditions. It is worth pointing out that the solutions of differential systems with impulses may experience pulse phenomena, namely, the solutions may hit a given surface a finite or infinite number of times, causing a rhythmical beating. This situation presents difficulties in the investigation of properties of solutions of such systems. In addition, it is not suitable for the stronger conditions of a control problem. Consequently, it is desirable to find weaker conditions that guarantee the absence or presence of pulse phenomena. More generally, it is significant to find conditions where the solution only meets a given surface $k \in \mathbb{N}$ times ($\mathbb{N}$ denote the set of natural numbers).

Before concluding this section, we review the previous literature on the qualitative analysis of impulsive differential equations. In fact, the qualitative analysis of impulsive differential equations can at least be traced back to the works by N.M. Kruylov and N.N. Bogolyubov [12] in 1937 in their classical monograph *Introduction to Nonlinear Mechanics*. A mathematical formulation of the differential equation with impulses at fixed times was first presented by A.M. Samoilenko and N.A. Perestyuk [13] in 1974. Since then, the qualitative theory on differential equation with impulses at fixed times in finite (or infinite) dimensional spaces has been extensively studied (see [14–17] and the references therein). For the differential equations with impulses at variable times, A.M. Samoilenko and N.A. Perestyuk [18] gave in 1981 the mathematical model

$$\begin{cases} \dot{x}(t) = f(t, x(t)), & t \neq \tau_i(x(t)), \\ x(t+) = x(t) + J_i(x(t)), & t = \tau_i(x(t)). \end{cases} \tag{2}$$

Later relevant works were published by D.D. Bainov and A.B. Dishliev [19] in 1984, S. Hu [20] in 1989, etc. For more details, one can see the monographs of V. Lakshmikantham [21] in 1989, A.M. Samoilenko [22] in 1995, D.D. Bainov [23] in 1995 and M. Benchohra [24] in 2006 and so on. In a word, these works established the qualitative theory of (2) under stronger conditions. However, they are not suitable for the stronger conditions of a control problem and impulsive differential equations in infinite dimensional spaces. At the same time, when $y_i, (\forall i \in \Lambda)$ is a one-to-one mapping, $x(t) = y_i(t)$ is equal to $t = y_i^{-1}(x(t))$. Hence, (2) can be treated as a simplified case of (1). For the linear case of (1), Peng et al. [25] obtained the existence and uniqueness of the solution and its properties.

The rest of the paper is organized as follows. Section 2 presents the main results. In Sections 3–5, the proofs of the three main theorems are given in turn. The periodicity of an autonomous impulsive system is presented in Section 6. As an application, the variation in the solution relative to the control is presented in Section 7, which is a foundation for studying optimal control problems of systems governed by differential equations with impulses at variable times. Finally, some new phenomena of impulsive differential systems are summarized.

2. Main Results

We present our main results in this section. To state the first one, some preliminaries are introduced. Throughout this paper, we fix $T > 0$ and assume that $T = +\infty$, $\mathbb{R}^+ = [0, \infty)$, $L^1_{loc}(\mathbb{R}^+; \mathbb{R}^{n \times n}) \triangleq \{x : (0, +\infty) \to \mathbb{R}^{n \times n} || x(\cdot)| \in L^1(0, T; \mathbb{R}^{n \times n}), \forall T > 0\}$. We first introduce several definitions. We define the function set $PC_Y([0, T), \mathbb{R}^n) = \{x : [0, T) \longrightarrow \mathbb{R}^n | x$ is continuous at t when $x(t) \notin Y(t)$, x is left continuous at t, and the right limit $x(t+)$ exists when $x(t) \in Y(t)\}$. For $x \in PC_Y([0, T), \mathbb{R}^n)$, $t \in [0, T)$ is called an irregular point if $x(t) \in Y(t)$. Otherwise, t is called a regular point. One can directly verify that the function set $PC_Y([0, T), \mathbb{R}^n)$ is not linear. Denoted by $B(z, \theta^2)$, the closed ball (in $\mathbb{R}^n$) is centered at z and has radius $\theta^2 > 0$.

Definition 1. *A piecewise continuous function x_θ is said to be an approximate PC-solution of (1) if $x_\theta(\cdot) \equiv x_\theta(\cdot; 0, x_0)$ satisfies the following integral equation with impulses*

$$x_\theta(t) = x_0 + \int_0^t f(\tau, x_\theta(\tau))d\tau + \sum_{\substack{0 \le t_j < t, \\ x_\theta(t_j) \in B(y_i(t_j), \theta^2)}} J_i(x_\theta(t_j)). \tag{3}$$

In particular, when $\theta = 0$, we call $x(\cdot) \equiv x_0(\cdot) \in PC_Y([0, T), \mathbb{R}^n)$ a PC-solution of (1).

Meanwhile, we introduce the following basic assumptions.

[F](1) $f : \mathbb{R}^+ \times \mathbb{R}^n \longrightarrow \mathbb{R}^n$ is measurable in t on $\mathbb{R}^+$ and locally Lipschitz continuous in x, i.e., for any $\rho > 0$, there exits $L(\rho) > 0$ such that for all $x, y \in \mathbb{R}^n$ with $|x|, |y| \le \rho$, we have

$$|f(t, x) - f(t, y)| \le L(\rho)|x - y| \text{ for any } t \in \mathbb{R}^+.$$

(2) There exists a constant $\tilde{k} > 0$ such that

$$|f(t, x)| \le \tilde{k}(1 + |x|) \text{ for any } t \in \mathbb{R}^+.$$

(3) f is continuous, partially differentiable in x, and $f_x(\cdot, x) \in L^1_{loc}(\mathbb{R}^+, \mathbb{R}^{n \times n})$.
[Y](1) $y_i \in C(\mathbb{R}^+, \mathbb{R}^n)$, and $y_i(t) \ne y_j(t)$ for all $t \in \mathbb{R}^+$ and $i \ne j$ $(i, j \in \Lambda)$.
(2) $y_i \in C^1([0, T], \mathbb{R}^n)$, and $f(t, y_i(t)) \ne \dot{y}_i(t)$ $(i \in \Lambda)$.
[J](1) $J_i : \mathbb{R}^n \longrightarrow \mathbb{R}^n$ is continuous, and

$$Y_i(t) \equiv y_i(t) + J_i(y_i(t)) \ne y_j(t) \text{ for all } t \in \mathbb{R}^+ \text{ and } i, j \in \Lambda. \tag{4}$$

(2) $J_i : \mathbb{R}^n \longrightarrow \mathbb{R}^n$ is continuous, partially differentiable.

It is clear that when assumptions [F](1)(2) hold, for any fixed $(s, z_s) \in \mathbb{R}^+ \times \mathbb{R}^n$, the differential equation

$$\begin{cases} \dot{z}(t) = f(t, z(t)), t > s, \\ z(s) = z_s, \end{cases}$$

has a unique solution $z(\cdot; s, z_s) \in C([s, +\infty), \mathbb{R}^n)$ given by

$$z(t; s, z_s) = z_s + \int_s^t f(\tau, z(\tau; s, z_s)) d\tau. \tag{5}$$

We define several functions:

$$F_i(t; s, z_s) = \langle z(t; s, z_s) - y_i(t), z_s - y_i(s) \rangle \quad (i = 1, 2, \cdots, p), t \geq s \tag{6}$$

and

$$F_{ij}(t; s, Y_i(s)) = \langle z(t; s, Y_i(s)) - y_j(t), Y_i(s) - y_j(s) \rangle \quad (i, j = 1, 2, \cdots, p), t \geq s, \tag{7}$$

where $\langle \cdot, \cdot \rangle$ denotes the inner product in $\mathbb{R}^n$.

The first main result is presented as follows.

Theorem 1. *Suppose assumptions [F](1)(2), [Y](1) and [J](1) hold.*

(1) The system (1) admits a unique PC-solution $x \in PC_Y(\mathbb{R}^+, \mathbb{R}^n)$.

(2) x has exactly one irregular point set $\{t_i | 0 \leq t_1 < t_2 < \cdots < t_k < +\infty\}$ over $\mathbb{R}^+$ if and only if there exists $l_i \in \Lambda$ $(i = 1, 2, \cdots, k)$ such that

$$F_{l_1}(t_1; 0, x_0) = 0, \quad F_{l_i l_{i+1}}(t_{i+1}; t_i, Y_{l_i}(t_i)) = 0 \text{ for } i = 1, 2, \cdots, k-1, \tag{8}$$

and

$$F_{l_k j}(t; t_k, Y_{l_k}(t_k)) > 0 \text{ for any } t \in [t_k, +\infty) \text{ for all } j \in \Lambda. \tag{9}$$

We have to point out that the necessary and sufficient conditions of a pulse phenomenon is also given in Theorem 1. Moreover, for the existence of a solution of system (2), in order to ensure $t_k = \tau_k(x)$ is monotonous with respect to k in [21], it requires that $\tau_k(x)$ be smooth and satisfy the corresponding inequality conditions. However, using Theorem 1, we can obtain immediately the following result.

Corollary 1. *Suppose assumptions [F](1)(2), [Y](1) and [J](1) hold. If y_i is invertible and $\tau_i = y_i^{-1}$ for any $i \in \Lambda$, then the system (2) admits a unique PC-solution $x \in PC_Y(\mathbb{R}^+, \mathbb{R}^n)$.*

Now, we state our second and third main results. It follows from Theorem 1 that for any fixed, sufficiently small $\theta > 0$, (1) has a unique approximate PC-solution x_θ provided that assumptions [F](1)(2), [Y](1) and [J](1) hold. Let $v \in \mathbb{R}^n$, $x_\theta(\cdot; \theta, x_0 + \theta v)$ be an approximate PC-solution of Equation (1) corresponding to $(\theta, x_0 + \theta v)$. We note that (1) is not well posed. Thus, we can never expect to have the continuity of the solution with respect to the initial value. We have to modify the classical definition of continuity and differentiability, respectively.

Definition 2. *Let $v \in \mathbb{R}^n$ be fixed. The PC-solution $x(\cdot; 0, x_0)$ of (1) is said to have a continuous dependence relative to the initial value $(0, x_0)$ if the following facts hold:*

(i) When $x(t; 0, x_0) \neq y_i(t)$ $(i \in \Lambda)$, $x_\theta(t; \theta, x_0 + \theta v) \longrightarrow x(t; 0, x_0)$ as $\theta \to 0$;

(ii) For any sufficient small $\varepsilon > 0$, there exist $\delta > 0$ and $I_\varepsilon \subseteq [0, T]$ such that

$$|x_\theta(t; \theta, x_0 + \theta v) - x(t; 0, x_0)| < \varepsilon \text{ for any } t \in I_\varepsilon, \tag{10}$$

when $\mu([0, T] \backslash I_\varepsilon) < \varepsilon$, $0 < \theta < \delta$, where μ denotes the Lebesgue measure.

Definition 3. *Let $v \in \mathbb{R}^n$ be fixed. The PC-solution $x(\cdot; 0, x_0)$ of (1) is said to be Gâteaux differentiable relative to the initial value $(0, x_0)$ if the Gâteaux derivative $\varphi(t)$ of $x(t; 0, x_0)$ exists at $(0, x_0)$ for all $t \in [0, T]$ with $x(t; 0, x_0) \neq y_i(t)$, otherwise,*

$$\varphi(t) = \lim_{s \nearrow t} \varphi(s),$$

where

$$\varphi(t) = \lim_{\varepsilon \to 0} \frac{x_\varepsilon(t; \varepsilon, x_0 + \varepsilon v) - x(t; 0, x_0)}{\varepsilon} \quad \text{when } x(t; 0, x_0) \neq y_i(t).$$

Let us state the following main results.

Theorem 2. *Suppose assumptions [F](1)(2), [Y](1) and [J](1) hold. Then, the PC-solution $x(\cdot; 0, x_0)$ of (1) has a continuous dependence relative to the initial value $(0, x_0)$ in the sense of Definition 2.*

Theorem 3. *Suppose assumptions [F], [Y] and [J] hold. Then, the PC-solution $x(\cdot; 0, x_0)$ of (1) is Gâteaux differentiable relative to the initial value $(0, x_0)$ in the sense of Definition 3. Moreover, its Gâteaux derivative φ is a PC-solution of the following differential equation with impulses*

$$\begin{cases} \dot{\varphi}(t) = f_x(t, x(t))\varphi(t), & t \in (0, T], x(t) \cap Y(t) = \varnothing, \\ \varphi(t+) = \varphi(t) + \nabla J_i(y_i(t))[\varphi(t) + \dot{h}_t(0)f(t, y_i(t))], & x(t) \cap Y(t) = y_i(t), \\ \varphi(0) = v - f(0, x_0). \end{cases}$$

Here, h_t denotes the solution of the equation $\{x_\varepsilon(t; \varepsilon, x_0 + \varepsilon v)\} \cap \partial B(y_i(t), \varepsilon^2) \neq \varnothing$ in ε for some $i \in \Lambda$.

3. Proof of Theorem 1

Throughout this section, we define the function $r : (0, +\infty) \longrightarrow \mathbb{R}^+$ given by

$$r(T) \triangleq \frac{1}{2} \inf_{s,t \in [0,T]} \left\{ |y_i(s) - y_j(t)|, |y_i(s) - Y_j(t)|, |y_i(s) - Y_i(t)| \,\Big|\, i, j \in \Lambda \text{ and } i \neq j \right\},$$

where Y_j is defined by (4). It is easy from assumptions [J](1) and [Y](1) to see $Y_i \in C([0, T], \mathbb{R}^n)$ for all $i \in \Lambda$. Hence, there exists a constant $M(T)$ such that

$$|Y_i(t)| \leq M(T) \text{ for any } t \in [0, T] \text{ and } i \in \Lambda \tag{11}$$

and

$$r(T) > 0 \text{ for all } T > 0. \tag{12}$$

To claim the existence and uniqueness of the solution of (1), we need the following Lemma.

Lemma 1. *If assumptions [F](1)(2), [Y](1) and [J](1) hold, then for any $(s, \xi) \in [0, T) \times \{Y_i(t) | t \in [0, T], i \in \Lambda\}$, there is a $\delta > 0$ which is independent of (s, ξ) such that the following differential equation*

$$\begin{cases} \dot{\phi}(t) = f(t, \phi(t)), t > s, \\ \phi(s) = \xi, \end{cases} \tag{13}$$

has a unique solution $\phi \in C([s, s + \delta], \mathbb{R}^n)$ and

$$|\phi(t) - y_i(t)| \geq \frac{r(T)}{2} \text{ for any } t \in [s, s + \delta] \text{ and } i \in \Lambda. \tag{14}$$

Proof. It follows from assumptions [F](1)(2) that (13) has a unique solution $\phi \in C([s,T],\mathbb{R}^n)$ and

$$|\phi(t)| \le |\xi| + \int_s^t \tilde{k}(1 + |\phi(\tau)|)d\tau.$$

Using Gronwall's inequality, we have

$$|\phi(t)| \le (|\xi| + \tilde{k}T)e^{\tilde{k}(t-s)}.$$

Together with (11), this means that

$$|\phi(t)| \le (M(T) + \tilde{k}T)e^{\tilde{k}T} \equiv \tilde{M}(T;\tilde{k}) \quad \text{for any } t \in [0,T].$$

Consequently, for any $t \in [0,T]$, we have

$$
\begin{aligned}
|\phi(t) - \xi| &\le \int_s^t |f(\tau,0) - f(\tau,0) + f(\tau,\phi(\tau))|d\tau \\
&\le \int_s^t |f(\tau,0)|d\tau + \int_s^t |f(\tau,\phi(\tau)) - f(\tau,0)|d\tau \\
&\le \int_s^t |f(\tau,0)|d\tau + \int_s^t L(\tilde{M}(T;\tilde{k}))|\phi(\tau)|d\tau \\
&\le \int_s^t |f(\tau,0)|d\tau + L(\tilde{M}(T;\tilde{k}))\tilde{M}(T;\tilde{k})|t - s| \\
&\le [\tilde{k} + L(\tilde{M}(T;\tilde{k}))\tilde{M}(T;\tilde{k})]|t - s|
\end{aligned}
$$

Together with (12) and

$$|\phi(t) - y_i(t)| \ge |y_i(t) - \xi| - |\phi(t) - \xi|,$$

we have

$$
\begin{aligned}
|\phi(t) - y_i(t)| &\ge |y_i(t) - \xi| - |\phi(t) - \xi| \\
&\ge |y_i(t) - \xi| - [\tilde{k} + L(\tilde{M}(T;\tilde{k}))\tilde{M}(T;\tilde{k})]|t - s| \qquad (15) \\
&\ge 2r(T) - [\tilde{k} + L(\tilde{M}(T;\tilde{k}))\tilde{M}(T;\tilde{k})]|t - s|
\end{aligned}
$$

and there exists a constant $\delta = \delta(T,\tilde{k}) = \dfrac{3r(T)}{2[\tilde{k}+L(\tilde{M}(T;\tilde{k}))\tilde{M}(T;\tilde{k})]} > 0$ such that (14) holds. $\square$

Now, we prove conclusion (1) of Theorem 1. For any $T > 0$, with respect to the number of irregular point of that system (1), there are only two possibilities: Case (1), x has no irregular point on $[0,T]$ and Case (2), x has at least one irregular point on $[0,T]$. For Case (1), it follows from assumptions [F](1)(2) that (1) has a unique solution $x \in C([0,T],\mathbb{R}^n)$. For Case (2), there exists $i \in \Lambda$ and $t_1 > 0$ such that $x(t_1;0,x_0) = y_i(t_1)$, and t_1 is the time of the first impulse. In a similar way, if no more impulse occurs, it follows from assumptions [F](1)(2) that (1) has a unique solution $x \in C([t_1,T],\mathbb{R}^n)$. If another impulse occurs, there exists $j \in \Lambda$ and $t_2 > t_1$, such that $x(t_2;t_1,y_i(t_1) + J_i(y_i(t_1))) = y_j(t_2)$, and t_2 is the time of the second impulse. At the same time, from Lemma 1, we have $|t_1 - t_2| > \delta$. By a mathematical induction method, the system (1) has a unique PC-solution $x \in PC_Y([0,T],\mathbb{R}^n)$. Thus, when $T \to \infty$, Equation (1) admits a unique PC-solution $x(\cdot;0,x_0)$ on $\mathbb{R}^+$.

Next, we discuss the number of irregular points for solution x of (1) over $\mathbb{R}^+$.

Lemma 2. *If assumptions [F](1)(2), [Y](1) and [J](1) hold, then solution x of (1) has no irregular point over $\mathbb{R}^+$ if and only if the following algebraic equations*

$$F_i(t;0,x_0) = 0 \ \text{ has no solution on } \ \mathbb{R}^+ \ \text{ for all } \ i \in \Lambda.$$

Proof. For the first step, we prove the sufficient condition. We assume solution x of (1) has an irregular point over $[0, +\infty)$, then there exist $i \in \Lambda$ and $t_1 \in [0, +\infty)$ such that $x(t_1; 0, x_0) = y_i(t_1)$, and together with (5) and (6), we have

$$
\begin{aligned}
F_i(t_1; 0, x_0) &= \langle x(t_1; 0, x_0) - y_i(t_1), x_0 - y_i(0) \rangle \\
&= \langle x_0 + \int_0^{t_1} f(\tau, x(\tau; 0, x_0)) d\tau - y_i(t_1), x_0 - y_i(0) \rangle \\
&= \langle x_0 - \left(y_i(t_1) + \int_{t_1}^0 f(\tau, x(\tau; 0, x_0)) d\tau \right), x_0 - y_i(0) \rangle \\
&= \langle x_0 - x(0; t_1, y_i(t_1)), x_0 - y_i(0) \rangle \\
&= \langle x_0 - x(0), x_0 - y_i(0) \rangle \\
&= 0
\end{aligned}
$$

This contradicts $F_i(t; 0, x_0) = 0$ has no solution on $\mathbb{R}^+$ for all $i \in \Lambda$. the proof of the sufficient condition is completed.

For the second step, we prove the necessary condition. In fact, we can prove that under assumptions [F](1)(2), [Y](1) and [J](1), if solution x of (1) has no irregular point over $\mathbb{R}^+$, then $F_i(t; 0, x_0) > 0$ on $\mathbb{R}^+$ for all $i \in \Lambda$. First of all, if solution x of (1) has no irregular point over $\mathbb{R}^+$, then for all $i \in \Lambda$, $F_i(t; 0, x_0) \in C([0, +\infty), \mathbb{R})$. In addition, for all $i \in \Lambda$, $F_i(0; 0, x_0) = \langle x_0 - y_i(0), x_0 - y_i(0) \rangle > 0$. Combined with the proof of the sufficient condition, we have $F_i(t; 0, x_0) > 0$ on $\mathbb{R}^+$ for all $i \in \Lambda$. The proof of the necessary condition is completed. $\square$

Now, we prove the necessary condition on (2) in Theorem 1. For convenience, we let $x(\cdot) = x(\cdot; 0, x_0)$ and $\{t_i | 0 \le t_1 < t_2 < \cdots < t_k < +\infty\}$ stand for the irregular point set of x over $\mathbb{R}^+$. Then, there exists $l_1 \in \Lambda$ such that

$$
x(t_1) = y_{l_1}(t_1).
$$

Together with (6), we can affirm

$$
F_{l_1}(t_1; 0, x_0) = 0.
$$

For the second irregular point t_2 of x, there exists $l_2 \in \Lambda$ such that

$$
x(t_2) = x(t_2; t_1, Y_{l_1}(y_{l_1}(t_1))) = y_{l_2}(t_2).
$$

Together with (7), it follows

$$
F_{l_1 l_2}(t_2; t_1, Y_{l_1}(y_{l_1}(t_1))) = 0.
$$

Similarly, for the irregular point t_k of x, there is an $l_k \in \Lambda$ such that

$$
F_{l_{k-1} l_k}(t_k; t_{k-1}, Y_{l_{k-1}}(t_{k-1})) = 0.
$$

Moreover, we can see from Lemma 2 that x has no irregular point on $[t_k, +\infty)$ if and only if

$$
F_{l_k j}(t; t_k, Y_{l_k}(t_k)) = 0 \text{ has no solution on } [t_k, +\infty) \text{ for all } j \in \Lambda. \tag{16}
$$

Combined with (7), it is easy from assumptions [J](1) and [Y](1) to see that $F_{l_k j}(\cdot; t_k, Y_{l_k}(t_k)) \in C([t_k, +\infty), \mathbb{R})$ and

$$
F_{l_k j}(t_k; t_k, Y_{l_k}(t_k)) = \langle z(t_k; t_k, Y_{k_k}(t_k)) - y_j(t_k), Y_{l_k}(t_k) - y_j(t_k) \rangle > 0 \text{ for all } j \in \Lambda.
$$

Therefore, together with (16), this means (8) and (9) hold.

For the sufficient condition on (2) in Theorem 1, suppose $\{t_i | 0 \le t_1 < t_2 < \cdots < t_k < +\infty\}$ satisfies (8) and (9). For t_k, take $F_{l_{k-1} l_k}(t_k; t_{k-1}, Y_{l_{k-1}}(t_{k-1})) = 0$ and $F_{l_k j}(t; t_k, Y_{l_k}(t_k)) > 0$ for any $t \in [t_k, +\infty)$ for all $j \in \Lambda$, and combine with Lemma 2, then, t_k is the irregular point. For t_{k-1}, take $F_{l_{k-2}l_{k-1}}(t_{k-1}; t_{k-2}, Y_{l_{k-2}}(t_{k-2})) = 0$ and $F_{l_{k-1}j}\left(t; t_{k-1}, Y_{l_{k-1}}(t_{k-1})\right) > 0$ for any $t \in [t_{k-1}, t_k)$ for all $j \in \Lambda$, and combine with Lemma 2, then, t_{k-1} is the irregular point. Analogously, $\{t_i | 0 \leq t_1 < t_2 < \cdots < t_k < +\infty\}$ is the irregular point set of x over $\mathbb{R}^+$. This completes the proof.

4. Proof of Theorem 2

Throughout this section, we fix $T > 0$ and vector $v \in \mathbb{R}^n$. It follows from Theorem 1 that the irregular points to the *PC*-solution x of (1) occur at most a finite number of times on the interval $[0, T]$. There are only two possibilities: Case (1), x has no irregular point on $[0, T]$ and Case (2), x has at least one irregular point on $[0, T]$.

In Case (1), the *PC*-solution x has a continuous dependence relative to the initial value in the sense of the classical definition, i.e.,

$$|x_\theta(\cdot; \theta, x_0 + \theta v) - x(\cdot; 0, x_0)|_{C([0,T],\mathbb{R}^n)} \longrightarrow 0 \text{ as } \theta \to 0.$$

In Case (2), if $x_0 = y_i(0)$ for some $i \in \Lambda$, we only study the *PC*-solution $x(\cdot; 0+, Y_i(0))$. Consequently, we may assume that $x(\cdot; 0, x_0)$ meets the movement obstacle set $Y(t)$ k times in $[0, T]$, and let $\bar{t}^i_j$ be the moments when $x(\cdot; 0, x_0)$ hits the movement obstacle line $y_i(\cdot)$, this moment is exactly the jth hits movement obstacle set $Y(t)$, ($i \in \Lambda$, $j = 1, 2, \cdots, k$). For convenience, let $\{\bar{t}^i_j | 0 < \bar{t}^i_1 < \cdots < \bar{t}^r_k < T\}$ denote the irregular point set of $x(\cdot; 0, x_0)$ on $[0, T]$. By Theorem 1, one can prove that the impulsive differential Equation (1) has a unique approximate *PC*-solution $x_\theta(\cdot; \theta, x_0 + \theta v)$ corresponding to the initial value $(\theta, x_0 + \theta v)$. Note that the approximate *PC*-solution (3) is the *PC*-solution of (1), as $\theta = 0$. According to the continuous dependence of the solution of an ODE on parameters, there exists $\bar{\bar{\delta}} > 0$, such that when $0 \leq \theta < \bar{\bar{\delta}}$, $x_\theta(\cdot; \theta, x_0 + \theta v)$ and $x_0(\cdot; 0, x_0)$ have the same number of irregular points on $[t_0, T]$. Let $t^i_j(\theta)$ be the irregular moments of $x_\theta(\cdot; \theta, x_0 + \theta v)$. Notice approximate *PC*-solution (3) is the *PC*-solution of (1), again, as $\theta = 0$, and using the continuous dependence of the solution of an ODE on parameters, there exists $\bar{\delta} > \bar{\bar{\delta}} > 0$, such that when $0 \leq \theta < \bar{\delta}$, $\max\{\bar{t}^i_j, t^i_j(\theta)\} < \min\{\bar{t}^r_{j+1}, t^r_{j+1}(\theta)\}$.

For a sufficient small $\varepsilon > 0$, the *PC*-solution $x_0(\cdot; 0, x_0)$ of (1) does not meet movement obstacle set $Y(t)$ on $[0, \bar{t}^i_1 - \frac{\varepsilon}{4k}]$. Similarly, using the continuous dependence of the solution of an ODE on parameters, approximate *PC*-solution (3) is the *PC*-solution of (1), as $\theta = 0$. It yields that there is a $\bar{\delta} > \delta_1 > 0$ such that for any $0 < \theta < \min\{\delta_1, \frac{\varepsilon}{4k}\}$, the inequality $|x_\theta(\cdot; \theta, x_0 + \theta v) - x_0(\cdot; 0, x_0)| < \varepsilon$ holds on $[0, \bar{t}^i_1 - \frac{\varepsilon}{4k}]$. Furthermore, together with $x(\bar{t}^i_1) = y_i(\bar{t}^i_1)$, we have $x_\theta(t^i_1(\theta)) = \tilde{y}_i \in \partial B^{\theta^2}_{y_i}$, this means

$$\lim_{\theta \to 0} t^i_1(\theta) = \bar{t}^i_1.$$

Together with the continuity of J_i, we have

$$\lim_{\theta \to 0} J_i\left(x_\theta\left(t^i_1(\theta); \theta, x_0 + \theta v\right)\right) = J_i\left(x\left(\bar{t}^i_1; 0, x_0\right)\right).$$

It follows from (4) that

$$\lim_{\theta \to 0} Y_i\left(t^i_1(\theta)\right) = Y_i\left(\bar{t}^i_1\right),$$

where

$$Y_i\left(t^i_1(\theta)\right) = x_\theta\left(t^i_1(\theta); \theta, x_0 + \theta v\right) + J_i\left(x_\theta\left(t^i_1(\theta); \theta, x_0 + \theta v\right)\right).$$

For the time interval $\left[\bar{t}^i_1 + \frac{\varepsilon}{4k}, \bar{t}^j_2 - \frac{\varepsilon}{4k}\right]$,

$$|x_\theta(t; \theta, x_0 + \theta v) - x(t; 0, x_0)|$$

$$
= \left| x_\theta\left(t; t_1^i(\theta), Y_i\left(t_1^i(\theta)\right)\right) - x\left(t; \bar{t}_1^i, Y_i\left(\bar{t}_1^i\right)\right) \right|
$$

$$
\leq \left| Y_i\left(t_1^i(\theta)\right) - Y_i\left(\bar{t}_1^i\right) \right| + \left| \int_{t_1^i(\theta)}^t f(\tau, x_\theta(\tau))d\tau - \int_{\bar{t}_1^i}^t f(\tau, x(\tau))d\tau \right|
$$

$$
\leq 2M(T) + \left| \int_{\min\{t_1^i(\theta),\, \bar{t}_1^i\}}^{\max\{t_1^i(\theta),\, \bar{t}_1^i\}} f(\tau, x_\theta(\tau))d\tau \right|
$$

$$
+ L(\tilde{M}(T;\tilde{k})) \int_{\max\{t_1^i(\theta),\, \bar{t}_1^i\}}^t |x_\theta(\tau) - x(\tau)|d\tau
$$

$$
\leq 2M(T) + \tilde{k}(1 + \tilde{M}(T;\tilde{k}))\left| t_1^i(\theta) - \bar{t}_1^i \right| + L(\tilde{M}(T;\tilde{k})) \int_{\max\{t_1^i(\theta),\, \bar{t}_1^i\}}^t |x_\theta(\tau) - x(\tau)|d\tau
$$

From Gronwall's inequality, we obtain the estimate

$$
|x_\theta(t; \theta, x_0 + \theta v) - x(t; 0, x_0)|
$$
$$
\leq \exp(L(\tilde{M}(T;\tilde{k}))[t - \max\{t_1^i(\theta),\, \bar{t}_1^i\}])\left(2M(T) + \tilde{k}(1 + \tilde{M}(T;\tilde{k}))\left| t_1^i(\theta) - \bar{t}_1^i \right|\right)
$$

which implies that there is a $\delta_2 > 0$ with $\delta_2 < \delta_1$ such that for any $\theta > 0$ with $\theta < \delta_2$,

$$
|x_\theta(t; \theta, x_0 + \theta v) - x(t; u, 0, x_0)| = \left| x_\theta\left(t; t_1^i(\theta), Y_i\left(t_1^i(\theta)\right)\right) - x\left(t; \bar{t}_1^i, Y_i\left(\bar{t}_1^i\right)\right) \right|
$$
$$
< \varepsilon \text{ for any } t \in \left[\bar{t}_1^i + \frac{\varepsilon}{4k}, \bar{t}_2^j - \frac{\varepsilon}{4k}\right]
$$

Let

$$
Y_i\left(t_j^i(\theta)\right) = x_\theta\left(t_j^i(\theta); \theta, x_0 + \theta v\right) + J_i\left(x_\theta\left(t_j^i(\theta); \theta, x_0 + \theta v\right)\right), j > 1, i \in \Lambda. \tag{17}
$$

In general, by repeating the above process, one can show that there is a $\delta_{j+1} > 0$ with $\delta_{j+1} < \delta_j$ such that for any $\theta > 0$ with $\theta < \delta_{j+1}$,

$$
|x_\theta(t; \theta, x_0 + \theta v) - x(t; 0, x_0)| = \left| x_\theta\left(t; t_j^i(\theta), Y_i\left(t_j^i(\theta)\right)\right) - x\left(t; \bar{t}_j^i, Y_i\left(\bar{t}_j^i\right)\right) \right|
$$
$$
< \varepsilon \text{ for any } t \in \left[\bar{t}_j^i + \frac{\varepsilon}{4k}, \bar{t}_{j+1}^r - \frac{\varepsilon}{4k}\right]
$$

and

$$
\lim_{\theta \to 0} t_{j+1}^r(\theta) = \bar{t}_{j+1}^r,
$$

$$
\lim_{\theta \to 0} J_r\left(x_\theta\left(t_{j+1}^r(\theta); \theta, x_0 + \theta v\right)\right) = J_r\left(x\left(\bar{t}_{j+1}^r; 0, x_0\right)\right),
$$

$$
\lim_{\theta \to 0} Y_r\left(t_{j+1}^r(\theta)\right) = Y_r\left(\bar{t}_{j+1}^r\right),
$$

where

$$
Y_r\left(t_{j+1}^r(\theta)\right) = x_\theta\left(t_{j+1}^r(\theta); \theta, x_0 + \theta v\right) + J_r\left(x_\theta\left(t_j^r(\theta); \theta, x_0 + \theta v\right)\right).
$$

In short, for any sufficient small $\varepsilon > 0$, there exists a $\delta > 0$ such that

$$
|x_\theta(t; \theta, x_0 + \theta v) - x(t; 0, x_0)| < \varepsilon \text{ for any } t \in I_\varepsilon \text{ when } \theta < \delta,
$$

and $\mu([0,T] \setminus I_\varepsilon) < \varepsilon$, where

$$I_\varepsilon = \left[0, \bar{t}_1^i - \frac{\varepsilon}{4k}\right] \cup \left(\bigcup_{j=1}^{k-1}\left[\bar{t}_j^i + \frac{\varepsilon}{4k}, \bar{t}_{j+1}^r - \frac{\varepsilon}{4k}\right]\right) \cup \left[\bar{t}_k^r + \frac{\varepsilon}{4k}, T\right].$$

This completes the proof.

5. Proof of Theorem 3

Throughout this section, we fix $T > 0$. It follows from Theorem 2 that there are only two possibilities: Case (i), $x(\cdot;0,x_0)$ has no irregular point on $[0,T]$ and Case (ii), $x(\cdot;0,x_0)$ has at least one irregular point on $[0,T]$.

In Case (i), one can directly check that $x(\cdot;0,x_0)$ of (1) is Gâteaux differentiable, and its Gâteaux derivative φ is a weak solution of the following differential equation

$$\begin{cases} \dot{\varphi}(t) = f_x(t, x(t;0,x_0))\varphi(t), t \in (0,T], \\ \varphi(0) = v - f(0,x_0). \end{cases}$$

To discuss Case (ii), we define function h_t given by

$$h_t(\varepsilon) \text{ denotes the solution of the equation } H(\varepsilon,t) = 0. \tag{18}$$

Here,

$$H(\varepsilon,t) = x_\varepsilon(t;\varepsilon, x_0 + \varepsilon v) - \tilde{y}(t,\varepsilon), \tag{19}$$

where $\tilde{y}(t,\varepsilon) = \tilde{y}_i(t,\varepsilon)$ for some $i \in \Lambda$, $\tilde{y}_i(t,\varepsilon) \in \partial B(y_i(t), \varepsilon^2)$. By Theorem 2, when $x(t;0,x_0) = y_i(t)$, there is a $\delta > 0$ such that definition (18) holds for all $\varepsilon \in [0,\delta]$, that is, $h_t : [0,\delta] \longrightarrow O(t)$ is a function, and $h_t(0) = t$, where $O(t)$ denotes some neighborhood of t. For convenience, let $\{t_j^i | 0 < t_1^i < \cdots < t_k^r < T\}$ denote the irregular point set of $x(\cdot;0,x_0)$ on $[0,T]$. If $y_i \in C^1([0,T], \mathbb{R}^n)$, it follows from Theorem 2 and (19) that there is an $\delta > 0$ such that

$$H \in C([0,\delta] \times [0,T]) \text{ and } H\left(\varepsilon, h_{t_j^i}(\varepsilon)\right) = 0 \text{ for any } \varepsilon \in [0,\delta], i \in \Lambda, j = 1,2,\cdots,k$$

and

$$H_t(\varepsilon,t) = f(t, x_\varepsilon(t;\varepsilon, x_0 + \varepsilon v)) - \tilde{y}_t(t,\varepsilon).$$

According to assumption [Y](2), $f\left(t_j^i, y_i\left(t_j^i\right)\right) \neq \dot{y}_i\left(t_j^i\right)$ $(j = 1,2,\cdots,k, i \in \Lambda)$, we have

$$H_t\left(\varepsilon, h_{t_j^i}(\varepsilon)\right) = f\left(h_{t_j^i}(\varepsilon), x_\varepsilon\left(h_{t_j^i}(\varepsilon);\varepsilon, x_0 + \varepsilon v\right)\right) - \dot{y}_i(h_{t_j^i}(\varepsilon)) \neq 0 \text{ in } \mathbb{R}^n, \ \forall \varepsilon \in [0,\delta],$$

where $j = 1,2,\cdots,k$. Let $f = (f^1, f^2, \cdots, f^n)^\top$, $y_i = (y_i^1, y_i^2, \cdots, y_i^n)^\top$ $(i \in \Lambda)$. Without loss of generality, we suppose

$$f^1\left(h_{t_j^i}(\varepsilon), x_\varepsilon\left(h_{t_j^i}(\varepsilon);\varepsilon, x_0 + \varepsilon v\right)\right) - \dot{y}_i^1(h_{t_j^i}(\varepsilon)) \neq 0 \text{ in } \mathbb{R}, \ \forall \varepsilon \in [0,\delta], j = 1,2,\cdots,k, \tag{20}$$

We introduce the following functions

$$\Phi_\varepsilon(t,s) = \exp\left(\int_s^t f_x(\tau, x_\varepsilon(\tau;\varepsilon, x_0 + \varepsilon v))d\tau\right); \tag{21}$$

then,

$$\Phi(t,s) = \lim_{\varepsilon \to 0} \Phi_\varepsilon(t,s) = \exp\left(\int_s^t f_x(\tau, x(\tau; 0, x_0)) d\tau \right).$$

We let

$$\Phi_\varepsilon^1(t,s) \quad \text{and} \quad \Phi^1(t,s) \quad \text{denote the first line vector of} \quad \Phi_\varepsilon(t,s) \quad \text{and} \quad \Phi(t,s), \quad \text{respectively.} \tag{22}$$

We first claim the following lemma.

Lemma 3. *Suppose assumption [F](3) holds. Then, h_t is differentiable over $[0, \delta]$ for some $\delta > 0$, and its derivative is given by*

$$\dot{h}_{t_j^i}(0) = \begin{cases} \dfrac{\Phi^1(t_1^i,0)(f(0,x_0)-v)}{f^1\left(t_1^i,y_i\left(t_1^i\right)\right)-\dot{y}_i^1\left(t_1^i\right)}, & j = 1, \\[3mm] \dfrac{\dot{h}_{t_{j-1}^r}(0)\Phi^1\left(t_j^i,t_{j-1}^r\right)\left[f\left(t_{j-1}^r,y_r\left(t_{j-1}^r\right)\right)-\left(I+\nabla J_r\left(y_r\left(t_{j-1}^r\right)\right)\right)\dot{y}_r\left(t_{j-1}^r\right)\right]}{f^1\left(t_j^i,y_i\left(t_j^i\right)\right)-\dot{y}_i^1\left(t_j^i\right)}, & j > 1. \end{cases}$$

Here, I is a unit matrix.

Proof. When $t \in \left(0, h_{t_1^i}(\varepsilon)\right)$, it follows from assumption [F](3), (10) and (3) that

$$\begin{aligned} H_\varepsilon(\varepsilon,t) &= \lim_{\zeta \to 0} \frac{x_{\varepsilon+\zeta}(t;\varepsilon+\zeta, x_0+(\varepsilon+\zeta)v) - x_\varepsilon(t;\varepsilon, x_0+\varepsilon v)}{\zeta} + \frac{\partial}{\partial \varepsilon}\tilde{y}_i(t,\varepsilon) \\[2mm] &= \lim_{\zeta \to 0} \int_{\varepsilon+\zeta}^t \int_0^1 f_x(s, x_\varepsilon(s;\varepsilon, x_0+\varepsilon v) + \theta(x_{\varepsilon+\zeta}(s;\varepsilon+\zeta, x_0+(\varepsilon+\zeta)v) \\[2mm] &\quad -x_\varepsilon(s;\varepsilon, x_0+\varepsilon v))) \frac{x_{\varepsilon+\zeta}(s;\varepsilon+\zeta, x_0+(\varepsilon+\zeta)v) - x_\varepsilon(s;\varepsilon, x_0+\varepsilon v)}{\zeta} d\theta ds \\[2mm] &\quad v - f(\varepsilon, x_0+\varepsilon v) + \frac{\partial}{\partial \varepsilon}\tilde{y}_i(t,\varepsilon). \end{aligned}$$

One can see from (21) and the above equality that

$$H_\varepsilon(\varepsilon,t) = \Phi_\varepsilon(t,\varepsilon)(v - f(\varepsilon, x_0+\varepsilon v)) + \frac{\partial}{\partial \varepsilon}\tilde{y}_i(t,\varepsilon).$$

Combining (20), (21) and (22), we have

$$\dot{h}_{t_1^i}(\varepsilon) = -\frac{\Phi_\varepsilon^1\left(h_{t_1^i}(\varepsilon),\varepsilon\right)(v - f(\varepsilon, x_0+\varepsilon v)) + \frac{\partial}{\partial \varepsilon}\tilde{y}_i^1(t,\varepsilon)}{f^1\left(h_{t_1^i}(\varepsilon), x_\varepsilon\left(h_{t_1^i}(\varepsilon);\varepsilon, x_0+\varepsilon v\right)\right) - \dot{y}_i^1\left(h_{t_1^i}(\varepsilon)\right)}$$

and

$$\dot{h}_{t_1^i}(0) = \frac{\Phi^1(t_1^i,0)(v - f(0,x_0))}{\dot{y}_i^1(t_1^i) - f^1(t_1^i,y_i(t_1^i))},$$

In general, when $t \in \left(h_{t_{j-1}^r}(\varepsilon), h_{t_j^i}(\varepsilon)\right)$, it follows from assumption [F](3), (10), (3) and (4) that

$$\begin{aligned} H_\varepsilon(\varepsilon,t) &= \lim_{\zeta \to 0} \frac{x_{\varepsilon+\zeta}(t;\varepsilon+\zeta, x_0+(\varepsilon+\zeta)v) - x_\varepsilon(t;\varepsilon, x_0+\varepsilon v)}{\zeta} + \frac{\partial}{\partial \varepsilon}\tilde{y}_i(t,\varepsilon) \\[2mm] &= \lim_{\zeta \to 0} \frac{x_{\varepsilon+\zeta}\left(t;h_{t_{j-1}^r}(\varepsilon+\zeta), Y_r\left(h_{t_{j-1}^r}(\varepsilon+\zeta)\right)\right) - x_\varepsilon\left(t;h_{t_{j-1}^r}(\varepsilon), Y_r\left(h_{t_{j-1}^r}(\varepsilon)\right)\right)}{\zeta} \end{aligned}$$

$$+ \frac{\partial}{\partial \varepsilon} \tilde{y}_i(t, \varepsilon)$$

$$= \lim_{\xi \to 0} \int_{h_{t^r_{j-1}}(\varepsilon+\xi)}^{t} \int_0^1 f_x(s, x_\varepsilon(s; \varepsilon, x_0 + \varepsilon v) + \theta(x_{\varepsilon+\xi}(s; \varepsilon+\xi, x_0 + (\varepsilon+\xi)v)$$

$$- x_\varepsilon(s; \varepsilon, x_0 + \varepsilon v))) \frac{x_{\varepsilon+\xi}(s; \varepsilon+\xi, x_0 + (\varepsilon+\xi)v) - x_\varepsilon(s; \varepsilon, x_0 + \varepsilon v)}{\xi} \, d\theta ds$$

$$+ \lim_{\xi \to 0} \frac{Y_r\left(h_{t^r_{j-1}}(\varepsilon+\xi), \varepsilon+\xi\right) - Y_r\left(h_{t^r_{j-1}}(\varepsilon), \varepsilon\right)}{\xi}$$

$$- \lim_{\xi \to 0} \frac{\int_{h_{t^r_{j-1}}(\varepsilon)}^{h_{t^r_{j-1}}(\varepsilon+\xi)} f(s, x(s; \varepsilon, x_0 + \varepsilon v)) ds}{\xi} + \frac{\partial}{\partial \varepsilon} \tilde{y}_r(t, \varepsilon)$$

$$= \lim_{\xi \to 0} \int_{h_{t^r_{j-1}}(\varepsilon+\xi)}^{t} \int_0^1 f_x(s, x_\varepsilon(s; \varepsilon, x_0 + \varepsilon v) + \theta(x_{\varepsilon+\xi}(s; \varepsilon+\xi, x_0 + (\varepsilon+\xi)v)$$

$$- x_\varepsilon(s; \varepsilon, x_0 + \varepsilon v))) \frac{x_{\varepsilon+\xi}(s; \varepsilon+\xi, x_0 + (\varepsilon+\xi)v) - x_\varepsilon(s; \varepsilon, x_0 + \varepsilon v)}{\xi} \, d\theta ds$$

$$+ \left(I + \nabla J_r\left(\tilde{y}_r\left(h_{t^r_{j-1}}(\varepsilon), \varepsilon\right)\right)\right) \left[\dot{h}_{t^r_{j-1}}(\varepsilon) \frac{\partial}{\partial t} \tilde{y}_r\left(h_{t^r_{j-1}}(\varepsilon), \varepsilon\right)\right.$$

$$\left. + \frac{\partial}{\partial \varepsilon} \tilde{y}_r\left(h_{t^r_{j-1}}(\varepsilon), \varepsilon\right)\right] - \dot{h}_{t^r_{j-1}}(\varepsilon) f\left(h_{t^r_{j-1}}(\varepsilon), \tilde{y}_r\left(h_{t^r_{j-1}}(\varepsilon), \varepsilon\right)\right) + \frac{\partial}{\partial \varepsilon} \tilde{y}_r(t, \varepsilon).$$

We can also infer from (21) and the above equality that

$$H_\varepsilon(\varepsilon, t) = \frac{\partial}{\partial \varepsilon} \tilde{y}_r(t, \varepsilon) + \Phi_\varepsilon\left(t, h_{t^r_{j-1}}(\varepsilon)\right) \left(I + \nabla J_r\left(\tilde{y}_r\left(h_{t^r_{j-1}}(\varepsilon), \varepsilon\right)\right)\right) \left[\dot{h}_{t^r_{j-1}}(\varepsilon) \frac{\partial}{\partial t} \tilde{y}_r\left(h_{t^r_{j-1}}(\varepsilon), \varepsilon\right)\right.$$

$$\left. + \frac{\partial}{\partial \varepsilon} \tilde{y}_r\left(h_{t^r_{j-1}}(\varepsilon), \varepsilon\right)\right] - \dot{h}_{t^r_{j-1}}(\varepsilon) \Phi_\varepsilon\left(t, h_{t^r_{j-1}}(\varepsilon)\right) f\left(h_{t^r_{j-1}}(\varepsilon), \tilde{y}_r\left(h_{t^r_{j-1}}(\varepsilon), \varepsilon\right)\right).$$

Together with (20) and (22), by the implicit function theorem, we have

$$\dot{h}_{t^i_j}(\varepsilon) = -\frac{\Phi^1_\varepsilon\left(h_{t^i_j}(\varepsilon), h_{t^r_{j-1}}(\varepsilon)\right) \left(I + \nabla J_r\left(\tilde{y}_r\left(h_{t^r_{j-1}}(\varepsilon), \varepsilon\right)\right)\right)}{f^1\left(h_{t^i_j}(\varepsilon), x_\varepsilon\left(h_{t^i_j}(\varepsilon); \varepsilon, x_0 + \varepsilon v\right)\right) - \dot{y}^1_i\left(h_{t^i_2}(\varepsilon)\right)}$$

$$\cdot \left[\dot{h}_{t^r_{j-1}}(\varepsilon) \frac{\partial}{\partial t} \tilde{y}_r\left(h_{t^r_{j-1}}(\varepsilon), \varepsilon\right) + \frac{\partial}{\partial \varepsilon} \tilde{y}_r\left(h_{t^r_{j-1}}(\varepsilon), \varepsilon\right)\right]$$

$$- \frac{\frac{\partial}{\partial \varepsilon} \tilde{y}^1_r(t, \varepsilon) - \dot{h}_{t^r_{j-1}}(\varepsilon) \Phi^1_\varepsilon\left(h_{t^i_j}(\varepsilon), h_{t^r_{j-1}}(\varepsilon)\right) f\left(h_{t^r_{j-1}}(\varepsilon), \tilde{y}_r\left(h_{t^r_{j-1}}(\varepsilon), \varepsilon\right)\right)}{f^1\left(h_{t^i_j}(\varepsilon), x_\varepsilon\left(h_{t^i_j}(\varepsilon); \varepsilon, x_0 + \varepsilon v\right)\right) - \dot{y}^1_i\left(h_{t^i_j}(\varepsilon)\right)}.$$

Further, this means that

$$\dot{h}_{t^i_j}(0) = \frac{\dot{h}_{t^r_{j-1}}(0) \Phi^1\left(t^i_j, t^r_{j-1}\right) \left[f\left(t^r_{j-1}, y_r\left(t^r_{j-1}\right)\right) - \left(I + \nabla J_r\left(y_r\left(t^r_{j-1}\right)\right)\right) \dot{y}_r\left(t^r_{j-1}\right)\right]}{f^1\left(t^i_j, y_i\left(t^i_j\right)\right) - \dot{y}^1_i\left(t^i_j\right)}.$$

This completes the proof. $\square$

Now, we claim Case (ii). For $t \in (0, t_1^i)$, similarly to Case (i), it is not difficult to check the following result

$$\begin{cases} \dot{\varphi}(t) = f_x(t, x(t; 0, x_0))\varphi(t), & t \in (0, t_1^i], \\ \varphi(0) = v - f(0, x_0), \end{cases} \tag{23}$$

Combining with Lemma 3, we first note that

$$\begin{aligned}
&\lim_{\varepsilon \to 0} \frac{x_\varepsilon\left(h_{t_j^i}(\varepsilon); \varepsilon, x_0 + \varepsilon v\right) - x\left(t_j^i; 0, x_0\right)}{\varepsilon} \\
=~ &\lim_{\varepsilon \to 0} \frac{x_\varepsilon\left(h_{t_j^i}(\varepsilon); \varepsilon, x_0 + \varepsilon v\right) - x_\varepsilon\left(t_j^i; \varepsilon, x_0 + \varepsilon v\right)}{\varepsilon} + \lim_{\varepsilon \to 0} \frac{x_\varepsilon\left(t_j^i; \varepsilon, x_0 + \varepsilon v\right) - x\left(t_j^i; 0, x_0\right)}{\varepsilon} \\
=~ &\varphi\left(t_j^i\right) + \dot{h}_{t_j^i}(0) f\left(t_j^i, y_i\left(t_j^i\right)\right). \tag{24}
\end{aligned}$$

Together with assumption [J](2), When $h_{t_j^i}(\varepsilon) > t_j^i$, we have

$$\begin{aligned}
\varphi\left(t_j^i+\right) =~ &\lim_{\varepsilon \to 0} \frac{x_\varepsilon\left(h_{t_j^i}(\varepsilon)+; \varepsilon, x_0 + \varepsilon v\right) - x\left(h_{t_j^i}(\varepsilon); 0, x_0\right)}{\varepsilon} \\
=~ &\lim_{\varepsilon \to 0} \frac{1}{\varepsilon}\left[x_\varepsilon\left(h_{t_j^i}(\varepsilon); \varepsilon, x_0 + \varepsilon v\right) + J_i\left(x_\varepsilon\left(h_{t_j^i}(\varepsilon); \varepsilon, x_0 + \varepsilon v\right)\right)\right. \\
&\left. -x\left(h_{t_j^i}(\varepsilon); t_j^i, x\left(t_j^i; 0, x_0\right) + J_i\left(x\left(t_j^i; 0, x_0\right)\right)\right)\right] \\
=~ &\lim_{\varepsilon \to 0} \frac{1}{\varepsilon}\left[x_\varepsilon\left(h_{t_j^i}(\varepsilon); \varepsilon, x_0 + \varepsilon v\right) + J_i\left(x_\varepsilon\left(h_{t_j^i}(\varepsilon); \varepsilon, x_0 + \varepsilon v\right)\right)\right. \\
&\left. -x\left(t_j^i; 0, x_0\right) - J_i\left(x\left(t_j^i; 0, x_0\right)\right) - \int_{t_j^i}^{h_{t_j^i}(\varepsilon)} f(s, x(s; 0, x_0))ds\right] \\
=~ &\left(I + \nabla J_i\left(y_i\left(t_j^i\right)\right)\right)\left[\varphi\left(t_j^i-\right) + \dot{h}_{t_j^i}(0) f\left(t_j^i, y_i\left(t_j^i\right)\right)\right] - \dot{h}_{t_j^i}(0) f\left(t_j^i, y_i\left(t_j^i\right)\right) \\
=~ &\varphi\left(t_j^i-\right) + \nabla J_i\left(y_i\left(t_j^i\right)\right)\left[\varphi\left(t_j^i-\right) + \dot{h}_{t_j^i}(0) f\left(t_j^i, y_i\left(t_j^i\right)\right)\right].
\end{aligned}$$

When $h_{t_j^i}(\varepsilon) < t_j^i$, we also have

$$\begin{aligned}
\varphi\left(t_j^i+\right) =~ &\lim_{\varepsilon \to 0} \frac{x_\varepsilon\left(t_j^i; \varepsilon, x_0 + \varepsilon v\right) - x\left(t_j^i+; 0, x_0\right)}{\varepsilon} \\
=~ &\lim_{\varepsilon \to 0} \frac{1}{\varepsilon}\left[x_\varepsilon\left(h_{t_j^i}(\varepsilon); \varepsilon, x_0 + \varepsilon v\right) + J_i\left(x_\varepsilon\left(h_{t_j^i}(\varepsilon); \varepsilon, x_0 + \varepsilon v\right)\right)\right. \\
&\left. -x\left(t_j^i; 0, x_0\right) - J_i\left(x\left(t_j^i; 0, x_0\right)\right) - \int_{t_j^i}^{h_{t_j^i}(\varepsilon)} f(s, x_\varepsilon(s; \varepsilon, x_0 + \varepsilon v))ds\right] \\
=~ &\varphi\left(t_j^i-\right) + \nabla J_i\left(y_i\left(t_j^i\right)\right)\left[\varphi\left(t_j^i-\right) + \dot{h}_{t_j^i}(0) f\left(t_j^i, y_i\left(t_j^i\right)\right)\right].
\end{aligned}$$

Consequently, we have

$$\varphi\left(t_j^i+\right) = \varphi\left(t_j^i\right) + \nabla J_i\left(y_i\left(t_j^i\right)\right)\left[\varphi\left(t_j^i\right) + \dot{h}_{t_j^i}(0) f\left(t_j^i, y_i\left(t_j^i\right)\right)\right], i \in \Lambda, j = 1, 2, \cdots, k. \tag{25}$$

Therefore, when $t \in \left(t_j^i, t_{j+1}^r\right)$ $(j = 1, 2, \cdots, k-1)$ or $t \in (t_k^r, T]$, it follows from assumption [F](3) and (10), (3), (4), (17), (22) and (24) that

$$
\begin{aligned}
\varphi(t) &= \lim_{\theta \to 0} \frac{x_\theta(t; \theta, x_0 + \theta v) - x(t; 0, x_0)}{\theta} \\
&= \lim_{\theta \to 0} \frac{x_\theta(t; h_{t_j^i}(\theta), Y_r(h_{t_j^i}(\theta))) - x(t; t_j^i, Y_r(t_j^i))}{\theta} \\
&= \lim_{\theta \to 0} \frac{Y_i(h_{t_j^i}(\theta)) - Y_i(t_j^i))}{\theta} + \lim_{\theta \to 0} \int_{h_{t_j^i}(\theta)}^{t} \int_0^1 f_x(s, x(s; 0, x_0) + \xi(x_\theta(s; \theta, x_0 + \theta v) \\
&\quad - x(s; 0, x_0))) \frac{x_\theta(s; \theta, x_0 + \theta v) - x(s; 0, x_0)}{\theta} d\xi ds - \lim_{\theta \to 0} \frac{1}{\theta} \int_{t_j^i}^{h_{t_j^i}(\theta)} f(s, x(s; 0, x_0)) ds \\
&= -\dot{h}_{t_j^i}(0) f\left(t_j^i, y_i\left(t_j^i\right)\right) + \lim_{\theta \to 0} \int_{h_{t_j^i}(\theta)}^{t} \int_0^1 f_x(s, x(s; 0, x_0) + \xi(x_\theta(s; \theta, x_0 + \theta v) \\
&\quad - x(s; 0, x_0))) \frac{x_\theta(s; \theta, x_0 + \theta v) - x(s; 0, x_0)}{\theta} d\xi ds \\
&\quad + \left(I + \nabla J_i\left(y_i\left(t_j^i\right)\right)\right)\left(\varphi\left(t_j^i\right) + \dot{h}_{t_j^i}(0) f\left(t_j^i, y_i\left(t_j^i\right)\right)\right).
\end{aligned}
$$

Thus, combining with (23) and (25), we obtain from the above equality that

$$
\begin{cases}
\dot{\varphi}(t) = f_x(t, x(t; 0, x_0))\varphi(t), t \in (0, T] \text{ and } t \neq t_j^i, i \in \Lambda, j = 1, 2, \cdots, k, \\
\varphi(0) = v - f(0, x_0), \\
\varphi\left(t_j^i+\right) = \varphi\left(t_j^i\right) + \nabla J_i\left(y_i\left(t_j^i\right)\right)\left(\varphi\left(t_j^i\right) + \dot{h}_{t_j^i}(0) f\left(t_j^i, y_i\left(t_j^i\right)\right)\right), j = 1, 2, \cdots, k.
\end{cases}
$$

This completes the proof of Theorem 3.

6. Periodicity of an Autonomous Impulsive System

As an application, in this section, we discuss the periodicity of the solution of the following impulsive differential equation

$$
\begin{cases}
\dot{x}(t) = g(x(t)), & x(t) \neq y_1, t \geq 0, \\
x(t+) = y_2, & x(t) = y_1, t \geq 0, \\
x(0) = x_0,
\end{cases} \tag{26}
$$

where $y_1, y_2 \in \mathbb{R}^n$, and $y_1 \neq y_2$. We introduce the function

$$
G(t; s, z_s) = \langle z(t, s, z_s) - y_1, z_s - y_1 \rangle \text{ for any } t \geq s \geq 0.
$$

Here,

$$
z(t, s, z_s) = z_s + \int_s^t g(z(\tau, s, z_s)) d\tau, \text{ for any } t \geq s \geq 0.
$$

For function $G(\cdot; 0, x_0)$, it is clear that

$$
G(t; 0, x_0) = 0 \text{ has no solution on } \mathbb{R}^+ \tag{27}
$$

or

$$
t_1 \text{ is the minimum solution of } G(t; 0, x_0) = 0 \text{ on } \mathbb{R}^+. \tag{28}
$$

Similarly, it is obvious that

$$
G(t; t_1, y_2) = 0 \text{ has no solution on } [t_1, +\infty) \tag{29}
$$

or

$$t_2 \text{ is the minimum solution of } G(t; t_1, y_2) = 0 \text{ on } [t_1, +\infty). \tag{30}$$

Let $PC_{y_1 y_2}(\mathbb{R}^+, \mathbb{R}^n) = \{x : [0, +\infty) \longrightarrow \mathbb{R}^n | x$ be continuous at t when $x(t) \neq y_1$, x is left-continuous at t and the right limit $x(t+)$ exists when $x(t) = y_1\}$. We check the following main result for autonomous impulsive system (26).

Theorem 4. *Suppose* $g : \mathbb{R}^n \longrightarrow \mathbb{R}^n$ *is locally Lipschitz continuous in* x, *and there exists a constant* $\tilde{k} > 0$ *such that*

$$|g(x)| \leq \tilde{k}(1 + |x|) \text{ for any } t \geq 0.$$

(1) If (27) holds, then (26) has a unique solution $x \in C(\mathbb{R}^+, \mathbb{R}^n)$.
(2) If (28) and (29) hold, then the solution of (26) has a unique irregular point t_1.
(3) If (29) and (30) hold, then the solution of (26) is a periodic function on $[t_1, +\infty)$.

Proof. Using Theorem 1, we directly check that autonomous impulsive system (26) has a unique solution $x \in PC_{y_1 y_2}(\mathbb{R}^+, \mathbb{R}^n)$. Further, there are only three possibilities for the solution: Case (i), x has not irregular point on $\mathbb{R}^+$; Case (ii), x has a unique irregular point on $\mathbb{R}^+$; and Case (iii), x has two irregular points on $\mathbb{R}^+$ at least.

For Case (i), it follows from (2) of Theorem 1 that x has no irregular point on $\mathbb{R}^+$ if and only if (27) holds. This means (26) has a unique solution $x \in C(\mathbb{R}^+, \mathbb{R}^n)$. Similarly, for Case (ii), together with (28) and (29), we can also infer that x only has a unique irregular point t_1.

For Case (iii), let t_1 and t_2 denote the smallest two irregular points of solution x on $\mathbb{R}^+$ and $T = t_2 - t_1$. We claim

$$x(t + T) = x(t) \text{ for any } t \in [t_1, +\infty). \tag{31}$$

By the definitions of t_1 and t_2 (see (28) and (30)), solution x of (26) has not irregular point on (t_1, t_2) and satisfies

$$x(t) = y_2 + \int_{t_1}^{t} g(x(s))ds \text{ for any } t \in (t_1, t_2] \text{ and } x(t_2) = x(t_1) = y_1. \tag{32}$$

When $t \in (t_1, t_2]$, we have $t + T \in (t_2, t_2 + T]$ and

$$x(t + T) = y_2 + \int_{t_1 + T}^{t+T} g(x(s))ds = y_2 + \int_{t_1}^{t} g(x(s + T))ds. \tag{33}$$

It is easy to see that by the assumption conditions of g, there exists $\rho > 0$ such that $|x(t)|$, $|x(T + t)| \leq \rho$ for every $t \in (t_1, t_2]$. Furthermore, we assert from (32) and (33) that

$$\begin{aligned} |x(t + T) - x(t)| &\leq \int_{t_1}^{t} |g(x(s + T)) - g(x(s))|ds \\ &\leq L(\rho) \int_{t_1}^{t} |x(s + T) - x(s)|ds. \end{aligned}$$

Together with Gronwall's inequality, one can verify that

$$x(t + T) = x(t) \text{ for any } t \in (t_1, t_2].$$

Consequently, we can infer that (31) holds. Thus, this means that solution x of (26) is a periodic function on $[t_1, +\infty)$ with period T. The proof is completed. $\square$

7. Application

As an application, in this section, we discuss the variation in the solution relative to the control for the following control impulsive differential equation

$$
\begin{cases}
\dot{x}(t) = f(t, x(t)) + B(t)u(t), & \{x(t)\} \cap Y(t) = \varnothing, t \geq 0, \\
x(t+) = J_i(x(t)) + x(t), & \{x(t)\} \cap Y(t) = y_i(t), t \geq 0, \\
x(0) = x_0,
\end{cases}
\tag{34}
$$

where control function $u \in L^1_{loc}(\mathbb{R}^+, \mathbb{R}^m)$, $B \in L^\infty_{loc}(\mathbb{R}^+, \mathbb{R}^{n \times m})$.

Using the idea of Theorems 1 and 2, for any $T > 0$ and $u \in L^1((0, T), \mathbb{R}^m)$, one can prove the following result.

Theorem 5. *Suppose assumptions [F](1)(2), [Y](1) and [J] hold. Then, system (34) has a unique PC-solution $x(\cdot; u) \equiv x(\cdot; u, 0, x_0) \in PC_Y([0, T], \mathbb{R}^n)$ given by*

$$
x(t; u) = x_0 + \int_0^t [f(\tau, x(\tau; u)) + B(\tau)u(\tau)]d\tau + \sum_{\substack{0 \leq t_j < t, \\ x(t_j; u) = y_i(t_j))}} J_i(x(t_j; u)).
$$

Moreover, solution $x(\cdot; u)$ has a continuous dependence relative to the control u in the sense of Definition 2.

Moreover, for any fixed sufficient small $\theta > 0$ and fixed $v \in L^1([0, T], \mathbb{R}^m)$, (34) has a unique PC-approximate solution $x_\theta(\cdot) \equiv x_\theta(\cdot; u + \theta v, 0, x_0)$ which satisfies

$$
x_\theta(t) = x_0 + \int_0^t [f(\tau, x_\theta(\tau)) + B(\tau)(u(\tau) + \theta v(\tau))]d\tau + \sum_{\substack{0 \leq t_j < t, \\ x_\theta(t_j) \in B(y_i(t_j), \theta^2)}} J_i(x_\theta(t_j)).
\tag{35}
$$

To discuss the variation in the solution relative to the control, we introduce the following definitions.

Definition 4. *The PC-solution $x(\cdot; u, 0, x_0)$ of (34) is said to be Gâteaux differentiable relative to the control u if the Gâteaux derivative $\psi(\cdot)$ of $x(t; u)$ exists at u for all $t \in [0, T]$ with $x(t; u, 0, x_0) \neq y_i(t)$; otherwise,*

$$
\psi(t) = \lim_{s \nearrow t} \psi(s),
$$

where

$$
\psi(t) = \lim_{\varepsilon \to 0} \frac{x_\varepsilon(t; u + \varepsilon v, 0, x_0) - x(t; u, 0, x_0)}{\varepsilon} \quad \text{when } x(t; u, 0, x_0) \neq y_i(t).
$$

Theorem 6. *Suppose assumptions [F], [Y] and [J] hold and $u \in C([0, T], \mathbb{R}^m)$, $B \in C([0, T], \mathbb{R}^{n \times m})$. The PC-solution $x(\cdot) = x(\cdot; u, 0, x_0)$ of (34) is Gâteaux differentiable relative to the control u in the sense of Definition 4. Moreover, its Gâteaux derivative ψ is a PC-solution of the following differential equation with impulses*

$$
\begin{cases}
\dot{\psi}(t) = f_x(t, x(t))\psi(t) + B(t)v(t), & t \in (0, T], x(t) \neq y_i(t), i \in \Lambda, \\
\psi(0) = 0, \\
\psi(t+) = \psi(t) + \nabla J_i(y_i(t))[\psi(t) + \dot{g}_t(0)(f(t, y_i(t)) + B(t)u(t)], x(t) = y_i(t), i \in \Lambda.
\end{cases}
$$

Proof. There are only two possibilities: Case (I), $x(\cdot; u, 0, x_0)$ has no irregular point on $[0, T]$ and Case (II), $x(\cdot; u, 0, x_0)$ has at least one irregular point on $[0, T]$.

In Case (I), one can directly check that $x(\cdot; u, 0, x_0)$ of (34) is Gâteaux differentiable, and its Gâteaux derivative ψ is a weak solution of the following differential equation

$$\begin{cases} \dot{\psi}(t) = f_x(t, x(t; u))\psi(t) + B(t)v(t), t \in (0, T], \\ \psi(0) = 0. \end{cases}$$

To discuss Case (II), we define function g_t given by

$$g_t(\varepsilon) \text{ denotes the solution of the equation } G(\varepsilon, t) = 0.$$

Here,

$$G(\varepsilon, t) = x_\varepsilon(t; u + \varepsilon v, 0, x_0) - \tilde{y}(t, \varepsilon).$$

By Theorem 5, when $x(t; u, 0, x_0) = y_i(t)$, there is a $\delta > 0$ such that for all $\varepsilon \in [0, \delta]$, $g_t : [0, \delta] \longrightarrow O(t)$ is a function and $g_t(0) = t$, where $O(t)$ denotes some neighborhood of t. For convenience, let $\{t_j^i | 0 < t_1^i < \cdots < t_k^r < T\}$ denote the irregular point set of $x(\cdot; u, 0, x_0)$ on $[0, T]$. If $y_i \in C^1([0, T], \mathbb{R}^n)$, it follows that there is a $\delta > 0$ such that

$$G_t(\varepsilon, t) = f(t, x_\varepsilon(t; u + \varepsilon v, 0, x_0)) + B(t)[u(t) + \varepsilon v(t)] - \tilde{y}_t(t, \varepsilon).$$

Further, when $f\left(t_j^i, y_i\left(t_j^i\right)\right) + B\left(t_j^i\right)u\left(t_j^i\right) \neq \dot{y}_i\left(t_j^i\right)$ $(j = 1, 2, \cdots, k, i \in \Lambda)$, without loss of generality, we assume

$$f^1\left(g_{t_j^i}(\varepsilon), x_\varepsilon\left(g_{t_j^i}(\varepsilon); u + \varepsilon v, 0, x_0\right)\right) + B^1\left(g_{t_j^i}(\varepsilon)\right)u\left(g_{t_j^i}(\varepsilon)\right) - \dot{y}_i^1(g_{t_j^i}(\varepsilon)) \neq 0 \text{ in } \mathbb{R},$$
$$i \in \Lambda, \forall \varepsilon \in [0, \delta], j = 1, 2, \cdots, k, \tag{36}$$

where B^1 denotes the first line vector of B. We introduce the following functions given by

$$\Psi_\varepsilon(t, s) = \exp\left(\int_s^t f_x(\tau, x_\varepsilon(\tau; u + \varepsilon v, 0, x_0))d\tau\right), \tag{37}$$

then

$$\Psi(t, s) = \lim_{\varepsilon \to 0} \Psi_\varepsilon(t, s) = \exp\left(\int_s^t f_x(\tau, x(\tau; u, 0, x_0))d\tau\right). \tag{38}$$

We let

$$\Psi_\varepsilon^1(t, s) \text{ and } \Psi^1(t, s) \text{ denote the first line vector of } \Psi_\varepsilon(t, s) \text{ and } \Psi(t, s), \text{ respectively.}$$

Now, we calculate the variation in the solution relative to the control in Case (II). For $t \in \left[0, t_1^i\right]$, similar to Case (I), it is not difficult to check the following result:

$$\begin{cases} \dot{\psi}(t) = f_x(t, x(t; u, 0, x_0))\psi(t) + B(t)v(t), \quad t \in (0, t_1^i], \\ \psi(0) = 0. \end{cases} \tag{39}$$

When $t \in \left(0, g_{t_1^i}(\varepsilon)\right)$, it follows from assumption [F](3), (35) and (10) that

$$\begin{aligned} G_\varepsilon(\varepsilon, t) &= \lim_{\xi \to 0} \frac{x_{\varepsilon + \xi}(t; u + (\varepsilon + \xi)v, 0, x_0) - x_\varepsilon(t; u + \varepsilon v, 0, x_0)}{\xi} + \frac{\partial}{\partial \varepsilon}\tilde{y}_i(t, \varepsilon) \\ &= \lim_{\xi \to 0} \int_0^t \int_0^1 f_x(s, x_\varepsilon(s; u + \varepsilon v, 0, x_0) + \theta(x_{\varepsilon + \xi}(s; u + (\varepsilon + \xi)v, 0, x_0) \\ &\quad - x_\varepsilon(s; u + \varepsilon v, 0, x_0)))\frac{x_{\varepsilon + \xi}(s; u + (\varepsilon + \xi)v, 0, x_0) - x_\varepsilon(s; u + \varepsilon v, 0, x_0)}{\xi}d\theta ds \end{aligned}$$

$$\int_0^t B(s)v(s)ds + \frac{\partial}{\partial\varepsilon}\tilde{y}_i(t,\varepsilon).$$

It follows from (37) and the above that

$$G_\varepsilon(\varepsilon,t) = \int_0^t \Psi_\varepsilon(t,s)B(s)v(s)ds + \frac{\partial}{\partial\varepsilon}\tilde{y}_i(t,\varepsilon).$$

Using the implicit function theorem, combined with (36), we have

$$\dot{g}_{t_1^i}(\varepsilon) = -\frac{\int_0^{g_{t_1^i}(\varepsilon)} \Psi_\varepsilon^1(g_{t_1^i}(\varepsilon),s)B(s)v(s)ds + \frac{\partial}{\partial\varepsilon}\tilde{y}_i^1(g_{t_1^i}(\varepsilon),\varepsilon)}{f^1\left(g_{t_1^i}(\varepsilon),x_\varepsilon\left(g_{t_1^i}(\varepsilon);u+\varepsilon v,0,x_0\right)\right) + B^1\left(g_{t_1^i}(\varepsilon)\right)u\left(g_{t_1^i}(\varepsilon)\right) - \dot{y}_i^1(g_{t_1^i}(\varepsilon))}.$$

In the above equation, the vector product is the inner product operation. In the following operations, the vector product is also the inner product operation. Together with Theorem 5, we obtain

$$\dot{g}_{t_1^i}(0) = -\frac{\int_0^{t_1^i} \Psi^1(t_1^i,s)B(s)v(s)ds}{f^1(t_1^i,x(t_1^i;u,0,x_0)) + B^1(t_1^i)u(t_1^i) - \dot{y}_i^1(t_1^i)}. \tag{40}$$

Further,

$$\begin{aligned}
&\lim_{\varepsilon\to 0} \frac{x_\varepsilon\left(g_{t_1^i}(\varepsilon);u+\varepsilon v,0,x_0\right) - x\left(t_1^i;u,0,x_0\right)}{\varepsilon} \\
&= \lim_{\varepsilon\to 0} \frac{x_\varepsilon\left(g_{t_1^i}(\varepsilon);u+\varepsilon v,0,x_0\right) - x_\varepsilon\left(t_1^i;u+\varepsilon v,0,x_0\right)}{\varepsilon} \\
&\quad + \lim_{\varepsilon\to 0} \frac{x_\varepsilon\left(t_1^i;u+\varepsilon v,0,x_0\right) - x\left(t_1^i;u,0,x_0\right)}{\varepsilon} \\
&= \psi\left(t_1^i\right) + \dot{g}_{t_1^i}(0)\left[f\left(t_1^i,y_i\left(t_1^i\right)\right) + B\left(t_1^i\right)u\left(t_1^i\right)\right].
\end{aligned} \tag{41}$$

Together with assumption [J](2), it follows from (40) and (41) that when $g_{t_1^i}(\varepsilon) > t_1^i$,

$$\begin{aligned}
\psi\left(t_1^i\right) &= \lim_{\varepsilon\to 0} \frac{x_\varepsilon\left(g_{t_1^i}(\varepsilon)+;u+\varepsilon v,0,x_0\right) - x\left(g_{t_1^i}(\varepsilon);u,0,x_0\right)}{\varepsilon} \\
&= \lim_{\varepsilon\to 0}\frac{1}{\varepsilon}\Big[x_\varepsilon\left(g_{t_1^i}(\varepsilon);u+\varepsilon v,0,x_0\right) + J_i\left(x_\varepsilon\left(g_{t_1^i}(\varepsilon);u+\varepsilon v,0,x_0\right)\right) \\
&\qquad -x\left(g_{t_1^i}(\varepsilon);u,t_1^i,x\left(t_1^i;u,0,x_0\right) + J_i\left(x\left(t_1^i;u,0,x_0\right)\right)\right)\Big] \\
&= \lim_{\varepsilon\to 0}\frac{1}{\varepsilon}\Big[x_\varepsilon\left(g_{t_1^i}(\varepsilon);u+\varepsilon v,0,x_0\right) + J_i\left(x_\varepsilon\left(g_{t_1^i}(\varepsilon);u+\varepsilon v,0,x_0\right)\right) \\
&\qquad -x\left(t_1^i;u,0,x_0\right) - J_i\left(x\left(t_1^i;u,0,x_0\right)\right) - \int_{t_1^i}^{g_{t_1^i}(\varepsilon)}[f(s,x(s;u,0,x_0)) + B(s)u(s)]ds\Big] \\
&= \left(I + \nabla J_i\left(y_i\left(t_1^i\right)\right)\right)\left[\psi\left(t_1^i-\right) + \dot{g}_{t_1^i}(0)\left(f\left(t_1^i,y_i\left(t_1^i\right)\right) + B\left(t_1^i\right)u\left(t_1^i\right)\right)\right] \\
&\qquad -\dot{g}_{t_1^i}(0)\left(f\left(t_1^i,y_i\left(t_1^i\right)\right) + B\left(t_1^i\right)u\left(t_1^i\right)\right) \\
&= \psi\left(t_1^i-\right) + \nabla J_i\left(y_i\left(t_1^i\right)\right)\left[\psi\left(t_1^j-\right) + \dot{g}_{t_1^i}(0)\left(f\left(t_1^i,y_i\left(t_1^i\right)\right) + B\left(t_1^i\right)u\left(t_1^i\right)\right)\right],
\end{aligned}$$

and when $g_{t_1^i}(\varepsilon) < t_1^i$, we also have

$$
\begin{aligned}
\psi\left(t_1^i+\right) &= \lim_{\varepsilon \to 0} \frac{x_\varepsilon\left(t_1^i; u + \varepsilon v, 0, x_0\right) - x\left(t_1^i+; u, 0, x_0\right)}{\varepsilon} \\
&= \lim_{\varepsilon \to 0} \frac{1}{\varepsilon} \left[x_\varepsilon\left(g_{t_1^i}(\varepsilon); u + \varepsilon v, 0, x_0\right) + J_i\left(x_\varepsilon\left(g_{t_1^i}(\varepsilon); u + \varepsilon v, 0, x_0\right)\right) \right. \\
&\qquad \left. - x\left(t_1^i; u, 0, x_0\right) - J_i\left(x\left(t_1^i; u, 0, x_0\right)\right) \right] \\
&\quad - \lim_{\varepsilon \to 0} \frac{1}{\varepsilon} \int_{t_1^i}^{g_{t_1^i}(\varepsilon)} [f(s, x_\varepsilon(s; u + \varepsilon v, 0, x_0)) + B(s)(u(s) + \varepsilon v(s))] ds \\
&= \psi\left(t_1^i-\right) + \nabla J_i\left(y_i\left(t_1^i\right)\right)\left[\psi\left(t_1^i-\right) + \dot{g}_{t_1^i}(0)\left(f\left(t_1^i, y_i\left(t_1^i\right)\right) + B\left(t_1^i\right)u\left(t_1^i\right)\right)\right].
\end{aligned}
$$

Consequently, we have

$$
\psi\left(t_1^i+\right) = \psi\left(t_1^i\right) + \nabla J_i\left(y_i\left(t_1^i\right)\right)\left[\psi\left(t_1^i\right) + \dot{g}_{t_1^i}(0) f\left(f\left(t_1^i, y_i\left(t_1^i\right)\right) + B\left(t_1^i\right)u\left(t_1^i\right)\right)\right], i \in \Lambda. \tag{42}
$$

Generally speaking, we first note that

$$
\begin{aligned}
&\lim_{\varepsilon \to 0} \frac{x_\varepsilon\left(g_{t_{j-1}^r}(\varepsilon); u + \varepsilon v, 0, x_0\right) - x\left(t_{j-1}^r; u, 0, x_0\right)}{\varepsilon} \\
&= \lim_{\varepsilon \to 0} \frac{x_\varepsilon\left(g_{t_{j-1}^r}(\varepsilon); u + \varepsilon v, 0, x_0\right) - x_\varepsilon\left(t_{j-1}^r; u + \varepsilon v, 0, x_0\right)}{\varepsilon} \\
&\quad + \lim_{\varepsilon \to 0} \frac{x_\varepsilon\left(t_{j-1}^r; u + \varepsilon v, 0, x_0\right) - x\left(t_{j-1}^r; u, 0, x_0\right)}{\varepsilon} \\
&= \varphi\left(t_{j-1}^r\right) + \dot{g}_{t_{j-1}^r}(0)\left[f\left(t_{j-1}^r, y_r\left(t_{j-1}^r\right)\right) + B\left(t_{j-1}^r\right)u\left(t_{j-1}^r\right)\right]. \tag{43}
\end{aligned}
$$

Further, when $t \in \left(g_{t_{j-1}^r}(\varepsilon), g_{t_j^i}(\varepsilon)\right)$, one can infer from assumption [F](3), (35), (10) and (43) that

$$
\begin{aligned}
G_\varepsilon(\varepsilon, t) &= \lim_{\xi \to 0} \frac{x_{\varepsilon+\xi}(t; u + (\varepsilon + \xi)v, 0, x_0) - x_\varepsilon(t; u + \varepsilon v, 0, x_0)}{\xi} + \frac{\partial}{\partial \varepsilon}\tilde{y}_i(t, \varepsilon) \\
&= \lim_{\xi \to 0} \frac{1}{\xi}\left[x_{\varepsilon+\xi}\left(t; u + (\varepsilon + \xi)v, g_{t_{j-1}^r}(\varepsilon + \xi), Y_r\left(g_{t_{j-1}^r}(\varepsilon + \xi)\right)\right) \right. \\
&\qquad \left. - x_\varepsilon\left(t; u + \varepsilon v, g_{t_{j-1}^r}(\varepsilon), Y_r\left(g_{t_{j-1}^r}(\varepsilon)\right)\right)\right] + \frac{\partial}{\partial \varepsilon}\tilde{y}_i(t, \varepsilon) \\
&= \lim_{\xi \to 0} \int_{g_{t_{j-1}^r}(\varepsilon+\xi)}^{t} \int_0^1 f_x(s, x_\varepsilon(s; u + \varepsilon v, 0, x_0) + \theta(x_{\varepsilon+\xi}(s; u + (\varepsilon + \xi)v, 0, x_0) \\
&\qquad - x_\varepsilon(s; u + \varepsilon v, 0, x_0))) \frac{x_{\varepsilon+\xi}(s; u + (\varepsilon + \xi)v, 0, x_0) - x_\varepsilon(s; u + \varepsilon v, 0, x_0)}{\xi} d\theta ds \\
&\quad + \lim_{\xi \to 0} \frac{Y_r\left(g_{t_{j-1}^r}(\varepsilon + \xi), \varepsilon + \xi\right) - Y_r\left(g_{t_{j-1}^r}(\varepsilon), \varepsilon\right)}{\xi} + \lim_{\xi \to 0} \int_{g_{t_{j-1}^r}(\varepsilon+\xi)}^{t} B(s)v(s) ds \\
&\quad - \lim_{\xi \to 0} \frac{\int_{g_{t_{j-1}^r}(\varepsilon)}^{g_{t_{j-1}^r}(\varepsilon+\xi)} [f(s, x(s; u + \varepsilon v, 0, x_0)) + B(s)(u(s) + \varepsilon v(s))] ds}{\xi} + \frac{\partial}{\partial \varepsilon}\tilde{y}_r(t, \varepsilon) \\
&= \lim_{\xi \to 0} \int_{g_{t_{j-1}^r}(\varepsilon+\xi)}^{t} \int_0^1 f_x(s, x_\varepsilon(s; u + \varepsilon v, 0, x_0) + \theta(x_{\varepsilon+\xi}(s; u + (\varepsilon + \xi)v, 0, x_0)
\end{aligned}
$$

$$-x_\varepsilon(s; u + \varepsilon v, 0, x_0)))\frac{x_{\varepsilon+\zeta}(s; u + (\varepsilon + \zeta)v, 0, x_0) - x_\varepsilon(s; u + \varepsilon v, 0, x_0)}{\zeta} d\theta ds$$

$$+ \int_{g_{t_{j-1}^r}(\varepsilon)}^t B(s)v(s)ds + \psi\Big(g_{t_{j-1}^r}(\varepsilon)\Big) + \frac{\partial}{\partial\varepsilon}\tilde{y}_r(t, \varepsilon)$$

$$+ \nabla J_r\Big(\tilde{y}_r\Big(g_{t_{j-1}^r}(\varepsilon), \varepsilon\Big)\Big)\Big[\psi\Big(g_{t_{j-1}^r}(\varepsilon)\Big)$$

$$+ \dot{g}_{t_{j-1}^r}(\varepsilon)\Big(f\Big(g_{t_{j-1}^r}(\varepsilon), \tilde{y}_r\Big(g_{t_{j-1}^r}(\varepsilon), \varepsilon\Big)\Big) + B\Big(g_{t_{j-1}^r}(\varepsilon)\Big)u\Big(g_{t_{j-1}^r}(\varepsilon)\Big)\Big)\Big].$$

Moreover, one can see from (37) and the above equality that

$$G_\varepsilon(\varepsilon, t) = \frac{\partial}{\partial\varepsilon}\tilde{y}_r(t, \varepsilon) + \Psi_\varepsilon\Big(t, g_{t_{j-1}^r}(\varepsilon)\Big)\nabla J_r\Big(\tilde{y}_r\Big(g_{t_{j-1}^r}(\varepsilon), \varepsilon\Big)\Big)\Big[\psi\Big(g_{t_{j-1}^r}(\varepsilon)\Big)$$

$$+ \dot{g}_{t_{j-1}^r}(\varepsilon)\Big(f\Big(g_{t_{j-1}^r}(\varepsilon), \tilde{y}_r\Big(g_{t_{j-1}^r}(\varepsilon), \varepsilon\Big)\Big) + B\Big(g_{t_{j-1}^r}(\varepsilon)\Big)u\Big(g_{t_{j-1}^r}(\varepsilon)\Big)\Big)\Big]$$

$$+ \Psi_\varepsilon\Big(t, g_{t_{j-1}^r}(\varepsilon)\Big)\psi\Big(g_{t_{j-1}^r}(\varepsilon)\Big) + \int_{g_{t_{j-1}^r}(\varepsilon)}^t \Psi_\varepsilon(t, s)B(s)v(s)ds.$$

Together with (36), by the implicit function theorem, we have

$$\dot{g}_{t_j^i}(\varepsilon) = -\frac{\Psi_\varepsilon^1\Big(g_{t_j^i}(\varepsilon), g_{t_{j-1}^r}(\varepsilon)\Big)\nabla J_r\Big(\tilde{y}_r\Big(g_{t_{j-1}^r}(\varepsilon), \varepsilon\Big)\Big)}{f^1\Big(g_{t_j^i}(\varepsilon), x_\varepsilon\Big(g_{t_j^i}(\varepsilon); u + \varepsilon v, 0, x_0\Big)\Big) + B^1\Big(g_{t_j^i}(\varepsilon)\Big)u\Big(g_{t_j^i}(\varepsilon)\Big) - \dot{y}_i^1(g_{t_j^i}(\varepsilon))}$$

$$\cdot\Big[\psi\Big(g_{t_{j-1}^r}(\varepsilon)\Big) + \dot{g}_{t_{j-1}^r}(\varepsilon)\Big(f\Big(g_{t_{j-1}^r}(\varepsilon), \tilde{y}_r\Big(g_{t_{j-1}^r}(\varepsilon), \varepsilon\Big)\Big) + B\Big(g_{t_{j-1}^r}(\varepsilon)\Big)u\Big(g_{t_{j-1}^r}(\varepsilon)\Big)\Big)\Big]$$

$$-\frac{\frac{\partial}{\partial\varepsilon}\tilde{y}_r^1\Big(g_{t_j^i}(\varepsilon), \varepsilon\Big) + \Psi_\varepsilon^1\Big(g_{t_j^i}(\varepsilon), g_{t_{j-1}^r}(\varepsilon)\Big)\psi\Big(g_{t_{j-1}^r}(\varepsilon)\Big) + \int_{g_{t_{j-1}^r}(\varepsilon)}^{g_{t_j^i}(\varepsilon)}\Psi_\varepsilon^1(t, s)B(s)v(s)ds}{f^1\Big(g_{t_j^i}(\varepsilon), x_\varepsilon\Big(g_{t_j^i}(\varepsilon); u + \varepsilon v, 0, x_0\Big)\Big) + B^1\Big(g_{t_j^i}(\varepsilon)\Big)u\Big(g_{t_j^i}(\varepsilon)\Big) - \dot{y}_i^1(g_{t_j^i}(\varepsilon))}.$$

Further, it follows from the above expression, (38) and Theorem 5 that

$$\dot{g}_{t_j^i}(0) = -\frac{\Psi^1\Big(t_j^i, t_{j-1}^r\Big)\nabla J_r\Big(y_r\Big(t_{j-1}^r\Big)\Big)}{f^1\Big(t_j^i, x\Big(t_j^i; u, 0, x_0\Big)\Big) + B^1\Big(t_j^i\Big)u\Big(t_j^i\Big) - \dot{y}_i^1\Big(t_j^i\Big)}$$

$$\cdot\Big[\psi\Big(t_{j-1}^r\Big) + \dot{g}_{t_{j-1}^r}(0)\Big(f\Big(t_{j-1}^r, y_r\Big(t_{j-1}^r\Big)\Big) + B\Big(t_{j-1}^r\Big)u\Big(t_{j-1}^r\Big)\Big)\Big] \tag{44}$$

$$-\frac{\Psi^1\Big(t_j^i, t_{j-1}^r\Big)\psi\Big(t_{j-1}^r\Big) + \int_{t_{j-1}^r}^{t_j^i}\Psi^1\Big(t_j^i, s\Big)B(s)v(s)ds}{f^1\Big(t_j^i, x\Big(t_j^i; u, 0, x_0\Big)\Big) + B^1\Big(t_j^i\Big)u\Big(t_j^i\Big) - \dot{y}_i^1\Big(t_j^i\Big)}, i \in \Lambda, j = 1, 2, \cdots, k.$$

Similar to (43), we can obtain

$$\lim_{\varepsilon\to 0}\frac{x_\varepsilon\Big(g_{t_j^i}(\varepsilon); u + \varepsilon v, 0, x_0\Big) - x\Big(t_j^i; u, 0, x_0\Big)}{\varepsilon}$$

$$= \psi\Big(t_j^i\Big) + \dot{g}_{t_j^i}(0)\Big[f\Big(t_j^i, y_i\Big(t_j^i\Big)\Big) + B\Big(t_j^i\Big)u\Big(t_j^i\Big)\Big], i \in \Lambda, j = 1, 2, \cdots, k. \tag{45}$$

Together with assumption [J](2), (45) and (44), it follows that when $g_{t_j^i}(\varepsilon) > t_j^i$,

$$
\begin{aligned}
\psi\!\left(t_j^i+\right) &= \lim_{\varepsilon\to 0}\frac{x_\varepsilon\!\left(g_{t_j^i}(\varepsilon)+;u+\varepsilon v,,x_0\right)-x\!\left(g_{t_j^i}(\varepsilon);u,0,x_0\right)}{\varepsilon}\\[4pt]
&= \lim_{\varepsilon\to 0}\frac{1}{\varepsilon}\Bigg[x_\varepsilon\!\left(g_{t_j^i}(\varepsilon);u+\varepsilon v,0,x_0\right)+J_i\!\left(x_\varepsilon\!\left(g_{t_j^i}(\varepsilon);u+\varepsilon v,0,x_0\right)\right)\\
&\qquad -x\!\left(g_{t_j^i}(\varepsilon);u,t_j^i,x\!\left(t_j^i;u,0,x_0\right)+J_i\!\left(x\!\left(t_j^i;u,0,x_0\right)\right)\right)\Bigg]\\[4pt]
&= \lim_{\varepsilon\to 0}\frac{1}{\varepsilon}\Bigg[x_\varepsilon\!\left(g_{t_j^i}(\varepsilon);u+\varepsilon v,0,x_0\right)+J_i\!\left(x_\varepsilon\!\left(g_{t_j^i}(\varepsilon);u+\varepsilon v,0,x_0\right)\right)\\
&\qquad -x\!\left(t_j^i;u,0,x_0\right)-J_i\!\left(x\!\left(t_j^i;u,0,x_0\right)\right)-\int_{t_j^i}^{g_{t_j^i}(\varepsilon)}[f(s,x(s;u,0,x_0))+B(s)u(s)]ds\Bigg]\\[4pt]
&= \left(I+\nabla J_i\!\left(y_i\!\left(t_j^i\right)\right)\right)\left[\psi\!\left(t_j^i-\right)+\dot g_{t_j^i}(0)\left[f\!\left(t_j^i,y_i\!\left(t_j^i\right)\right)+B\!\left(t_j^i\right)u\!\left(t_j^i\right)\right]\right]\\
&\qquad -\dot g_{t_j^i}(0)\left[f\!\left(t_j^i,y_i\!\left(t_j^i\right)\right)+B\!\left(t_j^i\right)u\!\left(t_j^i\right)\right]\\[4pt]
&= \psi\!\left(t_j^i-\right)+\nabla J_i\!\left(y_i\!\left(t_j^i\right)\right)\left[\psi\!\left(t_j^i-\right)+\dot g_{t_j^i}(0)\left[f\!\left(t_j^i,y_i\!\left(t_j^i\right)\right)+B\!\left(t_j^i\right)u\!\left(t_j^i\right)\right]\right],
\end{aligned}
$$

and when $g_{t_j^i}(\varepsilon)\leq t_j^i$,

$$
\begin{aligned}
\psi\!\left(t_j^i+\right) &= \lim_{\varepsilon\to 0}\frac{x_\varepsilon\!\left(t_j^i;u+\varepsilon v,0,x_0\right)-x\!\left(t_j^i+;u,0,x_0\right)}{\varepsilon}\\[4pt]
&= \lim_{\varepsilon\to 0}\frac{1}{\varepsilon}\Bigg[x_\varepsilon\!\left(g_{t_j^i}(\varepsilon);u+\varepsilon v,0,x_0\right)+J_i\!\left(x_\varepsilon\!\left(g_{t_j^i}(\varepsilon);u+\varepsilon v,0,x_0\right)\right)\\
&\qquad -x\!\left(t_j^i;u,0,x_0\right)-J_i\!\left(x\!\left(t_j^i;u,0,x_0\right)\right)\\
&\qquad -\int_{t_j^i}^{g_{t_j^i}(\varepsilon)}[f(s,x_\varepsilon(s;u+\varepsilon v,0,x_0))+B(s)(u(s)+\varepsilon v(s))]ds\Bigg]\\[4pt]
&= \psi\!\left(t_j^i-\right)+\nabla J_i\!\left(y_i\!\left(t_j^i\right)\right)\left[\psi\!\left(t_j^i-\right)+\dot g_{t_j^i}(0)\left[f\!\left(t_j^i,y_i\!\left(t_j^i\right)\right)+B\!\left(t_j^i\right)u\!\left(t_j^i\right)\right]\right].
\end{aligned}
$$

Consequently, we have

$$
\psi\!\left(t_j^i+\right)=\psi\!\left(t_j^i\right)+\nabla J_i\!\left(y_i\!\left(t_j^i\right)\right)\left[\psi\!\left(t_j^i\right)+\dot g_{t_j^i}(0)\left[f\!\left(t_j^i,y_i\!\left(t_j^i\right)\right)+B\!\left(t_j^i\right)u\!\left(t_j^i\right)\right]\right]\tag{46}
$$

for $i\in\Lambda,\ j=1,2,\cdots,k$. Therefore, when $t\in\left(t_j^i,t_{j+1}^r\right)$ $(j=1,2,\cdots,k-1)$ or $t\in\left(t_k^r,T\right]$, it follows from assumption [F](3), (10), (35), (3), (17), (44) and (45) that

$$
\begin{aligned}
\psi(t) &= \lim_{\theta\to 0}\frac{x_\theta(t;u+\theta v,0,x_0)-x(t;u,0,x_0)}{\theta}\\[4pt]
&= \lim_{\theta\to 0}\frac{x_\theta(t;u+\theta v,g_{t_j^i}(\theta),Y_i(g_{t_j^i}(\theta)))-x(t;u,t_j^i,Y_i(t_j^i))}{\theta}\\[4pt]
&= \lim_{\theta\to 0}\frac{Y_i(g_{t_j^i}(\theta))-Y_i(t_j^i)}{\theta}+\lim_{\theta\to 0}\int_{g_{t_j^i}(\theta)}^{t}\int_0^1 f_x(s,x(s;u,0,x_0)+\xi(x_\theta(s;u+\theta v,0,x_0)\\
&\qquad -x(s;u,0,x_0)))\frac{x_\theta(s;u+\theta v,0,x_0)-x(s;u,0,x_0)}{\theta}d\xi ds+\lim_{\theta\to 0}\int_{g_{t_j^i}(\theta)}^{t}B(s)v(s)ds
\end{aligned}
$$

$$
-\lim_{\theta \to 0} \frac{1}{\theta} \int_{t^i_j}^{g_{t^i_j}(\theta)} [f(s, x(s; u, 0, x_0)) + B(s)u(s)]ds
$$

$$
= \psi\left(t^i_j\right) + \nabla J_i\left(y_i\left(t^i_j\right)\right)\left[\psi\left(t^i_j\right) + \dot{g}_{t^i_j}(0)\left(f\left(t^i_j, y_i\left(t^i_j\right)\right) + B\left(t^i_j\right)u\left(t^i_j\right)\right)\right]
$$

$$
+ \int_{t^i_j}^{t} B(s)v(s)ds + \lim_{\theta \to 0} \int_{g_{t^i_j}(\theta)}^{t} \int_0^1 f_x(s, x(s; u, 0, x_0) + \xi(x_\theta(s; u + \theta v, 0, x_0)
$$

$$
- x(s; u, 0, x_0))) \frac{x_\theta(s; u + \theta v, 0, x_0) - x(s; u, 0, x_0)}{\theta} d\xi ds.
$$

Thus, it follows from (39), (42) and (46) that

$$
\begin{cases}
\dot{\psi}(t) = f_x(t, x(t; u, 0, x_0))\psi(t) + B(t)v(t), t \in (0, T] \text{ and } t \neq t^i_j, i \in \Lambda, j = 1, 2, \cdots, k, \\
\psi(0) = 0, \\
\psi\left(t^i_j +\right) = \left(I + \nabla J_i\left(y_i\left(t^i_j\right)\right)\right)\psi\left(t^i_j\right) \\
\qquad + \dot{g}_{t^i_j}(0)\nabla J_i\left(y_i\left(t^i_j\right)\right)\left[f\left(t^i_j, y_i\left(t^i_j\right)\right) + B\left(t^i_j\right)u\left(t^i_j\right)\right], j = 1, 2, \cdots, k.
\end{cases}
$$

This completes the proof of Theorem 6. $\square$

8. Conclusions

In this paper, we proposed a class of widely applied impulsive differential systems and gave its qualitative theory under some weaker conditions, including the existence, uniqueness, and periodicity of the solution, as well as the continuous dependence and differentiability of the solution on the initial value. For the pulse phenomena of the solution, it is significant to give the sufficient and necessary conditions. It is very interesting that the pulse may destroy the intrinsic properties of the system, such as the existence, the continuous dependence, and differentiability of solution. Moreover, these results also lay a theoretical foundation for the optimal control problem given by impulsive different systems with impulses at variable times and the applications of such systems.

Author Contributions: Conceptualization, H.X., Y.P. and P.Z.; Methodology, Y.P. and P.Z.; Writing—original draft, H.X. All authors have read and agreed to the published version of the manuscript.

Funding: This research was funded by the National Natural Science Foundation of China No. 12061021 and No. 11161009).

Data Availability Statement: No new data were created or analyzed in this study.

Acknowledgments: The authors would like to thank the anonymous reviewers and the editor of this journal for their valuable time and their careful comments and suggestions because of which the quality of this paper has been improved.

Conflicts of Interest: The authors declare there are no conflicts of interest.

References

1. Bensoussan, A.; Giuseppe, D.P.; Michel, C.D.; Sanjoy, K.M. *Representation and Control of Infinite Dimensional Systems*, 2nd ed.; Birkhäuser: Boston, MA, USA, 2007; p. 15.
2. Bainov, D.; Simeonov, P. *Impulsive Differential Equations: Periodic Solutions and Applications*, 1st ed.; Longman Scientific and Technical: New York, NY, USA, 1993; pp. 39–58.
3. Kobayashi, Y.; Nakano, H.; Saito, T. A simple chaotic circuit with impulsive switch depending on time and state. *Nonlinear Dyn.* **2006**, *44*, 73–79. [CrossRef]
4. Touboul, J.; Brette, R. Spiking dynamics of Bidimensional integrate-and-fire neurons. *SIAM J. Appl. Dyn. Syst.* **2009**, *8*, 1462–1506. [CrossRef]
5. Izhikevich, E.M. *Dynamical Systems in Neuroscience*, 1st ed.; MIT Press: Cambridge, MA, USA, 2007.
6. Huang, M.; Li, J.; Song, X.; Guo, H. Modeling impulsive injections of insulin: Towards artificial pancreas. *SIAM J. Appl. Math.* **2012**, *72*, 1524–1548. [CrossRef]
7. Zhang, Q.; Tang, B.; Cheng, T.; Tang, S. Bifurcation analysis of a generalized impulsive Kolmogorov model with applitions to pest and disease control. *SIAM J. Appl. Math.* **2020**, *80*, 1796–1819. [CrossRef]

8.	Catllá, A.J.; Schaeffer, D.G.; Witelski, T.P.; Monson, E.E. On spiking models for synaptic activity and impulsive differential equations. *SIAM Rev.* **2008**, *50*, 553–569. [CrossRef]
9.	Akhmet, M.; Yilmaz, E. impulsive differential equations. In *Neural Networks with Discontinuous/Impact Activations*; Akhmet, M., Yilmaz, E., Eds.; Springer: New York, NY, USA, 2014; pp. 67–83.
10.	Lions, P.L.; Perthame, B. Quasi-variational inequalities and ergodic impulse control. *SIAM J. Control Optim.* **1986**, *24*, 604–615. [CrossRef]
11.	Wang, Y.; Lu, J. Some recent results of analysis and control for impulsive systems. *Commun. Nonlinear Sci. Numer. Simulat.* **2019**, *80*, 104862. [CrossRef]
12.	Krylov, M.M.; Bogolyubov, N.N. *Introduction to Nonlinear Mechanics*; Academiya Nauk Ukrin: Kiev, Ukraine, 1937. (In Russian)
13.	Samoilenko, A.M.; Perestyuk, N.A. The method of averaging in systems with an impulsive action. *Ukr. Math. J.* **1974**, *26*, 342–347. [CrossRef]
14.	Ahmed, N.U. Existence of optimal controls for a general class of impulsive systems on Banach spaces. *SIAM J. Control Optim.* **2003**, *42*, 669–685. [CrossRef]
15.	Peng, Y.; Xiang, X. A class of nonlinear impulsive differential equation and optimal controls on time scales. *Discrete Cont. Dyn.-B* **2011**, *16*, 1137–1155. [CrossRef]
16.	Nain, A.K.; Vats, R.K.; Kumar, A. Caputo-Hadamard fractional differential equation with impulsive boundary conditions. *J. Math. Model.* **2021**, *9*, 93–106. [CrossRef]
17.	Malik, M.; Kumar, A. Existence and controllability results to second order neutral differential equation with non-instantaneous impulses. *J. Control Decis.* **2020**, *7*, 286–308. [CrossRef]
18.	Samoilenko, A.M.; Perestyuk, N.A. On stability of solutions of impulsive systems. *Differ. Uravn.* **1981**, *17*, 1995–2002. [CrossRef]
19.	Bainov, D.D.; Dishliev, A.B. Sufficient conditions for absence of "beating" in systems of differential equations with impulses. *Appl. Anal.* **1984**, *18*, 67–73. [CrossRef]
20.	Hu, S.; Lakshmikantham, V. Periodic boundary value problem for second order impulsive differential systems. *Nonlinear Anal. TMA* **1989**, *13*, 75–85. [CrossRef]
21.	Lakshmikantham, V.; Bainov, D.D.; Simenonov, P.S. *Theory of Impulsive Differential Equences*, 1st ed.; World Scientific: Hong Kong, China, 1989.
22.	Samoilenko, A.M. Application of the method of averaging for the investigation of vibrations excited by instantaneous impulses in self-vibrating systems of the second order with a small parameter. *Ukr. Math. J.* **1961**, *13*, 103–108.
23.	Bainov, D.; Simeonov, P. *Impulsive Differential Equations*, 1st ed.; World Scientific: Singapore, 1995.
24.	Benchohra, M.; Henderson, J.; Ntouyas, S. *Impulsive Differential Equations and Inclusions*, 1st ed.; Hindawi Publishing Corporation: New York, NY, USA, 2006.
25.	Peng, Y.; Wu, K.; Qin, S.; Kang, Y. Properties of solution of linear controlled systems with impulses at variable times. In Proceedings of the 36th Chinese Control Conference, Dalian, China, 26–28 July 2017. [CrossRef]

Article

New Conditions for Testing the Oscillation of Solutions of Second-Order Nonlinear Differential Equations with Damped Term

Asma Al-Jaser [1], Belgees Qaraad [2], Higinio Ramos [3,4] and Stefano Serra-Capizzano [5,6,*]

1   Department of Mathematical Science, College of Science, Princess Nourah Bint Abdulrahman University, P.O. Box 84428, Riyadh 11671, Saudi Arabia; ajaljaser@pnu.edu.sa

2   Department of Mathematics, Faculty of Science, Mansoura University, Mansoura 35516, Egypt; belgeesmath2016@gmail.com

3   Scientific Computing Group, Universidad de Salamanca, Plaza de la Merced, 37008 Salamanca, Spain; higra@usal.es

4   Department of Mathematics, Escuela Politecnica Superior de Zamora, Campus Viriato, 49022 Zamora, Spain

5   Department of Science and High Technology, University of Insubria, Via Valleggio 11, 22100 Como, Italy

6   Division of Scientific Computing, Department of Information Technology, Uppsala University, Lägerhyddsv 2, hus 2, SE-751 05 Uppsala, Sweden

*   Correspondence: s.serracapizzano@uninsubria.it

Abstract: This paper deals with the oscillatory behavior of solutions of a new class of second-order nonlinear differential equations. In contrast to most of the previous results in the literature, we establish some new criteria that guarantee the oscillation of all solutions of the studied equation without additional restrictions. Our approach improves the standard integral averaging technique to obtain simpler oscillation theorems for new classes of nonlinear differential equations. Two examples are presented to illustrate the importance of our findings.

Keywords: second order; damping term; oscillation; differential equations

MSC: 34C10; 34K11

Citation: Al-Jaser, A.; Qaraad, B.; Ramos, H.; Serra-Capizzano, S. New Conditions for Testing the Oscillation of Solutions of Second-Order Nonlinear Differential Equations with Damped Term. *Axioms* **2024**, *13*, 105. https://doi.org/10.3390/axioms13020105

Academic Editors: Feliz Manuel Minhós and Juan J. Nieto

Received: 31 December 2023
Revised: 26 January 2024
Accepted: 30 January 2024
Published: 4 February 2024

1. Introduction

In this work, we consider the asymptotic and oscillatory properties of solutions to a class of differential equations of the form

$$\left(r(\top)\left(y'(\top)\right)^{\xi}\right)' + p(\top)\left(y'(\top)\right)^{\xi} + q(\top)f(y(\top)) = 0, \quad \top \geq \top_0 > 0, \tag{1}$$

where $\xi \geq 1$ is a ratio of two odd positive integers, and

(H_1) $r(\top) \in C^1\left(I_{\top_0}, \mathbb{R}^+\right)$,

$$p(\top) \text{ and } q(\top) \in C\left(I_{\top_0}, \mathbb{R}\right), \tag{2}$$

where $I_{\top_0} = [\top_0, \infty)$;

(H_2) $f(\top) \in C(\mathbb{R}, \mathbb{R})$, $yf(y) > 0$ for $y \neq 0$, and $f(y)/y^{\xi} \geq \mu$, for $y \neq 0$ and for some $\mu > 0$.

Definition 1 ([1]). *By a solution y of Equation (1), we mean a function $y \in C([\top_y^*, \infty))$, $\top_y^* \in I_{\top_0}$, which satisfies (1) on $[\top_y^*, \infty)$ for every $\top \geq \top_y^* \geq \top_0$, and $r(\top)(y'(\top))^{\xi} \in C^1([\top_y^*, \infty))$. Our attention is restricted to those solutions y of (1) that exist on some half line I and satisfy*

$$\sup\left\{|y(\top)| : \top_y \leq \top < \infty\right\} > 0, \quad \top_y \geq \top_y^*.$$

Definition 2 ([2]). *A solution of Equation (1) is called oscillatory if it has arbitrarily large zeros; otherwise, it is called non-oscillatory. Moreover, we say that Equation (1) oscillates if all its solutions oscillate, otherwise we say that it does not oscillate.*

Oscillation theory is considered one of the most important theories in all fields of science, including physics and engineering. It also plays a crucial role in the advancement of science and technology and in developing solutions to contemporary challenges. Through continued research and development in this field, significant progress can be achieved in various scientific and applied fields. It attempts to explain how objects or phenomena can change over time and is used to understand advanced natural and technological phenomena in the modern world. Currently, oscillation theory is of particular importance because of its practical applications in various fields such as communications, astronomy, and others. Its importance is not diminished even in the field of medicine, as it contributes to examining and analysing vital signals such as heartbeats and brain waves, which enables doctors to better evaluate health conditions and diagnose diseases.

Both the concept of symmetry and the oscillation theory play pivotal roles in understanding nature at different levels, and there can be overlaps and interactions between them in certain contexts of physical research. Oscillations can be viewed as a kind of temporal symmetry in many dynamical systems. Likewise, a physical system that oscillates regularly can be described as a type of temporal symmetry in that phenomenon, where conditions repeat periodically. On the other hand, the concept of symmetry plays an important role in describing fundamental interactions and particle interactions. It is worth noting that in some cases, symmetries lead to phenomena such as oscillation between different types of particles, such as neutrino oscillation. Theories that combine symmetry and oscillation may reveal new and unexpected phenomena. For example, broken symmetry could be responsible for generating particle masses in the Standard Model of particle physics; see, for instance [3–9].

Their approximations lead to very large linear systems and many properties can be understood using the approximated solutions [10–12]. Damping is crucial in control systems to prevent and minimise feedback-induced oscillations, so the damping differential equation is used in the models of mechanical systems, electrical circuits, acoustics, civil engineering, and control theory (economic cycles). Second-order differential equations with a damping term play a central role in many scientific and engineering fields, helping to understand and analyse dynamical systems and develop new technologies. They are used in many different fields, and the analysis of solutions to these equations often includes the term "damping" to describe resistance to movement or the gradual degradation of energy, which may be the result of movement in an elastic medium or under the presence of friction. Second-order differential equations can also be used to study damping vibrations in structures and machines. Damping is also used to describe the effect that resistors, capacitors, and coils have on the current and voltage in the system. The term damping describes the interaction between particles and their surrounding environment, and its importance extends to planetary science and astronomy, as these equations are used in studying the motion of planets and other astronomical bodies and the damping effects resulting from gravity and resistance [13–18].

A number of authors, such as [19–23], have paid attention to the oscillation of equations of the form

$$(r(\top)\varphi(y(\top))y'(\top))' + p(\top)y'(\top) + q(\top)f(y(\top)) = 0.$$

On the other hand, the authors in [24–27] examined the oscillation of the following differential equation:

$$(r(\top)y'(\top))' + p(\top)y'(\top) + q(\top)f(y(\top)) = 0 \tag{3}$$

and some special cases under conditions

$$p(\top) \geq 0 \text{ and } q(\top) > 0. \tag{4}$$

Moreover, Rogovchenko [28] showed a sufficient condition for the oscillation of Equation (3) assuming that (2) is satisfied and

$$f'(x) \text{ exists, } f'(x) \geq k \text{ for some } k > 0.$$

Also, Grace [29] shed light on finding criteria that guarantee the oscillatory behavior of all solutions of Equation (3).

Motivation

Adding a damping term to a differential equation may change the character of the solutions, for example, giving rise to oscillations. For example, if we look at equation

$$y'''(\mathsf{T}) + \left(4\mathsf{T}^3\right)^{-1} y(\mathsf{T}) = 0, \tag{5}$$

we find that all of its solutions are non-oscillatory as follows: $y_1 = 1.2696$, $y_2 = 1.83763$ and $y_3 = -0.10716$. While if we introduce the damping term $\left(4\mathsf{T}^2\right)^{-1} y'(\mathsf{T})$ into Equation (5) it becomes as follows:

$$y'''(\mathsf{T}) + \left(4\mathsf{T}^2\right)^{-1} y'(\mathsf{T}) + \left(4\mathsf{T}^3\right)^{-1} y(\mathsf{T}) = 0.$$

We find that the behavior of its solutions is different, as we obtain two conjugate solutions (oscillatory solutions) and another solution (nonoscillatory solution) as follows: $y_{1,2} = 1.5490 \pm 0.3925i$ and $y_3 = -0.097912$. Thus, the study of this type of equations can be considered related to the oscillation theory. Through this work, we aim to establish new relationships that can be used to obtain new oscillation criteria for the solutions of the Equation (1). Our results are an extension of the findings presented in the previous literature, for example [19–22,28,30–32], which studied the Equation (1) with $\xi = 1$. On the other hand, our results work to develop and improve some of the previous findings; for instance, contrary to [24–27], we do not need additional constraints, including the constraints in (4). Therefore, the scope of application of our results extends to include more models that previous studies did not cover.

This paper is organized as follows. In Section 1, we present the significance of studying oscillations in many areas of life, which is the primary motivation for our study. In Section 2, we present previous findings and the abbreviations that will be used throughout the paper. Then, in Section 3, we provide some results of oscillation for the solutions of the studied equation. We also present and discuss some examples to illustrate the importance of our results in Section 4. Finally, in Section 5, we offer a brief overview of the main conclusions and present some suggestions and open problems for future work.

2. Preliminaries

Now, assume that $U \in C(D, \mathbb{R}^+)$ and

$$D = \{(\mathsf{T}, \varsigma) : \mathsf{T}_0 \leq \varsigma \leq \mathsf{T} < \infty\} \text{ and } D_0 = \{(\mathsf{T}, \varsigma) : \mathsf{T}_0 \leq \varsigma < \mathsf{T} < \infty\}.$$

If $U(\mathsf{T}, \mathsf{T}) = 0$, $U(\mathsf{T}, \varsigma) > 0$ and there is $(\mathsf{T}, \varsigma) \in D_0$ for U has a nonpositive continuous partial derivative with respect to ς, and there is there is a function $\tilde{u} \in l_{\{loc\}}(D, \mathbb{R})$ such that

$$\frac{\partial U(\mathsf{T}, \varsigma)}{\partial \varsigma} = -\tilde{u}(\mathsf{T}, \varsigma)(U(\mathsf{T}, \varsigma))^{\xi/(\xi+1)}, \tag{6}$$

then we say that $U \in W_\xi$.

Now we present some results obtained previously, in order to compare them with the main results we reached in this work.

Theorem 1 ([29], Theorem 6). *Assume that there exist functions $\rho \in C^1(I_{T_0}, \mathbb{R}^+)$, $\phi \in C(I_{T_0}, \mathbb{R})$, and $U \in W_\xi$, $\xi = 1$ and $f'(x) \geq K$. If*

$$0 < \inf_{\varsigma \geq T_0} \Phi(T) \leq \infty, \tag{7}$$

$$\limsup_{T \to \infty} U^{-1}(T, T^*) \int_{T^*}^{T} r(\varsigma)\rho(\varsigma)\left[\tilde{u}(T,\varsigma) - \pi(\varsigma)\sqrt{U(T,\varsigma)}\right]^2 d\varsigma < \infty,$$

$$\limsup_{T \to \infty} U^{-1}(T, T_0) \int_{T^*}^{T} (U(T,\varsigma)\rho(\varsigma)q(\varsigma) - F(T,\varsigma)) d\varsigma \geq \phi(T^*),$$

and

$$\lim_{T \to \infty} \int_{T_0}^{\infty} \phi_+^2(\varsigma)(v(\varsigma)r(\varsigma))^{-1/\xi} d\varsigma = \infty,$$

for $T > T_0$, and y $T^* \geq T_0$, where

$$\Phi(T) = \liminf_{T \to \infty} \frac{U(T,\varsigma)}{U(T,T_0)},$$

$$\phi_+(T) = \max(\phi(T), 0)$$

and

$$F(T,\varsigma) = (4K)^{-1}\rho(\varsigma)r(\varsigma)\left(\tilde{u}(T,\varsigma) - \pi(\varsigma)\sqrt{U(T,\varsigma)}\right)^2,$$

where $\pi(\varsigma) = (r(\varsigma)\rho'(\varsigma) - p(\varsigma)\rho(\varsigma))/(r(\varsigma)\rho(\varsigma))$, then (3) is oscillatory.

Theorem 2 ([28], Theorem 2). *Assume that there exist functions $g \in C^1(I_{T_0}, \mathbb{R}^+)$, $\phi \in C(I_{T_0}, \mathbb{R})$. Assume further that $U \in W_\xi$, $\xi = 1$ and $f'(x) \geq K$. Set*

$$\tilde{\rho}(T) = \exp\left(-2\int^{T} g(\varsigma)d\varsigma\right)$$

and

$$\Psi(T) = K^{-1}\tilde{\rho}(T)\left(Kq(T) - p(T)g(T) - [r(T)g(T)]' + r(T)g^2(T)\right).$$

If

$$\limsup_{T \to \infty} U^{-1}(T, T_0) \int_{T_0}^{T} r(\varsigma)\rho(\varsigma)\left(\tilde{u}(T,\varsigma) + \frac{p(\varsigma)}{r(\varsigma)}\sqrt{U(T,\varsigma)}\right)^2 d\varsigma < \infty,$$

$$\limsup_{T \to \infty} U^{-1}(T, T^*) \int_{T^*}^{T} U(T,\varsigma)\Psi(\varsigma) - \frac{r(\varsigma)\tilde{\rho}(\varsigma)}{4K}\left(\tilde{u}(T,\varsigma) + \frac{p(\varsigma)}{r(\varsigma)}\sqrt{U(T,\varsigma)}\right)^2 d\varsigma \geq \phi(T^*)$$

and

$$\limsup_{T \to \infty} \int_{T_0}^{T} \frac{\phi_+^2(\varsigma)}{\tilde{\rho}(\varsigma)r(\varsigma)} d\varsigma = \infty,$$

then (3) is oscillatory.

Now, define the functions

$$v(T) = \exp\left[-(\xi+1)\int_{T_0}^{T}\left(\rho^{1/\xi}(\varsigma) - \frac{p(\varsigma)}{(\xi+1)r(\varsigma)}\right)d\varsigma\right], \tag{8}$$

$$\psi(T) = v(T)\left[\mu q(T) + r(T)\rho^{(\xi+1)/\xi}(T) - (r(T)\rho(T))' - p(T)\rho(T)\right] \tag{9}$$

and

$$\tilde{F}(T,\varsigma) = U(T,\varsigma)\psi(\varsigma) - \beta^\xi(\xi+1)^{-(\xi+1)}v(\varsigma)r(\varsigma)\tilde{u}^{\xi+1}(T,\varsigma), \text{ for some } \beta \in [1,\infty)$$

3. Main Results

In this section we present two main results in the form of theorems. In the first theorem, using the Riccati technique, we obtained criteria that ensure the oscillation of all solutions of the studied equation. In the second theorem, using other analytical techniques, we present another criterion that reaches the same conclusion as in the first theorem.

Theorem 3. *Assume that there exists a function* $\rho \in C^1([T_0, \infty), \mathbb{R})$ *such that, for some* $\beta \in [1, \infty)$ *and* $U \in W_\xi$,

$$\limsup_{T \to \infty} U^{-1}(T, T_0) \int_{T_0}^{T} \left[U(T, \varsigma)\psi(\varsigma) - \beta^\xi(\xi + 1)^{-(\xi+1)} v(\varsigma) r(\varsigma) \tilde{u}^{\xi+1}(T, \varsigma) \right] d\varsigma = \infty \quad (10)$$

with $v(T)$ *and* $\psi(T)$ *given in (8) and (9), respectively. Then all solutions of Equation (1) are oscillatory.*

Proof. Let $x(T) > 0$ be a solution of (1) for $T \geq T_0^* \geq T_0$. Setting

$$u(T) = v(T)r(T)\left[\frac{(x'(T))^\xi}{x^\xi(T)} + \rho(T) \right], \quad T \geq T_0^*, \quad (11)$$

we have

$$\begin{aligned} u'(T) &= \frac{v'(T)}{v(T)} u(T) + v(T)\frac{\left(r(T)(x'(T))^\xi\right)'}{x^\xi(T)} \\ &\quad -\xi v(T) r(T)\left[\frac{u(T)}{v(T)r(T)} - \rho(T) \right]^{(\xi+1)/\xi} + v(T)(r(T)\rho(T))'. \end{aligned} \quad (12)$$

According to [33], it is

$$N_1^{1+1/\xi} - (N_1 - N_2)^{1+1/\xi} \leq \frac{N_2^{1/\xi}}{\xi}[(\xi + 1)N_1 - N_2]. \quad (13)$$

Taking

$$N_1 = u(T)/(v(T)r(T)) \text{ and } N_2 = \rho(T),$$

in (13), we obtain

$$\begin{aligned} (N_1 - N_2)^{(\xi+1)/\xi} &= \left[\frac{u(T)}{v(T)r(T)} - \rho(T) \right]^{(\xi+1)/\xi} \geq \left(\frac{u(T)}{v(T)r(T)} \right)^{(\xi+1)/\xi} \\ &\quad -\frac{\rho^{1/\xi}(T)}{\xi}\left[(\xi + 1)\frac{u(T)}{v(T)r(T)} - \rho(T) \right]. \end{aligned}$$

It follows from (1), (8), and (12) that

$$u'(T) \leq -\psi(T) - \xi\left(\frac{u^{\xi+1}(T)}{v(T)r(T)} \right)^{1/\xi}, \quad (14)$$

which we rewrite as

$$U(T, \varsigma)u'(T) \leq -U(T, \varsigma)\psi(T) - U(T, \varsigma)\xi\left(\frac{u^{\xi+1}(T)}{v(T)r(T)} \right)^{1/\xi}. \quad (15)$$

By integrating (15) from T_1^* to T, for all $\mathsf{T} \geq \mathsf{T}_1^* \geq \mathsf{T}_0^*$ and all $\beta \geq 1$, we have

$$\int_{\mathsf{T}_1^*}^{\mathsf{T}} U(\mathsf{T},\varsigma)\psi(\varsigma)\mathrm{d}\varsigma + \int_{\mathsf{T}_1^*}^{\mathsf{T}} \widetilde{u}(\mathsf{T},\varsigma)(U(\mathsf{T},\varsigma))^{\xi/(\xi+1)} u(\mathsf{T})\mathrm{d}\varsigma$$

$$+ \frac{\xi}{\beta}\int_{\mathsf{T}_1^*}^{\mathsf{T}} U(\mathsf{T},\varsigma)u^{\xi+1/\xi}(\varsigma)\frac{1}{(v(\varsigma)r(\varsigma))^{1/\xi}}\mathrm{d}\varsigma$$

$$\leq \quad U(\mathsf{T},\mathsf{T}_1^*)u(\mathsf{T}_1^*) - \xi\beta^{-1}(\beta-1)\int_{\mathsf{T}_1^*}^{\mathsf{T}} U(\mathsf{T},\varsigma)u^{\xi+1/\xi}(\varsigma)\frac{1}{(v(\varsigma)r(\varsigma))^{1/\xi}}\mathrm{d}\varsigma. \quad (16)$$

Also, according to [34], it is

$$M_1^{(\xi+1)/\xi} - \frac{\xi+1}{\xi}M_1^{1/\xi}M_2 \geq -\frac{1}{\xi}M_2^{(\xi+1)/\xi}. \quad (17)$$

Taking,

$$M_1^{(\xi+1)/\xi} = \frac{\xi}{\beta}\frac{U(\mathsf{T},\varsigma)u^{(\xi+1)/\xi}(\varsigma)}{(v(\varsigma)r(\varsigma))^{1/\xi}}$$

and

$$M_2^{(\xi+1)/\xi} = -\frac{\xi\beta^{\xi}}{(\xi+1)^{\xi+1}}v(\varsigma)r(\varsigma)\widetilde{u}^{(\xi+1)}(\mathsf{T},\varsigma),$$

in (17), we get

$$u(\varsigma)\widetilde{u}(\mathsf{T},\varsigma)(U(\mathsf{T},\varsigma))^{\xi/(\xi+1)} + \frac{\xi}{\beta}U(\mathsf{T},\varsigma)\left(\frac{u^{\xi+1}(\varsigma)}{v(\varsigma)r(\varsigma)}\right)^{1/\xi}$$

$$+ \frac{\beta^{\xi}}{(\xi+1)^{\xi+1}}v(\varsigma)r(\varsigma)\widetilde{u}^{\xi+1}(\mathsf{T},\varsigma) \leq 0. \quad (18)$$

Thus, it follows from (16) and (18) that

$$U(\mathsf{T},\mathsf{T}_1^*)u(\mathsf{T}_1^*) \quad \geq \quad \int_{\mathsf{T}_1^*}^{\mathsf{T}}\left(U(\mathsf{T},\varsigma)\psi(\varsigma) - \beta^{\xi}(\xi+1)^{-(\xi+1)}v(\varsigma)r(\varsigma)\widetilde{u}^{\xi+1}(\mathsf{T},\varsigma)\right)\mathrm{d}\varsigma$$

$$+ \xi\beta^{-1}(\beta-1)\int_{\mathsf{T}_1^*}^{\mathsf{T}} U(\mathsf{T},\varsigma)\left(\frac{u^{\xi+1}(\varsigma)}{v(\varsigma)r(\varsigma)}\right)^{1/\xi}\mathrm{d}\varsigma. \quad (19)$$

From property (6), we find

$$\int_{\mathsf{T}_1^*}^{\mathsf{T}}\left[U(\mathsf{T},\varsigma)\psi(\varsigma) - \frac{\beta^{\xi}}{(\xi+1)^{\xi+1}}v(\varsigma)r(\varsigma)\widetilde{u}^{\xi+1}(\mathsf{T},\varsigma)\right]\mathrm{d}\varsigma$$

$$\leq \quad U(\mathsf{T},\mathsf{T}_1^*)|u(\mathsf{T}_1^*)| \leq U(\mathsf{T},\mathsf{T}_0)|u(\mathsf{T}_1^*)|, \text{ for all } \mathsf{T} \geq \mathsf{T}_1^*.$$

Therefore, it is

$$\int_{\mathsf{T}_0}^{\mathsf{T}}\psi(\varsigma)U(\mathsf{T},\varsigma) - \beta^{\xi}(\xi+1)^{-(\xi+1)}v(\varsigma)r(\varsigma)\widetilde{u}^{\xi+1}(\mathsf{T},\varsigma)\mathrm{d}\varsigma$$

$$\leq \quad U(\mathsf{T},\mathsf{T}_0)\left(|u(\mathsf{T}_1^*)| + \int_{\mathsf{T}_0}^{\mathsf{T}_1^*}|\psi(\varsigma)|\mathrm{d}\varsigma\right).$$

Hence,

$$
\limsup_{\mathsf{T}\to\infty} U^{-1}(\mathsf{T},\mathsf{T}_0)\int_{\mathsf{T}_0}^{\mathsf{T}}\left[U(\mathsf{T},\varsigma)\psi(\varsigma)-\beta^{\xi}(\xi+1)^{-(\xi+1)}v(\varsigma)r(\varsigma)\widetilde{u}^{\xi+1}(\mathsf{T},\varsigma)\right]d\varsigma
$$

$$
\leq\ |u(\mathsf{T}_1^*)|+\int_{\mathsf{T}_0}^{\mathsf{T}_1^*}|\psi(\varsigma)|d\varsigma
$$

$$
<\ \infty,
$$

which contradicts (10). $\square$

Theorem 4. *Assume that there exist functions $\rho\in C^1(I_{\mathsf{T}_0},\mathbb{R})$, $\phi\in C(I_{\mathsf{T}_0},\mathbb{R})$ and U belonging to the class W_ξ such that, for some $\beta>1$ and for $\mathsf{T}^*\geq\mathsf{T}_0$,*

$$
\limsup_{\mathsf{T}\to\infty}U^{-1}(\mathsf{T},\mathsf{T}^*)\int_{\mathsf{T}^*}^{\mathsf{T}}\widetilde{F}(\mathsf{T},\varsigma)d\varsigma\geq\phi(\mathsf{T}^*)\tag{20}
$$

and

$$
0<\inf_{\mathsf{T}\geq\mathsf{T}_0}\widetilde{U}(\mathsf{T})\leq\infty.\tag{21}
$$

If

$$
\int_{\mathsf{T}_0}^{\infty}\phi_+^{\xi+1/\xi}(\varsigma)(v(\varsigma)r(\varsigma))^{-1/\xi}d\varsigma=\infty,\tag{22}
$$

then all solutions of Equation (1) are oscillatory.

Proof. Let $x(\mathsf{T})>0$ be a solution of (1) on $[\mathsf{T}_0^*,\infty)$, $\mathsf{T}_0^*\geq\mathsf{T}_0$. Proceeding exactly as in the proof of Theorem 3, we get the inequality (19), it is obvious that

$$
\phi(\mathsf{T}_1^*)\ \leq\ \limsup_{\mathsf{T}\to\infty}\frac{1}{U(\mathsf{T},\mathsf{T}_1^*)}\int_{\mathsf{T}_1^*}^{\mathsf{T}}\left[U(\mathsf{T},\varsigma)\psi(\varsigma)-\frac{\beta^{\xi}}{(\xi+1)^{\xi+1}}v(\varsigma)r(\varsigma)\widetilde{u}^{\xi+1}(\mathsf{T},\varsigma)\right]d\varsigma
$$

$$
\leq\ u(\mathsf{T}_1^*)-\frac{\xi(\beta-1)}{\beta}\liminf\frac{1}{U(\mathsf{T},\mathsf{T}_1^*)}\int_{\mathsf{T}_1^*}^{\mathsf{T}}U(\mathsf{T},\varsigma)\left(\frac{u^{\xi+1}(\varsigma)}{v(\varsigma)r(\varsigma)}\right)^{\frac{1}{\xi}}d\varsigma,
$$

for all $\mathsf{T}>\mathsf{T}_1^*$ and for any $\beta\geq1$. This implies that

$$
\phi(\mathsf{T}_1^*)+\xi\beta^{-1}(\beta-1)\liminf_{\mathsf{T}\to\infty}U^{-1}(\mathsf{T},\mathsf{T}_1^*)\int_{\mathsf{T}_1^*}^{\mathsf{T}}U(\mathsf{T},\varsigma)\frac{u^{\frac{\xi+1}{\xi}}(\varsigma)}{(v(\varsigma)r(\varsigma))^{\frac{1}{\xi}}}d\varsigma\leq u(\mathsf{T}_1^*)\tag{23}
$$

and

$$
\liminf_{\mathsf{T}\to\infty}U^{-1}(\mathsf{T},\mathsf{T}_1^*)\int_{\mathsf{T}_1^*}^{\mathsf{T}}U(\mathsf{T},\varsigma)\frac{u^{\frac{\xi+1}{\xi}}(\varsigma)}{(v(\varsigma)r(\varsigma))^{\frac{1}{\xi}}}d\varsigma
$$

$$
\leq\ \beta(\xi\beta-\xi)^{-1}(u(\mathsf{T}_1^*)-\phi(\mathsf{T}_1^*))
$$

$$
<\ \infty.\tag{24}
$$

It follows from (21) that there exists $v>0$ such that

$$
\widetilde{U}(\mathsf{T})>v(\mathsf{T}).\tag{25}
$$

Now, we claim that

$$
\int_{\mathsf{T}_1^*}^{\infty}\frac{u^{\frac{\xi+1}{\xi}}(\varsigma)}{(v(\varsigma)r(\varsigma))^{\frac{1}{\xi}}}d\varsigma=\infty.\tag{26}
$$

By (26) and for any constant $\eta > 0$, there exists a $T_2^* > T_1^*$ such that

$$\int_{T_1^*}^{T} \frac{u^{\frac{\xi+1}{\xi}}(\varsigma)}{(v(\varsigma)r(\varsigma))^{\frac{1}{\xi}}} \, d\varsigma > \frac{\eta}{v}, \text{ for all } T \geq T_2^*. \tag{27}$$

Integrating from T_1^* to T and using (27), we see that

$$U^{-1}(T, T_1^*) \int_{T_1^*}^{T} U(T, \varsigma) \frac{u^{\frac{\xi+1}{\xi}}(\varsigma)}{(v(\varsigma)r(\varsigma))^{\frac{1}{\xi}}} \, d\varsigma$$

$$= U^{-1}(T, T_1^*) \int_{T_1^*}^{T} U(T, \varsigma) d\left[\int_{T_1^*}^{\varsigma} \frac{u^{\frac{\xi+1}{\xi}}(\zeta)}{(v(\zeta)r(\zeta))^{\frac{1}{\xi}}} \, d\zeta \right],$$

for all $T \geq T_1^*$. Hence,

$$U^{-1}(T, T_1^*) \int_{T_1^*}^{T} U(T, \varsigma) \left(\frac{u^{\xi+1}(\varsigma)}{v(\varsigma)r(\varsigma)} \right)^{\frac{1}{\xi}} d\varsigma = U^{-1}(T, T_1^*) \int_{T_1^*}^{T} \left(-\frac{\partial U(T, \varsigma)}{\partial \varsigma} \right)$$

$$\times \left(\int_{T_1^*}^{\varsigma} \left(\frac{u^{\xi+1}(\zeta)}{v(\zeta)r(\zeta)} \right)^{\frac{1}{\xi}} d\zeta \right) d\varsigma$$

$$\geq \frac{\eta}{v} U^{-1}(T, T_1^*) \int_{T_2^*}^{T} \left(-\frac{\partial U(T, \varsigma)}{\partial \varsigma} \right) d\varsigma$$

$$= \frac{\eta}{v} U(T, T_2^*) U^{-1}(T, T_1^*)$$

$$\geq \frac{\eta}{v} U^{-1}(T, T_0) U(T, T_2^*).$$

In view of (25), there exists a $T_3^* \geq T_2^*$ such that

$$\frac{U(T, T_2^*)}{U(T, T_0)} \geq v(T), \text{ for all } T \geq T_3^*.$$

Thus, we have

$$U^{-1}(T, T_1^*) \int_{T_1^*}^{T} U(T, \varsigma) \left(\frac{u^{\xi+1}(\varsigma)}{v(\varsigma)r(\varsigma)} \right)^{\frac{1}{\xi}} d\varsigma \geq \eta \text{ for } T \geq T_2^*.$$

Since $\eta > 0$, we obtain

$$\liminf_{T \to \infty} U^{-1}(T, T_1^*) \int_{T_1^*}^{T} U(T, \varsigma) \left(\frac{u^{\xi+1}(\varsigma)}{v(\varsigma)r(\varsigma)} \right)^{\frac{1}{\xi}} d\varsigma = \infty.$$

But according to (24), we note that

$$\int_{T_1^*}^{\infty} u^{\frac{\xi+1}{\xi}}(\varsigma)(v(\varsigma)r(\varsigma))^{\frac{-1}{\xi}} d\varsigma = \infty,$$

and from (23), we get

$$\int_{T_1^*}^{\infty} \left(\frac{\phi^{\xi+1}(\varsigma)}{v(\varsigma)r(\varsigma)} \right)^{\frac{1}{\xi}} d\varsigma \leq \int_{T_1^*}^{\infty} \left(\frac{u^{\xi+1}(\varsigma)}{v(\varsigma)r(\varsigma)} \right)^{\frac{1}{\xi}} d\varsigma < \infty.$$

This completes the proof. $\square$

Remark 1. *We observe that the restrictions imposed in Theorem 4 are more tractable than those in [29] [Theorem 6], since we do not have the complex hypotheses that appear there.*

Corollary 1. *If one of the following statements is true*
(i) All conditions of Theorem 3 are satisfied;
(ii) All conditions of Theorem 4 are satisfied,
then the equation

$$\left(r(\mathsf{T})(y'(\mathsf{T}))^{\xi} \right)' + p(\mathsf{T})(y'(\mathsf{T}))^{\xi} + \mu q(\mathsf{T})y^{\xi}(\mathsf{T}) = 0, \tag{28}$$

where $\mu > 0$, is oscillatory.

4. Applications

Example 1. *Consider the following differential equation*

$$\left(\frac{1}{\mathsf{T}}(y'(\mathsf{T}))^{\xi} \right)' + \cos \mathsf{T} (y'(\mathsf{T}))^{\xi} + q(\mathsf{T})y^{\xi}(\mathsf{T}) = 0, \tag{29}$$

for $\mathsf{T} \geq 1$ and $\xi \geq 1$, where

$$
\begin{aligned}
q(\mathsf{T}) \;=\; & \frac{1}{\mathsf{T}^3} - \frac{\mathsf{T}\cos\mathsf{T} - 2\mathsf{T}^{-1}}{\mathsf{T}(\xi+1)} \left(\frac{\mathsf{T}\cos\mathsf{T} - 2\mathsf{T}^{-1}}{\xi+1} \right) + \left(\frac{\mathsf{T}\cos\mathsf{T} - 2\mathsf{T}^{-1}}{\xi+1} \right) \cos\mathsf{T} \\
& + \left(\frac{\mathsf{T}\cos\mathsf{T} - 2\mathsf{T}^{-1}}{\mathsf{T}^{\xi}(\xi+1)} \right)'.
\end{aligned}
$$

Let assume that

$$\rho(\mathsf{T}) = \left(\frac{\mathsf{T}\cos\mathsf{T} - 2\mathsf{T}^{-1}}{\xi+1} \right), \Psi(\mathsf{T}) = \mathsf{T}^{-1}, v(\mathsf{T}) = \mathsf{T}^3 \text{ and } \beta \geq 1.$$

By condition (10) in Corollary 1, we conclude that

$$
\begin{aligned}
& \limsup_{\mathsf{T}\to\infty} \frac{1}{U(\mathsf{T},\mathsf{T}_0)} \int_{\mathsf{T}_0}^{\mathsf{T}} \left[U(\mathsf{T},\varsigma)\psi(\varsigma) - \frac{\beta^{\xi}}{(\xi+1)^{\xi+1}} v(\varsigma)r(\varsigma)\tilde{u}^{\xi+1}(\mathsf{T},\varsigma) \right] d\varsigma \\
= \;& \limsup_{\mathsf{T}\to\infty} \frac{1}{\mathsf{T}^2} \int_{1}^{\mathsf{T}} \left[\frac{(\mathsf{T}-\varsigma)^2}{\varsigma} - \frac{2^{\xi+1}\beta^{\xi}}{(\xi+1)^{\xi+1}}\varsigma(\mathsf{T}-\varsigma)^{1-\xi} \right] d\varsigma = \infty.
\end{aligned}
$$

That is Equation (29) is oscillatory.

Example 2. *Consider the following differential equation*

$$0 = \left(\frac{(2\mathsf{T}^3+1)(2+\sin\mathsf{T})}{2\mathsf{T}^3}(x'(\mathsf{T}))^{\xi} \right)' + \left(\frac{3(2\mathsf{T}^3+1)(2+\sin\mathsf{T})}{2\mathsf{T}^4} \right)(x'(\mathsf{T}))^{\xi} + q(\mathsf{T})x^{\xi}(\mathsf{T}), \tag{30}$$

for $\mathsf{T} \geq 1$ and $\xi \geq 1$, where

$$q(\mathsf{T}) = \frac{1}{\mathsf{T}^3}\left(\left(1 - \mathsf{T}^3 + 2\mathsf{T}^2 - 6\mathsf{T}\right)\sin\mathsf{T} + 12\mathsf{T} \right).$$

Now, assume that

$$\rho(\mathsf{T}) = 0, \Psi(\mathsf{T}) = \left(1 - \mathsf{T}^3 + 2\mathsf{T}^2 - 6\mathsf{T}\right)\sin\mathsf{T} + 12\mathsf{T}, v(\mathsf{T}) = \mathsf{T}^3, \beta = 2^{-1}(1+\xi)^{(\xi+1)/\xi}.$$

Set $U(\mathsf{T},\varsigma) = (\mathsf{T}-\varsigma)^2, \tilde{u}(\mathsf{T},\varsigma) = 2(\mathsf{T}-\varsigma)^{(1-\xi)/(\xi+1)}.$

By condition (20) in Theorem 4, we find that

$$
\begin{aligned}
&\limsup_{\mathsf{T}\to\infty}\frac{1}{U(\mathsf{T},\mathsf{T}^*)}\int_{\mathsf{T}*}^{\mathsf{T}}\left[U(\mathsf{T},\varsigma)\psi(\varsigma)-\frac{\beta^{\xi}}{(\xi+1)^{\xi+1}}v(\varsigma)r(\varsigma)\tilde{u}^{\xi+1}(\mathsf{T},\varsigma)\right]d\varsigma \\
&=\ \limsup_{\mathsf{T}\to\infty}\frac{1}{\mathsf{T}^2}\int_{\mathsf{T}*}^{\mathsf{T}}[(\mathsf{T}-\varsigma)^2\left(\left(1-\varsigma^3+2\varsigma^2-6\varsigma\right)\sin\varsigma+12\varsigma\right)-2^{\xi}\beta^{\xi}(\xi+1)^{-(\xi+1)} \\
&\qquad\times\left(2\varsigma^3+1\right)(2+\sin\varsigma)(\mathsf{T}-\varsigma)^{1-\xi}]d\varsigma \\
&\geq\ \limsup_{\mathsf{T}\to\infty}\frac{1}{\mathsf{T}^2}\int_{\mathsf{T}*}^{\mathsf{T}}[(\mathsf{T}-\varsigma)^2\left(\left(1-\varsigma^3+2\varsigma^2-6\varsigma\right)\sin\varsigma+12\varsigma\right) \\
&\qquad-\left(2\varsigma^3+1\right)(2+\sin\varsigma)]d\varsigma \\
&=\ 16-\mathsf{T}^{*3}\cos\mathsf{T}^*+\mathsf{T}^{*2}(2\cos\mathsf{T}^*-6+3\sin\mathsf{T}^*)-4\mathsf{T}^*\sin\mathsf{T}^*-3\cos\mathsf{T}^*=\phi(\mathsf{T}^*).
\end{aligned}
$$

It is easy to see that condition (22) is satisfied. Therefore, Equation (30) is oscillatory.

Remark 2. *If condition (10) in Theorem 3 fails, we can use Theorem 4.*

Remark 3. *By applying Theorems 3 and 4 when $\xi = 1$, we obtain the results presented in references [24] [Theorems 17 and 19], Our results also improve those of [25,26], which imposed more restrictions on the sign of the coefficients p and q.*

5. Conclusions

Through this paper, we focus on studying some oscillatory properties of a particular class of differential equations with damping. We note that the conditions in Theorem 2 are less restrictive and more efficient than those in Theorem 1. The improvement is due to the fact that the oscillation criteria obtained in this paper are more flexible compared to those appearing [29,35], because there are no restrictions on the damping coefficient $p(\mathsf{T})$. Studying this type of equation without any restrictions imposed on the functions $p(\mathsf{T})$ and $q(\mathsf{T})$ is an extension and improvement of previous results. Defining the optional functions U and ρ and then using them in Theorems 3 and 4 to test the oscillatory behavior of Equation (1) (or its special cases) provide strong results for testing the oscillation of its solutions. Also, for $\xi = 1$, W_{ξ} generates the class of functions W, which was studied in [24]. On the other hand, our results do not need additional restrictions to ensure the oscillation of all solutions of Equation (1) [1,24–28]. It would be worth studying the following more general form of Equation (1):

$$
\left(r(\mathsf{T})(y'(\mathsf{T}))^{\xi}\right)'+p(\mathsf{T})(y'(\mathsf{T}))^{\beta}+q(\mathsf{T})f(y(\mathsf{T}))=0,
$$

where ξ and β are positive. Furthermore, introducing a delay term into the function $f(y(\mathsf{T}))$ so that it has the form $f(y(\tau(\mathsf{T})))$, where $\tau(\mathsf{T}) < \mathsf{T}$, will be a fertile field for researchers. Also, the possibility of providing different conditions without resorting to setting the restriction $\xi \geq 1$ remains an inspiring point for researchers as well.

Author Contributions: Conceptualization, A.A.-J. and B.Q.; methodology, B.Q., A.A.-J. and H.R.; investigation, A.A.-J. and B.Q.; writing—original draft preparation, A.A.-J., H.R., B.Q. and S.S.-C.; writing—review and editing, A.A.-J., B.Q., H.R. and S.S.-C.; presentation, and the revised content, S.S.-C. All authors have read and agreed to the published version of the manuscript.

Funding: Princess Nourah bint Abdulrahman University Researchers Supporting Project number (PNURSP2024R406), Princess Nourah bint Abdulrahman University, Riyadh, Saudi Arabia.

Data Availability Statement: Data sharing is not applicable to this article.

Acknowledgments: The authors would like to thank Princess Nourah bint Abdulrahman University Researchers Supporting Project number (PNURSP2024R406), Princess Nourah bint Abdulrahman University, Riyadh, Saudi Arabia.

Conflicts of Interest: The authors declare no conflicts of interest.

References

1. Al Themairi, A.; Qaraad, B.; Bazighifan, O.; Nonlaopon, K. Third-Order Neutral Differential Equations with Damping and Distributed Delay: New Asymptotic Properties of Solutions. *Symmetry* **2022**, *14*, 2192. [CrossRef]
2. Aldiaiji, M.; Qaraad, B.; Iambor, L.F.; Elabbasy, E.M. New Oscillation Theorems for Second-Order Superlinear Neutral Differential Equations with Variable Damping Terms. *Symmetry* **2023**, *15*, 1630. [CrossRef]
3. Sturm, C. Memoire sur les equations differentielles lineaires du second ordre. *J. Math. Pures Appl.* **1836**, *1*, 106–186.
4. Hale, J.K. Functional differential equations. In *Analytic Theory of Differential Equations*; Springer: New York, NY, USA, 1971; pp. 9–22.
5. Cesarano, C.; Moaaz, O.; Qaraad, B.; Alshehri, N.A.; Elagan, S.K.; Zakarya, M. New Results for Oscillation of Solutions of Odd-Order NeutralDifferential Equations. *Symmetry* **2021**, *13*, 1095. [CrossRef]
6. Al Themairi, A.; Qaraad, B.; Bazighifan, O.; Nonlaopon, K. Third-Order New Conditions for Testing the Oscillation of Third-Order Differential Equations with Distributed Arguments. *Symmetry* **2022**, *14*, 2416. [CrossRef]
7. Berezansky, L.; Domoshnitsky, A.; Koplatadze, R. *Oscillation, Nonoscillation, Stability and Asymptotic Properties for Second and Higher Order Functional Differential Equations*; CRC Press: New York, NY, USA, 2020. [CrossRef]
8. Grace, S.R.; Zurina, J.D.; Jadlovska, I.; Li, T. An improved approach for studying oscillation of second-order neutral delay differential equations. *J. Inequal. Appl.* **2018**, *2018*, 193. [CrossRef] [PubMed]
9. Erbe, L.; Kong, Q.; Zhang, B.G. *Oscillation Theory for Functional Differential Equations*; CRC Press: New York, NY, USA, 1994; Volume 190.
10. Cottrell, J.A.; Reali, A.; Bazilevs, Y.; Hughes, T.J.R. Isogeometric analysis of structural vibrations. *Comput. Methods Appl. Mech. Engrg.* **2006**, *195*, 5257–5296. [CrossRef]
11. Garoni, C.; Speleers, H.; Ekström, S.-E.; Reali, A.; Serra-Capizzano, S.; Hughes, T.J.R. Symbol based analysis of fiinite element and isogeometric B-spline discretizations of eigenvalue problems: exposition and review. *Arch. Comput. Methods Eng.* **2019**, *26*, 1639–1690. [CrossRef]
12. Dorostkar, A.; Neytcheva, M.; Serra-Capizzano, S. Spectral analysis of coupled PDEs and of their Schur complements via generalized locally Toeplitz sequences in 2D. *Comput. Methods Appl. Mech. Engrg.* **2016**, *309*, 74–105. [CrossRef]
13. Liu, Q.; Bohner, M.; Grace, R.S.; Li, T. Asymptotic behavior of even-order damped differential equations with p-Laplacian like operators and deviating arguments. *J. Inequal. Appl.* **2016**, *2016*, 321. [CrossRef]
14. Li, T.; Baculikova, B.; Džurina, J.; Zhang, C. Oscillation of fourth-order neutral differential equations with p-Laplacian like operators. *Bound. Value Probl.* **2014**, *2014*, 56. [CrossRef]
15. Zhang, C.; Agarwal, R.P.; Li, T. Oscillation and asymptotic behavior of higher-order delay differential equations with p-Laplacian like operators. *J. Math. Analy. Appl.* **2014**, *409*, 1093–1106. [CrossRef]
16. Ioannis, D.; Muhib, A.; El-Marouf, S.A.; Elagan, S.K. Oscillation of Neutral Differential Equations with Damping Terms. *Mathematics* **2023**, *11*, 447. [CrossRef]
17. Wu, Y.; Yu, Y.; Xiao, J. Oscillation of Second Order Nonlinear Neutral Differential Equations. *Mathematics* **2022**, *10*, 2739. [CrossRef]
18. Moaaz, O.; Elabbasy, E.M.; Qaraad, B. An improved approach for studying oscillation of generalized Emden–Fowler neutral differential equation. *J. Inequal. Appl.* **2020**, *2020*, 69. [CrossRef]
19. Grace, S.R. Oscillation theorems for second order nonlinear differential equations with damping. *Math. Nachr.* **1989**, *141*, 117–127. [CrossRef]
20. Grace, S.R.; Graef, J.R.; Tunc, E. Oscillatory behavior of second order damped neutral differential equations with distributed deviating arguments. *Miskolc Math. Notes* **2017**, *18*, 759–769. [CrossRef]
21. Grace, S.R.; Lalli, B.S. Oscillations in second order differential equations with alternating coefficients, Period. *Math. Hungar.* **1988**, *19*, 69–78. [CrossRef]
22. Grace, S.R.; Jadlovska, I. Oscillation criteria for second-order neutral damped differential equations with delay argument. In *Dynamical Systems—Analytical and Computational Techniques*; IntechOpen: London, UK, 2017; pp. 31–53.
23. Kirane, M.; Rogovchenko, Y.V. Oscillation results for a second order damped differential equation with nonmonotonous nonlinearity. *J. Math. Anal. Appl.* **2000**, *250*, 118–138. [CrossRef]
24. Rogovchenko, Y.; Tuncayay, F. Oscillation criteria for second-order nonlinear differential equations with damping. *Nonlinear Anal.* **2008**, *69*, 208–221. [CrossRef]
25. Liu, S.; Zhang, Q.; Yu, Y. Oscillation of even-order half-linear functional differential equations with damping. *Comput. Math. Appl.* **2011**, *61*, 2191–2196. [CrossRef]
26. Yamaoka, N. Oscillation criteria for second-order damped nonlinear differential equations with p-Laplacian. *J. Math. Anal. Appl.* **2007**, *325*, 932–948. [CrossRef]
27. Zhang, Q.; Liu, S.; Gao, L. Oscillation criteria for even-order half-linear functional differential equations with damping. *Appl. Math. Lett.* **2011**, *24*, 1709–1715. [CrossRef]

28. Rogovchenko, Y.V. Oscillation theorems for second-order equations with damping. *Nonlinear Anal.* **2000**, *41*, 1005–1028. [CrossRef]
29. Grace, S.R. Oscillation theorems for nonlinear differential equations of second order. *J. Math. Anal. Appl.* **1992**, *171*, 220–241. [CrossRef]
30. Elabbasy, E.M.; Hassan, T.S.; Saker, S.H. Oscillation of second-order nonlinear differential equations with a damping term. *Electron. J. Differ. Equ.* **2005**, *76*, 1–13. [CrossRef]
31. Kirane, M.; Rogovchenko, Y.V. On oscillation of nonlinear second order differential equation with damping term. *Appl. Math. Comput.* **2001**, *117*, 177–192. [CrossRef]
32. Li, W.T.; Agarwal, R.P. Interval oscillation criteria for second order nonlinear differential equations with damping. *Comput. Math. Appl.* **2000**, *40*, 217–230. [CrossRef]
33. Jiang, J.C.; Li, X.P. Oscillation of second order nonlinear neutral differential equations. *Appl. Math. Comput.* **2003**, *135*, 531–540. [CrossRef]
34. Hardy, G.H.; Littlewood, J.E.; Polya, G. *Inequalities*, 2nd ed.; Cambridge University Press: Cambridge, UK, 1988.
35. Grace, S.R.; Lalli, B.S. Integral averaging technique for the oscillation of second order nonlinear differential equations. *J. Math. Anal. Appl.* **1990**, *149*, 277–311. [CrossRef]

Article

The FitzHugh–Nagumo Model Described by Fractional Difference Equations: Stability and Numerical Simulation

Tareq Hamadneh [1], Amel Hioual [2,*], Omar Alsayyed [3], Yazan Alaya Al-Khassawneh [4], Abdallah Al-Husban [5] and Adel Ouannas [6]

1   Department of Mathematics, Faculty of Science, Al Zaytoonah University of Jordan, Amman 11733, Jordan; t.hamadneh@zuj.edu.jo
2   Laboratory of Dynamical Systems and Control, University of Oum EL-Bouaghi, Oum El Bouaghi 04000, Algeria
3   Department of Mathematics, Faculty of Science, The Hashemite University, P.O. Box 330127 Zarqa 13133, Jordan; Omarm_re@hu.edu.jo
4   Data Science and Artificial Intelligence Department, Zarqa University, Zarqa 13110, Jordan; ykhassawneh@zu.edu.jo
5   Department of Mathematics, Faculty of Science and Technology, Irbid National University, Irbid 21110, Jordan; dralhosban@inu.edu.jo
6   Department of Mathematics and Computer Science, University of Oum EL-Bouaghi, Oum El Bouaghi 04000, Algeria; ouannas.adel@univ-oeb.dz
*   Correspondence: amel.hioual@univ-oeb.dz

Abstract: The aim of this work is to describe the dynamics of a discrete fractional-order reaction–diffusion FitzHugh–Nagumo model. We established acceptable requirements for the local asymptotic stability of the system's unique equilibrium. Moreover, we employed a Lyapunov functional to show that the constant equilibrium solution is globally asymptotically stable. Furthermore, numerical simulations are shown to clarify and exemplify the theoretical results.

Keywords: fractional discrete reaction–diffusion equations; FitzHugh–Nagumo model; global asymptotic stability; Lyapunov functional

MSC: 39A12; 39A30; 39A60; 39B82

Citation: Hamadneh, T.; Hioual, A.; Alsayyed, O.; Al-Khassawneh, Y.A.; Al-Husban, A.; Ouannas, A. The FitzHugh–Nagumo Model Described by Fractional Difference Equations: Stability and Numerical Simulation. *Axioms* **2023**, *12*, 806. https://doi.org/10.3390/axioms12090806

Academic Editors: Azhar Ali Zafar and Nehad Ali Shah

Received: 26 May 2023
Revised: 5 July 2023
Accepted: 10 July 2023
Published: 22 August 2023

1. Introduction

Fractional calculus has been around for three centuries, and recently, it has become more frequently utilized in the scientific and technical fields. It investigates extensions of the basic calculus operators, differentiation and integration, defined by letting their order to roam outside of Z to more extended domains [1–3]. Such extensions are not only a mathematical novelty; differential equations containing the generalized operators have been employed in a wide range of scientific domains [4,5], from viscoelasticity [6] to epidemiology [7], economics [8,9], and electrical circuits [10].

Almost every mathematical theory has a discrete equivalent that enables it to be comprehended theoretically and practically in the modeling process of real-world issues. Owing to the availability of a coherent mathematical framework for continuous fractional calculus, the potential advancement of discrete fractional calculus has been inadequate until recently. However, there has been significant progress in the development of discrete fractional calculus. For example, Atici and Eloe [11] implemented a discrete Laplace transform technique for solving a series of fractional difference equations. Atici and Eloe [12] developed the triggers for the beginning value in discrete fractional calculus. With the nabla operator, Atici and Eloe [13] investigated the structure of a discrete fractional calculus. For additional information on recent advances in fractional discrete calculus, see [14–19].

Reaction–diffusion systems have acquired great theoretical attention and are of tremendous utility in many scientific and technical disciplines due to their capacity to simulate a range of real-world events and the intricacy of their solutions (see [20–23]). Meanwhile, the fractional partial differential equation is widely used in practice. Several papers on the subject have recently been published [24–27]. An effective and common application of fractional diffusion equations is the simulation of anomalous diffusion in porous media with rich nano–micro-size characteristics. However, many nonlinear systems in nature have discrete qualities, such as population models, brain networks, and gene information. Discrete models may be used to successfully identify parameters from experimental data. Fractional partial difference equations offer a separate time-discretization model, particularly for anomalous diffusion, or a time-discretization difference technique, which was recently described as a discrete fractional modeling [28]. The authors of [29] established a fractional time discretization diffusion model in the Caputo-like delta interpretation, and addressed diffusion concentration for various fractional difference orders. Alternatively, the authors of [30] proposed a variable-order fractional diffusion equation on discrete periods and created a variable-order function using a chaotic map.

Several neuron models have recently been proposed in the literature to describe neural dynamics. Among these models, one can find the reaction diffusion FitzHugh–Nagumo model, which is a classic standard model in neuroscience that has been extensively examined in periodical literature [31]. This model is a simplified variant of the well-known Hodgkin–Huxley model, which captures neuron dynamics and, more broadly, the dynamics of excitable systems in several domains such as chemical reaction kinetics and solid state physics [32–34]. It is made up of two differential equations that describe the voltage variable's temporal evolution. In recent years, FitzHugh–Nagumo has received a lot of attention, and several notable studies have been conducted to examine this system. For example, in [35], the global existence and asymptotic stability of solutions for a generalized Lengyel–Epstein and FitzHugh–Nagumo reaction–diffusion system were explored. In [36], synchronization and control of FitzHugh–Nagumo coupled reaction–diffusion systems are addressed. In addition, synchronization of the reaction–diffusion FitzHugh–Nagumo systems using a one-dimensional linear control law was investigated in [37]. Finite element analysis of a FitzHugh–Nagumo reaction–diffusion system with Robin boundary conditions was explored in [38]. Moreover, many papers examined the influence of the fractional derivative on the FitzHugh–Nagumo model. For example, in [39] the low-voltage, low-power sinh-domain implementations of the fractional-order FitzHugh–Nagumo neuron model have been presented, as well as the influence of fractional orders on the neuron's external excitation current and dynamics. In [40], the effect of the fractional order on the dynamics of action potentials in the FitzHugh–Nagumo model is discussed.

The goal of this paper is to study the stability of the equilibrium state of a discrete fractional-order reaction–diffusion FitzHugh–Nagumo model. Both local and global stability are explored for applicability in the above-mentioned neural model research. To the best of our knowledge, this is the first time a full theoretical stability study for a discrete fractional-order reaction–diffusion FitzHugh–Nagumo model has been conducted in which the effect of the fractional order on the dynamics of the model is investigated and discussed.

The paper is structured as follows. Section 2 is intended to provide some preliminary results as well as the discrete fractional-order dependent and independent outcomes. Section 3 describes the main findings of the study; the mathematical model is presented, the local stability of the equilibrium state is addressed, and global stability of the equilibrium state is examined, both dependently on the fractional orders of the considered model. The findings are corroborated by numerical simulations. Section 5 draws conclusions from the findings.

2. Preliminaries

This section begins by introducing the subject's required nomenclature and stability theory.

Definition 1 ([41]). *Assume* $x : \mathbb{N} \to \mathbb{R}$, *the forward difference operator* Δ *is then defined by*

$$\Delta x(\ell) = x(\ell + 1) - x(\ell); \quad \ell \in \mathbb{N}. \tag{1}$$

Next, the operators $\Delta^n, n = 1, 2, 3, \ldots$, *are recursively identified by*

$$\Delta^n x(\ell) = \Delta(\Delta^{n-1}x)(\ell), \quad \ell \in \mathbb{N}. \tag{2}$$

In particular, the second order difference operator of function $x(t)$ *is given by*

$$\Delta^2 x(\ell) = x(\ell + 2) - 2x(\ell + 1) + x(\ell). \tag{3}$$

Lemma 1 ([41]). *Here we give some properties of the difference operator* Δ,
- $\Delta c = 0$, *where* c *is a constant.*
- $\Delta(x + \kappa)(\ell) = \Delta x(\ell) + \Delta \kappa(\ell)$.
- $\Delta(x\kappa)(\ell) = x(\ell)\Delta\kappa(\ell) + \kappa(\ell + 1)\Delta x(\ell)$.

Theorem 1 ([41]). *Given two functions* $x; \kappa : \mathbb{R} \to \mathbb{R}$ *and* $a; b \in \mathbb{N}; \quad a < b; \quad$ *we have the summation by parts' formulas:*

$$\sum_{j=a}^{b-1} x(j)\Delta\kappa(j) = x(j)\kappa(j)\big|_a^b - \sum_{j=a}^{b-1} \kappa(j+1)\Delta x(j), \tag{4}$$

$$\sum_{j=a}^{b-1} x(j+1)\Delta\kappa(j) = x(j)\kappa(j)\big|_a^b - \sum_{j=a}^{b-1} \kappa(j)\Delta x(j). \tag{5}$$

Definition 2 ([42,43]). *Let* $x \in (h\mathbb{N})_a \to \mathbb{R}$. *For given* $\vartheta > 0$, *the* ϑ-*th order h-sum is given by*

$$_h\Delta_a^{-\vartheta}x(t) = \frac{h}{\Gamma(\vartheta)} \sum_{\frac{t}{h}-\vartheta}^{s=\frac{a}{h}} (t - \sigma(sh))^{(\vartheta-1)}x(sh), \quad \sigma(sh) = (s+1)h, \quad t \in (h\mathbb{N})_{a+\vartheta h}, \tag{6}$$

with $a \in \mathbb{R}$ *as the initial value and the* $\hbar$-*falling factorial function described by*

$$t_\hbar^{(\vartheta)} = \hbar^\vartheta \frac{\Gamma(\frac{t}{\hbar} + 1)}{\Gamma(\frac{t}{\hbar} + 1 - \vartheta)}, \tag{7}$$

while

$$(h\mathbb{N})_{a+\vartheta\hbar} = \{a + (1 - \vartheta)\hbar, a + (2 - \vartheta)\hbar, \ldots\}. \tag{8}$$

Definition 3 ([43,44]). *For a function* $x(t)$ *defined on* $(h\mathbb{N})_a$ *and for a certain* $\vartheta > 0$, *so that* $\vartheta \in \mathbb{N}$ *the Caputo* $\hbar$-*difference operator is expressed by*

$$^C_\hbar\Delta_a^\vartheta x(t) = {}_\hbar\Delta_a^{-(n-\vartheta)}\Delta_\hbar^n x(t), \tag{9}$$

where $\Delta_\hbar^n x(t) = \dfrac{x(t + \hbar) - x(t)}{\hbar}$.

Lemma 2 ([42]). *Here are some important properties employed in this work:*
- *Discrete Leibniz integral law:*

$$_\hbar\Delta_{a+(1-\vartheta)\hbar}^{-\vartheta} {}^C_\hbar\Delta^\vartheta x(t) = x(t) - x(a), \quad 0 < \vartheta \leq 1, \quad t \in (\hbar\mathbb{N})_{a+\hbar}. \tag{10}$$

- *Caputo fractional difference of a constant* x:

$$^C_\hbar\Delta^\vartheta x = 0, \quad 0 < \vartheta \leq 1. \tag{11}$$

Lemma 3 ([42]). *The following inequality holds:*

$$\,^{C}_{h}\Delta^{\vartheta}_{a}\mathsf{x}^2(t) \leq 2\mathsf{x}(t+\vartheta\hbar)\,^{C}_{h}\Delta^{\vartheta}_{a}\mathsf{x}(t), \quad t \in (\hbar\mathbb{N})_{a+\vartheta\hbar},\tag{12}$$

where $0 < \vartheta \leq 1$.

Let us consider the nonlinear fractional-order difference system.

$$\,^{C}_{h}\Delta^{\vartheta}_{a}\mathsf{x}(t) = \psi(t+\hbar\vartheta, \mathsf{x}(t+\hbar\vartheta)), \quad t \in (h\mathbb{N})_{a+\vartheta h}.\tag{13}$$

Theorem 2 ([42]). *Let $\mathsf{x} = 0$ be the system's equilibrium point (13). The equilibrium point is asymptotically stable if there exists a positive, definite, and declining scalar function. If all the eigenvalues of $\psi'(\mathsf{x}^*)$ are located in $S^{\vartheta}_{\hbar}$, then x^* is asymptotically stable, where $\,^{C}_{h}\Delta^{\vartheta}_{a}V(t,\mathsf{x}(t)) \leq 0$.*

Theorem 3 ([45]). *Let x^* be an equilibrium point of (13). If all the eigenvalues of $\psi'(\mathsf{x}^*)$ are located in $S^{\vartheta}_{\hbar}$, then x^* is asymptotically stable,*
where

$$S^{\vartheta}_{\hbar} = \left\{ w \in \mathbb{C} : |Arg(w)| > \frac{\vartheta\pi}{2} \quad or \quad |w| > \frac{2^{\vartheta}}{\hbar^{\vartheta}}\cos^{\vartheta}\left(\frac{Arg(w)}{\vartheta}\right) \right\}.\tag{14}$$

3. The Discrete Fractional-Order FitzHugh–Nagumo Reaction–Diffusion System

In this section, we present the model under discussion, which is approximated using two well known approaches. This discrete model is, to the best of our knowledge, the first in the literature.

The FitzHugh–Nagumo reaction–diffusion system, as is well known, was proposed in [46] as follows:

$$\begin{cases} \dfrac{\partial u}{\partial t} = d_1\Delta u - u^3 + (\beta+1)u^2 - \beta u - v, & x \in \Omega, t > 0, \\[2mm] \dfrac{\partial v}{\partial t} = d_2\Delta v + \epsilon u - \epsilon\gamma v, & x \in \Omega, t > 0, \\[2mm] \partial_u = \partial_v = 0 \quad, & x \in \partial\Omega, t > 0, \\[2mm] u(x,0) = u_0(x) > 0, \quad v(x,0) = v_0(x) > 0, & x \in \Omega. \end{cases}\tag{15}$$

where Ω is a bounded domain in $\mathbb{R}^n, n = 1$, with sufficiently smooth boundary $\partial\Omega$, $\Delta = \sum_{i=1}^{n}\dfrac{\partial^2}{\partial x_i^2}$. The state u corresponds to the membrane potential in this spatially extended system, whereas v reflects a combination of potassium activation and sodium inactivation at point $(x,t) \in \Omega \times (0,\infty)$. The parameters β, ϵ and γ are positive constants with values of $0 < \beta < \dfrac{1}{2}$ and $\epsilon << 1$.

Since time fractional systems have been extensively studied by researchers, the following time fractional FitzHugh–Nagumo reaction–diffusion system was presented in [47] as follows:

$$\begin{cases} \,^{C}_{0}D^{\delta}_{t}u - d_1\Delta u = -u^3 + (\beta+1)u^2 - \beta u - v, \\[2mm] \,^{C}_{0}D^{\delta}_{t}v - d_2\Delta v = \epsilon u - \epsilon\gamma v. \end{cases}\tag{16}$$

where $0 < \delta \leq 1$ is the fractional order and $\,^{C}_{0}D^{\delta}_{t}$ describes the Caputo fractional derivative, d_1, d_2 and σ are strictly positive constants with the same initial conditions and Neumann boundary conditions.

Based on the model (16) and with the discretization used in [29,48], and assuming that $x \in [0,L]$, we have $x_{i+1} = x_i + k, \quad i = 0,\ldots,m$, and using the central difference formula concerning x, $\dfrac{\partial^2 u(x,t)}{\partial x^2}$ and $\dfrac{\partial^2 v(x,t)}{\partial x^2}$ can be approximately expanded as

$$\begin{cases} \dfrac{\partial^2 u(x,t)}{\partial x^2} \approx \dfrac{u_{i+1}(t) - 2u_i(t) + u_{i-1}(t)}{k^2}, \\ \dfrac{\partial^2 v(x,t)}{\partial x^2} \approx \dfrac{v_{i+1}(t) - 2v_i(t) + v_{i-1}(t)}{k^2}. \end{cases}$$

Using the definition of the second order difference operator of u_i and v_i we obtain

$$\begin{cases} \dfrac{\partial^2 u(x,t)}{\partial x^2} \approx \dfrac{\Delta^2 u_{i-1}(t)}{k^2}, \\ \dfrac{\partial^2 v(x,t)}{\partial x^2} \approx \dfrac{\Delta^2 v_{i-1}(t)}{k^2}. \end{cases}$$

Therefore, we consider the following discrete-time reaction–diffusion fractional FitzHugh–Nagumo system

$$\begin{cases} {}^C_\hbar\Delta^\vartheta_{t_0} u_i(t) = \dfrac{d_1}{k^2}\Delta^2 u_{i-1}(t + \hbar\vartheta) - u^3(t + \hbar\vartheta) + (\beta + 1)u^2(t + \hbar\vartheta) - \beta u(t + \hbar\vartheta) - v_i(t + \hbar\vartheta), \\ {}^C_\hbar\Delta^\vartheta_{t_0} v_i(t) = \dfrac{d_2}{k^2}\Delta^2 v_{i-1}(t + \hbar\vartheta) + \epsilon u_i(t + \hbar\vartheta) - \epsilon\gamma v_i(t + \hbar\vartheta). \end{cases} \tag{17}$$

where ${}^C_\hbar\Delta^\vartheta_{t_0}$ is the Caputo-like difference, $0 < \vartheta \le 1, t \in (\hbar\mathbb{N})_{t_0}$.
With the periodic boundary conditions

$$\begin{cases} u_0(t) = u_m(t), \quad u_1(t) = u_{m+1}(t), \\ v_0(t) = v_m(t), \quad v_1(t) = v_{m+1}(t), \end{cases} \tag{18}$$

and the initial condition

$$u_i(t_0) = \phi_1(x_i) \ge 0, \quad v_i(t_0) = \phi_2(x_i) \ge 0.$$

4. Local Stability

In order to investigate the asymptotic stability of the considered discrete-time fractional FitzHugh–Nagumo system, we consider the unique equilibrium point, which is the solution of the following system:

$$\begin{cases} \dfrac{d_1}{k^2}\Delta^2 u^* - u^{*3} + (\beta + 1)u^{*2} - \beta u^* - v^* = 0, \\ \dfrac{d_2}{k^2}\Delta^2 v^* + \epsilon u^* - \epsilon\gamma v^* = 0. \end{cases} \tag{19}$$

As previously stated in [49], the system (17) may have many equilibriums depending on the sign of ξ, where ξ is determined by

$$\xi = (1 - \beta)^2 - \frac{4}{\gamma}. \tag{20}$$

Thus, we may have the three cases listed below:

- If $\xi < 0$, system (17) has the origin $(u_0^*, v_0^*) = (0,0)$ as its only fixed point.
- If $\xi = 0$, system (17) has two fixed points; the origin and $(u_1^*, v_1^*) = \left(-\dfrac{\beta + 1}{2}, \dfrac{u_1^*}{\gamma}\right)$.
- If $\xi > 0$, system (17) has three fixed points; the origin,

$$(u_2^*, v_2^*) = \left(-\frac{\beta}{2} - \sqrt{\xi}, \frac{u_2^*}{\gamma}\right) \quad \text{and} \quad (u_3^*, v_3^*) = \left(-\frac{\beta}{2} + \sqrt{\xi}, \frac{u_3^*}{\gamma}\right).$$

4.1. Local Stability of the Free Diffusions System

In this part, we develop suitable requirements for the local asymptotic stability of the following system:

$$\begin{cases} \frac{C}{\hbar}\Delta^{\vartheta}_{t_0} u(t) = -u^3(t+\hbar\vartheta) + (\beta+1)u^2(t+\hbar\vartheta) - \beta u(t+\hbar\vartheta) - v(t+\hbar\vartheta), \\ \frac{C}{\hbar}\Delta^{\vartheta}_{t_0} v(t) = \epsilon u(t+\hbar\vartheta) - \epsilon\gamma v(t+\hbar\vartheta). \end{cases} \tag{21}$$

The characteristic equation for the eigenvalues is obtained using linear stability analysis around the stable state:

$$J = \begin{pmatrix} \dfrac{\partial\psi}{\partial u} & \dfrac{\partial\psi}{\partial v} \\ \dfrac{\partial\Psi}{\partial u} & \dfrac{\partial\Psi}{\partial v} \end{pmatrix} = \begin{pmatrix} -3u^2 + 2(\beta+1)u - \beta & -1 \\ \epsilon\gamma & -\epsilon \end{pmatrix}, \tag{22}$$

where

$$\psi(u,v) = -u^3(t+\hbar\vartheta) + (1+\beta)u^2(t+\hbar\vartheta) - \beta u(t+\hbar\vartheta) - v(t+\hbar\vartheta), \tag{23}$$

and

$$\Psi(u,v) = \epsilon\gamma u(t+\hbar\vartheta) - \epsilon v(t+\hbar\vartheta). \tag{24}$$

We may deduce the following:

Theorem 4. *System (21) is locally asymptotically stable at the steady state according to the following cases:*

- *If $\xi = 0$, the equilibrium point (u_0^*, v_0^*) is locally asymptotically stable.*
- *If $\xi = 0$, the equilibrium points (u_0^*, v_0^*) and (u_1^*, v_1^*) are locally asymptotically stable.*
- *If $\xi > 0$, the equilibrium points (u_0^*, v_0^*) and (u_2^*, v_2^*) are locally asymptotically stable, and (u_3^*, v_3^*) is stable if the following hold true:*

$$\beta\left(\frac{7}{4}\beta + 2\right) - \sqrt{\xi}(5\beta + 2) + 3\xi > 0.$$

Proof. Since the system (21) might have many equilibriums depending on the sign of ξ, we shall analyze each one separately.

- Given that the origin (u_0^*, v_0^*) always represents an equilibrium point, we shall investigate the stability of the system (21) regardless of the sign of ξ.

The Jacobian matrix of the equilibrium point (u_0^*, v_0^*) may be expressed as follows:

$$J_{(u_0^*, v_0^*)} = \begin{pmatrix} -\beta & -1 \\ \epsilon\gamma & -\epsilon \end{pmatrix}, \tag{25}$$

The Jacobian matrix $J_{(u_0^*, v_0^*)}$ has the following characteristic equation:

$$\Lambda^2 - \text{tr}(J_{(u_3^*, v_3^*)})\Lambda + \det(J_{(u_3^*, v_3^*)}) = 0, \tag{26}$$

where

$$\text{tr}(J_{(u_0^*, v_0^*)}) = -\beta - \epsilon, \quad \det(J_{(u_0^*, v_0^*)}) = \beta\epsilon + \epsilon\gamma. \tag{27}$$

This might lead to the following discriminant

$$\Delta_\Lambda = \text{tr}^2(J_{(u_0^*, v_0^*)}) - 4\det(J_{(u_0^*, v_0^*)}) = (\beta+\epsilon)^2 - 4(\beta\epsilon + \epsilon\gamma) = (\beta-\epsilon)^2 - 4\epsilon\gamma.$$

The solutions of (26) are obviously dependent on the sing of Δ_Λ; therefore, we may analyze the stability in the following situations.

- If $(\beta - \epsilon)2 > 4\epsilon\gamma$, and since $\beta\epsilon + \epsilon\gamma > 0$, the negativity of the eigenvalues is determined by the sign of $\mathrm{tr}(J_{(u_0^*,v_0^*)})$. Furthermore, as $-\beta - \epsilon < 0$, and the eigenvalues Λ_1 and Λ_2 are real, thus we have

$$\Lambda_1 = \frac{\mathrm{tr}(J_{(u_0^*,v_0^*)}) - \sqrt{\Delta_\Lambda}}{2} < 0. \tag{28}$$

As a consequence of this, $Arg(\Lambda_1) = \pi$. It is self-evident that $Arg(\Lambda_1) = Arg(\Lambda_2) = \pi$. As a result, according to Theorem 3, the equilibrium (u_0^*, v_0^*) is asymptotically stable.
- If $(\beta - \epsilon)^2 < 4\epsilon\gamma$, then

$$\Lambda_1 = \frac{\mathrm{tr}(J_{(u_0^*v_0^*)}) - i\sqrt{-\Delta_\Lambda}}{2}, \qquad \Lambda_2 = \frac{\mathrm{tr}(J_{(u_0^*v_0^*)}) + i\sqrt{-\Delta_\Lambda}}{2}. \tag{29}$$

Since $-\beta - \epsilon < 0$, the system (21) is then asymptotically stable, based on the identical situation studied before.
- If $(\beta - \epsilon)^2 = 4\epsilon\gamma$, $\mathrm{tr}(J_{(u_0^*,v_0^*)})$ cannot be equal to zero. The sign of the eigenvalues is the same as the sign of $\mathrm{tr}(J_{(u_0^*,v_0^*)})$. As a result, (u_0^*, v_0^*) is asymptotically stable for all $\vartheta \in (0, 1]$.

We may deduce that the origin is locally asymptotically stable, regardless of the sing of Δ_Λ.
- Now, assuming that $\xi = 0$, and the origin is clearly stable according to the previous investigations, we can thus investigate the stability of the equilibrium point (u_1^*, v_1^*).

In this case, we have the Jacobian matrix of the equilibrium point (u_1^*, v_1^*) defined by

$$J_{(u_1^*,v_1^*)} = \begin{pmatrix} -3\left(\dfrac{\beta+1}{2}\right)^2 - 2\dfrac{(\beta+1)^2}{2} - \beta & -1 \\[2ex] \epsilon\gamma & -\epsilon \end{pmatrix}, \tag{30}$$

and we also have:

$$\mathrm{tr}(J_{(u_1^*,v_1^*)}) = \frac{-7(\beta+1)^2}{4} - \beta - \epsilon, \quad \det(J_{(u_1^*,v_1^*)}) = \left(\frac{7(\beta+1)^2}{4} + \beta\right)\epsilon + \epsilon\gamma. \tag{31}$$

This may lead us to the discriminant of the eigenvalue problem (26):

$$\Delta_\Lambda = \frac{7}{2}(\beta+1)^2\left(\frac{7}{8}(\beta+1)^2 - \epsilon + \beta\right) - 4\epsilon(\beta+\gamma) + (\beta+\epsilon)^2.$$

We notice that $\det(J_{(u_1^*,v_1^*)}) > 0$ and $\mathrm{tr}(J_{(u_1^*,v_1^*)}) < 0$, which indicates that, based on the results we have reached about the stability of the equilibrium point, (u_0^*, v_0^*), (u_1^*, v_1^*) is asymptotically stable.
- In the last case, we suppose that $\xi > 0$; thus, the equilibrium point (u_0^*, v_0^*) remains stable, and we will discuss the stability of the two other equilibriums.
  - Concering the equilibrium (u_2^*, v_2^*) we have

$$J_{(u_2^*,v_2^*)} = \begin{pmatrix} -3\left(-\dfrac{\beta}{2} - \sqrt{\xi}\right)^2 + 2(\beta+1)\left(-\dfrac{\beta}{2} - \sqrt{\xi}\right) - \beta & -1 \\[2ex] \epsilon\gamma & -\epsilon \end{pmatrix}. \tag{32}$$

This leads us to:

$$\mathrm{tr}(J_{(u_2^*,v_2^*)})= -3\left(-\frac{\beta}{2}-\sqrt{\xi}\right)^2 + 2(\beta+1)\left(-\frac{\beta}{2}-\sqrt{\xi}\right) - \beta - \epsilon,$$

$$= -\beta\left(\frac{7}{4}\beta+2\right) - \sqrt{\xi}(5\beta+2) - 3\xi - \epsilon,$$

$$\det(J_{(u_2^*,v_2^*)})= -\epsilon\left(-3\left(-\frac{\beta}{2}-\sqrt{\xi}\right)^2 + 2(\beta+1)\left(-\frac{\beta}{2}-\sqrt{\xi}\right) - \beta\right) + \epsilon\gamma,$$

$$= -\epsilon(\mathrm{tr}(J_{(u_2^*,v_2^*)}) + \epsilon) + \epsilon\gamma.$$

$$= \epsilon\left(\beta\left(\frac{7}{4}\beta+2\right) + \sqrt{\xi}(5\beta+2) + 3\xi + \gamma\right).$$

The discriminant of the eingenvalue problem (26) is as follows:

$$\Delta_\Lambda = \left(-\beta\left(\frac{7}{4}\beta+2\right) + \sqrt{\xi}(-3\beta+2) - 3\xi + \epsilon\right)^2 - 4\epsilon\gamma.$$

This case is identical to the case of the equilibrium point (u_1^*, v_1^*), since $\det(J_{(u_2^*,v_2^*)}) > 0$ and $\mathrm{tr}(J_{(u_2^*,v_2^*)}) < 0$, which leads us to the same results as the first and second cases of the demonstration. As a result, (u_2^*, v_2^*) is locally asymptotically stable. Finally, we investigate the stability of the equilibrium (u_3^*, v_3^*), and we have

$$J_{(u_3^*,v_3^*)} = \begin{pmatrix} -3\left(-\frac{\beta}{2}+\sqrt{\xi}\right)^2 + 2(\beta+1)\left(-\frac{\beta}{2}+\sqrt{\xi}\right) - \beta & -1 \\ \epsilon\gamma & -\epsilon \end{pmatrix}. \tag{33}$$

We might observe from the Jacobian matrix that

$$\mathrm{tr}(J_{(u_3^*,v_3^*)})= -3\left(-\frac{\beta}{2}+\sqrt{\xi}\right)^2 + 2(\beta+1)\left(-\frac{\beta}{2}+\sqrt{\xi}\right) - \beta - \epsilon,$$

$$= -\beta\left(\frac{7}{4}\beta+2\right) + \sqrt{\xi}(5\beta+2) - 3\xi - \epsilon,$$

$$\det(J_{(u_3^*,v_3^*)})= -\epsilon\left(-3\left(-\frac{\beta}{2}+\sqrt{\xi}\right)^2 + 2(\beta+1)\left(-\frac{\beta}{2}+\sqrt{\xi}\right) - \beta\right) + \epsilon\gamma,$$

$$= -\epsilon(\mathrm{tr}(J_{(u_3^*,v_3^*)}) + \epsilon) + \epsilon\gamma.$$

$$= \epsilon\left(\beta\left(\frac{7}{4}\beta+2\right) - \sqrt{\xi}(5\beta+2) + 3\xi + \gamma\right).$$

The characteristic equation (26) has the following discriminant

$$\Delta_\Lambda = \left(-\beta\left(\frac{7}{4}\beta+2\right) + \sqrt{\xi}(5\beta+2) - 3\xi + \epsilon\right)^2 - 4\epsilon\gamma. \tag{34}$$

Based on (34), we investigate each case independently.

* If $\Delta_\Lambda > 0$ and if $\det(J_{(u_3^*,v_3^*)}) > 0$, as a result, the eigenvalues' negativity is dependent on the sign of $\mathrm{tr}(J_{(u_3^*,v_3^*)})$, and the eigenvalues Λ_1 and Λ_2 are real and may be represented as

$$\Lambda_1 = \frac{\mathrm{tr}(J_{(u_3^*,v_3^*)}) - \sqrt{\Delta_\Lambda}}{2}, \qquad \Lambda_2 = \frac{\mathrm{tr}(J_{(u_3^*,v_3^*)}) + \sqrt{\Delta_\Lambda}}{2}. \tag{35}$$

- If $\mathrm{tr}(J_{(u_3^*,v_3^*)}) < 0$, then we have

$$\Lambda_1 = \frac{\mathrm{tr}(J_{(u_3^*,v_3^*)}) - \sqrt{\Delta_\Lambda}}{2} < 0. \tag{36}$$

As a result, $Arg(\Lambda_1) = \pi$. Since both eigenvalues are real, it is obvious that $Arg(\Lambda_1) = Arg(\Lambda_2) = \pi$. As a consequence, based on Theorem 3, the equilibrium $(u_3^*, {}^v *_3)$ is asymptotically stable.
- If $\mathrm{tr}(J_{(u_3^*,v_3^*)}) > 0$, then we have

$$\Lambda_2 = \frac{\mathrm{tr}(J_{(u_3^*,v_3^*)}) + \sqrt{\Delta_\Lambda}}{2} > 0. \tag{37}$$

Therefore, $Arg(\Lambda_2) = 0$, and based on Theorem 3, system (21) is unstable.

*   If $\Delta_\Lambda < 0$ and if $\det(J_{(u_3^*,v_3^*)}) > 0$, then

$$\Lambda_1 = \frac{\mathrm{tr}(J_{(u_3^*,v_3^*)}) - i\sqrt{-\Delta_\Lambda}}{2}, \qquad \Lambda_2 = \frac{\mathrm{tr}(J_{(u_3^*,v_3^*)}) + i\sqrt{-\Delta_\Lambda}}{2}. \tag{38}$$

We may discuss the solutions based on the sign of $\mathrm{tr}(J_{(u_3^*,v_3^*)})$.

- If $\mathrm{tr}(J_{(u_3^*,v_3^*)}) < 0$ or $\mathrm{tr}(J_{(u_3^*,v_3^*)}) > 0$, then, following the same case investigated previously, system (21) is asymptotically stable.
- If $\mathrm{tr}(J_{(u_3^*,v_3^*)}) = 0$, then

$$Arg\left(\frac{-i\sqrt{-\Delta_\Lambda}}{2}\right) = Arg\left(\frac{i\sqrt{-\Delta_\Lambda}}{2}\right) = \frac{\pi}{2},$$

and system (21) is asymptotically stable.

*   If $\Delta_\Lambda = 0$, and $\det(J_{(u_3^*,v_3^*)}) > 0$, $\mathrm{tr}(J_{(u_3^*,v_3^*)})$ cannot be equal to zero. The sign of the eigenvalues is the same as the sign of $\mathrm{tr}(J_{(u_3^*,v_3^*)})$. As a result, (u_3^*, v_3^*) is asymptotically stable for all $\vartheta \in (0,1]$ if $\mathrm{tr}(J_{(u_3^*,v_3^*)}) < 0$ and unstable if $\mathrm{tr}(J_{(u_3^*,v_3^*)}) > 0$.

The proof is completed. $\square$

4.2. Local Stability of the Diffusion System

We shall now show that in the presence of diffusion, the steady state (u^*, v^*) can be stable under certain parameter circumstances. We will adopt the same approach as in [50], first considering the eigenvalues of the following equation:

$$\Delta^2 x_{i-1}(t + h\vartheta) + \Lambda_i x_i(t + h\vartheta) = 0, \tag{39}$$

with the periodic boundary conditions:

$$x_0(t) = x_m(t), \quad x_1(t) = x_{m+1}(t). \tag{40}$$

We obtain

$$\begin{cases} {}_\hbar^C \Delta_{t_0}^\vartheta u_i(t) = -\dfrac{d_1}{k^2}\Lambda_i u_i(t + \hbar\vartheta) - u_i^3(t + \hbar\vartheta) + (\beta + 1)u_i^2(t + \hbar\vartheta) - \beta u_i(t + \hbar\vartheta) - v_i(t + \hbar\vartheta), \\[2mm] {}_\hbar^C \Delta_{t_0}^\vartheta v_i(t) = -\dfrac{d_2}{k^2}\Lambda_i v_i(t + \hbar\vartheta) + \epsilon u_i(t + \hbar\vartheta) - \epsilon\gamma v_i(t + \hbar\vartheta). \end{cases} \tag{41}$$

To explore the system's local asymptotic stability, we will linearize it. If the eigenvalues of the linearized system fulfill the conditions of Theorem 3, using fundamental linear operator theory and keeping the system's fractional structure in mind, we might state that (u^*, v^*) is asymptotically stable.

We derive the following by linearizing the reaction diffusion system (41) about the steady state, and we obtain

$$J_i = \begin{pmatrix} -\dfrac{d_1}{k^2}\Lambda_i - 3u_i^2(t + \hbar\vartheta) + 2(\beta + 1)u_i(t + \hbar\vartheta) - \beta & -1 \\[2ex] \epsilon\gamma & -\dfrac{d_2}{k^2}\Lambda_i - \epsilon \end{pmatrix}. \tag{42}$$

The following result is conducted.

Theorem 5. *System (17) is asymptotically stable if the following hold:*

- *We suppose that $\xi < 0$ and $(\beta - \epsilon)^2 > 4\epsilon\gamma$. System (17) is asymptotically stable at the steady state (u_0^*, v_0^*) if the following hold:*

  - *If $d_1 < d_2$ and $\frac{d_1}{k^2}\Lambda_i \leq -\beta$.*
  - *If $d_1 > d_2$ and $\frac{d_1}{k^2}\Lambda_i \leq -\beta$, and in addition, the eigenvalues*

  $$\mu_j(\Lambda_i) = \frac{\mathrm{tr}(J_{i(u_0^*, v_0^*)}) \pm \sqrt{\mathrm{tr}(J_{i(u_0^*, v_0^*)})^2 - 4\det(J_{i(u_0^*, v_0^*)})}}{2}, \quad j = 1, 2,$$

  satisfy $Arg(\mu_j(\Lambda_i)) > \dfrac{\vartheta\pi}{2}$.

- *We suppose that $\xi = 0$ and $(\frac{7}{2}(\beta + 1)^2\left(\frac{7}{8}(\beta + 1)^2 - \epsilon + \beta\right) > 4\epsilon(\beta + \gamma) - (\beta + \epsilon)^2$. System (17) is asymptotically stable at the steady state (u_1^*, v_1^*) if the following hold:*

  - *If $d_1 < d_2$ and $-\frac{d_1}{k^2}\Lambda_i \geq \frac{7}{4}(\beta + 1)^2 + \beta$.*
  - *If $d_1 > d_2$ and $-\frac{d_1}{k^2}\Lambda_i \geq \frac{7}{4}(\beta + 1)^2 + \beta$, and in addition, the eigenvalues*

  $$\mu_j(\Lambda_i) = \frac{\mathrm{tr}(J_{i(u_1^*, v_1^*)}) \pm \sqrt{\mathrm{tr}(J_{i(u_1^*, v_1^*)})^2 - 4\det(J_{i(u_1^*, v_1^*)})}}{2}, \quad j = 1, 2,$$

  satisfy $Arg(\mu_j(\Lambda_i)) > \dfrac{\vartheta\pi}{2}$.

- *We suppose that $\xi > 0$ and we have two cases:*

  - *If $\left(-\beta\left(\frac{7}{4}\beta + 2\right) - \sqrt{\xi}(3\beta + 2) - 3\xi + \epsilon\right)^2 > 4\epsilon\gamma$, system (17) is asymptotically stable at the steady state (u_2^*, v_2^*) if the following hold:*

    * *If $d_1 < d_2$ and $-\frac{d_1}{k^2}\Lambda_i \geq \beta\left(\frac{7}{4}\beta + 2\right) + \sqrt{\xi}(5\beta + 2) + 3\xi$.*

    * *If $d_1 > d_2$ and $-\frac{d_1}{k^2}\Lambda_i \geq \beta\left(\frac{7}{4}\beta + 2\right) + \sqrt{\xi}(5\beta + 2) + 3\xi$, and in addition, the eigenvalues*

    $$\mu_j(\Lambda_i) = \frac{\mathrm{tr}(J_{i(u_2^*, v_2^*)}) \pm \sqrt{\mathrm{tr}(J_{i(u_2^*, v_2^*)})^2 - 4\det(J_{i(u_2^*, v_2^*)})}}{2}, \quad j = 1, 2,$$

    satisfy $Arg(\mu_j(\Lambda_i)) > \dfrac{\vartheta\pi}{2}$.

  - *If $\left(-\beta\left(\frac{7}{4}\beta + 2\right) + \sqrt{\xi}(3\beta + 2) - 3\xi + \epsilon\right)^2 > 4\epsilon\gamma$, system (17) is asymptotically stable at the steady state (u_3^*, v_3^*) if the following hold:*

* If $d_1 < d_2$ and $\quad -\frac{d_1}{k^2}\Lambda_i \geq \beta\left(\frac{7}{4}\beta + 2\right) - \sqrt{\tilde{\zeta}}(5\beta + 2) + 3\tilde{\zeta}.$

* If $d_1 > d_2$ and $\quad -\frac{d_1}{k^2}\Lambda_i \geq \beta\left(\frac{7}{4}\beta + 2\right) - \sqrt{\tilde{\zeta}}(5\beta + 2) + 3\tilde{\zeta},$ *and in addition,*
  the eigenvalues

$$\mu_j(\Lambda_i) = \frac{\operatorname{tr}(J_{i(u_3^*,v_3^*)}) +-\sqrt{\operatorname{tr}(J_{i(u_3^*,v_3^*)})^2 - 4\det(J_{i(u_3^*,v_3^*)})}}{2}, \quad j = 1,2,$$

satisfy $\quad Arg(\mu_j(\Lambda_i)) > \dfrac{\vartheta\pi}{2}.$

Proof. The proof will be conducted following the same cases investigated in the free diffusion section.

* We first start with the origin (u_0^*, v_0^*), and we have

$$\begin{pmatrix} -\frac{d_1}{k^2}\Lambda_i - \beta & -1 \\ \epsilon\gamma & -\frac{d_2}{k^2}\Lambda_i - \epsilon \end{pmatrix} = J_{i(u_0^*,v_0^*)} - \lambda(\Lambda_i)I,$$

which has the eigenvalue equation

$$\mu^2(\Lambda_i) - \operatorname{tr}(J_{i(u_0^*,v_0^*)})\mu(\Lambda_i) + \det(J_{i(u_0^*,v_0^*)}) = 0, \tag{43}$$

where

$$\operatorname{tr}(J_{i(u_0^*,v_0^*)}) = -\left(\frac{d_1}{k^2} + \frac{d_2}{k^2}\right)\Lambda_i + \operatorname{tr}(J_{(u_0^*,v_0^*)}), \tag{44}$$

and

$$\det(J_{i(u_0^*,v_0^*)}) = \frac{d_1}{k^2}\frac{d_2}{k^2}\Lambda_i^2 + \left(\frac{d_1}{k^2}\epsilon + \frac{d_2}{k^2}\beta\right)\Lambda_i + \det(J_{(u_0^*,v_0^*)}),$$

and its discriminant is

$$\Delta_i = \operatorname{tr}^2(J_{i(u_0^*,v_0^*)}) - 4\det(J_{i(u_0^*,v_0^*)}) = \left(\frac{d_1}{k^2} - \frac{d_2}{k^2}\right)^2\Lambda_i^2 + 2\left(\frac{d_1}{k^2} - \frac{d_2}{k^2}\right)(\beta - \epsilon)\Lambda_i + \Delta_\Lambda.$$

The sign of Δ_i is important to the stability of (u_0^*, v_0^*). The discriminant of Δ_i in relation to Λ_i is

$$\Delta_{\Lambda_i} = \left(\left(\frac{d_1}{k^2} - \frac{d_2}{k^2}\right)(\beta - \epsilon)\Lambda_i\right)^2 - \left(\frac{d_1}{k^2} - \frac{d_2}{k^2}\right)^2\Lambda_i^2\Delta_\Lambda = 4\left(\frac{d_1}{k^2} - \frac{d_2}{k^2}\right)^2\epsilon\gamma.$$

Clearly, $\Delta_{\Lambda_i} > 0$, because with $d_1 \neq d_2$ we distinguish two cases:

− If $d_1 < d_2$, then $(\beta - \epsilon)^2 > 4\epsilon\gamma$, and the two solutions of the equation $\Delta_{\Lambda_i} = 0$ are both negative. Thus, $\Delta_i > 0$ and the roots of (43) are

$$\begin{cases} \mu_1(\Lambda_i) = \dfrac{\operatorname{tr}(J_{i(u_0^*,v_0^*)}) + \sqrt{\operatorname{tr}(J_i)^2 - 4\det(J_{i(u_0^*,v_0^*)})}}{2}, \\[3mm] \mu_2(\Lambda_i) = \dfrac{\operatorname{tr}(J_{i(u_0^*,v_0^*)}) - \sqrt{\operatorname{tr}(J_{i(u_0^*,v_0^*)})^2 - 4\det(J_{i(u_0^*,v_0^*)})}}{2}. \end{cases} \tag{45}$$

Note that the solutions are real, and also $\mu(\Lambda_i)_1 < 0$. In addition, if $-\frac{d_1}{k^2}\Lambda_1 \geq \beta$, then $\mu(\Lambda_i)_2 < 0$. This leads to

$$|Arg(\mu_1(\Lambda_i))| = |Arg(\mu_2(\Lambda_i)_2)| = \pi, \tag{46}$$

which ensures the asymptotic stability of (u_0^*, v_0^*).

- If $d_1 > d_2$, we have $(\beta - \epsilon)^2 > 4\epsilon\gamma$. This returns us to the previous scenario. Again, for $\frac{d_1}{k^2}\Lambda_1 \geq \beta$, $det(J_{i(u_0^*,v_0^*)}) > 0$; thus, $\mu_1(\Lambda_i)$ and $\mu_2(\Lambda_i)$ are negative and must meet the conditions of Theorem 3.

- Moving on to the second case where $\xi = 0$, we will investigate the stability of the equilibrium point (u_1^*, v_1^*), and in order to do so we consider the following:

$$\begin{pmatrix} -\frac{d_1}{k^2}\Lambda_i - \frac{7}{4}(\beta+1)^2 - \beta & -1 \\ \epsilon\gamma & -\frac{d_2}{k^2}\Lambda_i - \epsilon \end{pmatrix} = J_{i(u_1^*,v_1^*)} - \lambda(\Lambda_i)I,$$

where

$$\text{tr}(J_{i(u_1^*,v_1^*)}) = -\left(\frac{d_1}{k^2} + \frac{d_2}{k^2}\right)\Lambda_i + \text{tr}(J_{(u_1^*,v_1^*)}), \tag{47}$$

and

$$\det(J_{i(u_1^*,v_1^*)}) = \frac{d_1}{k^2}\frac{d_2}{k^2}\Lambda_i^2 + \left(\frac{d_1}{k^2}\epsilon + \frac{d_2}{k^2}\left(\frac{7}{4}(\beta+1) + \beta\right)\right)\Lambda_i + \det(J_{(u_1^*,v_1^*)}),$$

and its discriminant is

$$\Delta_i = \text{tr}^2(J_{i(u_0^*,v_0^*)}) - 4\det(J_{i(u_0^*,v_0^*)}) = \left(\frac{d_1}{k^2} - \frac{d_2}{k^2}\right)^2\Lambda_i^2 + 2\left(\frac{d_1}{k^2} - \frac{d_2}{k^2}\right)(\beta - \epsilon)\Lambda_i + \Delta_\Lambda.$$

In this case, we have the discriminant of Δ_i in relation to Λ_i, defined by

$$\Delta_{\Lambda_i} = \left(\left(\frac{d_1}{k^2} - \frac{d_2}{k^2}\right)(\beta - \epsilon)\Lambda_i\right)^2 - \left(\frac{d_1}{k^2} - \frac{d_2}{k^2}\right)^2\Lambda_i^2\Delta_\Lambda = 4\left(\frac{d_1}{k^2} - \frac{d_2}{k^2}\right)^2\epsilon\gamma.$$

We can clearly notice that the discriminant in this case is identical to the one calculated previously; therefore, we summarized the dynamics of the system concerning the (u_1^*, v_1^*) in Theorem 5.

- Moving on to the last case where $\xi > 0$, we will investigate the stability of the equilibrium points (u_2^*, v_2^*) and (u_3^*, v_3^*).

- We start by considering the Jacobian matrix of (u_2^*, v_2^*), and we have

$$\begin{pmatrix} -\frac{d_1}{k^2}\Lambda_i - \beta\left(\frac{7}{4}\beta + 2\right) - \sqrt{\xi}(5\beta + 2) - 3\xi & -1 \\ \epsilon\gamma & -\frac{d_2}{k^2}\Lambda_i - \epsilon \end{pmatrix} = J_{i(u_2^*,v_2^*)} - \lambda(\Lambda_i)I,$$

where

$$\text{tr}(J_{i(u_2^*,v_2^*)}) = -\left(\frac{d_1}{k^2} + \frac{d_2}{k^2}\right)\Lambda_i + \text{tr}(J_{(u_2^*,v_2^*)}), \tag{48}$$

and

$$\det(J_{i(u_2^*,v_2^*)}) = \frac{d_1}{k^2}\frac{d_2}{k^2}\Lambda_i^2 + \frac{d_1}{k^2}\epsilon + \frac{d_2}{k^2}\left(\beta\left(\frac{7}{4}\beta + 2\right) + \sqrt{\xi}(5\beta + 2) + 3\xi\right)\Lambda_i + \det(J_{(u_2^*,v_2^*)}),$$

and its discriminant is

$$\Delta_i = \left(\frac{d_1}{k^2} - \frac{d_2}{k^2}\right)^2\Lambda_i^2 + 2\left(\frac{d_1}{k^2} - \frac{d_2}{k^2}\right)\left(\beta\left(\frac{7}{4}\beta + 2\right) + \sqrt{\xi}(5\beta + 2) + 3\xi - \epsilon\right)\Lambda_i + \Delta_\Lambda.$$

The discriminant of Δ_i in relation to Λ_i is

$$\Delta_{\Lambda_i} = \left(\left(\frac{d_1}{k^2} - \frac{d_2}{k^2}\right)\left(\beta\left(\frac{7}{4}\beta + 2\right) + \sqrt{\xi}(5\beta + 2) + 3\xi - \epsilon\right)\right)^2 - \left(\frac{d_1}{k^2} - \frac{d_2}{k^2}\right)^2 \Lambda_i^2 \Delta_\Lambda,$$

$$= 4\left(\frac{d_1}{k^2} - \frac{d_2}{k^2}\right)^2 \epsilon\gamma.$$

The discriminant in this situation is obviously similar to the one determined previously; therefore, we summarized the dynamics of the system concerning the (u_2^*, v_2^*) in Theorem 5.

- Finally, let us consider the equilibrium point (u_3^*, v_3^*)

$$\begin{pmatrix} -\frac{d_1}{k^2}\Lambda_i - \beta\left(\frac{7}{4}\beta + 2\right) + \sqrt{\xi}(5\beta + 2) - 3\xi & -1 \\ \epsilon\gamma & -\frac{d_2}{k^2}\Lambda_i - \epsilon \end{pmatrix} = J_{i(u_3^*, v_3^*)} - \lambda(\Lambda_i)I,$$

where

$$\mathrm{tr}(J_{i(u_3^*, v_3^*)}) = -\left(\frac{d_1}{k^2} + \frac{d_2}{k^2}\right)\Lambda_i + \mathrm{tr}(J_{(u_3^*, v_3^*)}), \tag{49}$$

and

$$\det(J_{i(u_3^*, v_3^*)}) = \frac{d_1}{k^2}\frac{d_2}{k^2}\Lambda_i^2 + \frac{d_1}{k^2}\epsilon + \frac{d_2}{k^2}\left(\beta\left(\frac{7}{4}\beta + 2\right) - \sqrt{\xi}(5\beta + 2) + 3\xi\right)\Lambda_i + \det(J_{(u_3^*, v_3^*)}),$$

and its discriminant is

$$\Delta_i = \left(\frac{d_1}{k^2} - \frac{d_2}{k^2}\right)^2 \Lambda_i^2 + 2\left(\frac{d_1}{k^2} - \frac{d_2}{k^2}\right)\left(\beta\left(\frac{7}{4}\beta + 2\right) - \sqrt{\xi}(5\beta + 2) + 3\xi - \epsilon\right)\Lambda_i + \Delta_\Lambda.$$

The discriminant of Δ_i in relation to Λ_i is

$$\Delta_{\Lambda_i} = \left(\left(\frac{d_1}{k^2} - \frac{d_2}{k^2}\right)\left(\beta\left(\frac{7}{4}\beta + 2\right) + \sqrt{\xi}(5\beta + 2) + 3\xi - \epsilon\right)\right)^2 - \left(\frac{d_1}{k^2} - \frac{d_2}{k^2}\right)^2 \Lambda_i^2 \Delta_\Lambda,$$

$$= 4\left(\frac{d_1}{k^2} - \frac{d_2}{k^2}\right)^2 \epsilon\gamma.$$

We can easily see that the discriminant in this case is also similar to the one determined previously; thus, we outlined the dynamics of the system concerning the (u_3^*, v_3^*) in Theorem 5.

$\square$

5. Global Stability

In this part, we define the global asymptotic stability of the constant steady-state solution. It is possible to rewrite the discrete-time fractional FitzHugh–Nagumo system (17) as follows:

$$\begin{cases} {}^C_\hbar\Delta^\vartheta_{t_0} u_i(t) = \dfrac{k_1}{\Delta_x^2}\Delta^2 u_{i-1}(t + \hbar\vartheta) + (f(u_i) - f(u^*)) - (v_i(t + \hbar\vartheta) - v^*), \\[2mm] {}^C_\hbar\Delta^\vartheta_{t_0} v_i(t) = \dfrac{k_2}{\Delta_x^2}\Delta^2 v_{i-1}(t + \hbar\vartheta) + \epsilon\gamma\left(\dfrac{u_i(t + \hbar\vartheta)}{\vartheta} - \dfrac{u^*}{\vartheta} - (v_i(t + \hbar\vartheta) - v^*)\right). \end{cases} \tag{50}$$

We define the variables $U_i = u_i - u*$ and $V_i = v_i - v*$, such that the function $f(u_i)$ is defined as follows:

$$f(u_i) = -u_i^3 + (\beta + 1)u_i^2 - \beta u_i. \tag{51}$$

Theorem 6. *System (17) is globally asymptotically stable if the following holds:*

$$(u_i(t) - u^*)(f(u_i) - f(u^*)) > 0, \quad 1 \le i \le m. \tag{52}$$

Proof. To achieve the unique equilibrium point's global asymptotic stability (u^*, v^*), we evaluate the following function:

$$L(t) = \frac{1}{2} \sum_{i=1}^{m} \left(\left(\frac{u_i(t)}{\gamma} - \frac{u^*}{\gamma} \right)^2 + (v_i(t) - v^*)^2 \right). \tag{53}$$

Taking the Caputo h-difference operator and using Lemma 3, we have

$$
{}^{C}_{\hbar}\Delta^{\vartheta}_{t_0} L(t) = \frac{1}{2} \sum_{i=1}^{m} \left({}^{C}_{\hbar}\Delta^{\vartheta}_{t_0} \left(\frac{u_i(t)}{\gamma} - \frac{u^*}{\gamma} \right)^2 + {}^{C}_{\hbar}\Delta^{\vartheta}_{t_0} (v_i(t) - v^*)^2 \right),
$$

$$
\le \sum_{i=1}^{m} \left(\frac{u_i(t+\hbar\vartheta)}{\gamma} - \frac{u^*}{\gamma} \right) {}^{C}_{\hbar}\Delta^{\vartheta}_{t_0} \left(\frac{u_i(t)}{\gamma} - \frac{u^*}{\gamma} \right) + (v_i(t+\hbar\vartheta) - v^*) {}^{C}_{\hbar}\Delta^{\vartheta}_{t_0} (v_i(t) - v^*),
$$

$$
\le \sum_{i=1}^{m} \left(\frac{u_i(t+\hbar\vartheta)}{\gamma} - \frac{u^*}{\gamma} \right) \left(\frac{k_1}{\Delta_x^2} \Delta^2 u_{i-1}(t+\hbar\vartheta) + (f(u_i) - f(u^*)) \right.
$$

$$
\left. - (v_i(t+\hbar\vartheta) - v^*) \right) + (v_i(t+\hbar\vartheta) - v^*) \left(\frac{k_2}{\Delta_x^2} \Delta^2 v_{i-1}(t+\hbar\vartheta) \right.
$$

$$
\left. + \epsilon\gamma \left(\frac{u_i(t+\hbar\vartheta)}{\gamma} - \frac{u^*}{\gamma} - (v_i(t+\hbar\vartheta) - v^*) \right) \right),
$$

$$
\le \sum_{i=1}^{m} \frac{k_1}{\Delta_x^2} \left(\frac{u_i(t+\hbar\vartheta)}{\gamma} - \frac{u^*}{\gamma} \right) \Delta^2 u_{i-1}(t+\hbar\vartheta) + \frac{k_2}{\Delta_x^2} (v_i(t+\hbar\vartheta) - v^*) \Delta^2 v_{i-1}(t+\hbar\vartheta)
$$

$$
+ \sum_{i=1}^{m} \left(\frac{u_i(t+\hbar\vartheta)}{\gamma} - \frac{u^*}{\gamma} \right) \left((f(u_i) - f(u^*)) - (v_i(t+\hbar\vartheta) - v^*) \right)
$$

$$
+ \sum_{i=1}^{m} (v_i(t+\hbar\vartheta) - v^*) \left(\epsilon\gamma \left(\frac{u_i(t+\hbar\vartheta)}{\gamma} - \frac{u^*}{\gamma} - (v_i(t+\hbar\vartheta) - v^*) \right) \right),
$$

$$
= J_1(t) + J_2(t),
$$

where

$$J_1(t) = \sum_{i=1}^{m} \frac{k_1}{\Delta_x^2} \left(\frac{u_i(t+\hbar\vartheta)}{\gamma} - \frac{u^*}{\gamma} \right) \Delta^2 u_{i-1}(t+\hbar\vartheta) + \frac{k_2}{\Delta_x^2} (v_i(t+\hbar\vartheta) - v^*) \Delta^2 v_{i-1}(t+\hbar\vartheta), \tag{54}$$

$$J_2(t) = \sum_{i=1}^{m} \left(\frac{u_i(t+\hbar\vartheta)}{\gamma} - \frac{u^*}{\gamma} \right) \left((f(u_i) - f(u^*)) \right. \tag{55}$$

$$\left. - (v_i(t+\hbar\vartheta) - v^*) \right) + (v_i(t+\hbar\vartheta) - v^*) \left(\epsilon\gamma \left(\frac{u_i(t+\hbar\vartheta)}{\gamma} - \frac{u^*}{\gamma} - (v_i(t+\hbar\vartheta) - v^*) \right) \right). \tag{56}$$

We then examine the J_1 and J_2 signs:

$$J_1(t) = \sum_{i=1}^{m} \frac{k_1}{\Delta_x^2}\left(\frac{u_i(t+\hbar\vartheta)}{\gamma} - \frac{u^*}{\gamma}\right)\Delta^2 u_{i-1}(t+\hbar\vartheta) + \frac{k_2}{\Delta_x^2}(v_i(t+\hbar\vartheta) - v^*)\Delta^2 v_{i-1}(t+\hbar\vartheta),$$

$$= \sum_{i=1}^{m} \frac{k_1}{\gamma\Delta_x^2}(u_i(t+\hbar\vartheta) - u^*)\Delta^2(u_{i-1}(t+\hbar\vartheta) - u^*) + \frac{k_2}{\Delta_x^2}(v_i(t+\hbar\vartheta) - v^*)\Delta^2(v_{i-1}(t+\hbar\vartheta) - v^*)$$

$$= \sum_{i=1}^{m} \frac{k_1}{\gamma\Delta_x^2}(u_i(t+\hbar\vartheta) - u^*)\Delta(u_{i-1}(t+\hbar\vartheta) - u^*)|_1^{m+1}$$

$$+ \frac{k_2}{\Delta_x^2}(v_i(t+\hbar\vartheta) - v^*)\Delta(v_{i-1}(t+\hbar\vartheta) - v^*)|_1^{m+1} - \sum_{i=1}^{m} \frac{k_1}{\gamma\Delta_x^2}(\Delta(u_{i-1}(t+\hbar\vartheta) - u^*))^2$$

$$- \frac{k_2}{\Delta_x^2}(\Delta(v_{i-1}(t+\hbar\vartheta) - v^*))^2 < 0.$$

$$J_2(t) = \sum_{i=1}^{m}\left(\frac{u_i(t+\hbar\vartheta)}{\gamma} - \frac{u^*}{\gamma}\right)((f(u_i) - f(u^*)) - (v_i(t+\hbar\vartheta) - v^*))$$

$$+ (v_i(t+\hbar\vartheta) - v^*)(\epsilon\gamma(\frac{u_i(t+\hbar\vartheta)}{\gamma} - \frac{u^*}{\gamma} - (v_i(t+\hbar\vartheta) - v^*)))),$$

$$\leq \sum_{i=1}^{m}\left(\frac{u_i(t+\hbar\vartheta)}{\gamma} - \frac{u^*}{\gamma}\right)(f(u_i) - f(u^*)) - \frac{\epsilon}{\gamma}(u_i(t+\hbar\vartheta) - u^*)(v_i(t+\hbar\vartheta) - v^*)$$

$$+ \frac{\epsilon}{\gamma}(v_i(t+\hbar\vartheta) - v^*)(u_i(t+\hbar\vartheta) - u^*) - (v_i(t+\hbar\vartheta) - v^*)^2,$$

$$\leq \sum_{i=1}^{m}\left(\frac{u_i(t+\hbar\vartheta)}{\gamma} - \frac{u^*}{\vartheta}\right)(f(u_i) - f(u^*)) - (v_i(t+\hbar\vartheta) - v^*)^2.$$

Now, the following hold:

- If $u_i(t+\hbar\vartheta) \leq u^*$, then $\quad(u_i(t+\hbar\vartheta) - u^*)(f(u_i) - f(u*)) < 0.$
- If $u_i(t+\hbar\vartheta) \geq u^*$, then $\quad(u_i(t+\hbar\vartheta) - u^*)(f(u_i) - f(u*)) < 0.$

This means that $L(t) < 0$, and according to Theorem 2, the system is globally asymptotically stable. $\quad\square$

6. Numerical Simulations

In this part, we show some exemplary simulations of the theoretical properties of the stability of the discrete-time fractional FitzHugh–Nagumo reaction–diffusion system. We can observe the behavior of the system by modifying its parameters and order. We use the following numerical solution, and the system (17) appears as follows:

$$\begin{cases} u_i(n\hbar) = \phi_1(x_i) + \dfrac{\hbar^\vartheta}{\Gamma(\vartheta)}\sum_{j=1}^{n}\dfrac{\Gamma(n-j+\vartheta)}{\Gamma(n-j+1)}[s\dfrac{u_{i+1}((j-1)\hbar) - 2u_i((j-1)\hbar) + u_{i-1}((j-1)\hbar)}{k^2} \\ \quad -u^3((j-1)\hbar) + (\beta+1)u^2((j-1)\hbar) - \beta u((j-1)\hbar) - v_i((j-1)\hbar)], \\ v_i(n\hbar) = \phi_2(x_i) + \dfrac{\hbar^\vartheta}{\Gamma(\vartheta)}\sum_{j=1}^{n}\dfrac{\Gamma(n-j+\vartheta)}{\Gamma(n-j+1)}[\dfrac{v_{i+1}((j-1)\hbar) - 2v_i((j-1)\hbar) + v_{i-1}((j-1)\hbar)}{k^2} \\ \quad +\epsilon u_i((j-1)\hbar) - \epsilon\gamma v_i((j-1)\hbar)], \\ 1 \leq i \leq m, \\ n > 0. \end{cases} \tag{57}$$

Example 1. *Consider the following parameter values of model (17):* $N = 110$, $(\beta, \epsilon, \gamma, d_1, d_2) = (0.139, 0.7, 0.18, 2, 3)$ $\hbar = 0.18$, $t \in [0, 20]$, $x \in [0, 20]$, *and the boundary conditions* $(u_0(t), v_0(t)) = (2, 3)$, $(u_1(t), v_1(t)) = (2, 3)$, *with the initial conditions*

$$\begin{cases} \phi_1(x_i) = 1 - \sin(\pi x_i), \\ \phi_2(x_i) = 3 - \sin(\pi x_i). \end{cases}$$

We see that all of our model's solutions converge at some point to the equilibrium point $(u^*, v^*) = (0.64, 0.12)$. *The unique equilibrium is thus asymptotically stable. This numerical conclusion is consistent with our earlier theoretical results. Figures 1–3 display the results mentioned earlier for different orders.*

Example 2. *In this example, we set the following parameter of the model (17):* $N = 110$, $(\beta, \epsilon, \gamma, d_1, d_2) = (0.3, 0.01, 0.1, 0.1, 0.7)$ $\hbar = 0.4$, $t \in [0, 20]$, $x \in [0, 20]$ *and the boundary conditions* $(u_0(t), v_0(t)) = (1, 3)$, $(u_1(t), v_1(t)) = (1, 3)$, *with the initial conditions*

$$\begin{cases} \phi_1(x_i) = 3 + \cos\left(\dfrac{\pi x_i}{2}\right), \\ \phi_2(x_i) = 2 + \cos\left(\dfrac{\pi x_i}{2}\right). \end{cases}$$

We can observe that the solutions of the model converge to the equilibrium point $(u^*, v^*) = (0, 0)$. *As a result, the unique equilibrium is asymptotically stable. This numerical solution agrees with the theories provided in the previous sections, as displayed in Figures 4–6 for different fractional orders.*

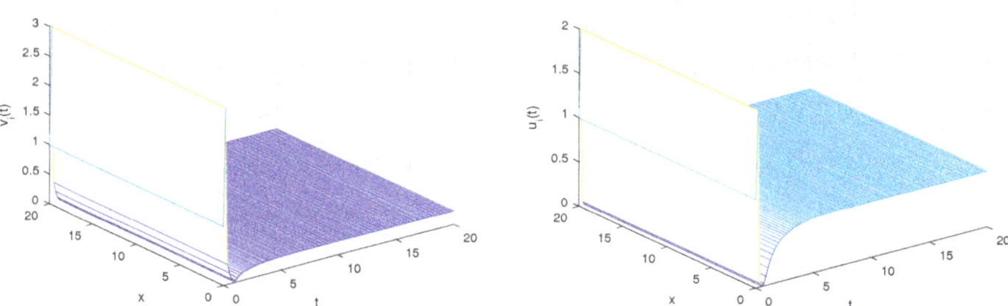

Figure 1. State trajectories of r $u_i(t)$ and $v_i(t)$ for $\vartheta = 0.3$.

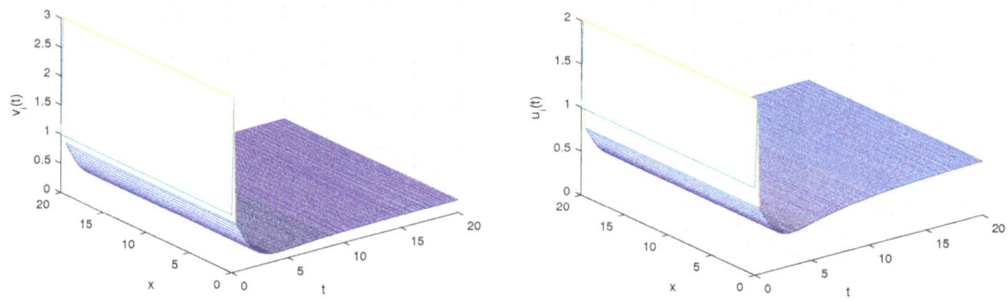

Figure 2. State trajectories of r $u_i(t)$ and $v_i(t)$ for $\vartheta = 0.05$.

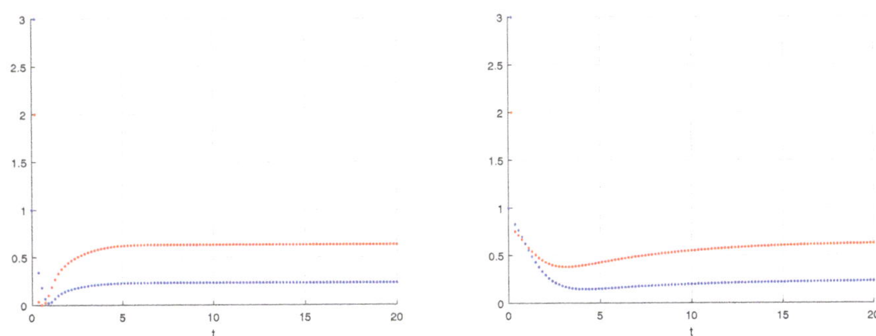

Figure 3. Dynamic behaviors of $u_i(t)$ and $v_i(t)$ $\vartheta = 0.3$ and $\vartheta = 0.05$.

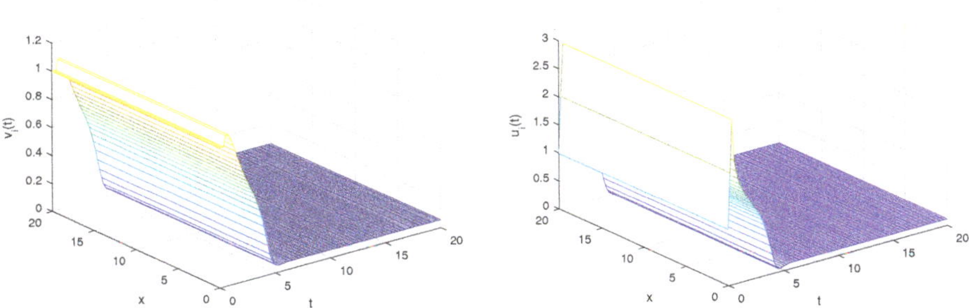

Figure 4. Numerical solution of $u_i(t)$ and $v_i(t)$ for $(\beta, \epsilon, \gamma, d_1, d_2) = (0.3, 0.01, 0.1, 0.1, 0.7)$ and $\vartheta = 0.2$.

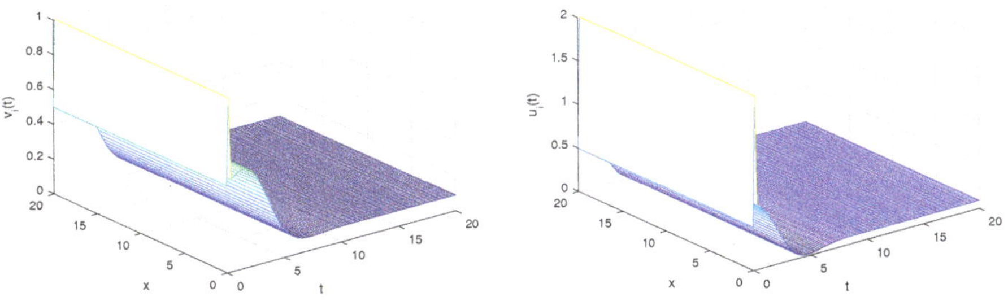

Figure 5. Numerical solution of $u_i(t)$ and $v_i(t)$ for $(\beta, \epsilon, \gamma, d_1, d_2) = (0.3, 0.01, 0.1, 0.1, 0.7)$ and $\vartheta = 0.8$.

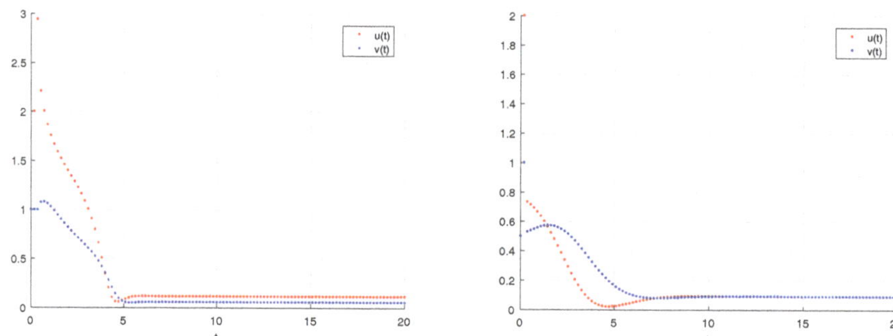

Figure 6. Dynamic behaviors of $u_i(t)$ and $v_i(t)$ $\vartheta = 0.8$ and $\vartheta = 0.2$.

7. Conclusions

In this paper, we looked at a discrete-time fractional-order variant of the reaction diffusion FitzHugh–Nagumo system. We provided adequate constraints for the unique equilibrium's local asymptotic stability. Moreover, with the help of the direct Lyapunov technique, the steady-state solution's global asymptotic stability was established. Finally, the simulation results illustrate all of the theoretical investigations' results. In the future, further research will be performed to examine this kind of discrete-time reaction–diffusion system.

Moreover, the linearization approach and the Lyapunov functional may be utilized to solve the issue of stability in discrete fractional reaction–diffusion models. In addition, the results of this study may be readily applicable to many various types of discrete fractional spatiotemporal systems with reaction–diffusion terms, as well as to other dynamical issues, such as chaos and synchronization control.

Author Contributions: T.H., A.H., O.A., Y.A.A.-K., A.A.-H. and A.O.; Conceptualization, T.H. and A.A.-H.; Formal analysis, O.A.; Investigation, T.H. and Y.A.A.-K.; Methodology, Y.A.A.-K.; Software, A.H.; Supervision, A.O.; Validation, O.A.; Visualization, A.A.-H.; Writing—original draft, A.H.; Writing—review and editing, A.O. All authors have read and agreed to the published version of the manuscript.

Funding: This research received no external funding.

Data Availability Statement: Not applicable.

References

1. Miller, K.S.; Ross, B. *An Introduction to the Fractional Calculus and Fractional Differential Equations*; Wiley: Hoboken, NJ, USA, 1993.
2. Oldham, K.B. *The Fractional Calculus*; Spanier, J., Ed.; Academic Press: New York, NY, USA, 1974.
3. Samko, S.G.; Kilbas, A.A.; Marichev, O.I. *Fractional Integrals and Derivatives*; Gordon and Breach Science Publishers: Cham, Switzerland, 1993.
4. Sun, H.; Zhang, Y.; Baleanu, D.; Chen, W.; Chen, Y. A new collection of real world applications of fractional calculus in science and engineering. *Commun. Nonlinear Sci. Numer. Simul.* **2018**, *64*, 213–231. [CrossRef]
5. Dababneh, A.; Djenina, N.; Ouannas, A.; Grassi, G.; Batiha, I.M.; Jebril, I.H. A new incommensurate fractional-order discrete COVID-19 model with vaccinated individuals compartment. *Fractal Fract.* **2022**, *6*, 456. [CrossRef]
6. Bonfanti, A.; Kaplan, J.L.; Charras, G.; Kabla, A. Fractional viscoelastic models for power-law materials. *Soft Matter* **2020**, *16*, 6002–6020. [CrossRef] [PubMed]
7. Skwara, U.; Martins, J.; Ghaffari, P.; Aguiar, M.; Boto, J.; Stollenwerk, N. Applications of fractional calculus to epidemiological models. *Aip Conf. Proc.* **2012**, *1479*, 1339–1342.
8. Acay, B.; Bas, E.; Abdeljawad, T. Fractional economic models based on market equilibrium in the frame of different type kernels. Solitons Fractals **2020**, *130*, 109438. [CrossRef]
9. Tarasov, V.E. Mathematical economics: Application of fractional calculus. *Mathematics* **2020**, *8*, 660. [CrossRef]
10. Acay, B.; Inc, M. Electrical circuits RC, LC, and RLC under generalized type non-local singular fractional operator. *Fractal Fract.* **2021**, *5*, 9. [CrossRef]

11. Atici, F.M.; Eloe, P.W. A transform method in discrete fractional calculus. *Int. J. Differ. Equ.* **2007**, *2*, 165–176.
12. Atici, F.; Eloe, P. Initial value problems in discrete fractional calculus. *Proc. Am. Math. Soc.* **2009**, *137*, 981–989. [CrossRef]
13. Atici, F. M.; Eloe, P. Discrete fractional calculus with the nabla operator. *Electron. J. Qual. Theory Differ. Equ.* **2009**, *2009*. [CrossRef]
14. Atıcı, F.M.; Şengül, S. Modeling with fractional difference equations. *J. Math. Anal. Appl.* **2010**, *369*, 1. [CrossRef]
15. Holm, M. Cubo Sum and difference compositions in discrete fractional calculus. *Temuco* **2011**, *13*, 153–184.
16. Atıcı, F.M.; Eloe, P.W. Two-point boundary value problems for finite fractional difference equations. *J. Differ. Equ. Appl.* **2011**, *17*, 445–456. [CrossRef]
17. Hioual, A.; Ouannas, A.; Grassi, G.; Oussaeif, T.E. Nonlinear nabla variable-order fractional discrete systems: Asymptotic stability and application to neural networks. *J. Comput. Appl. Math.* **2023**, *423*, 114939 [CrossRef]
18. Batiha, I.M.; Alshorm, S.; Ouannas, A.; Momani, S.; Ababneh, O.Y.; Albdareen, M. Modified Three-Point Fractional Formulas with Richardson Extrapolation. *Mathematics* **2022**, *10*, 3489. [CrossRef]
19. Saadeh, R.; Abbes, A.; Al-Husban, A.; Ouannas, A.; Grassi, G. The Fractional Discrete Predator–Prey Model: Chaos, Control and Synchronization. *Fractal Fract.* **2023**, *7*, 120. [CrossRef]
20. Ouannas, A.; Batiha, I.M.; Bekiros, S.; Liu, J.; Jahanshahi, H.; Aly, A.A.; Alghtani, A.H. Synchronization of the glycolysis reaction-diffusion model via linear control law. *Entropy* **2021**, *23*, 1516. [CrossRef]
21. Al Noufaey, K.S. Stability analysis for Selkov-Schnakenberg reaction-diffusion system. *Open Math.* **2021**, *19*, 46–62. [CrossRef]
22. Madzvamuse, A.; Gaffney, E.A.; Maini, P.K. Stability analysis of non-autonomous reaction-diffusion systems: The effects of growing domains. *J. Math. Biol.* **2010**, *61*, 133–164. [CrossRef]
23. Anakira, N.; Hioual, A.; Ouannas, A.; Oussaeif, T.E.; Batiha, I.M. Global Asymptotic Stability for Discrete-Time SEI Reaction-Diffusion Model. In Proceedings of the International Conference on Mathematics and Computations, Amman, Jordan, 11–13 May 2022; Springer Nature Singapore: Singapore, 2022; pp. 345–357.
24. Henry, B.I.; Wearne, S.L. Fractional reaction–diffusion. *Phys. A Stat. Mech. Its Appl.* **2000**, *276*, 448–455. [CrossRef]
25. Gafiychuk, V.; Datsko, B.; Meleshko, V. Mathematical modeling of time fractional reaction–diffusion systems. *J. Comput. Appl. Math.* **2008**, *220*, 215–225. [CrossRef]
26. Khan, H.; Gómez-Aguilar, J.F.; Khan, A.; Khan, T.S. Stability analysis for fractional order advection–reaction diffusion system. *Phys. A Stat. Mech. Its Appl.* **2019**, *521*, 737–751. [CrossRef]
27. Lu, Z.; Yu, Y.; Ren, G.; Xu, C.; Meng, X. Global dynamics for a class of reaction–diffusion multigroup SIR epidemic models with time fractional-order derivatives. *Nonlinear Anal. Model. Control* **2022**, *27*, 142–162. [CrossRef]
28. Almatroud, O.A.; Hioual, A.; Ouannas, A.; Grassi, G. On Fractional-Order Discrete-Time Reaction Diffusion Systems. *Mathematics* **2023**, *11*, 2447. [CrossRef]
29. Wu, G.C.; Baleanu, D.; Zeng, S.D.; Deng, Z.G. Discrete fractional diffusion equation. *Nonlinear Dyn.* **2015**, *80*, 281–286. [CrossRef]
30. Wu, G.C.; Baleanu, D.; Xie, H.P.; Zeng, S.D. Applications of variable-order fractional operators: A review. *Int. J. Bifurc. Chaos* **2016**, *26*, 1650013 [CrossRef]
31. Hodgkin, A.L.; Huxley, A.F. Current and Its Application to Conduction. *J. Physiol.* **1952**, *117*, 500–544. [CrossRef]
32. Pikovsky, A.S.; Kurths, J. Coherence resonance in a noise-driven excitable system. *Phys. Rev. Lett.* **1997**, *78*, 775. [CrossRef]
33. Makarov, V.A.; Nekorkin, V.I.; Velarde, M.G. Spiking behavior in a noise-driven system combining oscillatory and excitatory properties. *Phys. Rev. Lett.* **2001**, *86*, 3431. [CrossRef]
34. Lindner, B.; Garcıa-Ojalvo, J.; Neiman, A.; Schimansky-Geier, L. Effects of noise in excitable systems. *Phys. Rep.* **2004**, *392*, 321–424. [CrossRef]
35. Bendoukha, S.; Abdelmalek, S.; Kirane, M. Spiral-generation mechanism in the two-dimensional FitzHugh–Nagumo system. *Nonlinear Anal. Real World Appl.* **2020**, *53*, 103052 [CrossRef]
36. Ambrosio, B.; Aziz-Alaoui, M.A. Synchronization and control of coupled reaction–diffusion systems of the FitzHug–Nagumo type. *Comput. Math. Appl.* **2012**, *64*, 934–943.
37. Ouannas, A.; Mesdoui, F.; Momani, S.; Batiha, I.; Grassi, G. Synchronization of FitzHugh-Nagumo reaction-diffusion systems via one-dimensional linear control law. *Arch. Control. Sci.* **2021**, *31*, 1–13.
38. Al-Juaifri, G.A.; Harfash, A.J. Finite element analysis of nonlinear reaction–diffusion system of fitzhugh–nagumo type with robin boundary conditions. *Math. Comput. Simul.* **2023**, *203*, 486–517. [CrossRef]
39. Khanday, F.A.; Kant, N.A.; Dar, M.R.; Zulkifli, T.Z.A.; Psychalinos, C. Low-voltage low-power integrable CMOS circuit implementation of integer- and fractional-order FitzHugh–Nagumo neuron model. *IEEE Trans. Neural Netw. Learn. Syst.* **2018**, *30*, 2108–2122. [CrossRef]
40. Tabi, C.B. Dynamical analysis of the FitzHugh–Nagumo oscillations through a modified Van der Pol equation with fractional-order derivative term. *Int. J. Non-Linear Mech.* **2018**, *105*, 173–178. [CrossRef]
41. Kelley, W.G.; Peterson, A.C. *Difference Equations: An Introduction with Applications*; Academic Press: Cambridge, MA, USA, 2001.
42. Baleanu, D.; Wu, G.C.; Bai, Y.R.; Chen, F.L. Stability analysis of Caputo–like discrete fractional systems. *Commun. Nonlinear Sci. Numer. Simul.* **2017**, *48*, 520–530. [CrossRef]
43. Hioual, A.; Ouannas, A.; Oussaeif, T.E.; Grassi, G.; Batiha, I.M.; Momani, S. On variable-order fractional discrete neural networks: Solvability and stability. *Fractal Fract.* **2022**, *6*, 119. [CrossRef]
44. Abdeljawad, T. Different type kernel h-fractional differences and their fractional h-sums. *Chaos Solitons Fractals* **2018**, *116*, 146–156. [CrossRef]

45. Čermák, J.; Nechvátal, L. On a problem of linearized stability for fractional difference equations. *Nonlinear Dyn.* **2021**, *104*, 1253–1267. [CrossRef]
46. Zheng, Q.; Shen, J. Pattern formation in the FitzHugh–Nagumo model. *Comput. Math. Appl.* **2015**, *70*, 1082–1097. [CrossRef]
47. Tasbozan, O. A popular reaction-diffusion model fractional Fitzhugh-Nagumo equation: Analytical and numerical treatment. *Appl. Math. J. Chin. Univ.* **2021**, *36*, 218–228. [CrossRef]
48. Smith, G.D.; Smith, G.D.; Smith, G.D.S. *Numerical Solution of Partial Differential Equations: Finite Difference Methods*; Oxford University Press: Oxford, UK, 1985.
49. Ringqvist, M. On dynamical behaviour of FitzHugh-Nagumo systems. *Res. Rep. Math.* **2006**, *5*, 1–81. [CrossRef]
50. Xu, L.; Zhao, L.J.; Chang, Z.X.; Feng, J.T.; Zhang, G. Turing instability and pattern formation in a semi-discrete Brusselator model. *Mod. Phys. Lett.* **2013**, *27*, 1350006. [CrossRef]

Article

Synchronization of Fractional Partial Difference Equations via Linear Methods

Ibraheem Abu Falahah [1], Amel Hioual [2,*], Mowafaq Omar Al-Qadri [3], Yazan Alaya AL-Khassawneh [4], Abdallah Al-Husban [5], Tareq Hamadneh [6] and Adel Ouannas [7]

1.   Department of Mathematics, Faculty of Science, The Hashemite University, P.O. Box 330127, Zarqa 13133, Jordan; iabufalahah@hu.edu.jo
2.   Laboratory of Dynamical Systems and Control, University of Larbi Ben M'hidi, Oum El Bouaghi 04000, Algeria
3.   Department of Mathematics, Jerash University, Jerash 26150, Jordan; m.alqadri@jpu.edu.jo
4.   Data Science and Artificial Intelligence Department, Zarqa University, Zarqa 13110, Jordan; ykhassawneh@zu.edu.jo
5.   Department of Mathematics, Faculty of Science and Technology, Irbid National University, Irbid 2600, Jordan; dralhosban@inu.edu.jo
6.   Department of Mathematics, Faculty of Science, Al Zaytoonah University of Jordan, Amman 11733, Jordan; t.hamadneh@zuj.edu.jo
7.   Department of Mathematics and Computer Science, University of Larbi Ben M'hidi, Oum El Bouaghi 04000, Algeria; ouannas.adel@univ-oeb.dz
*   Correspondence: amel.hioual@univ-oeb.dz

Citation: Abu Falahah, I.; Hioual, A.; Al-Qadri, M.O.; AL-Khassawneh, Y.A.; Al-Husban, A.; Hamadneh, T.; Ouannas, A. Synchronization of Fractional Partial Difference Equations via Linear Methods. *Axioms* 2023, *12*, 728. https://doi.org/10.3390/axioms12080728

Academic Editors: Azhar Ali Zafar and Nehad Ali Shah

Received: 8 June 2023
Revised: 30 June 2023
Accepted: 3 July 2023
Published: 27 July 2023

Abstract: Discrete fractional models with reaction-diffusion have gained significance in the scientific field in recent years, not only due to the need for numerical simulation but also due to the stated biological processes. In this paper, we investigate the problem of synchronization-control in a fractional discrete nonlinear bacterial culture reaction-diffusion model using the Caputo h-difference operator and a second-order central difference scheme and an L1 finite difference scheme after deriving the discrete fractional version of the well-known Degn–Harrison system and Lengyel–Epstein system. Using appropriate techniques and the direct Lyapunov method, the conditions for full synchronization are determined. Furthermore, this research shows that the L1 finite difference scheme and the second-order central difference scheme may successfully retain the properties of the related continuous system. The conclusions are proven throughout the paper using two major biological models, and numerical simulations are carried out to demonstrate the practical use of the recommended technique.

Keywords: fractional discrete reaction-diffusion Degn-Harrison system; discrete-time fractional reaction-diffusion Lengyel–Epstein system; second-order difference operator; Caputo $\hbar$-difference operator; complete synchronization; Lyapunov method

MSC: 39A12; 39A30; 39A60; 34K24

1. Introduction

    One of the most essential components of dynamic system analysis is the construction of adequate functions identified as controllers to ensure synchronization. To understand how these systems achieve their distinctive synchronization behavior, a great variety of mathematical models have been suggested and studied. For continuous-space systems, mathematical modeling of oscillating biological or chemical media, for example, takes the form of reaction-diffusion equations. This type of model shows intricate dynamical structures such as bifurcations, spatial patterns, and turning instability. It has been demonstrated that reaction-diffusion systems, such as low-dimensional oscillators, may exhibit synchronization. For example, Mesdoui et al. [1] examined the synchronization of the

Degn–Harrison reaction-diffusion system. Ref. [2] was concerned with the synchronization control of the Lengyel–Epstein reaction-diffusion system. Furthermore, the synchronization of the FitzHugh–Nagumo reaction-diffusion model using a particular control rule was detailed in [3]. Other works regarding this subject may be found in [4,5].

In real-world applications, fractional-order nonlinear equations are frequently employed to describe a wide range of physical phenomena [6–9]. Scientists are still fascinated by fractional calculus because of its numerous applications in physics, chemistry, biology, electronics, electrical engineering, mechanics, signal processing, and control [10–15]. As a result, in recent years, scholars have grown particularly interested in it. However, over the last decade, there has been a spike in attention to fractional reaction-diffusion systems, particularly on the topic of synchronization. For instance, in [16], a hybrid technique for synchronizing between two integer and fractional-order reaction-diffusion systems is proposed, with applications to particular chemical models. Moreover, In [17], the dynamics of the activator–inhibitor system known as the Gierer–Meinhardt system, which is utilized to describe the interactions of chemical and biological phenomena, was investigated.

The discrete form of fractional calculus is a novel approach with enormous potential applications in a variety of scientific and industrial fields. The application has attracted tremendous attention in the past few years (see [18–25]). The purpose of the latest investigations in this area is fundamental. Fractional difference equations, on the one hand, enhance classical differential equations. In addition, they provide for a feasible comparison of the behaviors of fractional difference and fractional differential equations.

Many physical phenomena rely on spatially discrete systems, often known as discrete reaction-diffusion systems. In fact, the discreteness and structure of the underlying spatial domain influence dynamical behavior significantly. Active PIN-induced transport across cell membranes, for instance, is required for auxin spreading across plant leaves [26]. Peierls–Nabarro barriers are often used to prevent tiny faults from propagating across discrete media, although they can be avoided by carefully modifying system characteristics [27]. Discrete reaction-diffusion systems are more similar to biological systems than continuous ones, and certain investigations on the behavior of such systems are particularly fascinating (see [25,28–30]). Nevertheless, fractional discrete reaction-diffusion equations have not yet been extensively studied [31]. A fractional discrete diffusion equation was presented by [32]. In [33], the chaotic behavior of a variable fractional diffusion equation on discontinuous time scales is examined. Clearly, there is a gap in our comprehension of the dynamics of such systems.

To the best of the authors' knowledge, this is the first work dealing with the synchronization and control of discrete fractional reaction-diffusion systems. This has prompted us to investigate the issue of complete synchronization in coupled discrete fractional reaction-diffusion systems. With the help of the fractional Lyapunov approach, linear control laws for the discrete fractional reaction-diffusion Degn–Harrison system and Lengyel–Epstein systems have been proposed after driving the discrete version of the considered systems using the L1 finite difference scheme and the second-order central difference scheme. The following is how the paper is managed: Section 2 introduces some essential concepts and lemmas for discrete fractional calculus. Section 3 describes the models investigated in this study, which are the fractional discrete reaction-diffusion Lengyel–Epstein and Degn–Harrison systems, and presents a unique discrete temporal fractional reaction-diffusion system. Section 4 contains the discrete fractional Lengyel–Epstein reaction-diffusion system's master-slave formulation, along with unique control rules and demonstrations of convergence based on an appropriate Lyapunov functional. Section 5 employs the same approach to drive the master-slave discrete fractional Degn–Harrison reaction-diffusion system, as well as control laws and proofs of convergence. In Section 6, control laws are derived analytically and numerically in two dimensions to achieve synchronization between the master-slave systems of the investigated models.

2. Preliminaries

This part starts with an overview of some of the topic's primary concepts.

Definition 1 ([21]). *Assuming* $x : \mathbb{N} \to \mathbb{R}$, *the forward difference operator Delta is expressed by*

$$\Delta x(i) = x(i+1) - x(i), \quad i \in \mathbb{N}.$$

Additionally, the operators Δ^n; $n = 1; 2; 3; \dots$, *are recursively determined by*

$$\Delta^n x(i) = \Delta(\Delta^{n-1} x(i)), \quad i \in \mathbb{N}.$$

More specifically, the second-order difference operator of the function $x(i)$ *is provided by*

$$\Delta^2 x(i) = x(i+2) - 2x(i+1) + x(i). \tag{1}$$

Theorem 1 ([21]). *Given two functions* $x; y : \mathbb{N}_a \to \mathbb{R}$ *and* $a; b \in \mathbb{N}$; $a < b$; *we have the following formulae for summation by parts:*

$$\sum_{i=a}^{b-1} x(i)\Delta y(i) = x(i)y(i)\big|_a^b - \sum_{i=a}^{b-1} y(i+1)\Delta x(i),$$

$$\sum_{i=a}^{b-1} x(i+1)\Delta y(i) = x(i)y(i)\big|_a^b - \sum_{i=a}^{b-1} y(i)\Delta x(i).$$

Definition 2 ([22]). *Let* $x \in (\mathfrak{h}\mathbb{N})_a \to \mathbb{R}$. *The* $\mathfrak{h}$-*sum of the* ζ−*th order for each* $\zeta > 0$ *has been provided by*

$$\mathfrak{h}\Delta_a^{-\zeta} x(t) = \frac{\mathfrak{h}}{\Gamma(\zeta)} \sum_{s=\frac{a}{\mathfrak{h}}}^{\frac{t}{\mathfrak{h}}-\zeta} (t - \sigma(s\mathfrak{h}))_{\mathfrak{h}}^{(\zeta-1)} x(s\mathfrak{h}),$$

$$\sigma(s\mathfrak{h}) = (s+1)\mathfrak{h}, \quad t \in (\mathfrak{h}\mathbb{N})_{a+\zeta\mathfrak{h}}.$$

where $a \in \mathbb{R}$ *is the initial value and the* $\mathfrak{h}$-*falling factorial function is stated as*

$$t_{\mathfrak{h}}^{(\zeta)} = \mathfrak{h}^\zeta \frac{\Gamma(\frac{t}{\mathfrak{h}}+1)}{\Gamma(\frac{t}{\mathfrak{h}}+1-\zeta)}.$$

while

$$(\mathfrak{h}\mathbb{N})_{a+\zeta\mathfrak{h}} = \{a + (1-\zeta)\mathfrak{h}, a + (2-\zeta)\mathfrak{h}, \dots\}.$$

Definition 3 ([22]). *For* $x(t)$ *given on* $(\mathfrak{h}\mathbb{N})_a$ *and a stated* $0 < \zeta < 1$, *the Caputo* $\mathfrak{h}$-*difference operator is supplied:*

$$_{\mathfrak{h}}^{C}\Delta_a^\zeta x(t) = _{\mathfrak{h}}\Delta_a^{-(n-\zeta)}\Delta_{\mathfrak{h}}^n x(t).$$

where $\Delta_{\mathfrak{h}}^n x(t) = \dfrac{x(t+\mathfrak{h}) - x(t)}{\mathfrak{h}}.$

The following are a few essential properties that have been used in this work.

Lemma 1 ([22]). *For* $t \in (h\mathbb{N})_{a+\zeta\mathfrak{h}}$ *and* $0 < \zeta \le 1$, *the following proprieties hold:*

-

$$_{\mathfrak{h}}\Delta_{a+(1-\zeta)\mathfrak{h}}^{-\zeta}\,_{\mathfrak{h}}^{C}\Delta^\zeta x(t) = x(t) - x(a).$$

- *For a constant* x

$$_{\mathfrak{h}}^{C}\Delta^\zeta x = 0.$$

Lemma 2 ([22]). *For $t \in (h\mathbb{N})_{a+\zeta h}$, inequality (2) holds true.*

$$\,^{C}_{h}\Delta^{\zeta}_{a} x^{2}(t) \leq 2x(t + \zeta h)\,^{C}_{h}\Delta^{\zeta}_{a}x(t), \tag{2}$$

where $0 < \zeta \leq 1$.

Considering the fractional-order difference system:

$$\,^{C}_{h}\Delta^{\zeta}_{a}x(t) = \Phi(t + h\zeta, x(t + h\zeta)), \quad t \in (h\mathbb{N})_{a+\zeta h}, \tag{3}$$

Theorem 2 ([22]). *Suppose $x = 0$ is the equilibrium point of system (3). If a positively definite and decreasing scalar function $V(t, x(t))$ exists so that $\,^{C}_{h}\Delta^{\zeta}_{a}V(t, x(t)) \leq 0$, the equilibrium point is asymptotically stable.*

3. Model Description

The models in question are now approximated using two well-known approaches. These discrete models are, to our knowledge, the first in the literature. Wu et al. [32] proposed an interesting discretization of the fractional reaction equation shown below.

$$\begin{cases} \dfrac{\partial \varkappa}{\partial t} = K\Delta\varkappa, & x \in \Omega, t > 0, \\ \partial_{\varkappa} = 0, & x \in \partial\Omega, t > 0, \\ \varkappa(x, 0) = \varkappa(x) > 0, & x \in \Omega. \end{cases} \tag{4}$$

This equation represents a classical diffusion equation with the initial boundary conditions, 0 is the initial point, and K is the diffusion coefficient.

According to the structure of the model (4) and the discretization employed by Wu et al. [32,33]. Considering $x \in [0, L]$, we obtain $x_{i+1} = x_i + \Delta_x$, $i = 0, ..., m$, and by applying the central difference formula for x, $\dfrac{\partial^{2} u(x, t)}{\partial x^{2}}$ as well as $\dfrac{\partial^{2} w(x, t)}{\partial x^{2}}$ may be approximated as

$$\begin{cases} \dfrac{\partial^{2} u(x, t)}{\partial x^{2}} \approx \dfrac{u_{i+1}(t) - 2u_{i}(t) + u_{i-1}(t)}{\Delta^{2}_{x}}, \\ \dfrac{\partial^{2} w(x, t)}{\partial x^{2}} \approx \dfrac{w_{i+1}(t) - 2w_{i}(t) + w_{i-1}(t)}{\Delta^{2}_{x}}. \end{cases}$$

With the aid of the description of the second-order difference operator of u_i and w_i, we obtain:

$$\begin{cases} \dfrac{\partial^{2} u(x, t)}{\partial x^{2}} \approx \dfrac{\Delta^{2} u_{i-1}(t)}{\Delta^{2}_{x}}, \\ \dfrac{\partial^{2} w(x, t)}{\partial x^{2}} \approx \dfrac{\Delta^{2} w_{i-1}(t)}{\Delta^{2}_{x}}. \end{cases}$$

As a result, we may identify the previously mentioned model by Wu et al. [32,33].

$$\,^{C}_{h}\Delta^{\zeta}_{t_{0}} \varkappa_{i}(t) = \dfrac{1}{\Delta^{2}_{x}}\Delta^{2}\varkappa_{i-1}(t + h\zeta). \tag{5}$$

With the periodic boundary conditions

$$\varkappa_{0}(t) = \varkappa_{m}(t), \quad \varkappa_{1}(t) = \varkappa_{m+1}(t). \tag{6}$$

Moving on to the models in question, the Degn–Harrison model and the Lengyel–Epstein model, we present the discrete fractional version of each.

Mesdoui et al. [1] designed the reaction-diffusion model commonly referred to as the Degn–Harrison reaction-diffusion model, which is represented as

$$\begin{cases} \dfrac{\partial u}{\partial t} = k_1 \Delta u + a - u - \dfrac{wu}{1+qu^2}, & x \in \Omega,\ t > 0, \\[2mm] \dfrac{\partial w}{\partial t} = k_2 \Delta w + b - \dfrac{wu}{1+qu^2}, & x \in \Omega,\ t > 0, \\[2mm] \partial_u = \partial_w = 0, & x \in \partial\Omega,\ t > 0 \\[2mm] u(x,0) = u_0(x) > 0, & w(x,0) = w_0(x) > 0, \quad x \in \Omega. \end{cases} \tag{7}$$

where Ω is a bounded domain in $\mathbb{R}^n$, and $\partial\Omega$ is a suitably smooth border, while k_1 and k_2 are the respective diffusion coefficients of the reacting substances u and w, which are supposed to be positive constants throughout the reaction phase. The Laplace operator is given by $\Delta = \sum_{i=1}^{n} \dfrac{\partial^2}{\partial x_i^2}$.

Because time-fractional systems have been widely explored by scholars, Mesdoui et al. [1] presented the following fractional-time Degn–Harrison reaction-diffusion system.

$$\begin{cases} {}^{C}_{0}D_t^{\delta} u - k_1 \Delta u = a - u - \dfrac{uw}{1+qu^2}, \\[2mm] {}^{C}_{0}D_t^{\delta} w - k_2 \Delta w = b - \dfrac{uw}{1+qu^2}. \end{cases} \tag{8}$$

where $0 < \delta \leq 1$ is the fractional order, ${}^{C}_{0}D_t^{\delta}$ denotes the Caputo fractional derivative, k_1, k_2 and σ are strictly positive constants with the same initial conditions and Neumann boundary conditions considered by Mesdoui et al. [34].

Following the discretization defined previously, we may now provide the discrete fractional reaction-diffusion Degn–Harrison system.

$$\begin{cases} {}^{C}_{\hbar}\Delta_{t_0}^{\zeta} u_i(t) = \dfrac{k_1}{\Delta_x^2} \Delta^2 u_{i-1}(t+\hbar\zeta) + a - u_i(t+\hbar\zeta) - \dfrac{u_i(t+\hbar\zeta)w_i(t+\hbar\zeta)}{1+q(u_i(t+\hbar\zeta))^2}, \\[3mm] {}^{C}_{\hbar}\Delta_{t_0}^{\zeta} w_i(t) = \dfrac{k_2}{\Delta_x^2} \Delta^2 w_{i-1}(t+\hbar\zeta) + b - \dfrac{u_i(t+\hbar\zeta)w_i(t+\hbar\zeta)}{1+q(u_i(t+\hbar\zeta))^2}. \end{cases} \tag{9}$$

With the periodic boundary conditions

$$\begin{cases} u_0(t) = u_m(t), & u_1(t) = u_{m+1}(t), \\[2mm] w_0(t) = w_m(t), & w_1(t) = w_{m+1}(t), \end{cases} \tag{10}$$

and the initial condition

$$u_i(t_0) = \psi_1(x_i) \geq 0, \qquad w_i(t_0) = \psi_2(x_i) \geq 0.$$

Regarding the remaining model, the Lengyel–Epstein reaction-diffusion system was provided as a simulation of the chlorite-iodide-malonic-acid chemical reaction (CIMA). Yi et al. [35] investigated a specific model described by:

$$\begin{cases} \dfrac{\partial u}{\partial t} = \Delta u + a - u - \dfrac{uw}{1+u^2}, & x \in \Omega,\ t > 0, \\[2mm] \dfrac{\partial w}{\partial t} = \sigma\left(d\Delta w + b\left(u - \dfrac{uw}{1+u^2} \right) \right), & x \in \Omega,\ t > 0, \\[2mm] \partial_u = \partial_w = 0, & x \in \partial\Omega,\ t > 0, \\[2mm] u(x,0) = u_0(x) > 0, & w(x,0) = w_0(x) > 0, \quad x \in \Omega. \end{cases} \tag{11}$$

where Ω is a bounded domain in $\mathbb{R}^n$, with a properly smooth boundary $\partial\Omega$. u reflects the chemical concentration of the activator iodide, whereas w indicates the inhibitor chlorite at a point $x \in \Omega$, a and b are related to the supply concentration, d is the value of the ratio of the coefficient of diffusion, and $\sigma > 0$ is an adjusting parameter determined by the amount of starch concentration.

Given that fractional systems have been thoroughly studied over the years, the next fractional Lengyel–Epstein system was investigated:

$$\begin{cases} {}^{C}_{0}D^{\delta}_{t}u - d_1\Delta u = a - u - \dfrac{4uw}{1+u^2}, \\ {}^{C}_{0}D^{\delta}_{t}w - d_2\Delta w = \sigma b\left(u - \dfrac{uw}{1+u^2}\right), \end{cases} \tag{12}$$

where d_1, d_2 and σ are constants that are positive and have similar initial conditions and Neumann boundaries.

We analyze the discrete fractional reaction-diffusion Lengyel–Epstein system (15) via the model (12) and the discretization described above.

$$\begin{cases} {}^{C}_{\hbar}\Delta^{\zeta}_{t_0}u_i(t) = \dfrac{d_1}{\Delta^2_x}\Delta^2 u_{i-1}(t+\hbar\zeta) + a - u_i(t+\hbar\zeta) - \dfrac{4u_i(t+\hbar\zeta)w_i(t+\hbar\zeta)}{1+(u_i(t+\hbar\zeta))^2}, \\ {}^{C}_{\hbar}\Delta^{\zeta}_{t_0}w_i(t) = \dfrac{d_2}{\Delta^2_x}\Delta^2 w_{i-1}(t+\hbar\zeta) + \sigma b\left(u_i(t+\hbar\zeta) - \dfrac{u_i(t+\hbar\zeta)w_i(t+\hbar\zeta)}{1+(u_i(t+\hbar\zeta))^2}\right). \end{cases} \tag{13}$$

Using periodic boundary conditions:

$$\begin{cases} u_0(t) = u_m(t), \quad u_1(t) = u_{m+1}(t), \\ w_0(t) = w_m(t), \quad w_1(t) = w_{m+1}(t), \end{cases} \tag{14}$$

as well as the initial condition

$$u_i(t_0) = \psi_1(x_i) \geq 0, \quad w_i(t_0) = \psi_2(x_i) \geq 0.$$

4. Synchronization of Discrete-Time Fractional Reaction-Diffusion Lengyel–Epstein System

The most typical method for testing synchronization is to employ a controller to have the slave system output duplicate the master system output in some similar way. In this part, we create a controller that minimizes the state difference between synchronized systems to zero, which is known to be complete synchronization. Let the discrete reaction-diffusion master system (13) and the slave system be

$$\begin{cases} {}^{C}_{\hbar}\Delta^{\zeta}_{t_0}U_i(t) = \dfrac{d_1}{\Delta^2_x}\Delta^2 U_{i-1}(t+\hbar\zeta) + a - U_i(t+\hbar\zeta) - \dfrac{4U_i(t+\hbar\zeta)W_i(t+\hbar\zeta)}{1+(U_i(t+\hbar\zeta))^2} + V_1(t), \\ {}^{C}_{\hbar}\Delta^{\zeta}_{t_0}W_i(t) = \dfrac{d_2}{\Delta^2_x}\Delta^2 W_{i-1}(t+\hbar\zeta) + \sigma b\left(U_i(t+\hbar\zeta) - \dfrac{U_i(t+\hbar\zeta)W_i(t+\hbar\zeta)}{1+(U_i(t+\hbar\zeta))^2}\right) + V_2(t). \end{cases} \tag{15}$$

With the periodic boundary conditions

$$\begin{cases} U_0(t) = U_m(t), \quad U_1(t) = U_{m+1}(t), \\ W_0(t) = W_m(t), \quad W_1(t) = W_{m+1}(t), \end{cases} \tag{16}$$

and the initial condition

$$U_i(t_0) = \Phi_1(x_i) \geq 0, \quad W_i(t_0) = \Phi_2(x_i) \geq 0.$$

The purpose of synchronization is to reduce the error regarding the master and slave systems to zero, which is described as

$$(e_{1i}, e_{2i}) = (U_i - u_i, W_i - w_i). \tag{17}$$

In what follows, we will identify the linear controllers V_1 and V_2 that cause the error system solution to be 0 as t approaches $+\infty$. In other words, to be able to accomplish complete synchronization within the master-slave systems (13)–(15), we examine the asymptotical stability of the zero solution of the synchronization error system described in (17).

First, According to Ouannas et al. [2], it is easy to verify that

$$
\left| \frac{4U_i(t+\hbar\zeta)W_i(t+\hbar\zeta)}{1+(U_i(t+\hbar\zeta))^2} - \frac{4u_i(t+\hbar\zeta)w_i(t+\hbar\zeta)}{1+(u_i(t+\hbar\zeta))^2} \right| \leq |U_i - u_i| + 4|W_i - w_i|,
$$

$$
\left| \frac{\sigma b U_i(t+\hbar\zeta)W_i(t+\hbar\zeta)}{1+(U_i(t+\hbar\zeta))^2} - \frac{\sigma b u_i(t+\hbar\zeta)w_i(t+\hbar\zeta)}{1+(u_i(t+\hbar\zeta))^2} \right| \leq |U_i - u_i| + \sigma b|W_i - w_i|.
$$

Theorem 3. *If there is a control matrix $M = (m_{ij})_{2\times2}$ that satisfies $1 - m_1 > 0$ and $m_2 - \sigma b > 0$ the master-slave reaction-diffusion system identified in (13)–(15) is synchronized applying the linear control rule indicated below.*

$$
\begin{cases}
V_1(t) = -\left(m_1 + \dfrac{29}{4} \right)e_{1i}(t), \\
V_2(t) = -m_2 e_{2i} - (\sigma b + 1)e_{2i}(t).
\end{cases}
\tag{18}
$$

Proof. When (18) is substituted into the error system described in (17), the result is

$$
\begin{cases}
{}^C_\hbar\Delta^\zeta_{t_0}e_{1i}(t) = \dfrac{d_1}{\Delta^2_x}\Delta^2 e_{1,i-1}(t+\hbar\zeta) - e_{1i}(t+h\zeta) \\
\qquad - \left(\dfrac{4U_i(t+\hbar\zeta)W_i(t+\hbar\zeta)}{1+(U_i(t+\hbar\zeta))^2} - \dfrac{4u_i(t+\hbar\zeta)w_i(t+\hbar\zeta)}{1+(u_i(t+\hbar\zeta))^2} \right) - \left(m_1 + \dfrac{29}{4} \right)e_{1i}(t), \\
{}^C_\hbar\Delta^\zeta_{t_0}e_{2i}(t) = \dfrac{d_2}{\Delta^2_x}\Delta^2 e_{2,i-1}(t+\hbar\zeta) + \sigma b\left(e_{2i}(t+\hbar\zeta) \right. \\
\qquad \left. - \left(\dfrac{U_i(t+\hbar\zeta)W_i(t+\hbar\zeta)}{1+(U_i(t+\hbar\zeta))^2} - \dfrac{u_i(t+\hbar\zeta)w_i(t+\hbar\zeta)}{1+(u_i(t+\hbar\zeta))^2} \right) \right) - m_2 e_{2i} - (\sigma b + 1)e_{2i}(t).
\end{cases}
\tag{19}
$$

Developing a Lyapunov function of the type

$$
L(t) = \frac{1}{2}\sum_{i=1}^{m}\left(e^2_{1i}(t) + e^2_{2i}(t) \right),
\tag{20}
$$

gives

$$
{}^C_\hbar\Delta^\zeta_{t_0}L(t) \leq \sum_{i=1}^{m} e_{1i}(t+\hbar\zeta){}^C_h\Delta^\zeta_{t_0}e_{1i}(t) + e_{2i}(t+\hbar\zeta){}^C_h\Delta^\zeta_{t_0}e_{2i}(t),
$$

$$
= \sum_{i=1}^{m} e_{1i}(t+h\zeta)[\frac{d_1}{\Delta^2_x}\Delta^2 e_{1,i-1}(t+\hbar\zeta) - e_{1i}(t+\hbar\zeta) - (\frac{4U_i(t+\hbar\zeta)W_i(t+\hbar\zeta)}{1+(U_i(t+\hbar\zeta))^2}
$$

$$
- \frac{4u_i(t+\hbar\zeta)w_i(t+\hbar\zeta)}{1+(u_i(t+\hbar\zeta))^2} - \left(m_1 + \frac{29}{4} \right)e_{1i}] + \sum_{i=1}^{m} e_{2i}(t+\hbar\zeta)[\frac{d_2}{\Delta^2_x}\Delta^2 e_{2,i-1}(t+\hbar\zeta)
$$

$$
+ \sigma b e_{2i}(t+\hbar\zeta) - \left(\frac{\sigma b U_i(t+\hbar\zeta)W_i(t+\hbar\zeta)}{1+(U_i(t+\hbar\zeta))^2} - \frac{\sigma b u_i(t+\hbar\zeta)w_i(t+\hbar\zeta)}{1+(u_i(t+\hbar\zeta))^2} \right)
$$

$$
- (m_2 e_{2i} + (\sigma b + 1)e_{2i})],
$$

$$
\leq \sum_{i=1}^{m} \frac{d_1}{\Delta^2_x}e_{1i}(t+\hbar\zeta)\Delta^2 e_{1,i-1}(t+\hbar\zeta) + \frac{d_2}{\Delta^2_x}e_{2i}(t+\hbar\zeta)\Delta^2 e_{2,i-1}(t+\hbar\zeta)
$$

$$
- \sum_{i=1}^{m}(1 - m_1)e^2_{1i}(t) + |e_{1i}(t)|(|U_i - u_i| + 4|W_i - w_i|)
$$

$$
- \frac{29}{4}e^2_{1i}(t+\hbar\zeta) + \sum_{i=1}^{m}(\sigma b - m_2)e^2_{2i}(t+\hbar\zeta) + |e_{2i}(t+\hbar\zeta)|(|U_i(t+\hbar\zeta) - u_i(t+\hbar\zeta)|
$$

$$+ \sigma b|W_i(t + \hbar\zeta) - w_i(t + \hbar\zeta)|) - (\sigma b + 1)e_{2i}^2(t + \hbar\zeta),$$

$$\leq \frac{d_1}{\Delta_x^2}(\Delta e_{1,i-1}\Delta e_{1,i-1}(t + \hbar\zeta)|_{m+1}^1 - \sum_{i=1}^{m}(\Delta e_{1,i-1}(t + \hbar\zeta))^2) + \frac{d_2}{\Delta_x^2}(\Delta e_{2,i-1}\Delta e_{2,i-1}(t + \hbar\zeta)|_{m+1}^1$$

$$- \sum_{i=1}^{m}(\Delta e_{2,i-1}(t + \hbar\zeta))^2) - \sum_{i=1}^{m}(1 - m_1)e_{1i}^2(t) + (\sigma b - m_2)e_{2i}^2(t + \hbar\zeta)$$

$$+ e_{1i}^2(t) + 4|e_{1i}(t)||e_{2i}(t)| - \frac{29}{4}e_{1i}^2(t + \hbar\zeta) + |e_{1i}(t + \hbar\zeta)||e_{2i}(t + \hbar\zeta)| + \sigma b e_{2i}^2(t + \hbar\zeta)$$

$$- (\sigma b + 1)e_{2i}^2(t + \hbar\zeta),$$

$$\leq - \sum_{i=1}^{m}\left(\frac{d_1}{\Delta_x^2}(\Delta e_{1,i-1}(t + \hbar\zeta))^2 + \frac{d_2}{\Delta_x^2}(\Delta e_{2,i-1}(t + \hbar\zeta))^2\right) - \sum_{i=1}^{m}(1 - m_1)e_{1i}^2(t)$$

$$- \sum_{i=1}^{m}(m_2 - \sigma b)e_{2i}^2(t) - \sum_{i=1}^{m}\left(\frac{5}{2}|e_{1i}(t + \hbar\zeta)| - |e_{2i}(t + \hbar\zeta)|\right)^2 < 0.$$

This means the global asymptotic stability of the error system's zero solution (19), based on the Lyapunov stability theory presented in Theorem 2. As a result, the master-slave systems (13)–(15) are completely synchronized. $\square$

5. Synchronization of Discrete Fractional Degn–Harrison Reaction-Diffusion Systems

We investigate the synchronization of the fractional discrete Degn–Harrison models using the master-slave formalism, in which the discrete fractional Degn–Harrison reaction-diffusion systems are linked in such a way that the slave system asymptotically matches the master system. In this scenario, we create controllers that cause the difference between the states of synchronized systems to converge to zero, indicating that the systems are fully synchronized. The slave system that is linked to the master system (13) may be expressed as

$$\begin{cases} {}^{C}_{\hbar}\Delta_{t_0}^{\zeta}U_i(t) = \dfrac{k_1}{\Delta_x^2}\Delta^2 U_{i-1}(t + \hbar\zeta) + a - U_i(t + \hbar\zeta) - \dfrac{U_i(t + \hbar\zeta)W_i(t + \hbar\zeta)}{1 + q(U_i(t + h\zeta))^2} + S_1(t), \\[2mm] {}^{C}_{\hbar}\Delta_{t_0}^{\zeta}W_i(t) = \dfrac{k_2}{\Delta_x^2}\Delta^2 W_{i-1}(t + \hbar\zeta) + b - \dfrac{U_i(t + \hbar\zeta)W_i(t + \hbar\zeta)}{1 + q(U_i(t + \hbar\zeta))^2} + S_2(t). \end{cases} \tag{21}$$

With the periodic boundary conditions

$$\begin{cases} U_0(t) = U_m(t), & U_1(t) = U_{m+1}(t), \\ W_0(t) = W_m(t), & W_1(t) = W_{m+1}(t), \end{cases} \tag{22}$$

and the initial condition

$$U_i(t_0) = \Phi_1(x_i) \geq 0, \quad W_i(t_0) = \Phi_2(x_i) \geq 0.$$

The goal of this part is to identify a control S_i to induce the synchronization errors $e_i(x, t) = (e_i^1(x, t), e_i^2(x, t))$ described by

$$e_{1i}(x, t) = U_i(t, x) - u_i(t, x), \quad e_{2i}(x, t) = W_i(t, x) - w_i(t, x). \tag{23}$$

where $(u_i(x, t), w_i(x, t))$ and $(U(x, t), W(x, t))$ are the solutions of systems (13) and (21) that converge to zero as t approaches infinity.

The error system is given by

$$\begin{cases} {}^{C}_{\hbar}\Delta^{\zeta}_{t_0} e_{1i}(t) = \dfrac{k_1}{\Delta^2_x}\Delta^2 e_{1,i-1}(t+\hbar\zeta) + a - e_{1i}(t+\hbar\zeta) - \dfrac{U_i(t+\hbar\zeta)W_i(t+\hbar\zeta)}{1+q(U_i(t+\hbar\zeta))^2} \\ \qquad + \dfrac{u_i(t+\hbar\zeta)w_i(t+\hbar\zeta)}{1+q(u_i(t+\hbar\zeta))^2} + S_1(t), \\ {}^{C}_{\hbar}\Delta^{\zeta}_{t_0} e_{2i}(t) = \dfrac{k_2}{\Delta^2_x}\Delta^2 e_{2,i-1}(t+\hbar\zeta) + b - \dfrac{U_i(t+\hbar\zeta)W_i(t+\hbar\zeta)}{1+q(U_i(t+\hbar\zeta))^2} \\ \qquad + \dfrac{u_i(t+\hbar\zeta)w_i(t+\hbar\zeta)}{1+q(u_i(t+\hbar\zeta))^2} + S_2(t). \end{cases} \tag{24}$$

The error system (24) may be seen to satisfy the periodic boundary conditions.

$$\begin{cases} e_{1,0}(t) = U_0(t) - u_0(t) = U_m(t) - u_m(t) = e_{1m}(t), \\ e_{1,1}(t) = U_1(t) - u_1(t) = U_{m+1}(t) - u_{m+1}(t) = e_{1,m+1}(t), \\ e_{2,0}(t) = W_0(t) - w_0(t) = W_m(t) - w_m(t) = e_{2m}(t), \\ e_{2,1}(t) = W_1(t) - w_1(t) = W_{m+1}(t) - w_{m+1}(t) = e_{2,m+1}(t). \end{cases} \tag{25}$$

Before proceeding to the synchronization of master-slave systems, consider the following lemma.

Lemma 3 ([34]). *The following inequality holds*

$$\left| \frac{u_i(t+\hbar\zeta)w_i(t+\hbar\zeta)}{1+q(u_i(t+\hbar\zeta))^2} - \frac{U_i(t+\hbar\zeta)W_i(t+\hbar\zeta)}{1+q(U_i(t+\hbar\zeta))^2} \right| \leq Q(|U_i - u_i| + |W_i - w_i|), \tag{26}$$

where

$$Q \geq \max\left\{ \frac{5}{4}k, \frac{1}{2\sqrt{q}} \right\}, \quad |W_i| < k.$$

The controllers S_1 and S_2 are determined in the following Theorem to establish synchronization between the systems provided in (13) and (21).

Theorem 4. *Under the following control law, the master system (1) and slave system (2) are completely synchronized.*

$$\begin{cases} S_1(t) = (1 - 2Q)e_{1i}(t), \\ S_2(t) = -2Qe_{2i}(t). \end{cases} \tag{27}$$

Proof. By substituting the control described in the Theorem in the error system, we obtain

$$\begin{cases} {}^{C}_{\hbar}\Delta^{\zeta}_{t_0} e_{1i}(t) = \dfrac{k_1}{\Delta^2_x}\Delta^2 e_{1,i-1}(t+\hbar\zeta) - \dfrac{U_i(t+\hbar\zeta)W_i(t+\hbar\zeta)}{1+q(U_i(t+\hbar\zeta))^2} + \dfrac{u_i(t+\hbar\zeta)w_i(t+\hbar\zeta)}{1+q(u_i(t+\hbar\zeta))^2} \\ \qquad -2Qe_{1i}(t+\hbar\zeta), \\ {}^{C}_{\hbar}\Delta^{\zeta}_{t_0} e_{2i}(t) = \dfrac{k_2}{\Delta^2_x}\Delta^2 e_{2,i-1}(t+\hbar\zeta) - \dfrac{U_i(t+\hbar\zeta)W_i(t+\hbar\zeta)}{1+q(U_i(t+\hbar\zeta))^2} + \dfrac{u_i(t+\hbar\zeta)w_i(t+\hbar\zeta)}{1+q(u_i(t+\hbar\zeta))^2} \\ \qquad -2Qe_{2i}(t+\hbar\zeta). \end{cases} \tag{28}$$

Next, we design a Lyapunov function as

$$L(t) = \frac{1}{2}\sum_{i=1}^{m}\left((e_{1i}(t))^2 + (e_{2i}(t))^2 \right), \tag{29}$$

then, we have

$$
{}^{C}_{\hbar}\Delta^{\zeta}_{t_0} L(t) = \frac{1}{2}\,{}^{C}_{\hbar}\Delta^{\zeta}_{t_0} \sum_{i=1}^{m}(e_{1i}(t))^2 + (e_{2i}(t))^2,
$$

$$
\leq \sum_{i=1}^{m} e_{1i}(t+\hbar\zeta)\,{}^{C}_{\hbar}\Delta^{\zeta}_{t_0} e_{1i}(t) + e_{2i}(t+\hbar\zeta)\,{}^{C}_{\hbar}\Delta^{\zeta}_{t_0} e_{2i}(t),
$$

$$
= \sum_{i=1}^{m} e_{1i}(t+\hbar\zeta)\Big(\frac{k_1}{\Delta_x^2}\Delta^2 e_{1,i-1}(t+\hbar\zeta) - \frac{U_i(t+\hbar\zeta)W_i(t+\hbar\zeta)}{1+q(U_i(t+\hbar\zeta))^2} + \frac{u_i(t+\hbar\zeta)w_i(t+\hbar\zeta)}{1+q(u_i(t+\hbar\zeta))^2}
$$

$$
- 2Qe_i^1(t+\hbar\zeta)\Big) + e_{2i}(t+\hbar\zeta)\Big(\frac{k_2}{\Delta_x^2}\Delta^2 e_{2,i-1}(t+\hbar\zeta)
$$

$$
- \frac{U_i(t+\hbar\zeta)W_i(t+\hbar\zeta)}{1+q(U_i(t+\hbar\zeta))^2} + \frac{u_i(t+\hbar\zeta)w_i(t+\hbar\zeta)}{1+q(u_i(t+\hbar\zeta))^2} 2Qe_i^2(t+\hbar\zeta)\Big),
$$

$$
= \sum_{i=1}^{m} \frac{k_1}{\Delta_x^2}e_{1i}(t+\hbar\zeta)\Delta^2 e_{1,i-1}(t+\hbar\zeta) + \frac{k_2}{\Delta_x^2}e_{2i}(t+\hbar\zeta)\Delta^2 e_{2,i-1}(t+\hbar\zeta) - 2Q((e_{1i})^2 + (e_{2i})^2)
$$

$$
+ \left(\frac{U_i(t+\hbar\zeta)W_i(t+\hbar\zeta)}{1+q(U_i(t+\hbar\zeta))^2} + \frac{u_i(t+\hbar\zeta)w_i(t+\hbar\zeta)}{1+q(u_i(t+\hbar\zeta))^2}\right)(e_{1i}+e_{2i}),
$$

$$
\leq \frac{k_1}{\Delta_x^2}\sum_{i=1}^{m} e_{1i}(t+\hbar\zeta) - (\Delta\Delta e_{1,i-1}(t+\hbar\zeta)) + \frac{k_2}{\Delta_x^2}\sum_{i=1}^{m} e_{2i}(t+\hbar\zeta) - (\Delta\Delta e_{2,i-1}(t+\hbar\zeta))
$$

$$
- 2Q\sum_{i=1}^{m}((e_{1i})^2 + (e_{2i})^2) + \sum_{i=1}^{m}\left|\frac{U_i(t+\hbar\zeta)W_i(t+\hbar\zeta)}{1+q(U_i(t+\hbar\zeta))^2}\right| \frac{u_i(t+\hbar\zeta)w_i(t+\hbar\zeta)}{1+q(u_i(t+\hbar\zeta))^2}\Big|(|e_{1i}| + |e_{2i}|),
$$

$$
\leq \frac{k_1}{\Delta_x^2}\left(\Delta e_{1,i-1}\Delta e_{1,i-1}(t+\hbar\zeta)\big|_{m+1}^{1} - \sum_{i=1}^{m}(\Delta e_{1,i-1}(t+\hbar\zeta))^2\right) - 2Q\sum_{i=1}^{m}((e_{1i})^2 + (e_{2i})^2)
$$

$$
+ \frac{k_2}{\Delta_x^2}\left(\Delta e_{2,i-1}\Delta e_{2,i-1}(t+\hbar\zeta)\big|_{m+1}^{1} - \sum_{i=1}^{m}(\Delta e_{2,i-1}(t+\hbar\zeta))^2\right) + Q\sum_{i=1}^{m}(|e_{1i}| + |e_{2i}|)^2,
$$

$$
\leq -\frac{k_1}{\Delta_x^2}\sum_{i=1}^{m}(\Delta e_{1,i-1}(t+\hbar\zeta))^2 - \frac{k_2}{\Delta_x^2}\sum_{i=1}^{m}(\Delta e_{2,i-1}(t+\hbar\zeta))^2 - Q\sum_{i=1}^{m}(|e_{1i}| - |e_{2i}|)^2 \leq 0.
$$

According to the Lyapunov stability theory stated in Theorem 2, this implies the global asymptotic stability of the zero solution of the error system (24). Consequently, the master-slave systems (13) and (21) are completely synchronized. $\square$

6. Numerical Simulation

To demonstrate and confirm the synchronization techniques proposed in the preceding section. We provide the following examples with numerical simulations:

Example 1. *We consider the master-slave systems (13)–(15) with the following parameters:*
$(a, b, \sigma, d_1, d_2) = (10, 1, 2, 1, 1.5), N = 100, \hbar = 1.5, t \in [0, 150], x \in [0, 20],$ *the boundary conditions* $(u_0(t), w_0(t)) = (1, 5), (u_1(t), w_1(t)) = (1, 5)$ *and with the following initial conditions.*

$$
\begin{cases}
(\psi_1(x_i), \psi_2(x_i)) = (7 + 0.3\sin(5\pi x_i), 7 + 0.6\sin(5\pi x_i)), \\
(\Phi_1(x_i), \Phi_2(x_i)) = (7 + 0.2\cos(5\pi x_i), 7 + 0.2\cos(5\pi x_i)).
\end{cases}
$$

First, the assumptions given in Theorem 3 is satisfied for controlling the master-slave discrete fractional reaction-diffusion systems using the following linear controllers.

$$
M = \begin{pmatrix} 0.9 & 0 \\ 0 & 3 \end{pmatrix}.
$$

As a result, systems (13) and (15) are completely synchronized. We provide the numerical solution of the system (13) in (30). Moreover, Figures 1 and 2 show the solutions u_i, w_i, U_i and W_i, also, Figure 3 illustrate the time development of error system states e_{1i} and e_{2i} in this case.

$$\begin{cases} u_i(n\hbar) = \psi_1(x_i) + \dfrac{\hbar^\zeta}{\Gamma(\zeta)} \sum_{\mathbb{p}=1}^{n} \dfrac{\Gamma(n-\mathbb{p}+\zeta)}{\Gamma(n-\mathbb{p}+1)} \times \Big[\dfrac{u_{i+1}((\mathbb{p}-1)\hbar) - 2u_i((\mathbb{p}-1)\hbar) + u_{i-1}((\mathbb{p}-1)\hbar)}{\Delta_x^2} \\ \qquad +a - u_i((\mathbb{p}-1)\hbar) - \dfrac{4u_i((\mathbb{p}-1)\hbar)w_i((\mathbb{p}-1)\hbar)}{1+(u_i((\mathbb{p}-1)\hbar))^2} \Big], \\ w_i(n\hbar) = \psi_2(x_i) + \dfrac{\hbar^\zeta}{\Gamma(\zeta)} \sum_{\mathbb{p}=1}^{n} \dfrac{\Gamma(n-\mathbb{p}+\zeta)}{\Gamma(n-\mathbb{p}+1)} \times \Big[\dfrac{w_{i+1}((\mathbb{p}-1)\hbar) - 2w_i((\mathbb{p}-1)\hbar) + w_{i-1}((\mathbb{p}-1)\hbar)}{\Delta_x^2} \\ \qquad +\sigma b\Big(u_i((\mathbb{p}-1)\hbar) - \dfrac{u_i((\mathbb{p}-1)\hbar)w_i((\mathbb{p}-1)\hbar)}{1+(u_i((\mathbb{p}-1)\hbar))^2} \Big) \Big], \\ 1 \leq i \leq m, \\ n > 0. \end{cases} \tag{30}$$

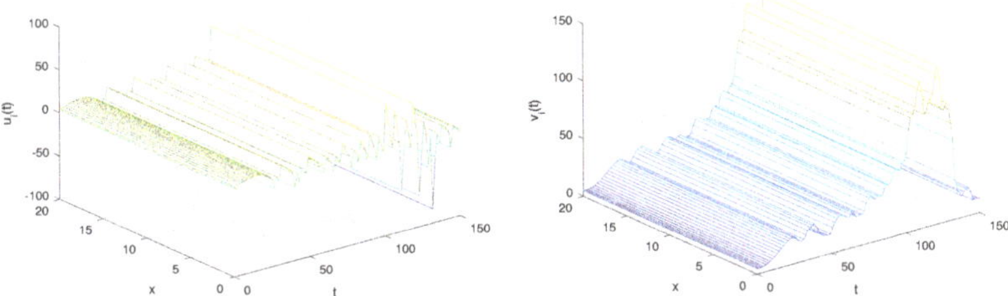

Figure 1. Dynamic behaviors of of the master system $u_i(t)$ and $w_i(t)$ for $N = 100$, $(a, b, \sigma, d_1, d_2) = (10, 1, 2, 1, 1.5)$ and $\zeta = 0.1$.

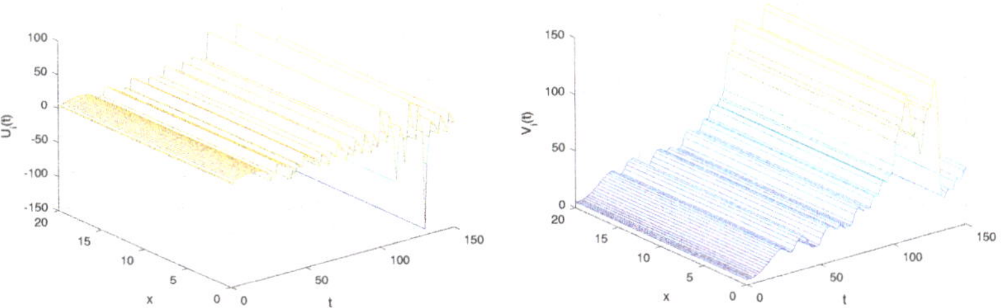

Figure 2. Dynamic behaviors of the slave system $U_i(t)$ and $W_i(t)$ for $N = 100$, $(a, b, \sigma, d_1, d_2) = (10, 1, 2, 1, 1.5)$ and $\zeta = 0.1$.

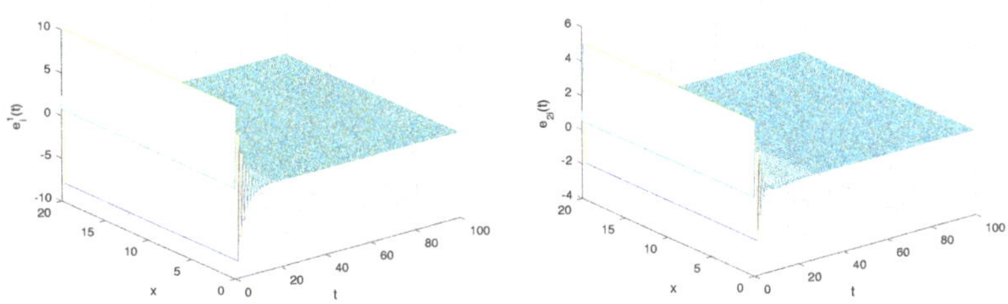

Figure 3. State trajectories of the error $e_{1i}(t)$ and $e_{2i}(t)$.

Example 2. *To keep track of the system's (13) performance, we alter the system's parameters and order, taking into account parameter values:* $(a, b, q, k_1, k_2, \zeta) = (1.2371, 0.1, 9, 3, 2, 0.35)$ *and*

$$
\begin{cases}
\psi_1(x_i) = 0.2(3 + 0.1\cos(0.5x_i)), \\
\psi_2(x_i) = 0.2(4 + 0.3\sin(0.2x_i)).
\end{cases}
\tag{31}
$$

Additionally, we set

$$
\begin{cases}
\Phi_1(x_i) = 0.7\sin(0.3x_i)), \\
\Phi_2(x_i) = 0.5\cos(0.3x_i)).
\end{cases}
\tag{32}
$$

With the periodic conditions $(u_0(t), w_0(t)) = (3, 1), (u_1(t), w_1(t)) = (3, 1)$ *and* $(U_0(t), W_0(t)) = (4, 2), (U_1(t), W_1(t)) = (4, 2)$.

As a consequence of the numerical simulations, we can see that by adding appropriate controllers as shown in (27), the dynamics of (13) and (21) are synchronized, and the zero constant state of the synchronization error system expressed in (28) is asymptotically stable. Figures 4 and 5 are numerical simulations of the master-slave systems under the considered parameters. Furthermore, Figure 6 indicates that the system's zero steady-state is asymptotically stable, moreover, Figure 7 shows the same results in the 2D spatial domain.

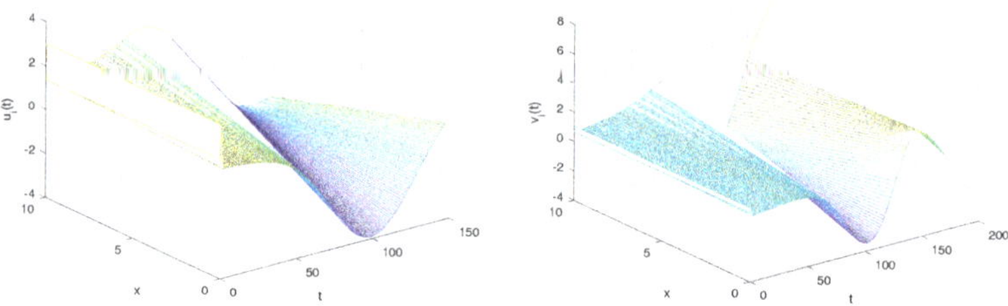

Figure 4. State trajectories of the master system (13).

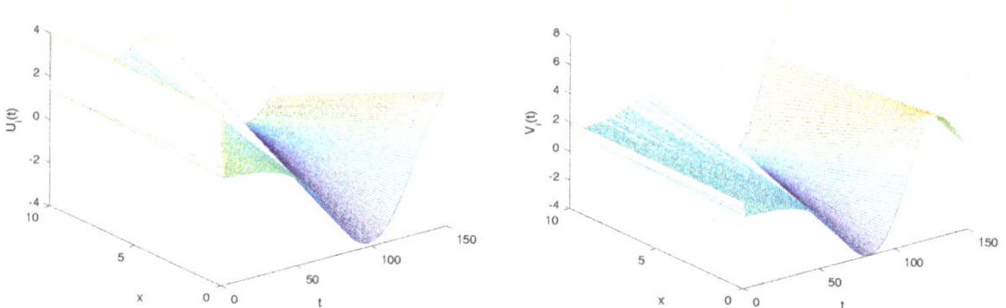

Figure 5. State trajectories of the master system (21).

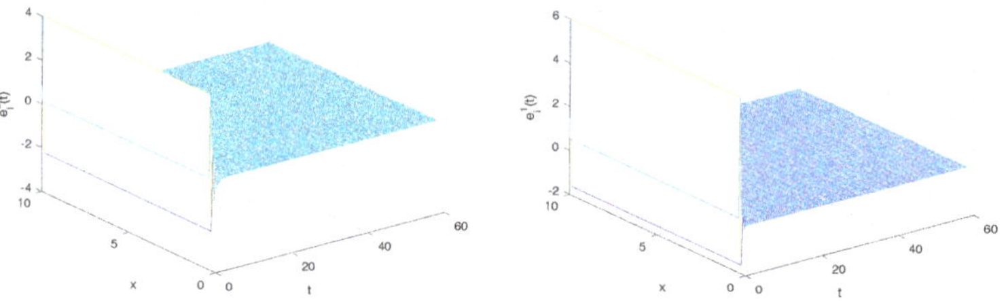

Figure 6. State trajectories of the error $e_i(t)$.

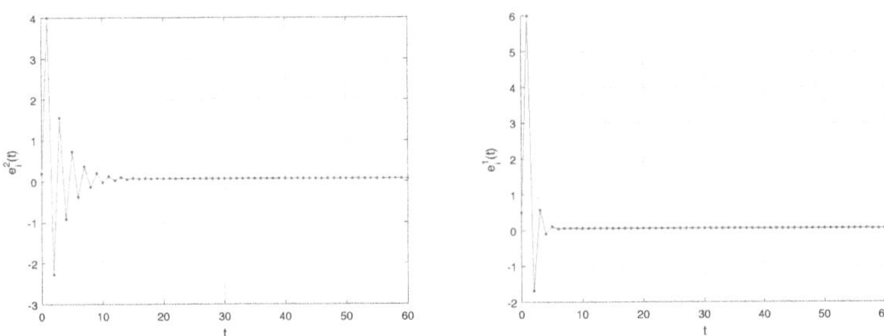

Figure 7. State trajectories of the error $e_i(t)$ in 2D.

7. Conclusions

In this study, we present a unique version of the Degn–Harrison reaction-diffusion systems and the Lengyel–Epstein reaction-diffusion systems that depend on the Caputo h-difference operator. We developed unique approaches for investigating synchronization in a spatiotemporal model of nonlinear bacterial colonies. First, for complete synchronization, suitable control schemes for synchronization are presented. The results of synchronization are based on Lyapunov theory and the master-slave formulation. To demonstrate the efficacy as well as the validity of the suggested synchronization schemas, numerical simulations of discrete time-fractional order Degn–Harrison systems and Lengyel–Epstein systems are provided. In the future, our plan is to further investigate bacterial colonies and the related reaction-diffusion synchronization phenomena, with the aim of developing sensor-based applications.

Author Contributions: Conceptualization, Y.A.A.-K.; Formal analysis, M.O.A.-Q. and T.H.; investigation, A.H.; Methodology, M.O.A.-Q. and A.A.-H.; Resources, I.A.F. and A.A.-H.; Supervision, A.O.; Validation, I.A.F.; Visualization, Y.A.A.-K. and T.H.; Writing—original draft, A.H.; Writing—review and editing, A.O. All authors have read and agreed to the published version of the manuscript.

Funding: This research received no external funding.

Data Availability Statement: Not applicable.

Conflicts of Interest: The authors declare no conflict of interest.

References

1. Mesdoui, F.; Ouannas, A.; Shawagfeh, N.; Grassi, G.; Pham, V.T. Synchronization methods for the Degn-Harrison reaction-diffusion systems. *IEEE Access* **2020**, *8*, 91829–91836. [CrossRef]
2. Ouannas, A.; Abdelli, M.; Odibat, Z.; Wang, X.; Pham, V.T.; Grassi, G.; Alsaedi, A. Synchronization control in reaction-diffusion systems: Application to Lengyel-Epstein system. *Complexity* **2019**, *2019*, 2832781. [CrossRef]
3. Ambrosio, B.; Aziz-Alaoui, M.A. Synchronization and control of coupled reaction–diffusion systems of the FitzHugh–Nagumo type. *Comput. Math. Appl.* **2012**, *64*, 934–943. [CrossRef]
4. Caraballo, T.; Chueshov, I.D.; Kloeden, P.E. Synchronization of a stochastic reaction-diffusion system on a thin two-layer domain. *SIAM J. Math. Anal.* **2007**, *38*, 1489–1507. [CrossRef]
5. Ambrosio, B.; Aziz-Alaoui, M.A.; Phan, V.L.E. Large time behaviour and synchronization of complex networks of reaction–diffusion systems of FitzHugh–Nagumo type. *IMA J. Appl. Math.* **2019**, *84*, 416–443. [CrossRef]
6. Miller, K.S.; Ross, B. *An Introduction to the Fractional Calculus and Fractional Differential Equations*; Wiley: New York, NY, USA, 1993.
7. Oldham, K.; Spanier, J. *The Fractional Calculus Theory and Applications of Differentiation and Integration to Arbitrary Order*; Elsevier: Amsterdam, The Netherlands, 1974.
8. Oldham, K.B. *The Fractional Calculus*; Spanier, J., Ed.; Academic Press: New York, NY, USA, 1974.
9. Samko, S.G.; Kilbas, A.A.; Marichev, O.I. *Fractional Integrals and Derivatives*; Gordon and Breach Science Publishers: Montreux, Switzerland, 1993.
10. Sun, H.; Zhang, Y.; Baleanu, D.; Chen, W.; Chen, Y. A new collection of real world applications of fractional calculus in science and engineering. *Commun. Nonlinear Sci. Numer. Simul.* **2018**, *64*, 213–231. [CrossRef]
11. Hilfer, R. (Ed.) *Applications of Fractional Calculus in Physics*; World Scientific: Singapore, 2000.
12. Silva, M.F.; Machado, J.T. Fractional order PD α joint control of legged robots. *J. Vib. Control.* **2006**, *12*, 1483–1501. [CrossRef]

13. Duarte, F.B.; Machado, J.T. Chaotic phenomena and fractional-order dynamics in the trajectory control of redundant manipulators. *Nonlinear Dyn.* **2002**, *29*, 315–342. [CrossRef]
14. Tenreiro Machado, J.A.; Silva, M.F.; Barbosa, R.S.; Jesus, I.S.; Reis, C.M.; Marcos, M.G.; Galhano, A.F. Some applications of fractional calculus in engineering. *Math. Probl. Eng.* **2010**, *2010*, 639801. [CrossRef]
15. Acay, B.; Inc, M. Electrical circuits RC, LC, and RLC under generalized type non-local singular fractional operator. *Fractal Fract.* **2021**, *5*, 9. [CrossRef]
16. Wang, B.; Ouannas, A.; Karaca, Y.; Xia, W.F.; Jahanshahi, H.; Alkhateeb, A.F.; Nour, M. A Hybrid Approach for Synchronizing between Two Reaction Diffusion Systems of Integer-and Fractional-Order Applied on Certain Chemical Models. *Fractals* **2022**, *30*, 2240145. [CrossRef]
17. Berkal, M.; Almatrafi, M.B. Bifurcation and stability of two-dimensional activator—Inhibitor model with fractional-order derivative. *Fractal Fract.* **2023**, *7*, 344. [CrossRef]
18. Abdeljawad, T. On Riemann and Caputo fractional differences. *Comput. Math. Appl.* **2011**, *62*, 1602–1611. [CrossRef]
19. Atici, F.M.; Eloe, P.W. A transform method in discrete fractional calculus. *Int. J. Differ. Equ.* **2007**, *2*, 165–176.
20. Goodrich, C.; Peterson, A.C. *Discrete Fractional Calculus*; Springer: Cham, Switzerland, 2015.
21. Kelley, W.G.; Peterson, A.C. *Difference Equations: An Introduction with Applications*; Academic Press: New York, NY, USA, 2001.
22. Baleanu, D.; Wu, G.C.; Bai, Y.R.; Chen, F.L. Stability analysis of Caputo–like discrete fractional systems. *Commun. Nonlinear Sci. Numer. Simul.* **2017**, *48*, 520–530. [CrossRef]
23. Atici, F.; Eloe, P. Initial value problems in discrete fractional calculus. *Proc. Am. Math. Soc.* **2009**, *137*, 981–989. [CrossRef]
24. Hamadneh, T.; Abbes, A.; Falahah, I.A.; AL-Khassawneh, Y.A.; Heilat, A.S.; Al-Husban, A.; Ouannas, A. Complexity and Chaos Analysis for Two-Dimensional Discrete-Time Predator–Prey Leslie–Gower Model with Fractional Orders. *Axioms* **2023**, *12*, 561. [CrossRef]
25. Saadeh, R.; Abbes, A.; Al-Husban, A.; Ouannas, A.; Grassi, G. The Fractional Discrete Predator–Prey Model: Chaos, Control and 252 Synchronization. *Fractal Fract.* **2023**, *7*, 120. [CrossRef]
26. Merks, R.M.; Van de Peer, Y.; Inzé, D.; Beemster, G.T. Canalization without flux sensors: A traveling-wave hypothesis. *Trends Plant Sci.* **2007**, *12*, 384–390. [CrossRef]
27. Cuevas, J.; English, L.Q.; Kevrekidis, P.G.; Anderson, M. Discrete breathers in a forced-damped array of coupled pendula: Modeling, computation, and experiment. *Phys. Rev. Lett.* **2009**, *102*, 224101. [CrossRef]
28. Nishiura, Y.; Ueyama, D.; Yanagita, T. Chaotic pulses for discrete reaction diffusion systems. *SIAM J. Appl. Dyn. Syst.* **2005**, *4*, 733–754. [CrossRef]
29. Li, M.; Han, B.; Xu, L.; Zhang, G. Spiral patterns near Turing instability in a discrete reaction diffusion system. *Chaos Solitons Fractals* **2013**, *49*, 1–6. [CrossRef]
30. Lee, I.H.; Jo, U.I. Pattern formations with Turing and Hopf oscillating pattern in a discrete reaction-diffusion system. *Bull. Korean Chem. Soc.* **2000**, *21*, 1213–1216.
31. Almatroud, O.A.; Hioual, A.; Ouannas, A.; Grassi, G. On Fractional-Order Discrete-Time Reaction Diffusion Systems. *Mathematics* **2023**, *11*, 2447. [CrossRef]
32. Wu, G.C.; Baleanu, D.; Zeng, S.D.; Deng, Z.G. Discrete fractional diffusion equation. *Nonlinear Dyn.* **2015**, *80*, 281–286. [CrossRef]
33. Wu, G.C.; Baleanu, D.; Xie, H.P.; Zeng, S.D. Discrete fractional diffusion equation of chaotic order. *Int. J. Bifurc. Chaos* **2016**, *26*, 1650013. [CrossRef]
34. Mesdoui, F.; Shawagfeh, N.; Ouannas, A. Global synchronization of fractional-order and integer-order N component reaction diffusion systems: Application to biochemical models. *Math. Methods Appl. Sci.* **2021**, *44*, 1003–1012. [CrossRef]
35. Yi, F.; Wei, J.; Shi, J. Global asymptotical behavior of the Lengyel–Epstein reaction–diffusion system. *Appl. Math. Lett.* **2009**, *22*, 52–55. [CrossRef]

Article

Solvability of a Boundary Value Problem Involving Fractional Difference Equations

Zhiwei Lv [1], Chun Wu [2,*], Donal O'Regan [3] and Jiafa Xu [2]

1. School of Sciences and Arts, Suqian University, Suqian 223800, China; sdlllzw@mail.ustc.edu.cn
2. School of Mathematical Sciences, Chongqing Normal University, Chongqing 401331, China; 20150028@cqnu.edu.cn
3. School of Mathematical and Statistical Sciences, University of Galway, H91 TK33 Galway, Ireland; donal.oregan@universityofgalway.ie
* Correspondence: wuchun@cqnu.edu.cn

Abstract: In this current work, we apply the topological degree and fixed point theorems to investigate the existence, uniqueness, and multiplicity of solutions for a boundary value problem associated with a fractional-order difference equation. Moreover, we provide some appropriate examples to verify our main conclusions.

Keywords: fractional difference equations; boundary value problems; solvability; fixed-point theory

MSC: 34B10; 34B18; 34A34; 45G15; 45M20

Citation: Lv, Z.; Wu, C.; O'Regan, D.; Xu, J. Solvability of a Boundary Value Problem Involving Fractional Difference Equations. *Axioms* **2023**, *12*, 650. https://doi.org/10.3390/axioms12070650

Academic Editors: Azhar Ali Zafar and Nehad Ali Shah

Received: 8 June 2023
Revised: 25 June 2023
Accepted: 28 June 2023
Published: 29 June 2023

1. Introduction

Let $[\kappa, \delta]_{\mathbb{N}_\kappa} := \{\kappa, \kappa+1, \kappa+2, \cdots, \delta\}$ $(\delta - \kappa \in \mathbb{N}_1)$, where $\mathbb{N}_\kappa := \{\kappa, \kappa+1, \kappa+2, \cdots\}$. In the current work, we shall discuss the solvability of the fractional difference boundary value problem

$$\begin{cases} -\Delta_{v-3}^v \psi(t) = g(t+v-1, \psi(t+v-1)), \quad t \in [0, \mathfrak{b}+2]_{\mathbb{N}_0}, \\ \psi(v-3) = \left[\Delta_{v-3}^\alpha \psi(t)\right]\big|_{t=v-\alpha-2} = \left[\Delta_{v-3}^\beta \psi(t)\right]\big|_{t=v+\mathfrak{b}+2-\beta} = 0, \end{cases} \tag{1}$$

where $v \in (2,3]$, $\beta \in (1,2)$, $v - \beta \in (1, +\infty)$, $\alpha \in (0,1)$, $\mathfrak{b} \in (3, +\infty)$ $(\mathfrak{b} \in \mathbb{N})$, and Δ_{v-3}^v is a discrete fractional-order operator defined by

$$\Delta_a^v \psi(t) := \begin{cases} \frac{1}{\Gamma(-v)} \sum_{s=a}^{t+v} (t-s-1)^{\underline{-v-1}} \psi(s), & N-1 < v < N, \\ \Delta^N \psi(t), & v = N, \end{cases}$$

where $N \in \mathbb{N}$ with $0 \leqslant N-1 < v \leqslant N$. As in [1], this definition is equivalent to (2) in Section 2.

The theory of fractional calculus has been widely used in modern mathematics for more than 300 years, and the study of solutions of fractional differential (difference) equations arises in real-world problems in the field of physics, mechanics, chemistry, and engineering. For example, in [2], the authors extended the variational approach to the fractional discrete case and introduced the Gompertz fractional difference equation

$$\Delta_0^\alpha \ln \mathcal{G}(t - \alpha + 1) = (b-1) \ln \mathcal{G}(t) + a,$$

which can be used to describe tumor growth, a special relationship between tumor size and time, and is of special interest since growth estimation is very critical in clinical practice. Here, a, b are parameters and $\alpha \in (0,1]$. One can also find some other applications for the

Gompertz fractional difference equation in [1]. In [3], the authors introduced the following discrete logistic map and investigated the chaotic behavior:

$$\begin{cases} {}^{C}\Delta_a^v \psi(t) = \mu \psi(t+v-1)(1-\psi(t+v-1)), t \in \mathbb{N}_{a+1-v}, 0 < v \le 1, \\ \psi(a) = c, \end{cases}$$

where ${}^{C}\Delta_a^v$ is the left Caputo-like delta difference defined by

$$ {}^{C}\Delta_a^v \psi(t) = \frac{1}{\Gamma(m-v)} \sum_{s=a}^{t-(m-v)} (t-s-1)^{\underline{m-v-1}} \Delta_s^m \psi(s), $$

where $t \in \mathbb{N}_{a+m-v}, m = [v] + 1$.

We note that in [4], the author mentioned that discretization is inevitable for fractional differential equations. To date, they are only used as the starting point for approximate solution calculations, and there is no special research on fractional difference equations. Therefore, from the perspective of theory and application, this is a big gap. Many developments in the theory are now taking place, and two books [5,6] are sources for mathematicians who are interested in this area. However, we still note that most works focus on fractional-order differential equations, while the research on fractional-order difference equations is quite small (we refer the reader to [5–26]). In [7], the authors investigated positive solutions for the discrete fractional boundary value problems

$$\begin{cases} -\Delta_{v-2}^v \chi(t) = \mathcal{F}(t+v-1, \chi(t+v-1)), 1 < v \le 2, \\ \chi(v-2) = \Delta_{v-1}^{v-1}\chi(v+N) = 0, \end{cases}$$

where $t \in [0, N+1]_{\mathbb{N}_0}$ and $\mathcal{F} : [v-1, v+N]_{\mathbb{N}_{v-1}} \times \mathbb{R} \to \mathbb{R}^+$ satisfies some superlinear or sublinear conditions. In [8], the authors utilized fixed-point methods to investigate the solvability of a fractional difference equation with a p-Laplacian operator

$$\begin{cases} \Delta^\beta [\phi_p(\Delta^\alpha \chi)](t) + \mathcal{F}(\alpha+\beta+t-1, \chi(\alpha+\beta+t-1)) = 0, t \in [0, \mathfrak{b}]_{\mathbb{N}_0}, \\ \Delta^\alpha \chi(\beta-2) = \Delta^\alpha \chi(\beta+\mathfrak{b}) = 0, \\ \chi(\alpha+\beta-4) = \chi(\alpha+\beta+\mathfrak{b}) = 0, \end{cases}$$

where $\mathcal{F} : [\alpha+\beta-4, \alpha+\beta+\mathfrak{b}]_{\mathbb{N}_{\alpha+\beta-4}} \times \mathbb{R} \to \mathbb{R}$ satisfies a Lipschitz condition, and $\phi_p(z) = |z|^{p-2}z, p > 1, z \in \mathbb{R}$. In [9], the authors utilized the fixed point index to consider the solvability of the system of fractional-order difference boundary value problems

$$\begin{cases} \Delta^v \chi_1(t) = \mathcal{F}_1(t+v-1, \chi_1(t+v-1), \chi_2(t+v-1)), t \in [0, T]_{\mathbb{Z}}, \\ \Delta^v \chi_2(t) = \mathcal{F}_2(t+v-1, \chi_1(t+v-1), \chi_2(t+v-1)), t \in [0, T]_{\mathbb{Z}}, \\ \chi_1(v-1) = \chi_1(v+T), \chi_2(v-1) = \chi_2(v+T), \end{cases}$$

where $\mathcal{F}_i(i = 1, 2)$ are semipositone nonlinearities.

We note that usually one expresses the solutions of fractional-order equations by a Green's function. However, not all fractional-order difference equations can be obtained in this way, for example, in [10], the authors studied the problem

$$\begin{cases} \Delta^\alpha \chi(t) = \mathcal{F}(t+\alpha-1, \chi(t+\alpha-1)), \ t \in [0, T]_{\mathbb{N}_0}, \alpha \in (1, 2], \\ \chi(\alpha-2) = 0, \chi(\alpha+T) = \Delta^{-\beta}\chi(\zeta+\beta), \ \zeta \in \mathbb{N}_{\alpha-2, \alpha+T-1}, \beta > 0, \end{cases}$$

and showed it is equivalent to

$$\chi(t) = -\frac{t^{\alpha-1}}{\Theta\Gamma(\alpha)}\left[\frac{1}{\Gamma(\beta)}\sum_{s=\alpha}^{\zeta}\sum_{\xi=0}^{s-\alpha}(\zeta+\beta-\sigma(s))^{\underline{\beta-1}}(s-\sigma(\xi))^{\underline{\alpha-1}}\mathcal{F}(\xi+\alpha-1,\chi(\xi+\alpha-1))\right.$$

$$\left.-\sum_{s=0}^{T}(T+\alpha-\sigma(s))^{\underline{\alpha-1}}\mathcal{F}(s+\alpha-1,\chi(s+\alpha-1))\right]+\frac{1}{\Gamma(\alpha)}\sum_{s=0}^{t-\alpha}(t-\sigma(s))^{\underline{\alpha-1}}\mathcal{F}(s+\alpha-1,\chi(s+\alpha-1)),$$

where

$$\Theta = \sum_{s=1}^{\zeta-\alpha+2}\frac{(\zeta+\beta-s-\alpha+1)^{\underline{\beta-1}}\Gamma(s+\alpha-1)}{\Gamma(\beta)\Gamma(s)} - \frac{\Gamma(\alpha+T+1)}{\Gamma(T+2)}.$$

Clearly, the integral form is very complicated and cannot be formulated via some suitable Green's function.

Inspired by the aforementioned works, in this paper, via a Green's function, we use the topological degree and fixed point theorems to consider the existence, uniqueness, and multiplicity of solutions to (1). Furthermore, we present some examples to illustrate our main results.

2. Preliminary

In this section, we first offer some basic materials for discrete fractional calculus; see [5–26] and the references therein.

Definition 1. *Let*
$t^{\underline{v}} := \frac{\Gamma(t+1)}{\Gamma(t+1-v)}, \forall t, v \in \mathbb{R}$. *If $t+1-v$ is a pole of $\Gamma(\cdot)$ and $t+1$ is not a pole, then $t^{\underline{v}} = 0$.*

Definition 2. *For $v > 0$, a function $\mathcal{F}$'s v-th fractional sum is defined by*

$$\Delta_a^{-v}\mathcal{F}(t) = \frac{1}{\Gamma(v)}\sum_{s=a}^{t-v}(t-s-1)^{\underline{v-1}}\mathcal{F}(s), \quad t \in \mathbb{N}_{a+v}.$$

$\mathcal{F}$'s v-th fractional difference is defined by

$$\Delta_a^v\mathcal{F}(t) = \Delta^N\Delta_a^{v-N}\mathcal{F}(t), \quad t \in \mathbb{N}_{a+N-v}, \tag{2}$$

where $N \in \mathbb{N}$ with $0 \leqslant N-1 < v \leqslant N$.

Let $\chi : [v-1, \mathfrak{b}+v+1]_{\mathbb{N}_{v-1}} \to \mathbb{R}$ be a given function. Then, we consider the problem

$$\begin{cases} -\Delta_{v-3}^v\psi(t) = \chi(t+v-1), & t \in [0, \mathfrak{b}+2]_{\mathbb{N}_0}, \\ \psi(v-3) = \left[\Delta_{v-3}^\alpha\psi(t)\right]\big|_{t=v-\alpha-2} = \left[\Delta_{v-3}^\beta\psi(t)\right]\big|_{t=v+\mathfrak{b}+2-\beta} = 0, \end{cases} \tag{3}$$

where $v, \alpha, \beta, \mathfrak{b}$ can be founded in (1).

Lemma 1 (see [11]). *Problem (3) has a unique solution*

$$\psi(t) = \sum_{s=0}^{\mathfrak{b}+2}\mathbb{G}(t,s)\chi(s+v-1), \quad t \in [v-1, \mathfrak{b}+v+1]_{\mathbb{N}_{v-1}},$$

where $\mathbb{G}$ is the Green's function given by

$$\mathbb{G}(t,s) = \frac{1}{\Gamma(v)}\begin{cases} \frac{t^{\underline{v-1}}(v+\mathfrak{b}-\beta-s+1)^{\underline{v-\beta-1}}}{(v+\mathfrak{b}-\beta+2)^{\underline{v-\beta-1}}} - (t-s-1)^{\underline{v-1}}, 0 \leq s < t-v+1 \leq \mathfrak{b}+2, \\ \frac{t^{\underline{v-1}}(v+\mathfrak{b}-\beta-s+1)^{\underline{v-\beta-1}}}{(v+\mathfrak{b}-\beta+2)^{\underline{v-\beta-1}}}, 0 \leq t-v+1 \leq s \leq \mathfrak{b}+2. \end{cases} \tag{4}$$

Lemma 2 (see [11]). *The Green's function (4) has the properties*
(G1) $\mathbb{G}(t,s) > 0, (t,s) \in [v-1, \mathfrak{b}+v+1]_{\mathbb{N}_{v-1}} \times [0, \mathfrak{b}+2]_{\mathbb{N}_0}$,

$(G2)$ $\frac{t^{v-1}\mathbb{G}(\mathfrak{b}+v+1,s)}{(\mathfrak{b}+v+1)^{\underline{v-1}}} \leqslant \mathbb{G}(t,s) \leqslant \frac{t^{v-1}(v+\mathfrak{b}-\beta-s+1)^{\underline{v-\beta-1}}}{\Gamma(v)(v+\mathfrak{b}-\beta+2)^{\underline{v-\beta-1}}}, (t,s) \in [v-1,\mathfrak{b}+v+1]_{\mathbb{N}_{v-1}} \times [0,\mathfrak{b}+2]_{\mathbb{N}_0}$,

$(G3)$ $q(t)\mathbb{G}(\mathfrak{b}+v+1,s) \leqslant \mathbb{G}(t,s) \leqslant \mathbb{G}(\mathfrak{b}+v+1,s), q(t) = \frac{t^{v-1}}{(\mathfrak{b}+v+1)^{\underline{v-1}}}, (t,s) \in [v-1,\mathfrak{b}+v+1]_{\mathbb{N}_{v-1}} \times [0,\mathfrak{b}+2]_{\mathbb{N}_0}$.

Lemma 3 (see [11]). *Let $\varphi(s+v-1) = \mathbb{G}(\mathfrak{b}+v+1,s), s \in [0,\mathfrak{b}+2]_{\mathbb{N}_0}$. Then, the following inequalities hold:*

$$\sum_{t=v-1}^{\mathfrak{b}+v+1} \mathbb{G}(t,s)\varphi(t) \leqslant \kappa_2\varphi(s+v-1), \kappa_2 = \sum_{t=v-1}^{\mathfrak{b}+v+1} \varphi(t), s \in [0,\mathfrak{b}+2]_{\mathbb{N}_0}, \tag{5}$$

and

$$\sum_{s=0}^{\mathfrak{b}+2} \mathbb{G}(t,s)q(s+v-1) \geq \kappa_1 q(t), \kappa_1 = \sum_{s=0}^{\mathfrak{b}+2} \mathbb{G}(\mathfrak{b}+v+1,s)q(s+v-1), t \in [v-1,\mathfrak{b}+v+1]_{\mathbb{N}_{v-1}}. \tag{6}$$

Let E be a set of all maps from $[v-3,\mathfrak{b}+v+1]_{\mathbb{N}_{v-3}}$ to $\mathbb{R}$, and $\|\psi\| = \max_{t \in [v-3,\mathfrak{b}+v+1]_{\mathbb{N}_{v-3}}} |\psi(t)|$. Then, E is a Banach space. Moreover, define a set $P = \{\psi \in E : \psi(t) \geqslant 0, t \in [v-1,\mathfrak{b}+v+1]_{\mathbb{N}_{v-1}}\}$. Then, P is a cone on E. Lemma 3 enables us to obtain that (1) is equivalent to the sum equation

$$\psi(t) = \sum_{s=0}^{\mathfrak{b}+2} \mathbb{G}(t,s)g(s+v-1,\psi(s+n-1)) - (\mathcal{B}\psi)(t), \quad t \in [v-1,\mathfrak{b}+v+1]_{\mathbb{N}_{v-1}},$$

where G is defined in Lemma 3. Obviously, $\psi \in E\backslash\{0\}$ is a solution for (1) when $\psi \in E\backslash\{0\}$ is a fixed point of $\mathcal{B}$.

Lemma 4. *Let $P_0 = \{\psi \in P : \psi(t) \geqslant q(t)\|\psi\|, \forall t \in [v-1,\mathfrak{b}+v+1]_{\mathbb{N}_{v-1}}\}$. Then, $\mathcal{L}(P) \subset P_0$, where*

$$(\mathcal{L}\psi)(t) = \sum_{s=0}^{\mathfrak{b}+2} \mathbb{G}(t,s)\psi(s+v-1), \quad t \in [v-1,\mathfrak{b}+v+1]_{\mathbb{N}_{v-1}}.$$

Lemma 5 (see [27] Theorem A.3.3). *Let E be a Banach space, $\Omega \subset E$ a bounded open set, and $\mathcal{T} : \Omega \to E$ be a continuous compact operator. If there is an $\mathfrak{x}_0 \in E\backslash\{0\}$ such that*

$$\mathfrak{x} - \mathcal{T}\mathfrak{x} \neq \mu\mathfrak{x}_0, \forall\mathfrak{x} \in \partial\Omega, \mu \geq 0,$$

then $\deg(I-\mathcal{T},\Omega,0) = 0$, where deg denotes the topological degree.

Lemma 6 (see [27] Lemma 2.5.1). *Let E be a Banach space, $\Omega \subset E$ a bounded open set with $0 \in \Omega$, and $\mathcal{T} : \Omega \to E$ be a continuous compact operator. If*

$$\mathcal{T}\mathfrak{x} \neq \mu\mathfrak{x}, \forall\mathfrak{x} \in \partial\Omega, \mu \geq 1,$$

then $\deg(I-\mathcal{T},\Omega,0) = 1$.

Lemma 7 (see [28,29]). *Let X be a Banach space and P be a cone on X. Define functionals as follows: $\alpha, \gamma : P \to \mathbb{R}^+$ are continuous increasing and $\beta : P \to \mathbb{R}^+$ is continuous. Moreover, there exists $M > 0, 0 < \widetilde{a} < \widetilde{c}$ such that*

$$\alpha(0) < \widetilde{a}, \gamma(\mathfrak{x}) \leq \beta(\mathfrak{x}) \leq \alpha(\mathfrak{x}) \text{ and } \|\mathfrak{x}\| \leq M\gamma(\mathfrak{x}), \forall\mathfrak{x} \in \overline{P(\gamma,\widetilde{c})} := \overline{\{\mathfrak{x} \in P : \gamma(\mathfrak{x}) < \widetilde{c}\}}.$$

Furthermore, there is a completely continuous operator $\mathcal{T} : \overline{P(\gamma,\widetilde{c})} \to P$ and a constant $\widetilde{b} > 0$ with $0 < \widetilde{a} < \widetilde{b} < \widetilde{c}$ such that $\beta(\lambda\mathfrak{x}) \leq \lambda\beta(\mathfrak{x})$ for $\lambda \in (0,1], \mathfrak{x} \in \partial P(\beta,\widetilde{b})$, and

(E1) $\gamma(\mathcal{T}\mathfrak{x}) < \widetilde{c}, \forall \mathfrak{x} \in \partial P(\gamma, \widetilde{c})$;
(E2) $\beta(\mathcal{T}\mathfrak{x}) > \widetilde{b}, \forall \mathfrak{x} \in \partial P(\beta, \widetilde{b})$;
(E3) $\alpha(\mathcal{T}\mathfrak{x}) < \widetilde{a}, \forall \mathfrak{x} \in \partial P(\alpha, \widetilde{a})$.
Then, $\mathcal{T}$ *has at least three fixed points* $\mathfrak{x}_1, \mathfrak{x}_2, \mathfrak{x}_3 \in \overline{P(\gamma, \widetilde{c})}$ *such that*

$$0 \leq \alpha(\mathfrak{x}_1) < \widetilde{a} < \alpha(\mathfrak{x}_2), \beta(\mathfrak{x}_2) < \widetilde{b} < \beta(\mathfrak{x}_3), \gamma(\mathfrak{x}_3) < \widetilde{c}.$$

In the following, we present some lemmas involving the theory of mixed monotone operators. Let $(E, \|\cdot\|)$ *be a real Banach space which is partially ordered by a cone* $P \subset E$, *i.e.,* $x \leq y \Leftrightarrow y - x \in P$. *If* $x \leq y$ *and* $x \neq y$, *then we mean that* $x < y$ *or* $y > x$. *Moreover, for a fixed* $h > 0$, *we define* $P_h = \{x \in E \mid x \sim h\}$, *in which* $\sim$ *is an equivalence relation, i.e.,* $x \sim y$ *implies that there are* $\lambda, \mu > 0$ *such that* $\lambda x \geq y \geq \mu x, \forall x, y \in E$.

Definition 3 (see [30,31]). *If* $\mathfrak{u}_i, \mathfrak{v}_i (i = 1, 2) \in P, \mathfrak{u}_1 < \mathfrak{u}_2, \mathfrak{v}_1 > \mathfrak{v}_2$ *imply* $A(\mathfrak{u}_1, \mathfrak{v}_1) \leq A(\mathfrak{u}_2, \mathfrak{v}_2)$, *then* $A : P \times P \to P$ *is called a mixed monotone operator.*

Definition 4 (see [30,31]). *If* $A(t\mathfrak{x}) \geq tA\mathfrak{x}, \forall t \in (0, 1), \mathfrak{x} \in P$, *then* $A : P \to P$ *is said to be sub-homogeneous.*

Lemma 8 (see [30,31]). *Let* $\mathcal{B} : P \to P$ *be an increasing sub-homogeneous operator,* $\mathcal{A} : P \times P \to P$ *a mixed monotone operator and satisfy*

$$\mathcal{A}\left(t\mathfrak{x}, t^{-1}\mathfrak{y}\right) \geq t^\alpha \mathcal{A}(\mathfrak{x}, \mathfrak{y}), \ t, \alpha \in (0, 1), \mathfrak{x}, \mathfrak{y} \in P. \tag{7}$$

If
(C1) There is a $\mathfrak{h}_0 \in P_\mathfrak{h}$ *such that* $\mathcal{A}(\mathfrak{h}_0, \mathfrak{h}_0) \in P_\mathfrak{h}$ *and* $\mathcal{B}\mathfrak{h}_0 \in P_\mathfrak{h}$;
(C2) There is a constant $\delta_0 > 0$ *such that* $\mathcal{A}(\mathfrak{x}, \mathfrak{y}) \geq \delta_0 \mathcal{B}\mathfrak{x}, \forall \mathfrak{x}, \mathfrak{y} \in P$.
Then,
(D1) $\mathcal{A} : P_\mathfrak{h} \times P_\mathfrak{h} \to P_\mathfrak{h}, \mathcal{B} : P_\mathfrak{h} \to P_\mathfrak{h}$;
(D2) There are $\mathfrak{u}_0, \mathfrak{v}_0 \in P_\mathfrak{h}$ *and* $r \in (0, 1)$ *such that* $r\mathfrak{v}_0 \leq \mathfrak{u}_0 < \mathfrak{v}_0, \mathfrak{u}_0 \leq \mathcal{A}(\mathfrak{u}_0, \mathfrak{v}_0) + \mathcal{B}\mathfrak{u}_0 \leq \mathcal{A}(\mathfrak{v}_0, \mathfrak{u}_0) + \mathcal{B}(\mathfrak{v}_0) \leq \mathfrak{v}_0$;
(D3) $\mathcal{A}(\mathfrak{x}, \mathfrak{x}) + \mathcal{B}\mathfrak{x} = \mathfrak{x}$ *has a unique solution* $\mathfrak{x}^*$ *in* $P_\mathfrak{h}$;
(D4) For any initial values $\mathfrak{x}_0, \mathfrak{y}_0 \in P_\mathfrak{h}$, *the sequences* $\mathfrak{x}_n = \mathcal{A}(\mathfrak{x}_{n-1}, \mathfrak{y}_{n-1}) + \mathcal{B}\mathfrak{x}_{n-1}, \mathfrak{y}_n = \mathcal{A}(\mathfrak{y}_{n-1}, \mathfrak{x}_{n-1}) + \mathcal{B}\mathfrak{y}_{n-1}$ *converge to* $\mathfrak{x}^*$ *as* $n \to \infty$.

3. Main Results

In the section, we will state our main theorems and give their proof. In the first theorem, we obtain an existence result on nontrivial solutions for (1) when the nonlinearity can change sign.

Theorem 1. *Suppose that the following assumptions hold:*
(H1) $g(t, \psi) : [v - 1, \mathfrak{b} + v + 1]_{\mathbb{N}_{v-1}} \times \mathbb{R} \to \mathbb{R}$ *is a continuous function;*
(H2) There are nonnegative continuous functions $\gamma_1(t), \gamma_2(t)$ *and* $\mathcal{M}(\psi)$ *with* $\gamma_2(t) \not\equiv 0$, $t \in [v - 1, \mathfrak{b} + v + 1]_{\mathbb{N}_{v-1}}$ *such that*

$$g(t, \psi) \geq -\gamma_1(t) - \gamma_2(t)\mathcal{M}(\psi), (t, \psi) \in [v - 1, \mathfrak{b} + v + 1]_{\mathbb{N}_{v-1}} \times \mathbb{R};$$

(H3) $\lim_{|\psi| \to +\infty} \frac{\mathcal{M}(\psi)}{|\psi|} = 0$;
(H4) $\liminf_{|\psi| \to +\infty} \frac{g(t, \psi)}{|\psi|} > \kappa_1^{-1}$, *uniformly in* $t \in [v - 1, \mathfrak{b} + v + 1]_{\mathbb{N}_{v-1}}$;
(H5) $\liminf_{|\psi| \to 0^+} \frac{|g(t, \psi)|}{|\psi|} < \kappa_2^{-1}$, *uniformly in* $t \in [v - 1, \mathfrak{b} + v + 1]_{\mathbb{N}_{v-1}}$.
Then, (1) has one nontrivial solution.

Proof. From (H3), for any given $\varepsilon > 0$, there exists $Y_0 > 0$ such that $\mathcal{M}(\psi) \leq \varepsilon|\psi|$ for $|\psi| > Y_0$. Let $\mathcal{M}^* = \max_{|\psi| \in [0, Y_0]} \mathcal{M}(\psi)$. Then, we have

$$\mathcal{M}(\psi) \leq \varepsilon|\psi| + \mathcal{M}^*, \ \psi \in \mathbb{R}. \tag{8}$$

By (H4), there exist $\delta_1 > 0$ and $Y_1 \geq Y_0$ such that $g(t, \psi) \geq (\kappa_1^{-1} + \delta_1)|\psi|$ for $|\psi| > Y_1$ and $t \in [v - 1, \mathfrak{b} + v + 1]_{\mathbb{N}_{v-1}}$. Furthermore, let $\widetilde{C}_g = \max_{(t,\psi) \in [v-1, \mathfrak{b}+v+1]_{\mathbb{N}_{v-1}} \times [0, Y_1]} |g(t, \psi)|$. Then, we obtain

$$g(t, \psi) \geq (\kappa_1^{-1} + \delta_1)|\psi| - \widetilde{C}_g, \ t \in [v - 1, \mathfrak{b} + v + 1]_{\mathbb{N}_{v-1}}, \psi \in \mathbb{R}.$$

Note that δ_1 can be greater than $\varepsilon\|\gamma_2\|$; then, from (H2) and (H3) and (8), we have

$$g(t, \psi) \geq (\kappa_1^{-1} + \delta_1 - \varepsilon\|\gamma_2\|)|\psi| - \gamma_1(t) - C_g, \ t \in [v - 1, \mathfrak{b} + v + 1]_{\mathbb{N}_{v-1}}, \psi \in \mathbb{R}, \tag{9}$$

where $C_g = \widetilde{C}_g + \|\gamma_2\|\mathcal{M}^*$. Let

$$\mathcal{R} > \max\left\{ \frac{\kappa_2(\|\gamma_1\| + \|\gamma_2\|\mathcal{M}^* + C_g)}{1 - \varepsilon\kappa_2\|\gamma_2\|}, \frac{(\|\gamma_1\| + \|\gamma_2\|\mathcal{M}^* + C_g)\left[\frac{\kappa_2(\delta_1 - \varepsilon\|\gamma_2\|)}{(\mathfrak{b}+v+1)^{v-1}} + (\kappa_1^{-1} + \delta_1 - \varepsilon\|\gamma_2\|)\mathcal{N}_1\right]}{\frac{\delta_1 - \varepsilon\|\gamma_2\|}{(\mathfrak{b}+v+1)^{v-1}}(1 - \varepsilon\kappa_2\|\gamma_2\|) - \varepsilon\|\gamma_2\|\mathcal{N}_1(\kappa_1^{-1} + \delta_1 - \varepsilon\|\gamma_2\|)} \right\}, \tag{10}$$

where

$$\mathcal{N}_1 = \sum_{\tau=0}^{\mathfrak{b}+2} \frac{(v + \mathfrak{b} - \beta - \tau + 1)^{\underline{v-\beta-1}}}{(v + \mathfrak{b} - \beta + 2)^{\underline{v-\beta-1}}\Gamma(v)}.$$

We prove that

$$\psi - \mathcal{B}\psi \neq \mu q, \ \psi \in \partial B_{\mathcal{R}}, \mu \geq 0, \tag{11}$$

where q is given in Lemma 4, and

$$B_{\mathcal{R}} = \{\psi \in E : \|\psi\| < \mathcal{R}\}, \ \partial B_{\mathcal{R}} = \{\psi \in E : \|\psi\| = \mathcal{R}\}.$$

Proof by contradiction. Then, there are $\psi \in \partial B_{\mathcal{R}}, \mu \geq 0$ such that

$$\psi - \mathcal{B}\psi = \mu q. \tag{12}$$

Note that if $\mu = 0$ and $\psi \in \partial B_{\mathcal{R}}$ is a nontrivial solution to (1), the theorem has been obtained. So, we only consider the case $\mu > 0$. Moreover, we also find that

$$q \in P_0.$$

In order to prove our theorem, we need to define a function $\widetilde{\psi}$ as follows:

$$\widetilde{\psi}(t) = \sum_{s=0}^{\mathfrak{b}+2} \mathbb{G}(t, s)\left[\gamma_1(s + v - 1) + \gamma_2(s + v - 1)\mathcal{M}(\psi(s + v - 1)) + C_g\right], t \in [v - 1, \mathfrak{b} + v + 1]_{\mathbb{N}_{v-1}}, \psi \in \partial B_{\mathcal{R}}.$$

Then, we get the following claims:

Claim i. Note that $\gamma_1 + \gamma_2\mathcal{M}(\psi) + C_g \in P$, and Lemma 6 implies that

$$\widetilde{\psi} \in P_0. \tag{13}$$

Claim ii. From (12), we find

$$\psi(t) + \widetilde{\psi}(t) = (\mathcal{B}\psi)(t) + \widetilde{\psi}(t) + \mu q(t)$$

$$= \sum_{s=0}^{\mathfrak{b}+2} \mathbb{G}(t, s)\left[g(s + v - 1, \psi(s + v - 1)) + \gamma_1(s + v - 1) + \gamma_2(s + v - 1)\mathcal{M}(\psi(s + v - 1)) + C_g\right] + \mu q(t),$$

for all $t \in [v-1, \mathfrak{b}+v+1]_{\mathbb{N}_{v-1}}$. Note that $g + \gamma_1 + \gamma_2 \mathcal{M} + C_g \in P$ and $q \in P_0$, and we have

$$\psi + \widetilde{\psi} \in P_0. \tag{14}$$

Claim iii. From (8) and (10), we have

$$\|\widetilde{\psi}\| \leq \sum_{s=0}^{\mathfrak{b}+2} \mathbb{G}(\mathfrak{b}+v+1, s)\left[\|\gamma_1\| + \|\gamma_2\|(\varepsilon\|\psi\| + \mathcal{M}^*) + C_g\right]$$
$$= \kappa_2\left[\|\gamma_1\| + \|\gamma_2\|(\varepsilon\|\psi\| + \mathcal{M}^*) + C_g\right]$$
$$< \mathcal{R}.$$

From Claim ii and (9), we have

$$(\mathcal{B}\psi)(t) + \widetilde{\psi}(t) = \sum_{s=0}^{\mathfrak{b}+2} \mathbb{G}(t,s)\left[g(s+v-1, \psi(s+v-1)) + \gamma_1(s+v-1) + \gamma_2(s+v-1)\mathcal{M}(\psi(s+v-1)) + C_g\right]$$

$$\geq \sum_{s=0}^{\mathfrak{b}+2} \mathbb{G}(t,s)\left[g(s+v-1, \psi(s+v-1)) + \gamma_1(s+v-1) + C_g\right]$$

$$\geq \sum_{s=0}^{\mathfrak{b}+2} \mathbb{G}(t,s)\left[(\kappa_1^{-1} + \delta_1 - \varepsilon\|\gamma_2\|)|\psi(s+v-1)| - \gamma_1(s+v-1) - C_g + \gamma_1(s+v-1) + C_g\right] \tag{15}$$

$$\geq (\kappa_1^{-1} + \delta_1 - \varepsilon\|\gamma_2\|)\sum_{s=0}^{\mathfrak{b}+2} \mathbb{G}(t,s)\psi(s+v-1)$$

$$= (\kappa_1^{-1} + \delta_1 - \varepsilon\|\gamma_2\|)\left[\sum_{s=0}^{\mathfrak{b}+2} \mathbb{G}(t,s)\left[\psi(s+v-1) + \widetilde{\psi}(s+v-1)\right] - \sum_{s=0}^{\mathfrak{b}+2} \mathbb{G}(t,s)\widetilde{\psi}(s+v-1)\right]$$

$$\geq \kappa_1^{-1}\sum_{s=0}^{\mathfrak{b}+2} \mathbb{G}(t,s)\left[\psi(s+v-1) + \widetilde{\psi}(s+v-1)\right].$$

The last inequality in (15) holds if

$$(\delta_1 - \varepsilon\|\gamma_2\|)\sum_{s=0}^{\mathfrak{b}+2} \mathbb{G}(t,s)\left[\psi(s+v-1) + \widetilde{\psi}(s+v-1)\right] - (\kappa_1^{-1} + \delta_1 - \varepsilon\|\gamma_2\|)\sum_{s=0}^{\mathfrak{b}+2} \mathbb{G}(t,s)\widetilde{\psi}(s+v-1) \geq 0, \tag{16}$$

for $t \in [v-1, \mathfrak{b}+v+1]_{\mathbb{N}_{v-1}}$. In what follows, we prove (16). Indeed, from Claim ii we have
$\psi(t) + \widetilde{\psi}(t) \geq q(t)\|\psi + \widetilde{\psi}\| \geq q(t)(\|\psi\| - \|\widetilde{\psi}\|), t \in [v-1, \mathfrak{b}+v+1]_{\mathbb{N}_{v-1}}$. Therefore, from (4) and (10), we obtain

$$(\delta_1 - \varepsilon\|\gamma_2\|)\sum_{s=0}^{\mathfrak{b}+2} \mathbb{G}(t,s)\left[\psi(s+v-1) + \widetilde{\psi}(s+v-1)\right] - (\kappa_1^{-1} + \delta_1 - \varepsilon\|\gamma_2\|)\sum_{s=0}^{\mathfrak{b}+2} \mathbb{G}(t,s)\widetilde{\psi}(s+v-1)$$

$$\geq (\delta_1 - \varepsilon\|\gamma_2\|)\sum_{s=0}^{\mathfrak{b}+2} \mathbb{G}(t,s)q(s+v-1)(\|\psi\| - \|\widetilde{\psi}\|)$$

$$- (\kappa_1^{-1} + \delta_1 - \varepsilon\|\gamma_2\|)\sum_{s=0}^{\mathfrak{b}+2} \mathbb{G}(t,s)\sum_{\tau=0}^{\mathfrak{b}+2} \mathbb{G}(s+v-1, \tau)\left[\gamma_1(\tau+v-1) + \gamma_2(\tau+v-1)\mathcal{M}(\psi(\tau+v-1)) + C_g\right]$$

$$\geq (\delta_1 - \varepsilon\|\gamma_2\|)\sum_{s=0}^{\mathfrak{b}+2} \mathbb{G}(t,s)\frac{(s+v-1)^{\underline{v-1}}}{(\mathfrak{b}+v+1)^{\underline{v-1}}}(\|\psi\| - \|\widetilde{\psi}\|)$$

$$- (\kappa_1^{-1} + \delta_1 - \varepsilon\|\gamma_2\|)\sum_{s=0}^{\mathfrak{b}+2} \mathbb{G}(t,s)\sum_{\tau=0}^{\mathfrak{b}+2} \frac{(s+v-1)^{\underline{v-1}}(v+\mathfrak{b}-\beta-\tau+1)^{\underline{v-\beta-1}}}{(v+\mathfrak{b}-\beta+2)^{\underline{v-\beta-1}}\Gamma(v)}\left[\|\gamma_1\| + \|\gamma_2\|(\varepsilon\|\psi\| + \mathcal{M}^*) + C_g\right]$$

$$\geq \sum_{s=0}^{\mathfrak{b}+2} \mathbb{G}(t,s)(s+v-1)^{\underline{v-1}}\left[\frac{\delta_1 - \varepsilon\|\gamma_2\|}{(\mathfrak{b}+v+1)^{\underline{v-1}}}\left(\mathcal{R} - \kappa_2[\|\gamma_1\| + \|\gamma_2\|(\varepsilon\mathcal{R} + \mathcal{M}^*) + C_g]\right)\right.$$

$$\left. - (\kappa_1^{-1} + \delta_1 - \varepsilon\|\gamma_2\|)[\|\gamma_1\| + \|\gamma_2\|(\varepsilon\mathcal{R} + \mathcal{M}^*) + C_g]\sum_{\tau=0}^{\mathfrak{b}+2} \frac{(v+\mathfrak{b}-\beta-\tau+1)^{\underline{v-\beta-1}}}{(v+\mathfrak{b}-\beta+2)^{\underline{v-\beta-1}}\Gamma(v)}\right]$$

$$\geq 0.$$

This implies that (15) holds, as required. Consequently, we have

$$(\mathcal{B}\psi)(t) + \widetilde{\psi}(t) \geq \kappa_1^{-1}\mathcal{L}(\psi + \widetilde{\psi})(t), t \in [v - 1, \mathfrak{b} + v + 1]_{\mathbb{N}_{v-1}}.$$

Using (12), we obtain

$$\psi + \widetilde{\psi} = \mathcal{B}\psi + \widetilde{\psi} + \mu q \geq \kappa_1^{-1}\mathcal{L}(\psi + \widetilde{\psi}) + \mu q \geq \mu q, \ \psi \in \partial B_{\mathcal{R}}, \mu > 0.$$

Define

$$\mu^* = \sup\{\mu > 0 : \psi + \widetilde{\psi} \geq \mu q\}.$$

Note that $\mu^* \geq \mu$ and $\psi + \widetilde{\psi} \geq \mu^* q$, and from (6), we have

$$\psi + \widetilde{\psi} \geq \kappa_1^{-1}\mathcal{L}(\mu^* q) + \mu q = \kappa_1^{-1}\mu^*\mathcal{L}q + \mu q \geq (\mu^* + \mu)q,$$

which contradicts the definition of μ^*. Hence, (11) holds, and Lemma 7 enables us to find

$$\deg(I - \mathcal{B}, B_{\mathcal{R}}, 0) = 0. \tag{17}$$

From (H5), there exist $\delta_2 \in (0, \kappa_2^{-1})$ and $r > 0$ such that

$$|g(t, \psi)| \leq (\kappa_2^{-1} - \delta_2)|\psi|, \ |\psi| \in [0, r], t \in [v - 1, \mathfrak{b} + v + 1]_{\mathbb{N}_{v-1}}. \tag{18}$$

For this r, we prove that

$$\mathcal{B}\psi \neq \mu\psi, \psi \in \partial B_r, \mu \geq 1. \tag{19}$$

Proof by contradiction. Then, there are $\psi \in \partial B_r, \mu \geq 1$ such that

$$\mathcal{B}\psi = \mu\psi \Rightarrow |\psi| = \frac{1}{\mu}|\mathcal{B}\psi| \leq |\mathcal{B}\psi|.$$

This, together with (18), implies that

$$|\psi(t)| \leq \sum_{s=0}^{\mathfrak{b}+2} \mathbb{G}(t,s)|g(s + v - 1, \psi(s + v - 1))| \leq (\kappa_2^{-1} - \delta_2)\sum_{s=0}^{\mathfrak{b}+2} \mathbb{G}(t,s)|\psi(s + v - 1)|. \tag{20}$$

Multiplying by $\varphi(t)$ on the both sides of (20) and summing over $[v - 1, \mathfrak{b} + v + 1]$, then (5) implies that

$$\sum_{t=v-1}^{\mathfrak{b}+v+1} |\psi(t)|\varphi(t) \leq (\kappa_2^{-1} - \delta_2)\sum_{t=v-1}^{\mathfrak{b}+v+1}\sum_{s=0}^{\mathfrak{b}+2} \mathbb{G}(t,s)\varphi(t)|\psi(s + v - 1)|$$

$$\leq (\kappa_2^{-1} - \delta_2)\kappa_2 \sum_{s=0}^{\mathfrak{b}+2} |\psi(s + v - 1)|\varphi(s + v - 1)$$

$$= (\kappa_2^{-1} - \delta_2)\kappa_2 \sum_{t=v-1}^{\mathfrak{b}+v+1} |\psi(t)|\varphi(t).$$

This implies that $\sum_{t=v-1}^{\mathfrak{b}+v+1} |\psi(t)|\varphi(t) = 0$, and thus $\psi(t) \equiv 0, t \in [v - 1, \mathfrak{b} + v + 1]_{\mathbb{N}_{v-1}}$. Clearly, this is contradictory to $\psi \in \partial B_r$. Hence, Lemma 8 shows that

$$\deg(I - \mathcal{B}, B_r, 0) = 1. \tag{21}$$

Equations (17) and (21) enable us to obtain

$$\deg(I - \mathcal{B}, B_{\mathcal{R}} \setminus \overline{B}_r, 0) = \deg(I - \mathcal{B}, B_{\mathcal{R}}, 0) - \deg(I - \mathcal{B}, B_r, 0) = -1.$$

This implies that $\mathcal{B}$ has a fixed point in $B_{\mathcal{R}} \backslash \overline{B}_r$, and (1) has a nontrivial solution. $\square$

In the following theorem, using the generalized Avery–Henderson fixed point theorem (Lemma 9), we obtain triple positive solutions for (1) when the nonlinearity satisfies some bounded conditions.

Theorem 2. *Suppose that there exist positive constants* $\widetilde{a}, \widetilde{b}, \widetilde{c}$ *with* $\widetilde{a} \; < \; \widetilde{b} \; < \; \widetilde{c}$,

$$\frac{\widetilde{c}}{\widetilde{b}} > \frac{\sum\limits_{s=0}^{\mathfrak{b}+2} G(\mathfrak{b}+v+1,s)}{\sum\limits_{t=r}^{\mathfrak{b}+v+1} G(\mathfrak{b}+v+1,t-v+1)} \; (r \text{ is a fixed point in } (v-1, \mathfrak{b}+v+1)_{\mathbb{N}_{v-1}}) \text{ such that}$$

(H6) $g(t,\psi) : [v-1, \mathfrak{b}+v+1]_{\mathbb{N}_{v-1}} \times \mathbb{R}^+ \to \mathbb{R}^+$ *is a continuous function, and* $g(t,0) \not\equiv 0$, $t \in [v-1, \mathfrak{b}+v+1]_{\mathbb{N}_{v-1}}$;

(H7) $g(t,\psi) < \dfrac{\widetilde{c}}{q_0 \sum\limits_{s=0}^{\mathfrak{b}+2} G(\mathfrak{b}+v+1,s)}$, *for* $t \in [v-1, \mathfrak{b}+v+1]_{\mathbb{N}_{v-1}}, \psi \in [0, \widetilde{c}q_0^{-2}]$;

(H8) $g(t,\psi) > \dfrac{\widetilde{b}}{q_0 \sum\limits_{t=r}^{\mathfrak{b}+v+1} G(\mathfrak{b}+v+1,t-v+1)}$ *for* $t \in [r, \mathfrak{b}+v+1]_{\mathbb{N}_{v-1}}, \psi \in [\widetilde{b}, \widetilde{b}q_0^{-2}]$;

(H9) $g(t,\psi) < \dfrac{\widetilde{a}}{\sum\limits_{s=0}^{\mathfrak{b}+2} G(\mathfrak{b}+v+1,s)}$ *for* $t \in [v-1, \mathfrak{b}+v+1]_{\mathbb{N}_{v-1}}, \psi \in [0, \widetilde{a}]$.

Then, (1) has at least three positive solutions $\mathfrak{y}_1, \mathfrak{y}_2$ *and* $\mathfrak{y}_3$ *satisfying*

$$0 < \alpha(\mathfrak{y}_1) < \widetilde{a} < \alpha(\mathfrak{y}_2), \beta(\mathfrak{y}_2) < \widetilde{b} < \beta(\mathfrak{y}_3), \gamma(\mathfrak{y}_3) < \widetilde{c}.$$

Proof. Note that if $q_0 = \min_{t \in [v-1, \mathfrak{b}+v+1]_{\mathbb{N}_{v-1}}} q(t) > 0$, then from Lemma 6 and (H6) we have

$$\mathcal{B}(P) \subset P_0.$$

Let $\alpha(\psi) \; = \; \max_{t \in [v-1, \mathfrak{b}+v+1]_{\mathbb{N}_{v-1}}} \psi(t), \; \beta(\psi) \; = \; \min_{t \in [r, \mathfrak{b}+v+1]_{\mathbb{N}_{v-1}}} \psi(t)$ and $\gamma(\psi) = q_0 \max_{t \in [v-1, r]_{\mathbb{N}_{v-1}}} \psi(t)$. We easily know that $\alpha, \gamma : P \to \mathbb{R}^+$ are continuous, increasing functionals with $\alpha(0) = 0$, $\forall t \in [v-1, \mathfrak{b}+v+1]_{\mathbb{N}_{v-1}}, \psi \in P$ and $\beta(\lambda\psi) = \lambda\beta(\psi)$. Moreover, for $\psi \in P_0$, we have

$$\gamma(\psi) = q_0 \max_{t \in [v-1, r]_{\mathbb{N}_{v-1}}} \psi(t) \leq q_0 \|\psi\| \leq \min_{t \in [v-1, \mathfrak{b}+v+1]_{\mathbb{N}_{v-1}}} \psi(t) \leq \min_{t \in [r, \mathfrak{b}+v+1]_{\mathbb{N}_{v-1}}} \psi(t) = \beta(\psi) \leq \alpha(\psi),$$

and

$$\gamma(\psi) \geq q_0 \min_{t \in [v-1, r]_{\mathbb{N}_{v-1}}} \psi(t) \geq q_0 \min_{t \in [v-1, \mathfrak{b}+v+1]_{\mathbb{N}_{v-1}}} \psi(t) \geq q_0^2 \|\psi\|,$$

i.e.,

$$\|\psi\| \leq \frac{1}{q_0^2} \gamma(\psi).$$

(i) For $\psi \in \partial P(\gamma, \widetilde{c})$, we have

$$\widetilde{c} = \gamma(\psi) \geq q_0^2 \|\psi\|,$$

which implies that

$$0 \leq \psi(t) \leq \widetilde{c}q_0^{-2}, \; t \in [v-1, \mathfrak{b}+v+1]_{\mathbb{N}_{v-1}}.$$

By (H7), we find

$$\gamma(\mathcal{B}\psi) = q_0 \max_{t\in[v-1,r]_{\mathbb{N}_{v-1}}} \sum_{s=0}^{b+2} \mathbb{G}(t,s)g(s+v-1,\psi(s+v-1))$$

$$\leq q_0 \max_{t\in[v-1,b+v+1]_{\mathbb{N}_{v-1}}} \sum_{s=0}^{b+2} \mathbb{G}(t,s)g(s+v-1,\psi(s+v-1))$$

$$< \frac{\widetilde{c}}{q_0 \sum_{s=0}^{b+2} G(b+v+1,s)} q_0 \sum_{s=0}^{b+2} \mathbb{G}(b+v+1,s)$$

$$= \widetilde{c}.$$

(ii) For $\psi \in \partial P(\beta,\widetilde{b})$, we have

$$\widetilde{b} = \beta(\psi) = \min_{t\in[r,b+v+1]_{\mathbb{N}_{v-1}}} \psi(t) \leq \|\psi\| \leq \frac{1}{q_0^2}\gamma(\psi) \leq \frac{1}{q_0^2}\beta(\psi) = \frac{\widetilde{b}}{q_0^2}.$$

This implies that

$$\widetilde{b} \leq \psi(t) \leq \frac{\widetilde{b}}{q_0^2}, \psi \in \partial P(\beta,\widetilde{b}), t \in [r, b+v+1]_{\mathbb{N}_{v-1}}.$$

This, combined with (H8), enables us to obtain

$$\beta(\mathcal{B}\psi) = \min_{t\in[r,b+v+1]_{\mathbb{N}_{v-1}}} \sum_{s=0}^{b+2} \mathbb{G}(t,s)g(s+v-1,\psi(s+v-1))$$

$$\geq \sum_{s=0}^{b+2} \min_{t\in[r,b+v+1]_{\mathbb{N}_{v-1}}} q(t)\mathbb{G}(b+v+1,s)g(s+v-1,\psi(s+v-1))$$

$$\geq \sum_{s=0}^{b+2} \min_{t\in[v-1,b+v+1]_{\mathbb{N}_{v-1}}} q(t)\mathbb{G}(b+v+1,s)g(s+v-1,\psi(s+v-1))$$

$$= q_0 \sum_{s=0}^{b+2} \mathbb{G}(b+v+1,s)g(s+v-1,\psi(s+v-1))$$

$$= q_0 \sum_{t=v-1}^{b+v+1} \mathbb{G}(b+v+1,t-v+1)g(t,\psi(t))$$

$$\geq q_0 \sum_{t=r}^{b+v+1} \mathbb{G}(b+v+1,t-v+1)g(t,\psi(t))$$

$$> \frac{\widetilde{b}}{q_0 \sum_{t=r}^{b+v+1} \mathbb{G}(b+v+1,t-v+1)} q_0 \sum_{t=r}^{b+v+1} \mathbb{G}(b+v+1,t-v+1)$$

$$= \widetilde{b}.$$

(iii) For $\psi \in \partial P(\alpha,\widetilde{a})$, we have

$$0 \leq \alpha(\psi) = \max_{t\in[v-1,b+v+1]_{\mathbb{N}_{v-1}}} \psi(t) = \widetilde{a},$$

and

$$0 \leq \psi(t) \leq \widetilde{a}, \ \psi \in \partial P(\alpha,\widetilde{a}), t \in [v-1, b+v+1]_{\mathbb{N}_{v-1}}.$$

This, together with (H9), implies that

$$\alpha(\mathcal{B}\psi) = \max_{t \in [v-1, b+v+1]_{\mathbb{N}_{v-1}}} \sum_{s=0}^{b+2} \mathbb{G}(t,s) g(s+v-1, \psi(s+v-1))$$

$$< \frac{\widetilde{a}}{\sum\limits_{s=0}^{b+2} \mathbb{G}(b+v+1,s)} \sum_{s=0}^{b+2} \mathbb{G}(b+v+1,s)$$

$$= \widetilde{a}.$$

Now, we have established that all the conditions in Lemma 9 hold, and note that $\mathcal{B}0 \neq 0$, so we conclude that (1) has at least three positive solutions $\eta_i \in P\backslash\{0\}$ such that $0 < \alpha(\eta_1) < \widetilde{a} < \alpha(\eta_2), \beta(\eta_2) < \widetilde{b} < \beta(\eta_3), \gamma(\eta_3) < \widetilde{c}.$ $\quad\square$

In what follows, we study the problem

$$\begin{cases} -\Delta_{v-3}^v \psi(t) = f(t+v-1, \psi(t+v-1), \psi(t+v-1)) + g(t+v-1, \psi(t+v-1)), & t \in [0, b+2]_{\mathbb{N}_0}, \\ \psi(v-3) = \left[\Delta_{v-3}^\alpha \psi(t)\right]\big|_{t=v-\alpha-2} = \left[\Delta_{v-3}^\beta \psi(t)\right]\big|_{t=v+b+2-\beta} = 0, \end{cases} \tag{22}$$

where v, α, β, b are founded in (1). By Lemma 3, (22) is equivalent to the following equation

$$\psi(t) = \sum_{s=0}^{b+2} \mathbb{G}(t,s)[f(s+v-1, \psi(s+v-1), \psi(s+v-1)) + g(s+v-1, \psi(s+v-1))], \, t \in [v-1, b+v+1]_{\mathbb{N}_{v-1}},$$

and let $\mathcal{A}: P \times P \to P$ and $\mathcal{B}: P \times P \to P$ be defined by

$$\mathcal{A}(\eta, \mathfrak{x})(t) = \sum_{s=0}^{b+2} \mathbb{G}(t,s) f(s+v-1, \eta(s+v-1), \mathfrak{x}(s+v-1)), \, (\mathcal{B}\eta)(t) = \sum_{s=0}^{b+2} \mathbb{G}(t,s) g(s+v-1, \eta(s+v-1)).$$

Obviously, η^* is a solution of (1) when $\eta^* = \mathcal{A}(\eta^*, \eta^*) + \mathcal{B}\eta^*$. In the following theorem, we study the operators $\mathcal{A}, \mathcal{B}$ to help us to obtain the existence of solutions to (22). Moreover, the positive solution is unique, and it can be uniformly approximated by two appropriate iterative sequences.

Now, we list some assumptions for our nonlinearities f, g as follows:

(H10) $f(t, u, v) : [v-1, b+v+1]_{\mathbb{N}_{v-1}} \times \mathbb{R}^+ \times \mathbb{R}^+ \to \mathbb{R}^+, g(t, u) : [v-1, b+v+1]_{\mathbb{N}_{v-1}} \times \mathbb{R}^+ \to \mathbb{R}^+$ are continuous functions;

(H11) $f(t, u, v)$ is increasing about $u \in \mathbb{R}^+$ for fixed $t \in [v-1, b+v+1]_{\mathbb{N}_{v-1}}$ and $v \in \mathbb{R}^+$ and decreasing about $v \in \mathbb{R}^+$ for fixed $t \in [v-1, b+v+1]_{\mathbb{N}_{v-1}}$ and $u \in \mathbb{R}^+$, and $g(t, u)$ is increasing about $u \in \mathbb{R}^+$ for fixed $t \in [v-1, b+v+1]_{\mathbb{N}_{v-1}}$;

(H12) For every $t \in [v-1, b+v+1]_{\mathbb{N}_{v-1}}, \gamma \in (0, 1), u, v \in \mathbb{R}^+$, there is a constant $\xi \in (0, 1)$ such that $f(t, \gamma u, \gamma^{-1} v) \geq \gamma^\xi f(t, u, v)$ and $g(t, \gamma u) \geq \gamma g(t, u)$;

(H13) For every $t \in [v-1, b+v+1]_{\mathbb{N}_{v-1}}$ and $u, v \in \mathbb{R}^+$, there is a constant $\delta_0 > 0$ such that $f(t, u, v) \geq \delta_0 g(t, u)$.

Theorem 3. *Suppose that (H10)–(H13) hold. Then, we get*

(T1) There are $\eta_0, \mathfrak{x}_0 \in P_{\mathfrak{h}}$ and $r \in (0, 1)$ such that $r\mathfrak{x}_0 \leq \eta_0 < \mathfrak{x}_0$,

$$\eta_0(t) \leq \sum_{s=0}^{b+2} \mathbb{G}(t,s)[f(s+v-1, \eta_0(s+v-1), \mathfrak{x}_0(s+v-1)) + g(s+v-1, \eta_0(s+v-1))],$$

and

$$\mathfrak{x}_0(t) \geq \sum_{s=0}^{b+2} \mathbb{G}(t,s)[f(s+v-1, \mathfrak{x}_0(s+v-1), \eta_0(s+v-1)) + g(s+v-1, \mathfrak{x}_0(s+v-1))],$$

where $\mathfrak{h}(t) = t^{\underline{v-1}}$;

    (T2) (22) has a unique positive solution $\mathfrak{y}^* \in P_\mathfrak{h}$;

    (T3) For each initial value $\mathfrak{x}_0, \mathfrak{y}_0 \in P_\mathfrak{h}$, *the sequences*

$$\mathfrak{x}_n = \sum_{s=0}^{\mathfrak{b}+2} \mathbb{G}(t,s)[f(s+v-1, \mathfrak{x}_{n-1}(s+v-1), \mathfrak{y}_{n-1}(s+v-1)) + g(s+v-1, \mathfrak{x}_{n-1}(s+v-1))],$$

$$\mathfrak{y}_n = \sum_{s=0}^{\mathfrak{b}+2} \mathbb{G}(t,s)[f(s+v-1, \mathfrak{y}_{n-1}(s+v-1), \mathfrak{x}_{n-1}(s+v-1)) + g(s+v-1, \mathfrak{y}_{n-1}(s+v-1))]$$

converge to $\mathfrak{y}^*$ *as* $n \to \infty$.

Proof. From (H10) and (H11), we know that $\mathcal{A} : P \times P \to P$ is a mixed monotone operator and $\mathcal{B} : P \to P$ is an increasing operator. Using (H12), for all $\gamma \in (0,1)$ and $\mathfrak{x}, \mathfrak{y} \in P$, we obtain

$$\mathcal{A}(\gamma\mathfrak{y}, \gamma^{-1}\mathfrak{x})(t) = \sum_{s=0}^{\mathfrak{b}+2} \mathbb{G}(t,s)f(s+v-1, \gamma\mathfrak{y}(s+v-1), \gamma^{-1}\mathfrak{x}(s+v-1))$$

$$\geq \gamma^{\xi} \sum_{s=0}^{\mathfrak{b}+2} \mathbb{G}(t,s)f(s+v-1, \mathfrak{y}(s+v-1), \mathfrak{x}(s+v-1))$$

$$= \gamma^{\xi}\mathcal{A}(\mathfrak{y}, \mathfrak{x})(t),$$

and hence $\mathcal{A}$ satisfies (7) in Lemma 12. In addition, for any $\mathfrak{y} \in P$ and $\gamma \in (0,1)$ we find

$$(\mathcal{B}\gamma\mathfrak{y})(t) = \sum_{s=0}^{\mathfrak{b}+2} \mathbb{G}(t,s)g(s+v-1, \gamma\mathfrak{y}(s+v-1))$$

$$\geq \gamma \sum_{s=0}^{\mathfrak{b}+2} \mathbb{G}(t,s)g(s+v-1, \mathfrak{y}(s+v-1))$$

$$= \gamma(\mathcal{B}\mathfrak{y})(t).$$

Thus, $\mathcal{B}$ is a sub-homogeneous operator.

Let $\mathfrak{h}_0 = \mathfrak{h} = t^{\underline{v-1}}$, and $\mathfrak{h}_0 \in P_h$. From Lemma 4, we have

$$\mathcal{A}(\mathfrak{h}_0, \mathfrak{h}_0)(t) = \sum_{s=0}^{\mathfrak{b}+2} \mathbb{G}(t,s)f(s+v-1, (s+v-1)^{\underline{v-1}}, (s+v-1)^{\underline{v-1}})$$

$$\leq \sum_{s=0}^{\mathfrak{b}+2} \frac{t^{\underline{v-1}}(v+\mathfrak{b}-\beta-s+1)^{\underline{v-\beta-1}}}{\Gamma(v)(v+\mathfrak{b}-\beta+2)^{\underline{v-\beta-1}}} f(s+v-1, (s+v-1)^{\underline{v-1}}, (s+v-1)^{\underline{v-1}})$$

$$\leq \sum_{s=0}^{\mathfrak{b}+2} \frac{t^{\underline{v-1}}(v+\mathfrak{b}-\beta-s+1)^{\underline{v-\beta-1}}}{\Gamma(v)(v+\mathfrak{b}-\beta+2)^{\underline{v-\beta-1}}} f(s+v-1, (\mathfrak{b}+v+1)^{\underline{v-1}}, 0)$$

$$= \sum_{s=0}^{\mathfrak{b}+2} \frac{(v+\mathfrak{b}-\beta-s+1)^{\underline{v-\beta-1}}}{\Gamma(v)(v+\mathfrak{b}-\beta+2)^{\underline{v-\beta-1}}} f(s+v-1, (\mathfrak{b}+v+1)^{\underline{v-1}}, 0) \cdot \mathfrak{h}_0,$$

and

$$\mathcal{A}(\mathfrak{h}_0, \mathfrak{h}_0)(t) = \sum_{s=0}^{\mathfrak{b}+2} \mathbb{G}(t,s)f(s+v-1, (s+v-1)^{\underline{v-1}}, (s+v-1)^{\underline{v-1}})$$

$$\geq \sum_{s=0}^{\mathfrak{b}+2} \frac{t^{\underline{v-1}}\mathbb{G}(\mathfrak{b}+v+1, s)}{(\mathfrak{b}+v+1)^{\underline{v-1}}} f(s+v-1, (s+v-1)^{\underline{v-1}}, (s+v-1)^{\underline{v-1}})$$

$$\geq \sum_{s=0}^{\mathfrak{b}+2} \frac{t^{\underline{v-1}}\mathbb{G}(\mathfrak{b}+v+1, s)}{(\mathfrak{b}+v+1)^{\underline{v-1}}} f(s+v-1, 0, (\mathfrak{b}+v+1)^{\underline{v-1}})$$

$$= \sum_{s=0}^{\mathfrak{b}+2} \frac{\mathbb{G}(\mathfrak{b}+v+1, s)}{(\mathfrak{b}+v+1)^{\underline{v-1}}} f(s+v-1, 0, (\mathfrak{b}+v+1)^{\underline{v-1}}) \cdot \mathfrak{h}_0.$$

Let $l = \sum\limits_{s=0}^{\mathfrak{b}+2} \frac{\mathbb{G}(\mathfrak{b}+v+1,s)}{(\mathfrak{b}+v+1)^{\underline{v-1}}} f(s+v-1,0,(\mathfrak{b}+v+1)^{\underline{v-1}}), L = \sum\limits_{s=0}^{\mathfrak{b}+2} \frac{(v+\mathfrak{b}-\beta-s+1)^{\underline{v-\beta-1}}}{\Gamma(v)(v+\mathfrak{b}-\beta+2)^{\underline{v-\beta-1}}} f(s+$
$v-1,(\mathfrak{b}+v+1)^{\underline{v-1}},0)$. Then, we have $l\mathfrak{h}_0 \leq \mathcal{A}(\mathfrak{h}_0,\mathfrak{h}_0) \leq L\mathfrak{h}_0$, i.e., $\mathcal{A}(\mathfrak{h}_0,\mathfrak{h}_0) \in P_{\mathfrak{h}_0}$.
Similarly, from (H11), we have

$$t^{\underline{v-1}} \sum_{s=0}^{\mathfrak{b}+2} \frac{\mathbb{G}(\mathfrak{b}+v+1,s)}{(\mathfrak{b}+v+1)^{\underline{v-1}}} g(s+v-1,0)$$

$$\leq (\mathcal{B}\mathfrak{h}_0)(t) = \sum_{s=0}^{\mathfrak{b}+2} \mathbb{G}(t,s)g(s+v-1,(s+v-1)^{\underline{v-1}})$$

$$\leq t^{\underline{v-1}} \sum_{s=0}^{\mathfrak{b}+2} \frac{(v+\mathfrak{b}-\beta-s+1)^{\underline{v-\beta-1}}}{\Gamma(v)(v+\mathfrak{b}-\beta+2)^{\underline{v-\beta-1}}} g(s+v-1,(\mathfrak{b}+v+1)^{\underline{v-1}}).$$

Thus, we obtain $\mathcal{B}\mathfrak{h}_0 \in P_{\mathfrak{h}_0}$. Therefore, (C1) in Lemma 12 holds.
Finally, for every $\mathfrak{x},\mathfrak{y} \in P$, from (H13) we have

$$\mathcal{A}(\mathfrak{y},\mathfrak{x})(t) = \sum_{s=0}^{\mathfrak{b}+2} \mathbb{G}(t,s)f(s+v-1,\mathfrak{y}(s+v-1),\mathfrak{x}(s+v-1))$$

$$\geq \delta_0 \sum_{s=0}^{\mathfrak{b}+2} \mathbb{G}(t,s)g(s+v-1,\mathfrak{y}(s+v-1))$$

$$= \delta_0(\mathcal{B}\mathfrak{y})(t).$$

Thus, (C2) in Lemma 12 holds. Then, our conclusions are true from Lemma 12. $\quad\square$

4. Examples

In this section, we will provide some examples to verify our main results.

Example 1. *Let* $g(t,\psi) = a|\psi| - b\mathcal{M}(\psi), \mathcal{M}(\psi) = \ln(|\psi|+1), \psi \in \mathbb{R}, t \in [v-1,\mathfrak{b}+$
$v+1]_{\mathbb{N}_{v-1}}$, *where* $a \in \left(\kappa_1^{-1},+\infty\right)$ *and* $b \in \left(a,a+\kappa_2^{-1}\right)$. *Then,* $\lim_{|\psi|\to+\infty} \frac{\mathcal{M}(\psi)}{|\psi|} = 0$, *and*
$\lim_{|\psi|\to+\infty} \frac{a|\psi|-b\mathcal{M}(\psi)}{|\psi|} = a > \kappa_1^{-1}$, $\lim_{|\psi|\to0^+} \frac{|a|\psi|-b\mathcal{M}(\psi)|}{|\psi|} = |a-b| < \kappa_2^{-1}$. *Therefore,*
(H1)–(H5) hold.

Example 2. *Let* $\mathfrak{b} = 4, v = 2.5, \alpha = 0.5, \beta = 1.4$. *Then,* $[v-1,\mathfrak{b}+v+1]_{\mathbb{N}_{v-1}} = \{1.5,2.5,3.5,4.5,5.5,6.5,7.5\}$, $[0,\mathfrak{b}+2]_{\mathbb{N}_0} = \{0,1,2,3,4,5,6\}$, q_0
$= \min_{t\in[v-1,\mathfrak{b}+v+1]_{\mathbb{N}_{v-1}}} \frac{t^{1.5}}{7.5^{1.5}} = 0.068$, *and if* $r = 6.5$ *we also obtain*

$$\sum_{s=0}^{6} \mathbb{G}(7.5,s) = \sum_{s=0}^{6} \frac{7.5^{1.5}(6.1-s)^{0.1}}{7.1^{0.1}} - 5.5^{1.5} = 112.26,$$

$$\sum_{t=r}^{\mathfrak{b}+v+1} \mathbb{G}(\mathfrak{b}+v+1,t-v+1) = \sum_{t=r+1-v}^{\mathfrak{b}+2} \mathbb{G}(\mathfrak{b}+v+1,t) = \sum_{t=5}^{6} \mathbb{G}(7.5,t) = 19.86.$$

Let $\widetilde{a} = 1, \widetilde{b} = 4, \widetilde{c} = 24$, *and*

$$g(t,\psi) = \begin{cases} 0.008, & \psi \in [0,1], \\ \psi - 0.992, & \psi \in [1,4], \\ 3.008, & \psi \in [4,+\infty). \end{cases}$$

Then, g satisfies
(I) $g(t,\psi) < \dfrac{\widetilde{c}}{q_0 \sum\limits_{s=0}^{\mathfrak{b}+2} \mathbb{G}(\mathfrak{b}+v+1,s)} = 3.144, \textit{for } t \in [v-1,\mathfrak{b}+v+1]_{\mathbb{N}_{v-1}}, \psi \in [0,5190.3];$

$(II)\ g(t,\psi) > \dfrac{\widetilde{b}}{q_0 \sum\limits_{t=r}^{\mathfrak{b}+v+1} G(\mathfrak{b}+v+1,t-v+1)} = 2.96\ \text{for } t \in [r, \mathfrak{b}+v+1]_{\mathbb{N}_{v-1}}, \psi \in [4, 865.1];$

$(III)\ g(t,\psi) < \dfrac{\widetilde{a}}{\sum\limits_{s=0}^{\mathfrak{b}+2} G(\mathfrak{b}+v+1,s)} = 0.009\ \text{for } t \in [v-1, \mathfrak{b}+v+1]_{\mathbb{N}_{v-1}}, \psi \in [0,1].$

Therefore, (H6)–(H9) hold.

Example 3. *Let* $f(t,\mathfrak{u},\mathfrak{v}) = (\mathfrak{b}+v+1-t)^{-\frac{1}{3}} t^{-\frac{2}{3}} \mathfrak{u}^{\frac{1}{3}} + \mathfrak{v}^{-\frac{1}{5}}, g(t,\mathfrak{u}) = (\mathfrak{b}+v+1-t)^{-\frac{1}{3}} t^{-\frac{2}{3}} \mathfrak{u}^{\frac{1}{3}},$
$(t,\mathfrak{u},\mathfrak{v}) \in [v-1, \mathfrak{b}+v+1]_{\mathbb{N}_{v-1}} \times \mathbb{R}^+ \times \mathbb{R}^+.$ *Then, f is increasing about $\mathfrak{u}$ and decreasing about*
$\mathfrak{v}$, and g is increasing about $\mathfrak{u}$. For any $\gamma \in (0,1), \mathfrak{u},\mathfrak{v} \in \mathbb{R}^+$, taking $\xi = \frac{1}{2}$, then $\gamma^\xi \in (\gamma, 1)$ and
we obtain

$$f\left(t, \gamma\mathfrak{u}, \gamma^{-1}\mathfrak{v}\right) = (\mathfrak{b}+v+1-t)^{-\frac{1}{3}} t^{-\frac{2}{3}} (\gamma\mathfrak{u})^{\frac{1}{3}} + \left(\gamma^{-1}\mathfrak{v}\right)^{-\frac{1}{5}}$$

$$= \gamma^{\frac{1}{3}} (\mathfrak{b}+v+1-t)^{-\frac{1}{3}} t^{-\frac{2}{3}} \mathfrak{u}^{\frac{1}{3}} + \gamma^{\frac{1}{5}} \mathfrak{v}^{-\frac{1}{5}}$$

$$\geq \gamma^{\frac{1}{2}} \left[(\mathfrak{b}+v+1-t)^{-\frac{1}{3}} t^{-\frac{2}{3}} \mathfrak{u}^{\frac{1}{3}} + \mathfrak{v}^{-\frac{1}{5}} \right]$$

$$= \gamma^\xi f(t,\mathfrak{u},\mathfrak{v}),$$

and

$$g(t, \gamma\mathfrak{u}) = (\mathfrak{b}+v+1-t)^{-\frac{1}{3}} t^{-\frac{2}{3}} (\gamma\mathfrak{u})^{\frac{1}{3}}$$

$$= \gamma^{\frac{1}{3}} (\mathfrak{b}+v+1-t)^{-\frac{1}{3}} t^{-\frac{2}{3}} \mathfrak{u}^{\frac{1}{3}}$$

$$\geq \gamma \left[(\mathfrak{b}+v+1-t)^{-\frac{1}{3}} t^{-\frac{2}{3}} \mathfrak{u}^{\frac{1}{3}} \right]$$

$$= \gamma g(t, \mathfrak{u}).$$

Moreover, it is easy to see that $f(t,\mathfrak{u},\mathfrak{v}) \geq g(t,\mathfrak{u})$ for $(t,\mathfrak{u},\mathfrak{v}) \in [v-1, \mathfrak{b}+v+1]_{\mathbb{N}_{v-1}} \times$
$\mathbb{R}^+ \times \mathbb{R}^+$. Therefore, (H10)–(H13) hold.

Example 4. *In [31], the authors consider nonlinearities like:*

$$f(t,\mathfrak{u},\mathfrak{v}) = \mathfrak{u}^{\frac{1}{4}} + [\mathfrak{v}+2]^{-\frac{1}{3}} + b(t) + d, \ g(t,\mathfrak{u}) = \frac{\mathfrak{u}}{1+\mathfrak{u}} a(t) + c - d, \ (t,\mathfrak{u},\mathfrak{v}) \in [v-1, \mathfrak{b}+v+1]_{\mathbb{N}_{v-1}} \times \mathbb{R}^+ \times \mathbb{R}^+,$$

where $a,b : [v-1, \mathfrak{b}+v+1]_{\mathbb{N}_{v-1}} \to \mathbb{R}^+$ with $a \not\equiv 0$, and c,d are positive constants with
$c > d > 0$. Note that f is increasing about $\mathfrak{u}$ and decreasing about $\mathfrak{v}$, and g is increasing about $\mathfrak{u}$.
Moreover, for $\gamma \in (0,1), t \in [v-1, \mathfrak{b}+v+1]_{\mathbb{N}_{v-1}}, \mathfrak{u}, \mathfrak{v}s. \in \mathbb{R}^+$, we have

$$g(t, \gamma\mathfrak{u}) = \frac{\gamma\mathfrak{u}}{1+\gamma\mathfrak{u}} a(t) + c - d \geq \frac{\gamma\mathfrak{u}}{1+\mathfrak{u}} a(t) + \gamma(c-d) = \gamma g(t,\mathfrak{u}),$$

and

$$f\left(t, \gamma\mathfrak{u}, \gamma^{-1}\mathfrak{v}\right) = \gamma^{\frac{1}{4}} \mathfrak{u}^{\frac{1}{4}} + \gamma^{\frac{1}{3}} [\mathfrak{v}+2\gamma]^{-\frac{1}{3}} + b(t) + d \geq \gamma^{\frac{1}{3}} \left\{ \mathfrak{u}^{\frac{1}{4}} + [\mathfrak{v}+2]^{-\frac{1}{3}} + b(t) + d \right\} = \gamma^\xi f(t,\mathfrak{u},\mathfrak{v}).$$

Furthermore, we note that

$$f(t,\mathfrak{u},\mathfrak{v}) \geq d = \frac{d}{\max_{t \in [v-1,\mathfrak{b}+v+1]_{\mathbb{N}_{v-1}}} a(t) + c - d} \times \left(\max_{t \in [v-1,\mathfrak{b}+v+1]_{\mathbb{N}_{v-1}}} a(t) + c - d \right)$$

$$\geq \frac{d}{\max_{t \in [v-1,\mathfrak{b}+v+1]_{\mathbb{N}_{v-1}}} a(t) + c - d} \times \left(\frac{\mathfrak{u}}{1+\mathfrak{u}} a(t) + c - d \right)$$

$$:= \delta_0 g(t,\mathfrak{u}), \ (t,\mathfrak{u},\mathfrak{v}) \in [v-1, \mathfrak{b}+v+1]_{\mathbb{N}_{v-1}} \times \mathbb{R}^+ \times \mathbb{R}^+.$$

Therefore, (H10)–(H13) hold.

5. Conclusions

Fractional-order difference equations are a new form of differential equation that have wider applications compared to traditional integer-order differential equations. They are generalized differential equations whose derivative index can be a decimal or a fraction, rather than an integer. This form of differential equation has wide applications in fields such as physics, engineering, and finance. Therefore, the importance of studying fractional difference equations is now becoming apparent. In this paper, we consider a boundary value problem with a fractional-order difference equation and use Green's function to express its solution. Moreover, we obtain some existence theorems for the considered problem, i.e., when the nonlinearities satisfy some appropriate conditions, we study the existence, uniqueness, and multiplicity of solutions via the topological degree and fixed point theorems. Finally, we provide some examples to verify our main results.

Author Contributions: Conceptualization, Z.L.; methodology, Z.L., C.W., D.O. and J.X.; validation, Z.L., C.W., D.O. and J.X.; formal analysis, Z.L., C.W., D.O. and J.X.; investigation, D.O. and J.X. All authors have read and agreed to the published version of the manuscript.

Funding: This work was supported by the Suqian Sci and Tech Program (grant no. K202134) anf the Natural Science Foundation of Chongqing (grant no. cstc2019jcyj-msxmX0390).

Data Availability Statement: Not applicable.

Conflicts of Interest: The authors declare no conflict of interest.

References

1. Atıcı, F.M.; Atıcı, M.; Belcher, M.; Marshall D. A new approach for modeling with discrete fractional equations. *Fund. Inform.* **2017**, *151*, 313–324. [CrossRef]
2. Atıcı, F.M.; Senguel, S. Modeling with fractional difference equations. *J. Math. Anal. Appl.* **2010**, *369*, 1–9. [CrossRef]
3. Wu, G.C.; Baleanu, D. Discrete fractional logistic map and its chaos. *Nonlinear Dyn.* **2014**, *75*, 283–287. [CrossRef]
4. Zheng, Z.X. On the developments and applications of fractional differential equations. *J. Xuzhou Normal Univ.* **2008**, *26*, 1–10.
5. Goodrich, C.S.; Peterson, A.C. *Discrete Fractional Calculus*; Springer: Berlin/Heidelberg, Germany, 2015.
6. Cheng, J. *The Theory of Fractional-Order Difference Equations*; Xiamen University Press: Xiamen, China, 2011.
7. Rehman, M.; Lqbal, F.; Seemab, A. On existence of positive solutions for a class of discrete fractional boundary value problems. *Positivity* **2017**, *21*, 1173–1187. [CrossRef]
8. Zhao, Y.; Sun, S.; Zhang, Y. Existence and uniqueness of solutions to a fractional difference equation with p-Laplacian operator. *J. Appl. Math. Comput.* **2017**, *54*, 183–197. [CrossRef]
9. Xu, J.; Goodrich, C.S.; Cui, Y. Positive solutions for a system of first-order discrete fractional boundary value problems with semipositone nonlinearities. *Rev. R. Acad. Cienc. Exactas Fís. Nat. Ser. A Mater.* **2019**, *113*, 1343–1358. [CrossRef]
10. Sitthiwirattham, T.; Tariboon, J.; Ntouyas, S.K. Boundary value problems for fractional difference equations with three-point fractional sum boundary conditions. *Adv. Differ. Equ.* **2013**, *2013*, 296. [CrossRef]
11. Xu, J.; O'Regan, D.; Hou, C.; Cui, Y. Positive solutions for a class of fractional difference boundary value problems. *Differ. Equ. Appl.* **2017**, *9*, 479–493.
12. Cheng, W.; Xu, J.; O'Regan, D.; Cui, Y. Positive solutions for a nonlinear discrete fractional boundary value problems with a p-Laplacian operator. *J. Anal. Appl. Comput.* **2019**, *9*, 1959–1972.
13. Cheng, W.; Xu, J.; Cui, Y.; Ge, Q. Positive solutions for a class of fractional difference systems with coupled boundary conditions. *Adv. Differ. Equ.* **2019**, *2019*, 249. [CrossRef]
14. Xu, J.; O'Regan, D. Existence and uniqueness of solutions for a first-order discrete fractional boundary value problem. *Rev. R. Acad. Cienc. Exactas Fís. Nat. Ser. A Mat.* **2018**, *112*, 1005–1016. [CrossRef]
15. Bohner, M.; Fewster-Young, N. Discrete fractional boundary value problems and inequalities. *Fract. Calc. Appl. Anal.* **2021**, *24*, 1777–1796. [CrossRef]
16. Eralp, B.; Topal, F.S. Monotone method for discrete fractional boundary value problems. *Int. J. Nonlinear Anal. Appl.* **2022**, *13*, 1989–1997.
17. Bourguiba, R.; Cabada, A.; Kalthoum, W.O. Existence of solutions of discrete fractional problem coupled to mixed fractional boundary conditions. *Rev. Real Acad. Cienc. Exactas Fis. Nat. Ser. A Mat.* **2022**, *116*, 175. [CrossRef]
18. Gopal, N.S.; Jonnalagadda, J.M. Positive solutions of nabla fractional boundary value problem. *Cubo Math. J.* **2022**, *24*, 467–484. [CrossRef]
19. Dahal, R.; Duncan, D.; Goodrich, C.S. Systems of semipositone discrete fractional boundary value problems. *J. Differ. Equ. Appl.* **2014**, *20*, 473–491. [CrossRef]

20. Goodrich, C.S. Systems of discrete fractional boundary value problems with nonlinearities satisfying no growth conditions. *J. Differ. Equ. Appl.* **2015**, *21*, 437–453. [CrossRef]
21. Lv, W. Existence of solutions for discrete fractional boundary value problems with a *p*-Laplacian operator. *Adv. Differ. Equ.* **2012**, *2012*, 163. [CrossRef]
22. Ferreira, R.A.C. Existence and uniqueness of solution to some discrete fractional boundary value problems of order less than one. *J. Differ. Equ. Appl.* **2013**, *19*, 712–718. [CrossRef]
23. Goodrich, C.S. On a first-order semipositone discrete fractional boundary value problem. *Arch. Math.* **2012**, *99*, 509–518. [CrossRef]
24. Goodrich, C.S. On discrete sequential fractional boundary value problems. *J. Math. Anal. Appl.* **2012**, *385*, 111–124. [CrossRef]
25. Sitthiwirattham, T. Boundary value problem for *p*-Laplacian Caputo fractional difference equations with fractional sum boundary conditions. *Math. Methods Appl. Sci.* **2016**, *39*, 1522–1534. [CrossRef]
26. Kunnawuttipreechachan, E.; Promsakon, C.; Sitthiwirattham, T. Nonlocal fractional sum boundary value problem for a coupled system of fractional sum-difference equations. *Dyn. Syst. Appl.* **2019**, *28*, 73–92. [CrossRef]
27. Guo, D.; Lakshmikantham, V. *Nonlinear Problems in Abstract Cones*; Academic Press: Orlando, FL, USA, 1988.
28. Zhang, W.; Ni, J. New multiple positive solutions for Hadamard-type fractional differential equations with nonlocal conditions on an infinite interval. *Appl. Math. Lett.* **2021**, *118*, 107165. [CrossRef]
29. Xu, J.; Jiang, J.; O'Regan, D. Positive solutions for a class of *p*-Laplacian Hadamard fractional-order three-point boundary value problems. *Mathematics* **2020**, *8*, 308. [CrossRef]
30. Zhai, C.; Hao, M. Fixed point theorems for mixed monotone operators with perturbation and applications to fractional differential equation boundary value problems. *Nonlinear Anal.* **2012**, *75*, 2542–2551. [CrossRef]
31. Zhai, C.; Hao, M. Mixed monotone operator methods for the existence and uniqueness of positive solutions to Riemann–Liouville fractional differential equation boundary value problems. *Bound. Value Probl.* **2013**, *2013*, 85. [CrossRef]

Article

The Dynamics of a General Model of the Nonlinear Difference Equation and Its Applications

Osama Moaaz [1,2,*] and Aseel A. Altuwaijri [1]

[1] Department of Mathematics, College of Science, Qassim University, P.O. Box 6644, Buraydah 51452, Saudi Arabia
[2] Department of Mathematics, Faculty of Science, Mansoura University, Mansoura 35516, Egypt
* Correspondence: o.refaei@qu.edu.sa or o_moaaz@mans.edu.eg

Abstract: This article investigates the qualitative properties of solutions to a general difference equation. Studying the properties of solutions to general difference equations greatly contributes to the development of theoretical methods and provides many pieces of information that may help to understand the behavior of solutions of some special models. We present the sufficient and necessary conditions for the existence of prime period-two and -three solutions. We also obtain a complete perception of the local stability of the studied equation. Then, we investigate the boundedness and global stability of the solutions. Finally, we support the validity of the results by applying them to some special cases, as well as numerically simulating the solutions.

Keywords: difference equations; qualitative properties; stability; periodicity; boundedness; numerical simulations

MSC: 34C10; 34K11

Citation: Moaaz, O.; Altuwaijri, A.A. The Dynamics of a General Model of the Nonlinear Difference Equation and Its Applications. *Axioms* **2023**, *12*, 598. https://doi.org/10.3390/axioms12060598

Academic Editors: Azhar Ali Zafar and Nehad Ali Shah

Received: 9 May 2023
Revised: 8 June 2023
Accepted: 13 June 2023
Published: 16 June 2023

1. Introduction

In both pure and applied mathematics, meteorology, physics, population dynamics, and engineering, there are many applications for the study of functional differential equations (FDEs) and difference equations (DIEs). The properties of these equations of different sorts are a topic that is addressed by all of these fields. For global existence and uniqueness theorems for differential equations, see books [1], and for the fundamentals of DIEs, see books [2–5]. Pure mathematics is concerned with the existence and uniqueness of solutions. The rigorous justification of the qualitative properties of solutions, such as oscillation, periodicity, stability (local and global), Hopf bifurcation, control, etc., is emphasized in applied mathematics [4,6–8].

DIEs are used to describe how a phenomena evolves in the real world when most observations of a temporally changing variable are discrete. These equations consequently become essential in mathematical models. Applications heavily rely on nonlinear DIEs of an order larger than one. Additionally, these equations naturally occur as discrete analogs and numerical answers to differential and delay differential equations that model a variety of diverse phenomena in different sciences; see [5,9–15].

Investigation of the qualitative properties of the DIE

$$u_{n+1} = \frac{u_{n-1}}{\mathcal{P}(u_n, u_{n-1})} \tag{1}$$

is the focus of this paper, where $\mathcal{P}(t, s) : [0, \infty)^2 \to (0, \infty)$ is continuous and homogenous with degree α, where α is a non-negative real number. Furthermore, the initial conditions u_{-1}, u_0 are nonnegative real numbers.

The study of the qualitative properties of solutions of DIEs was and still is a vital and active research field. As a result of the rapid development of science and technology, many biological, technological, geological and other issues have arisen. Many mathematical models have emerged with these issues. Studying the qualitative behavior of the general DIEs may significantly contribute to eliciting the characteristics of the solutions of these new models.

In this work, we are interested in investigating some qualitative properties of solutions to the general DIE (1). We begin by deducing the sufficient and necessary conditions for the existence of prime period-two solutions of DIE (1). Then, we investigate the local asymptotic stability of a two-cycle solution of DIE (1). Moreover, we obtain criteria that guarantee the existence of prime period-three solutions, and apply the results in this section to some special cases to support the theoretical results. We also study the local and global stability of solutions to DIE (1). We present several lemmas and theorems that set sufficient criteria for the convergence of solutions to the equilibrium point. Finally, through examples and numerical simulations, we present some theoretical results for some special cases of the studied equation and simulate the results numerically through the MATHEMATICA program.

In order to verify the periodicity of solutions, the methodology of this study is based on the use of an improved technique discussed in [16,17]. Using some theorems in [18], we investigate the local and global stability of the equilibrium points of the studied equation.

In the following, we review some of the previous results in the literature, which contributed significantly to the development of the study of the qualitative properties of solutions of DIEs.

The Riccati DIEs model

$$u_{n+1} = \frac{a_1 + a_2 u_n}{a_3 + a_4 u_n},\qquad (2)$$

is one of the most intriguing ones, where $a_i \in \mathbb{R}$, for $i = 1,2,3,4$, see [12]. A special application of DIE (2) offers the traditional Beverton–Holt model on the dynamics of exploited fish populations [10]. In [19], Kuruklis et al. examined some properties of solutions of the Pielou's discrete logistic model [20]

$$u_{n+1} = \frac{a u_n}{1 + u_{n-1}},\qquad (3)$$

where $a \le 1$. May [21] offered the DIE

$$u_{n+1} = \frac{u_n \exp(c(1 - 2u_n))}{1 - u_n + u_n \exp(c(1 - 2u_n))},\qquad (4)$$

where $c > 0$, as an illustration of a map produced by a straightforward model for frequency-dependent natural selection. The model of the expansion of the flour beetle population

$$u_{n+1} = a_1 u_n + a_2 u_{n-2} \exp(-a_3 u_n - a_4 u_{n-2}),$$

was proven to be globally stable by Kuang et al. [22], where $a_1 \in (0,1)$, $a_2, a_3, a_4 \in [0, \infty)$, $a_2 \ne 0$ and $a_3 + a_4 > 0$.

Many researchers have been interested in studying general models of DIEs. In [23], Stevic studied the periodic nature of the general DIE

$$u_{n+1} = \frac{F(u_n, u_{n-1})}{a + u_n},$$

where $a, u_{-1}, u_0 \in \mathbb{R}^+$ and $F \in \mathbf{C}(\mathbb{R}^+ \times \mathbb{R}^+, \mathbb{R}^+)$ and

$$F(k,l) - F(l,m) = (k - m)G(k,l,m) - a(k - l),$$

for some $G \in\in \mathbf{C}(\mathbb{R}^+ \times \mathbb{R}^+, \mathbb{R}^+)$, such that

$$\frac{1}{k} G(k, l, m) \to 0 \ \text{ as } \ k, l, m \to \infty \ \text{ and } \ \sup \frac{1}{a+k} G(k, l, m) < \infty.$$

Karakostas and Stevic [24] studied the qualitative properties of solutions to the general DIE

$$u_{n+1} = a + \frac{u_{n-r}}{F(u_n, u_{n-1}, \ldots, u_{n-r+1})}$$

where $a \geq 0$. In [25], the global stability of solutions to the general DIE

$$u_{n+} = F(u_{n-k}, u_{n-l}),$$

has been studied, where $k, l \in \mathbb{N}$, $k < l$. Moaaz et al. [26] discussed the qualitative properties of solutions to the DIE

$$u_{n+1} = f(u_{n-l}, u_{n-k}) \tag{5}$$

where $k, l \in \mathbb{N}$, and f is a homogenous function with degree *zero*.

Recently, Elsayed et al. [27–29], Al-Basyouni and Elsayed [30], and Kara and Yazlik [31] established solutions to for certain categories of DIEs. In [27], Elsayed and Alofi studied the properties of solutions to a system of DIEs and provided solutions to this system. Elsayed et al. [28] considered the DIE

$$u_{n+1} = a u_{n-1} + \frac{b u_{n-1} u_{n-4}}{c u_{n-4} + k u_{n-2}},$$

and provided solutions to this DIE. The periodic properties and construction of the solution for some rational system of DIEs were presented in [29,30]. Moreover, for fractional difference equations and systems, there are many interesting results in [32,33].

2. Definitions and Preliminary Results

The fundamental definitions, including equilibrium points, local and global stability, boundedness, and periodicity, are presented in this section. We also review some basic theorems.

Consider a DIE in the form

$$u_{n+1} = \psi(u_{n-l}, u_{n-k}), \ n = 0, 1, \ldots, \tag{6}$$

where $\psi \in \mathbf{C}(I \times I, I)$, $l, k \in \mathbb{Z}^+ \cup \{0\}$, I is some interval of $\mathbb{R}$, and $m = \max\{l, k\}$.

Definition 1. *If a point u_e is a fixed point of ψ, then it is said to be an equilibrium point (EQP) of DIE (6).*

Definition 2. *Assume that u_e is an EQP of (6).*

S1. *If for all $\epsilon > 0$ there is a $\delta > 0$ such that $|u_n - u_e| < \epsilon$ for all $n \geq -m$, for $u_{-j} \in I$, $j = 0, 1, \ldots, m$ with $\sum_{j=0}^{m} |u_{-j} - u_e| < \delta$, then u_e is said to be locally stable.*

S2. *If u_e is locally stable and there is $\gamma > 0$ such that $\lim_{n \to \infty} u_n = u_e$ for $u_{-j} \in I, j = 0, 1, \ldots, m$ with $\sum_{j=0}^{m} |u_{-j} - u_e| < \delta$, then u_e is said to be locally asymptotically stable.*

S3. *If $\lim_{n \to \infty} u_n = u_e$ for all $u_{-j} \in I, j = 0, 1, \ldots, m$, then u_e is said to be a global attractor.*

S4. *If u_e is locally stable and a global attractor, then it is said to be globally asymptotically stable.*

S5. *If u_e is not locally stable, then it is said to be unstable.*

Definition 3. *A sequence $\{u_n\}_{n=-m}^{\infty}$ is called a periodic solution with period ℓ if $u_{n+\ell} = u_n$ for all $n \geq -m$.*

Definition 4. *A sequence $\{u_n\}_{n=-m}^{\infty}$ is called a periodic solution with prime period ℓ if $\ell = \min\{s \in \mathbb{Z}^+ : u_{n+s} = u_n \text{ for all } n \geqslant -m\}$.*

Definition 5. *The linearized equation of (6) about the EQP u_e is defined by $\mathcal{Z}_{n+1} = \sum_{i=0}^{m} \lambda_i \mathcal{Z}_{n-i}$ where*

$$\lambda_i = \frac{\partial \psi(u_e, u_e)}{\partial u_{n-i}}.$$

Theorem 1 ([18], Theorem 1.4.6). *Suppose that $\psi \in \mathbf{C}(\mathcal{I}^2, \mathcal{I})$, where $\mathcal{I} \subset \mathbb{R}$, and $\psi(\mathsf{t}, \mathsf{s})$ satisfies the following properties:*
(a) $\psi_{\mathsf{t}} \leq 0$ and $\psi_{\mathsf{s}} \geq 0$, for all $(\mathsf{t}, \mathsf{s}) \in \mathcal{I}^2$,
(b) The DIE

$$u_{n+1} = \psi(u_n, u_{n-1}) \tag{7}$$

has no solutions of prime period two in $\mathcal{I}$.
Then, DIE (7) has a unique EQP u_e and all solutions of (7) converge to u_e.

Theorem 2 ([18], Theorem 1.4.5). *Suppose that $\psi \in \mathbf{C}(\mathcal{I}^2, \mathcal{I})$, where $\mathcal{I} \subset \mathbb{R}$, and $\psi(\mathsf{t}, \mathsf{s})$ satisfies the following properties:*
(a) $\psi_{\mathsf{t}} \geq 0$ and $\psi_{\mathsf{s}} \leq 0$, for all $(\mathsf{t}, \mathsf{s}) \in \mathcal{I}^2$,
(b) If $(s, B) \in \mathcal{I}^2$ is a solution of the system

$$\begin{cases} \psi(s, B) = s, \\ \psi(B, s) = B, \end{cases}$$

then $s = B$.
Then, DIE (7) has a unique EQP u_e and all solutions of (7) converge to u_e.

3. Dynamics of Equation (1)

In the following, we study the behavior of solutions to DIE (1). Through the next results, we need to define the following functions:

$$\mathcal{P}_1(\mathsf{t}, \mathsf{s}) = \frac{\partial}{\partial \mathsf{t}} \mathcal{P}(\mathsf{t}, \mathsf{s})$$

and

$$\mathcal{P}_2(\mathsf{t}, \mathsf{s}) = \frac{\partial}{\partial \mathsf{s}} \mathcal{P}(\mathsf{t}, \mathsf{s}).$$

3.1. Periodic Behavior of Solutions

In the following, we provide the necessary and sufficient conditions for the existence of prime period-two and -three solutions to DIE (1).

3.1.1. Existence of Prime Period-Two Solutions

Theorem 3. *Suppose that $\alpha > 0$. The necessary and sufficient condition for the existence of periodic solutions with period-two of DIE (1) is the existence of a constant $\ell \in \mathbb{R}^+ / \{1\}$ that satisfies $\mathcal{P}(\ell, 1) = \mathcal{P}(1, \ell)$.*

Proof. Suppose that DIE (1) has the solution of the form $\ldots, \sigma, \varrho, \sigma, \varrho, \ldots$. Then, we can obtain

$$\sigma = \frac{\sigma}{\mathcal{P}(\varrho, \sigma)};$$

$$\varrho = \frac{\varrho}{\mathcal{P}(\sigma, \varrho)}.$$

Therefore,

$$\varrho^{\alpha}\mathcal{P}\left(1,\frac{\sigma}{\varrho}\right) = 1,$$

and

$$\varrho^{\alpha}\mathcal{P}\left(\frac{\sigma}{\varrho},1\right) = 1.$$

Hence, there is a $\ell = \sigma/\varrho$ such that $\mathcal{P}(\ell,1) = \mathcal{P}(1,\ell)$.

On the other hand, we suppose that $\mathcal{P}(\ell,1) = \mathcal{P}(1,\ell)$. Now, we choose $u_{-1} = \ell\mathcal{P}^{-1/\alpha}(1,\ell)$ and $u_0 = \mathcal{P}^{-1/\alpha}(1,\ell)$, where $\ell \in \mathbb{R}^+/\{1\}$. Thus,

$$\begin{aligned}
u_1 &= \frac{u_{-1}}{\mathcal{P}(u_0,u_{-1})} \\
&= \frac{\ell\mathcal{P}^{-1/\alpha}(1,\ell)}{\mathcal{P}\left(\mathcal{P}^{-1/\alpha}(1,\ell),\ell\mathcal{P}^{-1/\alpha}(1,\ell)\right)} \\
&= \frac{\ell\mathcal{P}^{-1/\alpha}(1,\ell)}{\mathcal{P}^{-1}(1,\ell)\mathcal{P}(1,\ell)} \\
&= \ell\mathcal{P}^{-1/\alpha}(1,\ell) \\
&= u_{-1}.
\end{aligned}$$

Also,

$$\begin{aligned}
u_2 &= \frac{u_0}{\mathcal{P}(u_1,u_0)} \\
&= \frac{\mathcal{P}^{-1/\alpha}(1,\ell)}{\mathcal{P}^{-1}(1,\ell)\mathcal{P}(\ell,1)} \\
&= \mathcal{P}^{-1/\alpha}(1,\ell) \\
&= u_0.
\end{aligned}$$

Similarly, we have $u_{2r} = u_0$ and $u_{2r+1} = u_{-1}$ for all $r = 1,2,\ldots$.

Then, the proof is complete. $\square$

Theorem 4. *Suppose that $\alpha = 0$. The necessary and sufficient condition for the existence of periodic solutions with period-two of DIE (1) is the existence of a constant $\ell \in \mathbb{R}^+/\{1\}$ that satisfies $\mathcal{P}(\ell,1) = 1 = \mathcal{P}(1,\ell)$.*

Proof. Proceeding as in the proof of Theorem 1, we can prove that the condition is necessary.

On the other hand, we suppose that $\mathcal{P}(\ell,1) = \mathcal{P}(1,\ell)$. Now, we choose $u_{-1} = c$ and $u_0 = ck$, where $\ell \in \mathbb{R}^+/\{1\}$. Thus,

$$u_1 = \frac{c}{\mathcal{P}(c\ell,c)} = \frac{c}{\mathcal{P}(\ell,1)} = c$$

Also,

$$u_2 = \frac{c\ell}{\mathcal{P}(c,c\ell)} = \frac{c\ell}{\mathcal{P}(1,\ell)} = c\ell.$$

Similarly, we have $u_{2r} = c$ and $u_{2r+1} = c\ell$ for all $r = 1,2,\ldots$.

Then, the proof is complete. $\sqcup$

Example 1. *Let the DIE*

$$u_{n+1} = \frac{u_{n-1}}{au_n + bu_{n-1}}, \tag{8}$$

where $a, b \in \mathbb{R}^+$. We note that $\mathcal{P}(t,s) = at + bs$ is homogenous with degree one. Using Theorem 3, the necessary and sufficient condition for the existence of periodic solutions with period-

two of DIE (1) is the existence of a constant $\ell \in \mathbb{R}^+ / \{1\}$ that satisfies $a\ell + b = a + b\ell$, and so $(a - b)(\ell - 1) = 0$, i.e., $a = b$, see Figure 1.

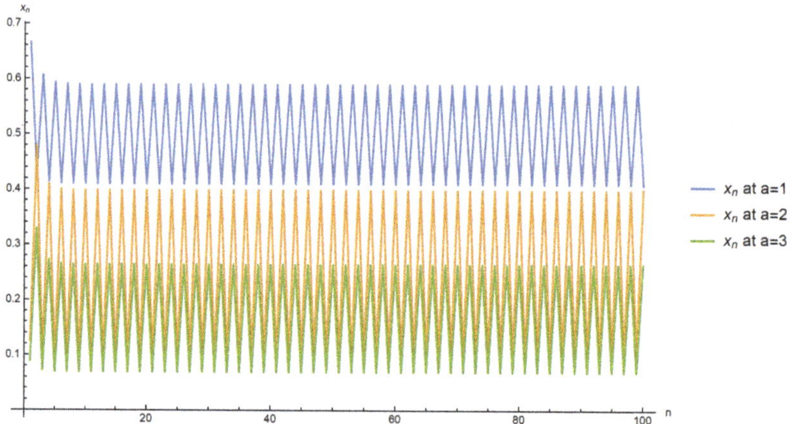

Figure 1. Periodic solutions of DIE (8) at $a = b = 1, 2,$ or 3.

3.1.2. Local Asymptotic Stability of a Two Cycle

Suppose that DIE (1) has a solution with two cycle $\ldots, \sigma, \varrho, \sigma, \varrho, \ldots$. Now, we set

$$t_n = u_{n-1} \text{ and } s_n = u_n.$$

Then, DIE (1) is equivalent to the system

$$\begin{cases} t_{n+1} = s_n, \\ s_{n+1} = \dfrac{t_n}{\mathcal{P}(s_n, t_n)}. \end{cases}$$

Next, we define $F : [0, \infty)^2 \to [0, \infty)^2$ by

$$F\begin{pmatrix} t \\ s \end{pmatrix} = \begin{pmatrix} s \\ \dfrac{t}{\mathcal{P}(s, t)} \end{pmatrix}.$$

Therefore, we have that

$$\begin{pmatrix} \sigma \\ \varrho \end{pmatrix}$$

is a fixed point of $F^{[2]} := F \circ F$, where

$$F^{[2]}\begin{pmatrix} t \\ s \end{pmatrix} = \begin{pmatrix} \dfrac{t}{\mathcal{P}(s, t)} \\ \dfrac{s}{\mathcal{P}\left(\frac{t}{\mathcal{P}(s,t)}, s\right)} \end{pmatrix}.$$

The Jacobian matrix $J_{F^{[2]}}$ at (σ, ϱ) takes the form

$$J_{F^{[2]}}\begin{pmatrix} \sigma \\ \varrho \end{pmatrix} = \begin{pmatrix} A & B \\ C & D \end{pmatrix},$$

where

$$A \quad : \quad = \frac{\mathcal{P}(\varrho,\sigma) - \sigma \mathcal{P}_2(\varrho,\sigma)}{\mathcal{P}^2(\varrho,\sigma)},$$

$$B \quad : \quad = \frac{-\sigma \mathcal{P}_1(\varrho,\sigma)}{\mathcal{P}^2(\varrho,\sigma)},$$

$$C \quad : \quad = \frac{-A\varrho}{\mathcal{P}^2\left(\frac{\sigma}{\mathcal{P}(\varrho,\sigma)},\varrho\right)} \mathcal{P}_1\left(\frac{\sigma}{\mathcal{P}(\varrho,\sigma)},\varrho\right),$$

and

$$D := \frac{1}{\mathcal{P}^2\left(\frac{\sigma}{\mathcal{P}(\varrho,\sigma)},\varrho\right)} \left[\mathcal{P}\left(\frac{\sigma}{\mathcal{P}(\varrho,\sigma)},\varrho\right) - \varrho \left[B\mathcal{P}_1\left(\frac{\sigma}{\mathcal{P}(\varrho,\sigma)},\varrho\right) + \mathcal{P}_2\left(\frac{\sigma}{\mathcal{P}(\varrho,\sigma)},\varrho\right) \right] \right].$$

In the event that the eigenvalues of $J_{F^{[2]}}$ at (σ,ϱ) are inside the unit disk, the two-cycle solution is locally asymptotically stable. Using Theorem 1.1.1 (c) in [18], the eigenvalues of $J_{F^{[2]}}$ at (σ,ϱ) are inside the unit disk if

$$\mathcal{K} < 1 + \mathcal{L} \text{ and } \mathcal{L} < 1,$$

where

$$\mathcal{K} = A + D$$

and

$$\mathcal{L} = AD - BC.$$

Example 2. *Consider the DIE (8) where $a, b \in \mathbb{R}^+$. From Theorem 3, for $\ell \in \mathbb{R}^+ / \{1\}$, there is a prime period two solution*

$$\ldots, \frac{\ell}{a(1+\ell)}, \frac{1}{a(1+\ell)}, \frac{\ell}{a(1+\ell)}, \frac{1}{a(1+\ell)}, \ldots . \tag{9}$$

It is easy to verify that

$$A = \frac{1}{1+\ell}, \ B = -\frac{\ell}{1+\ell}, \ C = -\frac{\ell}{1+\ell},$$

and

$$D = \frac{\ell(2+\ell)}{(1+\ell)^2}.$$

The two cycle solution (9) of DIE (8) is locally asymptotically stable if $\ell(1+\ell) < 1$.

3.1.3. Existence of Prime Period-Three Solutions

Theorem 5. *Assume that $\alpha > 0$. Then, DIE (1) has a prime period-three solution if and only if the system*

$$\begin{cases} \mathcal{P}(l,1) = k^{2-\alpha} l \mathcal{P}(k,1), \\ \mathcal{P}(1/kl,1) = \frac{l^{1-\alpha}}{k} \mathcal{P}(l,1), \\ \mathcal{P}(k,1) = k^{2-1} l^{2-2} \mathcal{P}(1/kl,1), \end{cases} \tag{10}$$

has a solution (k,l), where $k, l \in \mathbb{R}^+$, and at least one of $\{k,l\}$ is not equal to one.

Proof. Suppose that DIE (1) has the solution $\ldots, \delta, \beta, \gamma, \delta, \beta, \gamma, \ldots$. Then, we can obtain

$$\gamma = \frac{\delta}{\mathcal{P}(\beta, \delta)},$$

$$\delta = \frac{\beta}{\mathcal{P}(\gamma, \beta)},$$

$$\beta = \frac{\gamma}{\mathcal{P}(\delta, \gamma)}.$$

Set $\beta/\delta = k$ and $\gamma/\beta = l$, we arrive at

$$\gamma = \frac{\delta^{1-\alpha}}{\mathcal{P}(k, 1)},$$

$$\delta = \frac{\beta^{1-\alpha}}{\mathcal{P}(l, 1)},$$

$$\beta = \frac{\gamma^{1-\alpha}}{\mathcal{P}(1/kl, 1)}.$$

Thus, we obtain

$$\mathcal{P}(l, 1) = k^{2-\alpha} l \mathcal{P}(k, 1),$$

and

$$\mathcal{P}(1/kl, 1) = \frac{l^{1-\alpha}}{k} \mathcal{P}(l, 1).$$

Then, system (10) has the solution $(\beta/\delta, \gamma/\beta)$.

On the other hand, we suppose that system (10) has a solution (k, l), where $k, l \in \mathbb{R}^+$, and at least one of $\{k, l\}$ is not equal to one. Now, we choose

$$u_{-1} = \left(\frac{1}{kl\mathcal{P}(k, 1)} \right)^{1/\alpha},$$

$$u_0 = \left(\frac{k}{\mathcal{P}(l, 1)} \right)^{1/\alpha}.$$

Thus, by using (10), we have

$$
\begin{aligned}
u_1 &= \frac{u_{-1}}{\mathcal{P}(u_0, u_{-1})} \\
&= \frac{1}{k^{1/\alpha} l^{1/\alpha} \mathcal{P}^{1/\alpha}(k, 1)} \frac{1}{\mathcal{P}\left(\frac{k^{1/\alpha}}{\mathcal{P}^{1/\alpha}(l, 1)}, \frac{1}{k^{1/\alpha} l^{1/\alpha} \mathcal{P}^{1/\alpha}(k, 1)} \right)} \\
&= \frac{kl}{k^{1/\alpha} l^{1/\alpha} \mathcal{P}^{1/\alpha}(k, 1)} \\
&= \frac{kl}{k^{1/\alpha} l^{1/\alpha} \frac{1}{k^{\frac{1-\alpha}{\alpha}} l^{\frac{2-\alpha}{\alpha}}} \mathcal{P}^{1/\alpha}(1/kl, 1)} \\
&= \left(\frac{l}{\mathcal{P}(1/kl, 1)} \right)^{1/\alpha}.
\end{aligned}
$$

Additionally,

$$
\begin{aligned}
u_2 &= \frac{u_0}{\mathcal{P}(u_1, u_0)} \\
&= \frac{k^{1/\alpha}}{\mathcal{P}^{1/\alpha}(l,1)} \, \frac{1}{\mathcal{P}\left(\frac{l^{1/\alpha}}{\mathcal{P}^{1/\alpha}(1/kl,1)}, \frac{k^{1/\alpha}}{\mathcal{P}^{1/\alpha}(l,1)}\right)} \\
&= \frac{k^{1/\alpha}}{\mathcal{P}^{1/\alpha}(l,1)} \, \frac{1}{k} \\
&= \frac{k^{1/\alpha}}{k^{\frac{2-\alpha}{\alpha}} l^{1/\alpha}} \, \frac{1}{k} \, \frac{1}{\mathcal{P}^{1/\alpha}(k,1)} \\
&= \left(\frac{1}{kl\mathcal{P}(k,1)}\right)^{1/\alpha} \\
&= u_{-1}
\end{aligned}
$$

Similarly, we can prove that $u_3 = u_0$. Proceeding with the same approach, we conclude that

$$
u_{3r-1} = u_{-1}, \; u_{3r} = u_0, \text{and } u_{3r+1} = u_1, \text{ for all } r = 1, 2, \ldots .
$$

Therefore, the proof is complete. $\square$

Theorem 6. *Suppose that* $\alpha = 0$. *DIE (1) has a prime period-three solution if and only if the system*

$$
\begin{cases}
0 = 1 - kl\mathcal{P}(k,1), \\
0 = k - \mathcal{P}(l,1), \\
0 = l - \mathcal{P}(1/kl,1)
\end{cases}
\tag{11}
$$

has a solution (k, l, m), *where* $k, l, m \in \mathbb{R}^+$, *and at least one of* $\{k, l, m\}$ *is not equal to one.*

Proof. Suppose that DIE (1) has the solution $\ldots, \delta, \beta, \gamma, \delta, \beta, \gamma, \ldots$. As in the proof of Theorem 5, we arrive at

$$
\begin{aligned}
\gamma &= \frac{\delta}{\mathcal{P}(k,1)}, \\
\delta &= \frac{\beta}{\mathcal{P}(l,1)}, \\
\beta &= \frac{\gamma}{\mathcal{P}(1/kl,1)}.
\end{aligned}
$$

Thus, we obtain

$$
kl\mathcal{P}(k,1) = 1
$$

$$
k = \mathcal{P}(l,1)
$$

and

$$
l = \mathcal{P}(1/kl,1).
$$

Then, system (10) has the solution $(\beta/\delta, \gamma/\beta)$.

On the other hand, we assume that (10) has a solution (k, l), where $k, l \in \mathbb{R}^+$, and at least one of $\{k, l\}$ is not equal to one. Now, we choose $u_{-1} = c$ and $u_0 = ck$, where $k \in \mathbb{R}^+$ and c is an arbitrary positive real number. Therefore,

$$
\begin{aligned}
u_1 &= \frac{c}{\mathcal{P}(ck, c)} = \frac{c}{\mathcal{P}(k,1)} = ckl, \\
u_2 &= \frac{ck}{\mathcal{P}(ckl, ck)} = \frac{ck}{\mathcal{P}(l,1)} = c = u_{-1},
\end{aligned}
$$

and

$$u_3 = \frac{u_1}{\mathcal{P}(u_2, u_1)} = \frac{ckl}{\mathcal{P}(c, ckl)} = \frac{ckl}{\mathcal{P}(1/kl, 1)} = ck = u_0.$$

Proceeding with the same approach, we conclude that

$$u_{3r-1} = u_{-1}, \ u_{3r} = u_0, \text{and } u_{3r+1} = ckl, \text{ for all } r = 1, 2, \ldots .$$

Therefore, the proof is complete. $\square$

Example 3. *Consider the DIE*

$$u_{n+1} = \frac{u_n u_{n-1}^2}{a u_n u_{n-1} + b u_n^2 + c u_{n-1}^2}, \tag{12}$$

where a, b and $c \in \mathbb{R}/\{0\}$. We note that

$$\mathcal{P}(t, s) = a + b\frac{t}{s} + c\frac{s}{t}$$

is homogenous with degree zero. Using Theorem 5, DIE (12) has a prime period-three solution if the system

$$0 = 1 - kl\left(a + bk + c\frac{1}{k}\right),$$
$$0 = k - \left(a + bl + c\frac{1}{l}\right),$$
$$0 = l - \left(a + b\frac{1}{kl} + ckl\right)$$

has the solution.
Consider the special case when $a = -\frac{2521}{561}, b = \frac{380}{187}$, and $c = \frac{223}{187}$. DIE (12) has a prime period-three solution $\ldots, 1, 2, 6, 1, 2, 6, \ldots$, see Figure 2.

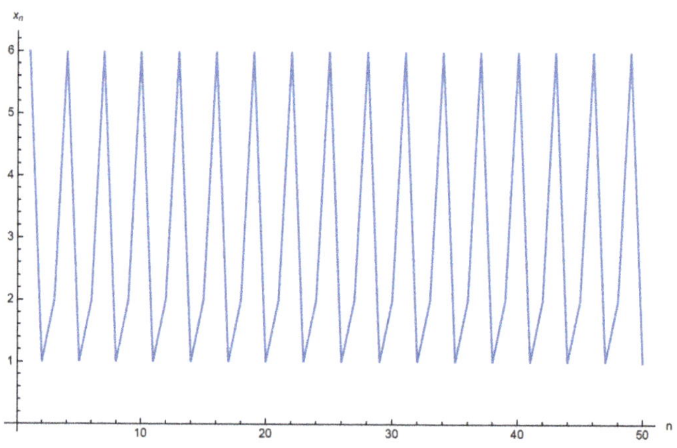

Figure 2. Prime period-three solution of DIE (12).

3.2. Stability Behavior of Solutions

Now, we define $\phi : (0, \infty)^2 \to (0, \infty)$ by

$$\phi(t, s) = \frac{s}{\mathcal{P}(t, s)}.$$

The EQP of DIE (1) is given by $u_e = \phi(u_e, u_e)$. Therefore,

$$\left[\frac{1}{\mathcal{P}(u_e, u_e)} - 1\right] u_e = 0,$$

this implies that the positive EQP

$$u_e = \frac{1}{\mathcal{P}^{1/\alpha}(1, 1)}, \quad \alpha > 0. \tag{13}$$

The linearized equation of DIE (1) is

$$\mathcal{L}_{n+1} - \lambda \mathcal{L}_n - \mu \mathcal{L}_{n-1} = 0, \tag{14}$$

where

$$\lambda = \frac{\partial \phi(u_e, u_e)}{\partial t} = \frac{-u_e \mathcal{P}_1(u_e, u_e)}{\mathcal{P}^2(u_e, u_e)} = -\frac{\mathcal{P}_1(1, 1)}{u_e^\alpha \mathcal{P}^2(1, 1)}$$

and

$$\mu = \frac{\partial \phi(u_e, u_e)}{\partial s} = \frac{\mathcal{P}(u_e, u_e) - u_e \mathcal{P}_2(u_e, u_e)}{\mathcal{P}^2(u_e, u_e)} = \frac{\mathcal{P}(1, 1) - \mathcal{P}_2(1, 1)}{u_e^\alpha \mathcal{P}^2(1, 1)}.$$

From (13), we obtain $u_e^\alpha = 1/\mathcal{P}(1, 1)$, and so

$$\lambda = -\frac{\mathcal{P}_1(1, 1)}{\mathcal{P}(1, 1)} \quad \text{and} \quad \mu = 1 - \frac{\mathcal{P}_2(1, 1)}{\mathcal{P}(1, 1)}.$$

Remark 1. *Since $\mathcal{P}(t, s)$ is homogenous with degree α, we have $\mathcal{P}_1(t, s)$ and $\mathcal{P}_2(t, s)$ are homogenous with degree $\alpha - 1$. Moreover, from Euler Theorem for homogeneous functions $t\mathcal{P}_1(t, s) + s\mathcal{P}_2(t, s) = \alpha \mathcal{P}(t, s)$. Thus, $\mathcal{P}_1(1, 1) + \mathcal{P}_2(1, 1) = \alpha \mathcal{P}(1, 1)$.*

Lemma 1. *The EQP u_e of DIE (1) is locally asymptotically stable (sink) if*

$$|\eta| < \rho < 2\kappa, \tag{15}$$

otherwise it is unstable. Furthermore, it has the following unstable cases:
(a) u_e is repeller if
$$|\kappa - \rho| > \kappa \text{ and } |\eta| < |\rho|,$$

(b) u_e is a saddle point if
$$\eta^2 + 4\kappa^2 > 4\kappa\rho \text{ and } |\eta| > |\rho|,$$

(c) u_e is a nonhyperbolic point if
$$\eta = |\rho|,$$

or

$$2\kappa = \rho \text{ and } |\eta| \leq 2\kappa,$$

where $\kappa = \mathcal{P}(1, 1)$, $\eta = \mathcal{P}_1(1, 1)$, and $\rho = \mathcal{P}_2(1, 1)$.

Proof. The proof results directly from Theorem 1.1.1 in [18], so it was deleted. $\square$

Lemma 2. *Assume that $\mathcal{P}_1(t, s) \geq 0$, $\mathcal{P}_2(t, s) \leq 0$, and*

$$\mathcal{P}(\ell, 1) = \mathcal{P}(1, \ell) \rightarrow \ell = 1. \tag{16}$$

Then, all solutions of DIE (1) converge to u_e.

Proof. From the definition of the function ϕ, it is easy to conclude that

$$\frac{\partial\phi(t,s)}{\partial t} = \frac{-s\mathcal{P}_1(t,s)}{\mathcal{P}^2(t,s)} \leq 0,$$

$$\frac{\partial\phi(t,s)}{\partial s} = \frac{\mathcal{P}(t,s) - s\mathcal{P}_2(t,s)}{\mathcal{P}^2(t,s)} \geq 0.$$

Since $\mathcal{P}(\ell,1) \neq \mathcal{P}(1,\ell)$ for all $\ell \in \mathbb{R}^+/\{1\}$, we obtain from Theorem 3 that DIE (1) has no solutions of prime period two. Therefore, from Theorem 1, all solutions of DIE (1) converge to u_e. Hence, the proof is complete. $\square$

Lemma 3. *Assume that $\alpha \leq 1$, $\mathcal{P}_1(t,s) \geq 0$, and (16) holds. Then, all solutions of DIE (1) converge to u_e.*

Proof. From Remark 1, we have $\alpha\mathcal{P}(t,s) - s\mathcal{P}_2(t,s) \geq 0$, which with the fact that $\alpha \leq 1$ gives $\mathcal{P}(t,s) \geq s\mathcal{P}_2(t,s)$. The rest of the proof is exactly as the proof of Theorem 2. $\square$

Lemma 4. *Assume that $\alpha \geq 1$, $\mathcal{P}_1(t,s) \leq 0$, and*

$$\mathcal{P}(1,\ell) = \ell^2\mathcal{P}(\ell,1) \to \ell = 1. \tag{17}$$

Then, all solutions of DIE (1) converge to u_e.

Proof. From Remark 1 and the fact that $\alpha \geq 1$, we get $\mathcal{P}(t,s) \leq \alpha\mathcal{P}(t,s) \leq s\mathcal{P}_2(t,s)$. From the definition of the function ϕ, it is easy to conclude that $\partial\phi/\partial t \geq 0$ and $\partial\phi/\partial s \leq 0$.

Now, we suppose that (s,B) is a solution of the system

$$\begin{cases} \phi(s,B) = s, \\ \phi(B,s) = B. \end{cases}$$

Thus, we obtain

$$B = s\,\mathcal{P}(s,B) \text{ and } s = B\,\mathcal{P}(B,s).$$

Hence, we conclude that

$$B = s\,s^{\alpha}\mathcal{P}\left(1,\frac{B}{s}\right) \text{ and } s = B\,s^{\alpha}\mathcal{P}\left(\frac{B}{s},1\right).$$

Set $B/s = \ell$, we arrive at

$$\mathcal{P}(1,\ell) = \ell^2\mathcal{P}(\ell,1).$$

Using (17), we obtain that $\ell = 1$, and so $B = s$. Therefore, it follows from Theorem 2 that all solutions of DIE (1) converge to u_e. This completes the proof. $\square$

Lemma 5. *Assume that $\mathcal{P}_1(t,s) \geq 0$, $\mathcal{P}(\ell,1) \geq \mathcal{P}_2(\ell,1)$ for all $\ell \in \mathbb{R}$, and (16) holds. Then, all solutions of DIE (1) converge to u_e.*

Proof. From the definition of the function ϕ, it is easy to note that $\partial\phi/\partial t \leq 0$, and

$$\frac{\partial\phi(t,s)}{\partial s} = \frac{\mathcal{P}(t,s) - s\mathcal{P}_2(t,s)}{\mathcal{P}^2(t,s)} = \frac{s^{\alpha}\left[\mathcal{P}(\frac{t}{s},1) - \mathcal{P}_2(\frac{t}{s},1)\right]}{\mathcal{P}^2(t,s)} \geq 0.$$

The rest of the proof is exactly as the proof of Theorem 2. $\square$

Lemma 6. *Assume that $\alpha = 0$, and there is a $h_0 \in \mathbb{R}^+$ such that $\mathcal{P}(\ell,1) \geq h_0 > 1$ for all $\ell \in \mathbb{R}^+$. If $\{u_n\}_{n=-1}^{\infty}$ is a solution of DIE (1), then $\lim_{n\to\infty} u_n = 0$.*

Proof. From DIE (1), we have

$$0 < u_{n+1} \;=\; \frac{u_{n+1}}{\mathcal{P}(u_n, u_{n-1})} \;=\; \frac{1}{u_{n-1}^{\alpha-1}\,\mathcal{P}\!\left(\frac{u_n}{u_{n-1}}, 1\right)} \;\leq\; \frac{1}{h_0}\, u_{n-1}^{1-\alpha} \tag{18}$$

$$\leq\; \frac{1}{h_0}\, u_{n-1}. \tag{19}$$

Now, let $y_{n+1} = \frac{1}{h_0} y_{n-1}$. Then,

$$y_n = \begin{cases} \dfrac{1}{h_0^{n/2}}\, y_0, & \text{if } n \text{ is even,} \\[2ex] \dfrac{1}{h_0^{(n+1)/2}}\, y_{-1}, & \text{if } n \text{ is odd.} \end{cases}$$

Therefore,

$$\lim_{n\to\infty} y_n = 0, \text{ if } h_0 > 1.$$

which with (19) gives $\lim_{n\to\infty} u_n = 0$. This completes the proof. $\square$

Lemma 7. *Assume that $\alpha = 1$, and there is a $h_0 \in \mathbb{R}^+$ such that $\mathcal{P}(\ell, 1) \geq h_0$ for all $\ell \in \mathbb{R}^+$. Then, all solutions of DIE (1) are bounded.*

Proof. From DIE (1), we have that (18) holds. Thus, $u_{n+1} \leq 1/h_0$ for all $n \geq 0$. Hence,

$$u_n \leq \max\left\{ \frac{1}{h_0}, u_0, u_{-1} \right\} \text{ for all } n \geq -1.$$

This completes the proof. $\square$

Theorem 7. *Assume that $\alpha \leq 1$, $\mathcal{P}_1(\mathsf{t}, \mathsf{s}) \geq 0$ and (16) holds. Then, the EQP of (1) is globally asymptotically stable if (15) holds.*

Theorem 8. *Assume that $\mathcal{P}_1(\mathsf{t}, \mathsf{s}) \geq 0$, $\mathcal{P}(\ell, 1) \geq \mathcal{P}_2(\ell, 1)$ for all $\ell \in \mathbb{R}$, and (16) holds. Then, the EQP of (1) is globally asymptotically stable if (15) holds.*

3.3. Examples and Numerical Simulations

In this part, we provide some examples that support the previous theoretical results. Examples are presented later, including what has been studied and what has not been studied before.

3.3.1. Special Case 1

Consider the DIE

$$u_{n+1} = \frac{a u_{n-1}}{b u_n + c u_{n-1}}, \tag{20}$$

where a, b, and c are positive real numbers. Using the substitution $u_n = \frac{a}{b z_n}$, DIE (20) reduces to $z_{n+1} = \frac{c}{b} + \frac{z_{n-1}}{z_n}$, and this equation has been studied in [34].

It is easy to notice that $\mathcal{P}(\mathsf{t}, \mathsf{s}) = \frac{b}{a}\mathsf{t} + \frac{c}{a}\mathsf{s}$ is homogenous with degree *one*. Using our previous results, the following information can be obtained

1. DIE (20) has a prime period-two solution $\iff b = c$.
2. The positive EQP of DIE (20) is $u_e = a/(b+c)$.
3. The EQP u_e of DIE (20) is locally asymptotically stable (sink) if $b < c$.
4. If $b < c$, then EQP of DIE (20) is globally asymptotically stable.
5. We note that $\mathcal{P}(\ell, 1) = \frac{1}{a}c + \frac{1}{a}b\ell \geq c/a$. Then, all solutions of DIE (20) are bounded if $c > a$.

3.3.2. Special Case 2

Consider the DIE

$$u_{n+1} = u_{n-1}\exp\left(-a - b\frac{u_n}{u_{n-1}} - c\frac{u_{n-1}}{u_n}\right), \tag{21}$$

where a, b and c are real numbers. It is easy to notice that

$$\mathcal{P}(t,s) = \exp\left(a + b\frac{t}{s} + c\frac{s}{t}\right)$$

is homogenous with degree *zero*.

1. DIE (21) has a prime period-two solution $\Longleftrightarrow$ there is a $\ell \in \mathbb{R}^+/\{1\}$ such that

$$b\ell + c\frac{1}{\ell} = \left(b\frac{1}{\ell} + c\ell\right),$$

i.e., $b = c < 0$, see Figure 3.

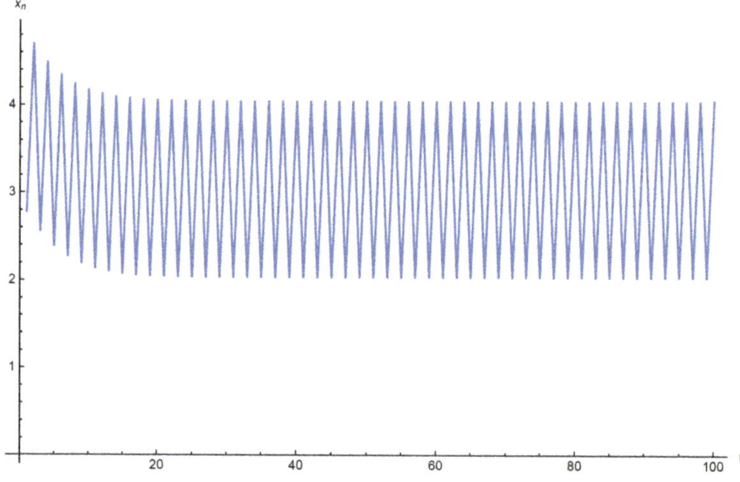

Figure 3. Periodic solutions of DIE (21) at $a = 1$, and $b = c = -2/5$.

2. DIE (21) has a prime period-three solution $\Longleftrightarrow$ there is a $\ell, l \in \mathbb{R}^+/\{1\}$ such that

$$\begin{aligned}
bk^2 + ak + c &= -k\ln(kl), \\
bl^2 + al + c &= l\ln k, \\
ck^2 + akl + bl^2 &= kl\ln l,
\end{aligned}$$

see Figure 4.

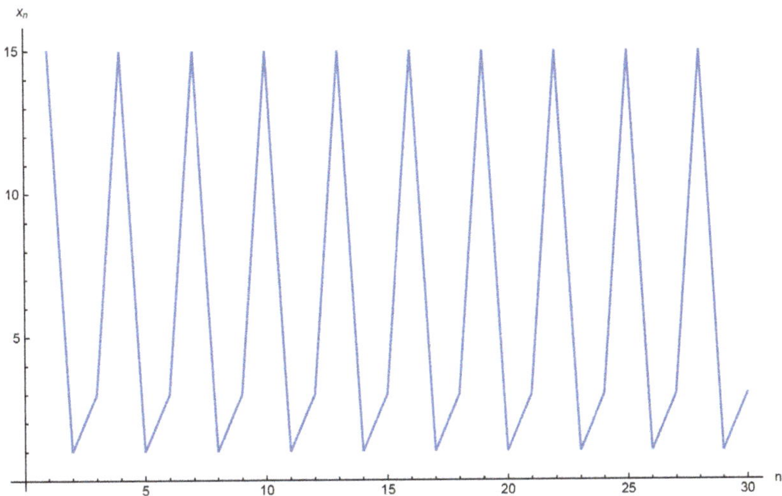

Figure 4. Periodic solutions of DIE (21) at $a = -8.7829$, $b = 1.9489$, and $c = 0.684\,16$.

3. Assume that $b, c \in \mathbb{R}^+$. We note that $\mathcal{P}(\ell, 1) = e^{a+b\ell+\frac{c}{\ell}} \geq e^a$. Then, every solution of DIE (22) converges to *zero* if $a > 0$.

3.3.3. Special Case 3

Consider the DIE

$$u_{n+1} = \frac{u_{n-1}}{au_n^2 + bu_nu_{n-1} + cu_{n-1}^2},\tag{22}$$

where a, b and c are real numbers, and one of them is not equal to zero at least. It is easy to notice that

$$\mathcal{P}(t,s) = at^2 + bts + cs^2$$

is homogenous with degree *two*.

1. DIE (22) has a prime period-two solution $\Longleftrightarrow$ there is a $\ell \in \mathbb{R}^+/\{1\}$ such that

$$(a-c)\left(\ell^2 - 1\right) = 0$$

i.e., $a = c$, see Figure 5.

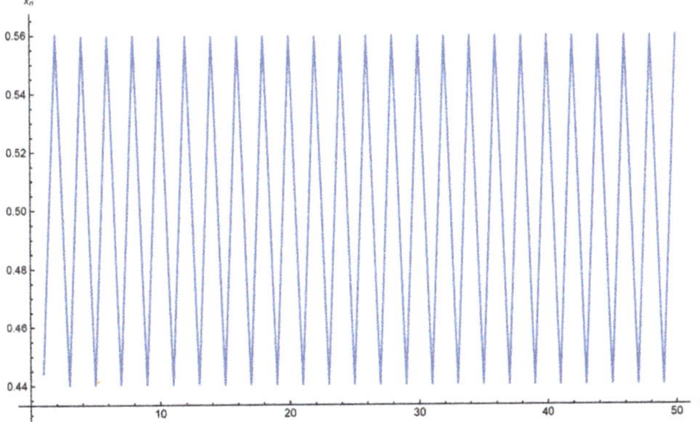

Figure 5. Periodic solutions of DIE (22) at $b = 2$, and $a = c = 1$.

2. DIE (22) has a prime period-three solution $\Longleftrightarrow$ there is a $\ell, l \in \mathbb{R}^+ / \{1\}$ such that

$$
\begin{aligned}
c + al^2 + bl - cl - ak^2l - bkl &= 0, \\
a - akl^3 - bkl^2 + ck^2l^2 + bkl - ckl &= 0, \\
a - ckl^2 - ak^3l^2 - bk^2l^2 + ck^2l^2 + bkl &= 0,
\end{aligned}
$$

see Figure 6.

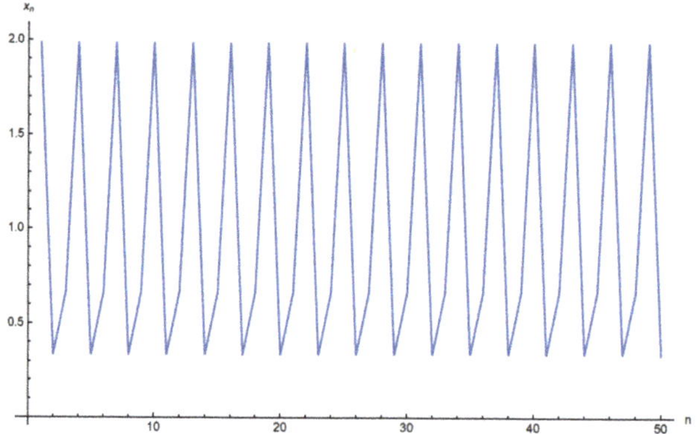

Figure 6. Periodic solutions of DIE (22) at $a = \frac{38}{11}$, $b = -\frac{196}{125}$, and $c = 1$.

3. The positive EQP of DIE (22) is

$$
u_e = \frac{1}{\sqrt{a+b+c}}, \ a+b+c > 0.
$$

4. The EQP u_e of DIE (22) is locally asymptotically stable (sink) if

$$
|2a + b| < b + 2c < 2(a + b + c).
$$

If a, b, and c are positive, then u_e is locally asymptotically stable (sink) if $a < c$, is a saddle point if $c < a$, and is a nonhyperbolic point if $a = c$, see Figure 7.

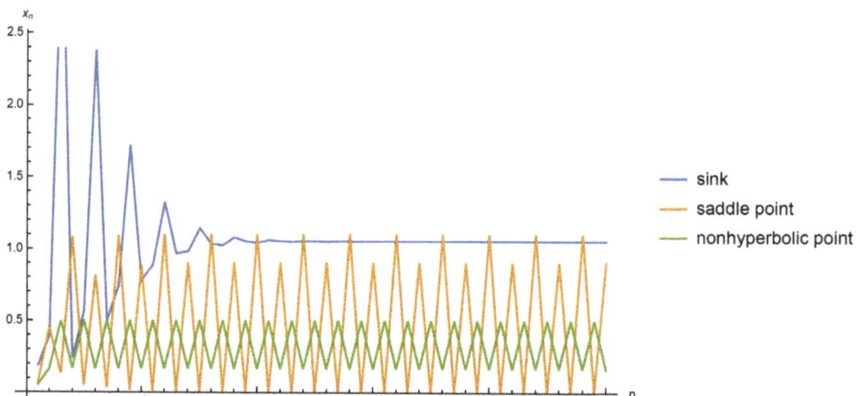

Figure 7. Stability behavior of solutions (22).

4. Conclusions

Our interest in this work was centered on the examination of some features of solutions to the general DIE (1). We considered the periodic behavior, stability, and boundedness of solutions to DIE (1). In detail, we fulfilled the sufficient and necessary conditions for the existence of periodic solutions with periods two and three. We then obtained a complete perception of the local stability of the EQPs for DIE (1). Moreover, we presented a number of lemma and theorems that discuss the global stability and boundedness of the studied equation. Finally, we obtained many properties of the solutions for some special cases of the studied equation, and we showed numerical simulations of their solutions.

Studying the qualitative behavior of the general DIEs may significantly contribute to eliciting the characteristics of the solutions of some new models that appear as a result of scientific and technological development in various fields. It is interesting, as an extension of our results in this work, to study the qualitative properties of solutions to the general DIE $u_{n+1} = \mathcal{K}(u_n, u_{n-1})$, where $\mathcal{K} = \mathcal{G}(\mathcal{P}(t, s))$ is a homothetic function.

Author Contributions: Conceptualization, O.M. and A.A.A.; methodology, O.M. and A.A.A.; formal analysis, O.M. and A.A.A.; investigation, O.M. and A.A.A.; writing—original draft preparation, O.M. and A.A.A.; writing—review and editing, O.M. All authors have read and agreed to the published version of the manuscript.

Funding: This research received no external funding.

Acknowledgments: The authors gratefully acknowledge Qassim University, represented by the Deanship of Scientific Research, on the financial support for this research under the number (COS-2022-1-1-J-27924) during the academic year 1444 AH/2022 AD.

Conflicts of Interest: The authors declare no conflict of interest.

References

1. Kiguradze, I.T.; Chaturia, T.A. *Asymptotic Properties of Solutions of Nonatunomous Ordinary Differential Equations*; Kluwer Academic Publishers: Drodrcht, The Netherlands, 1993.
2. Agarwal, R.P. *Difference Equations and Inequalities, Theory, Methods and Applications*, 2nd ed.; Marcel Dekker: New York, NY, USA, 2000.
3. Ahlabrandt, C.D.; Peterson, A.C. *Discrete Hamiltonian Systems: Difference Equations, Continued Fractions and Reccati Equations*; Kluwer Academic Publishers: Drodrcht, The Netherlands, 1996.
4. Elaydi, S. *An Introduction to Difference Equations*; Springer: New York, NY, USA, 1999.
5. Sharkovsky, A.N.; Maistrenko, Y.L.; Romanenko, E.Y. *Difference Equations and Their Applications*; Springer: Dordrecht, The Netherlands, 1993.
6. Diekmann, O.; Verduyn Lunel, S.M.; Gils, S.A.; Walther, H.-O. *Delay Equations, Functional, Complex and Nonlinear Analysis*; Springer: New York, NY, USA, 1995.
7. Kolmonovskii, V.; Myshkis, A. *Introduction to the Theory and Applications of Functional Differential Equations*; Kluwer Academic Publishers: Drodrcht, The Netherlands, 1999.
8. Kelley, W.G.; Peterson, A.C. *Difference Equations; An Introduction with Applications*, 2nd ed.; Academic Press: New York, NY, USA, 2000.
9. Allman, E.S.; Rhodes, J.A. *Mathematical Models in Biology: An Introduction*; Cambridge University Press: New York, NY, USA, 2003.
10. Beverton, R.J.H.; Holt, S.J. *On the Dynamics of Exploited Fish Populations*; Springer: Dordrecht, The Netherlands, 1993; Volume 11.
11. Cooke, K.L.; Calef, D.F.; Level, E.V. Stability or chaos in discrete epidemic models. In *Nonlinear Systems and Applications*; Academic Press: New York, NY, USA, 1977.
12. Cull, P.; Flahive, M.; Robson, R. *Difference Equations, From Rabbits to Chaos*; Undergraduate Texts in Mathematics; Springer: New York, NY, USA, 2005.
13. Din, Q. A novel chaos control strategy for discrete-time Brusselator models. *J. Math. Chem.* **2018**, *56*, 3045–3075. [CrossRef]
14. Din, Q. Bifurcation analysis and chaos control in discrete-time glycolysis models. *J. Math. Chem.* **2018**, *56*, 904–931. [CrossRef]
15. Din, Q.; Elsayed, E.M. Stability analysis of a discrete ecological model. *Comput. Ecol. Softw.* **2014**, *4*, 89–103.
16. Elsayed, E.M. New method to obtain periodic solutions of period two and three of a rational difference equation. *Nonlinear Dyn.* **2015**, *79*, 241–250. [CrossRef]
17. Moaaz, O. Comment on New method to obtain periodic solutions of period two and three of a rational difference equation [Nonlinear Dyn 79: 241–250]. *Nonlinear Dyn.* **2017**, *88*, 1043–1049. [CrossRef]
18. Kulenovic, M.R.S.; Ladas, G. *Dynamics of Second Order Rational Difference Equations with Open Problems and Conjectures*; Chapman & Hall/CRC Press: Boca Raton, FL, USA, 2001.

19. Kuruklis, S.; Ladas, G. Oscillation and global attractivity in a discrete delay logistic model. *Quart. Appl. Math.* **1992**, *50*, 227–233. [CrossRef]
20. Pielou, E.C. *An Introduction to Mathematical Ecology*; John Wiley & Sons: New York, NY, USA, 1965.
21. May, R.M. Nonlinear problems in ecology and resource management. *Chaotic Behav. Determ. Syst.* **1983**, 389–439.
22. Kuang, Y.K.; Cushing, J.M. Global stability in a nonlinear difference-delay equation model of flour beetle population growth. *J. Differ. Equ. Appl.* **1996**, *2*, 31–37. [CrossRef]
23. Stevo, S. The recursive sequence $u_{n+1} = g(u_n, u_{n-1})/(A + u_n)$. *Appl. Math. Lett.* **2002**, *15*, 305–308. [CrossRef]
24. Karakostas, G.L.; Stevic, S. On the recursive sequence $u_{n+1} = \alpha + u_{n-k}/f(u_n, u_{n-1}, \ldots, u_{n-k+1})$. *Demonstr. Math.* **2005**, *38*, 595.
25. Sun, S.; Xi, H. Global behavior of the nonlinear difference equation $u_{n+1} = f(u_{n-s}, u_{n-t})$. *J. Math. Anal. Appl.* **2005**, *311*, 760–765. [CrossRef]
26. Moaaz, O. Dynamics of difference equation $u_{n+1} = f(u_{n-l}, u_{n-k})$. *Adv. Differ. Equ.* **2018**, *2018*, 447. [CrossRef]
27. Elsayed, E.M.; Alofi, B.S. Dynamics and solutions structures of nonlinear system of difference equations. *Math. Method. Appl. Sci.* **2022**, *2022*, 1–18. [CrossRef]
28. Elsayed, E.M.; Aloufi, B.S.; Moaaz, O. The behavior and structures of solution of fifth-order rational recursive sequence. *Symmetry* **2022**, *14*, 641. [CrossRef]
29. Elsayed, E.M.; Alofi, B.S. The periodic nature and expression on solutions of some rational systems of difference equations. *Alex. Eng. J.* **2023**, *74*, 269–283. [CrossRef]
30. Al-Basyouni, K.S.; Elsayed, E.M. On some solvable systems of some rational difference equations of third order. *Mathematics* **2023**, *11*, 1047. [CrossRef]
31. Kara, M.; Yazlik, Y. On the solutions of three-dimensional system of difference equations via recursive relations of order two and applications. *J. Appl. Anal. Comput.* **2022**, *12*, 736–753. [CrossRef] [PubMed]
32. Al-Khedhairi, A.; Elsadany, A.A.; Elsonbaty, A. On the dynamics of a discrete fractional-order cournot–bertrand competition duopoly game. *Math. Probl. Eng.* **2022**, *2022*, 8249215. [CrossRef]
33. Khaliq, A.; Mustafa, I.; Ibrahim, T.F.; Osman, W.M.; Al-Sinan, B.R.; Dawood, A.A.; Juma, M.Y. Stability and bifurcation analysis of fifth-order nonlinear fractional difference equation. *Fractal Fract.* **2023**, *7*, 113. [CrossRef]
34. Amleh, A.M.; Georgiou, D.A.; Grove, E.A.; Ladas, G. On the recursive sequence $u_{n+1} = \alpha + u_{n-1}/u_n$. *J. Math. Anal. Appl.* **1999**, *233*, 790–798. [CrossRef]

Article

Study of Burgers–Huxley Equation Using Neural Network Method

Ying Wen [1,*,†] and **Temuer Chaolu** [2,†]

1   College of Information Engineering, Shanghai Maritime University, Shanghai 201306, China
2   College of Sciences and Arts, Shanghai Maritime University, Shanghai 201306, China; tmchaolu@shmtu.edu.cn
*   Correspondence: 201840310002@stu.shmtu.edu.cn
†   These authors contributed equally to this work.

Abstract: The study of non-linear partial differential equations is a complex task requiring sophisticated methods and techniques. In this context, we propose a neural network approach based on Lie series in Lie groups of differential equations (symmetry) for solving Burgers–Huxley nonlinear partial differential equations, considering initial or boundary value terms in the loss functions. The proposed technique yields closed analytic solutions that possess excellent generalization properties. Our approach differs from existing deep neural networks in that it employs only shallow neural networks. This choice significantly reduces the parameter cost while retaining the dynamic behavior and accuracy of the solution. A thorough comparison with its exact solution was carried out to validate the practicality and effectiveness of our proposed method, using vivid graphics and detailed analysis to present the results.

Keywords: Burgers–Huxley equation; optimization; neural network method; Lie groups; Lie series

MSC: 65M99

Citation: Wen, Y.; Chaolu, T. Study of Burgers–Huxley Equation Using Neural Network Method. *Axioms* **2023**, *12*, 429. https://doi.org/10.3390/axioms12050429

Academic Editor: Azhar Ali Zafar and Nehad Ali Shah

Received: 15 March 2023
Revised: 20 April 2023
Accepted: 25 April 2023
Published: 26 April 2023

1. Introduction

Partial differential equations (PDEs) are ubiquitous and fundamental to understanding and modeling the complexities of natural phenomena. From mathematics to physics to economics and beyond, PDEs play a critical role in virtually all fields of engineering and science [1–3]. Through their mathematical representation of physical phenomena, PDEs provide a powerful means of gaining insight into complex systems, enabling researchers and engineers to predict behavior and uncover hidden relationships. However, solving PDEs can be a daunting and challenging task. The complexity of these equations often requires sophisticated numerical methods that must balance accuracy and efficiency while solving high-dimensional PDEs. Despite these challenges, PDEs remain a cornerstone of modern science, enabling researchers to unlock discoveries and technological advancements across disciplines.

As numerical and computational techniques continue to rapidly develop, the study of PDEs has become increasingly vital. In recent years, advances in numerical methods and high-performance computing techniques have made it possible to solve complex PDEs more accurately and efficiently than ever before. These new tools can precisely solve specific problems across a broader range of equations while simultaneously computing data faster, reducing the time and cost of solving pending problems. Moreover, these new techniques have allowed researchers to gain deeper insights into the physical meaning behind PDEs, enabling them to revisit natural phenomena from fresh perspectives and explore those that prove challenging to explain by traditional methods. This has led to groundbreaking research discoveries and innovations in various fields of science and engineering.

Machine learning methods [4,5], particularly in the area of artificial neural networks (ANNs) [6,7], have piqued considerable interest in recent years due to their potential to solve differential equations. ANNs are well-known for their exceptional approximation capabilities and have emerged as a promising alternative to traditional algorithms [8] These methods have a significantly smaller memory footprint and generate numerical solutions that are both closed and continuous over the integration domain without requiring interpolation. ANNs have been applied to differential equations, including ordinary differential equations (ODEs) [9,10], PDEs [11,12], and stochastic differential equations (SDEs) [13,14], making them a valuable tool for researchers and engineers alike. Neural networks have become a powerful and versatile tool for solving differential equations due to their ability to learn intricate mappings from input–output data, further cementing their role as a critical component in the machine learning fields.

In recent years, the application of neural networks in solving differential equations has gained significant attention in the scientific community. One prominent model is the neural ordinary differential equations, which approximates the derivative of an unknown solution using neural networks, parameterizing the derivatives of the hidden states of the network with the help of the differential equation, thus creating a new type of neural network [15]. Another approach is the deep Galerkin method [16], which uses neural networks to approximate the solution of the differential equation in a bid to minimize error Gorikhovskii et al. [17] introduced a practical approach for solving ODEs using neural networks in the TensorFlow machine-learning framework. In addition, Huang et al. [18] introduce an additive self-attention mechanism to the numerical solution of differential equations based on the dynamical system perspective of the residual neural network.

By utilizing neural network functions to approximate the solutions, neural networks have also been used to solve PDEs. The physics-informed neural network (PINN) method uses the underlying physics of the problem to incorporate constraints into the solution of the neural network, resulting in successful applications to various PDEs such as the Burgers and Poisson equations [19]. Compared to traditional numerical methods, PINNs offer several advantages, including higher accuracy and more efficient computation. Berg et al. [20] introduced a new deep learning-based approach to solve PDEs on complex geometries. They use a feed-forward neural network and an unconstrained gradient-based optimization method to predict PDE solutions. Furthermore, Another exciting development in the field of neural networks and PDEs is the use of convolutional neural networks (CNNs). Ruthotto et al. [21] used a CNN to learn to solve elliptic PDEs and incorporated a residual block structure to improve network performance. Quan et al. [22] presented an innovative approach to addressing the challenge of solving diffusion PDEs, by introducing a novel learning method built on the foundation of the extreme learning machine algorithm. By leveraging this advanced technique, the parameters of the neural network are precisely calculated by solving a linear system of equations. Furthermore, the loss function is ingeniously constructed from three crucial components: the PDE, initial conditions, and boundary conditions. Tang et al. [23] demonstrate through numerical cases that the proposed depth adaptive sampling (DAS-PINNs) method can be used for solving PDEs. Overall, the advancements made in the domain of neural networks have revolutionized how we approach solving complex PDEs in unimaginable ways. These developments suggest that neural networks are a promising tool for solving complex PDEs and that there is great potential for further research and innovation in this area.

This paper proposes a novel approach for solving the Burgers–Huxley equation , which uses a neural network based on the Lie series in the Lie groups of differential equations, adding initial or boundary value terms to the loss function to approximate the solution of the equation by minimization. Slavova et al. [24] constructed a cellular neural network model to study the Burgers–Huxley equation. Shagun et al. [25] employed a feed-forward neural network to solve the Burgers-Huxley equation and investigated the impact of the number of training points on the accuracy of the solution. Kumar et al. [26] proposed a deep learning algorithm based on the deep Galerkin method for solving the

Burgers–Huxley equation, which outperformed traditional numerical methods. These studies demonstrate the potential of neural networks in solving differential equations. Nonetheless, it is simple to ignore the underlying nature of these equations, in other words, to fail to capture the nonlinear nature of the equations, which is essential to comprehend the behavior of complex systems. To address this issue, the aim of our proposed method is to approximate the solution of the differential equations by combining the Lie series in Lie groups of differential equations and the power of neural networks. Our proposed method accurately simulates the physical behavior of complicated systems, and the first part of the constructed solution has well captured the nonlinear nature of the equation while reducing the parameter cost of the subsequent neural network and by minimizing the loss function, making the solution converge quickly by introducing initial or boundary value terms required for exact approximation. This work demonstrates the effectiveness of combining neural networks with Lie series to solve differential equations and provides insights into the physical behavior of complex dynamical systems.

The essay is set up as follows. The basic framework and fundamental theory of neural network algorithms based on Lie series in Lie groups of differential equations are introduced in Section 2. The specific steps for the Lie-series-based neural network method to solve the Burgers–Huxley equation are described in Section 3. The method is also applied to the Burgers–Fisher equation and the Huxley equation. Summary and outlook are presented in Section 4.

2. Basic Idea of a Lie-Series-Based Neural Network Algorithm

2.1. Differential Forms and Lie Series Solution

With respect to the Lie group transformation of the parameter ε,

$$u^* = T(\varepsilon; u) \in G, \quad u^*(0) = u \tag{1}$$

where G is a Lie group, and ε is a group parameter.

By employing Taylor expansion about neighborhood of $\varepsilon = 0$,

$$u^* = T(\varepsilon; u) = u + \left.\frac{\partial T(\varepsilon; u)}{\partial \varepsilon}\right|_{\varepsilon=0} \varepsilon + O\left(\varepsilon^2\right). \tag{2}$$

Then, $u^* = u + \varepsilon\zeta$ is known as the infinitesimal transformation. $D = \zeta(u)\partial u$ is called the infinitesimal operator, where $\zeta(u) = \left.\frac{\partial T(\varepsilon; u)}{\partial \varepsilon}\right|_{\varepsilon=0}$.

The following differential equation is given

$$u' = F(\xi, u), \quad u(0) = u_0 \tag{3}$$

$F(\xi, u)$ is a differentiable function, and if (2) is a symmetry of (3), then it has a Lie series solution to the initial value problem (3) and can be written as [27]

$$u = e^{\xi D}u\big|_{\xi=0} \tag{4}$$

2.2. Algorithm of a Lie-Series-Based Neural Network

The idea of Lie groups is based on the study of continuous symmetry, which at first may seem abstract and complex. However, in the realm of solving differential equations, Lie group methods are a unique approach that goes beyond traditional mathematical techniques. Lie series in the Lie transform groups of differential equations can be used to construct approximate solutions of PDEs and to study their symmetries and other properties. Lie series provide a powerful framework for studying the behavior of differential equations and have many important applications in various fields of science and engineering.

From [28], it is known that

$$D = D_1 + D_2 \tag{5}$$

The solution of (3) can be written as $u = e^{\xi D} u|_{\xi=0} = e^{\xi(D_1+D_2)} u|_{\xi=0}$.

Theorem 1. $\bar{u}(\xi; u) = e^{\xi D_1} u|_{\xi=0}$, $\xi \in \mathbb{R}^n$, *is the decomposition part of D. The solution of problem (3) belonging to D expanded as follows:*

$$u = \bar{u}(\xi; u) + \int_0^{\xi} D_2\left(e^{(\xi-\tau)D} u\right)\big|_{u \to \bar{u}(\tau;u)} d\tau \tag{6}$$

The proof is given below and is detailed in the literature [28].

Proof.

$$u = e^{\xi D} u = e^{\xi(D_1+D_2)} u = \sum_{v=0}^{\infty} \frac{\xi^v}{v!} D_1^v u + \sum_{v=1}^{\infty} \frac{\xi^v}{v!} D_1^{v-1} D_2 u$$

$$+ \sum_{v=2}^{\infty} \frac{\xi^v}{v!} D_1^{v-2} D_2 D u + \ldots + \sum_{v=\alpha}^{\infty} \frac{\xi^v}{v!} D_1^{v-\alpha} D_2 D^{\alpha-1} u + \ldots \tag{7}$$

It is known that

$$\frac{\xi^v}{v!} = \int_0^{\xi} \frac{(\xi-\tau)^{\alpha-1}}{(\alpha-1)!} \frac{\tau^{v-\alpha}}{(v-\alpha)!} d\tau, \quad (v \geq \alpha \geq 1, integers)$$

Equation (7) is rewritten as

$$u = \bar{u} + \int_0^{\xi} \sum_{v=0}^{\infty} \frac{\tau^v}{v!} D_1^v D_2 u \, d\tau + \int_0^{\xi} (\xi-\tau) \sum_{v=0}^{\infty} \frac{\tau^v}{v!} D_1^v D_2 D u \, d\tau + \ldots$$

$$+ \int_0^{\xi} \frac{(\xi-\tau)^{\alpha-1}}{(\alpha-1)!} \sum_{v=0}^{\infty} \frac{\tau^v}{v!} D_1^v D_2 D^{\alpha-1} u \, d\tau + \ldots$$

From the form of the series solution [27], it follows that

$$\sum_{v=0}^{\infty} \frac{\tau^v}{v!} D_1^v \left(D_2 D^{\alpha-1} u\right) = \left(D_2 D^{\alpha-1} u\right)_{u \to \bar{u}(\tau;u)}$$

Hence,

$$u = \bar{u} + \sum_{\alpha=1}^{\infty} \int_0^{\xi} \frac{(\xi-\tau)^{\alpha-1}}{(\alpha-1)!} \left(D_2 D^{\alpha-1} u\right)_{u \to \bar{u}(\tau;u)} d\tau$$

after commuting the signs of the series and the integral which is allowed within the circle of absolute convergence, the formula

$$u = \bar{u} + \int_0^{\xi} \left(D_2 \sum_{\alpha=0}^{\infty} \frac{(\xi-\tau)^{\alpha}}{\alpha!} D^{\alpha} u\right)_{u \to \bar{u}(\tau;u)} d\tau \tag{8}$$

is obtained, which may also be written as follows:

$$e^{\xi D} u = e^{\xi D_1} u + \int_0^{\xi} \left(D_2 e^{(\xi-\tau)D} u\right)_{u \to \bar{u}(\tau;u)} d\tau \tag{9}$$

$\square$

The complexities inherent in the integration of the second component, as elucidated by Equation (6), necessitates a sophisticated approach to computation. To tackle this daunting challenge head-on, as elaborated in the reference [29] of our previous work, the functional form of the neural network is utilized to simplify this part and ensure the accuracy of our results.

From [29], $\hat{u} = e^{\xi D} u|_{\xi=0} = \bar{u} + \xi N(\theta; \xi)$. The determination of $\bar{u}$ from the equation $\bar{u}' = D_1 \bar{u}$ is inspired by the idea of the Lie series solution of the first-order ODE, where the initial value of $\bar{u}(0) = u(0) = u_0$ is kept constant throughout the process, ensuring the reliability and truthfulness of our results. $N(\theta; \xi)$ is a single output neural network with a single input of ξ, the parameter θ consists of the weight $\mathbf{W}$ and the bias $\mathbf{b}$. The Algorithm 1 is described in detail below, as shown in Figure 1.

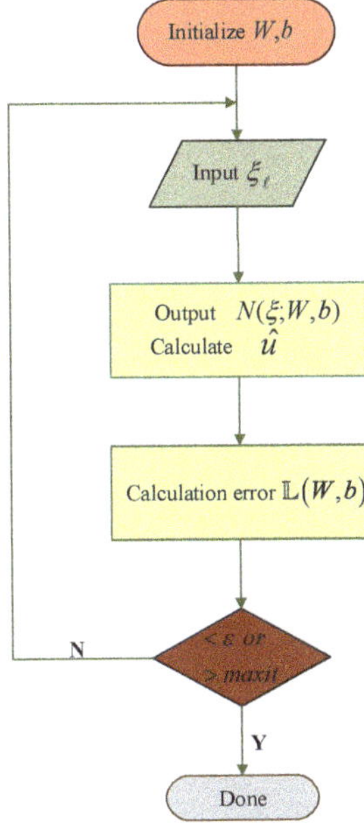

Figure 1. Flow chart of Lie-series-based neural network algorithm.

Algorithm 1: A Lie-series-based neural network algorithm for problem (3)

Require Determine the operator D according to (3), and solve it with the decomposed part D_1 to obtain $\bar{u}$.

Begin

1. Consider a uniformly spaced distribution of discrete points within the initial condition $\xi_\ell (\ell = 1, 2, \ldots, \lambda)$.

2. Determining the structure of a neural network. (The number of hidden layers and the number of neurons, the selection of the activation function σ.)

3. Initialization of the neural networks parameters $\mathbf{W}, \mathbf{b}$.

4. Get $\hat{u} = \bar{u} + \xi N(\theta; \xi)$ and substitute back into (3).

5. Minimize the loss function $\mathbb{L}(\theta)$.

6. Update the parameter θ so that $\hat{u}$ approximates the solution u of problem (3).

End

In general, the loss function $\mathbb{L}(\theta)$ is defined as follows:

$$\mathbb{L}(\theta) = \mathbb{L}_F + \mathbb{L}_I$$

$$= \frac{1}{\lambda} \sum_{\ell=1}^{\lambda} \sum_{i=1}^{n} \left\| \frac{\partial}{\partial \xi} \hat{u}_i(\xi, \theta) \right|_{\xi=\xi_\ell} - F_i(\hat{u}_1, \hat{u}_2, \ldots, \hat{u}_i) \right\|_2^2$$

$$+ \frac{1}{2} \sum_{l=1}^{p} \sum_{i=1}^{n} \left\| \left(\hat{u}_i(\xi, \theta) |_{\xi=\xi_l} - K(\xi) |_{\xi=\xi_l} \right) \right\|_2^2 \tag{10}$$

as additional terms with $K(\xi_l), l = 1, 2, \ldots, p$ as initial value or boundary conditions. The $\mathbb{L}_F$ part of the loss function is derived by substituting the network solution $\hat{u}$ into the mean squared error generated on both sides of the problem (3). In addition, the mean squared error generated by the network solution $\hat{u}$ under the initial or boundary value terms are also used to derive the $\mathbb{L}_I$ component of our loss function. By constructing the components of $\mathbb{L}_F$ and $\mathbb{L}_I$, we can satisfy both the differential equations and the initial values or boundary conditions of the problem under study.

The above algorithm also applies to the system of differential equations $\frac{du_i}{d\xi} = F_i(u_1, u_2, \ldots, u_n)$, $u_i(0) = \alpha_i \in \mathbb{R}^1, i = 1, 2, \ldots, n$, where $D = \sum_{i=1}^{n} F_i(u_i) \frac{\partial}{\partial u_i}$. For higher-order ODEs or PDEs, the above form can also be transformed with the help of some transformations or calculations.

2.3. The General Structure of the Neural Network

As depicted in Figure 2, our study delves into the complexities of multilayer perceptrons and their unique characteristics, with a particular emphasis on those with a single input unit, m hidden layers of H neurons, a neural network with activation function σ in the hidden layer, and a linear output unit. We present a detailed analysis of this neural network architecture. Specifically, for a given input vector $\xi_\ell (\ell = 1, 2, \ldots, \lambda)$, the output of the network $N = \sum_{i=1}^{H} \mathbf{W}^{m+1} \sigma(Z_i^m) + \mathbf{b}^{m+1}$, $Z_i^m = \sum_{j=1}^{H} w_{ji}^m \sigma(Z_j^{m-1}) + b_i^m$, where w_{ji}^m is the weight of the *jth* neuron in layer $m-1$ to the *ith* neuron in layer m, and b_i^m is the bias of the *ith* neuron in layer m. It can be seen that $Z_1^1 = w_{11}^1 \xi_\ell + b_1^1$. In this paper, the activation function σ is chosen $\tanh(Z) = \frac{e^Z - e^{-Z}}{e^Z + e^{-Z}}$.

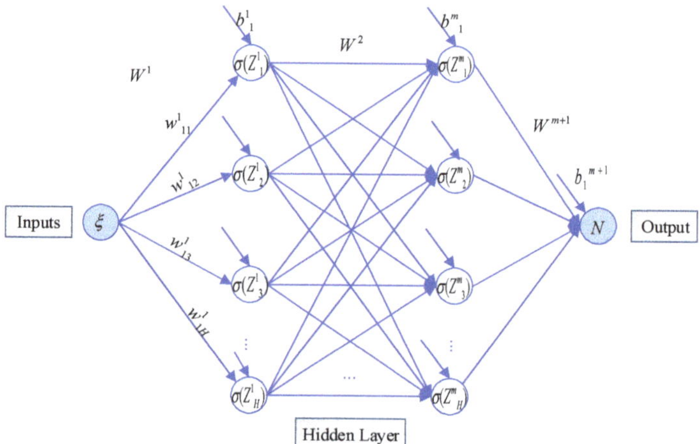

Figure 2. Neural network structure.

3. Lie-Series-Based Neural Network Algorithm for Solving Burgers Huxley Equation

The generalized Burgers–Huxley equation [30] is a nonlinear PDE that describes the propagation of electrical impulses in excitable media, such as nerve and muscle cells. It is a widely used mathematical framework for modeling intricate dynamical phenomena and has been instrumental in advancing research across multiple domains including physics, biology, economics, and ecology. The equation takes the form

$$\frac{\partial u}{\partial t} + \alpha u^{\delta}\frac{\partial u}{\partial x} - \frac{\partial^2 u}{\partial x^2} = \beta u\left(1 - u^{\delta}\right)\left(\eta u^{\delta} - \lambda\right) \tag{11}$$

where α, β, λ, η are constants and δ is a positive constant.

When $\alpha = -1$, $\beta = 1$, $\lambda = 1$, $\eta = 1$, $\delta = 1$, the Burgers–Huxley equation is as follows:

$$\frac{\partial u}{\partial t} = \frac{\partial^2 u}{\partial x^2} + u\frac{\partial u}{\partial x} + u(1 - u)(u - 1), \quad u(0, x) = \frac{1}{2}\left(1 - \tanh\frac{x}{4}\right) \tag{12}$$

The exact solution of (12) is $u(t, x) = \frac{1}{2}\left(1 - \tanh\left(\frac{x}{4} + \frac{3t}{8}\right)\right)$. Using the traveling wave transform $\xi = x - ct$, problem (12) is transformed into an ODE, $u'' + cu' + uu' + u(1 - u)(u - 1) = 0$. Naturally, it is transformed into the form of the following system of ODEs

$$u_1' = u_2, \ u_2' = \frac{3}{2}u_2 - u_1 u_2 - u_1(1 - u_1)(u_1 - 1) \tag{13}$$

with $c = -\frac{3}{2}$, $u_1(\xi) = u$ and initial values $u_1(0) = \frac{1}{2}$, $u_2(0) = -\frac{1}{8}$.

In this study, we address the problem of solving the Burgers–Huxley equation using a Lie-series-based neural network algorithm. The operator $D = u_2 \partial_{u_1} + (\frac{3}{2}u_2 - u_1 u_2 - u_1(1 - u_1)(u_1 - 1))\partial_{u_2}$ of (13) is chosen as $D_1 = u_2 \partial_{u_1} + \frac{3}{2}u_2 \partial_{u_2}$, and the solution of the corresponding initial value problem is $\bar{u}_1(\xi) = \frac{1}{12}\left(7 - \cosh\left(\frac{3\xi}{2}\right) - \sinh\left(\frac{3\xi}{2}\right)\right)$, $\bar{u}_2(\xi) = -\frac{1}{8}\cosh\left(\frac{3\xi}{2}\right) - \frac{1}{8}\sinh\left(\frac{3\xi}{2}\right)$. The solution of this part has been able to capture the nonlinear nature of the equation within a certain range, as shown in Figure 3. To minimize the loss function $\mathbb{L}(\theta)$, we employ two structurally identical neural networks and boundary value terms, each with 30 neurons in a single hidden layer, and the input $\xi_{\ell}(\ell = 1, 2, \ldots, 100)$ is 100 training points spaced equally in the interval $[-5, 3]$, making $\hat{u}_1(\xi)$ as close as possible to the exact solution $u(\xi)$ of the equation. The generalization ability of the neural network was confirmed in 120 test points at equidistant intervals of $\xi_{\ell} \in [-5, 3.3]$. The Lie-series-based neural network algorithm solves the Burgers–Huxley equation model as shown in Figure 4. Furthermore, we demonstrate the ability of neural networks to fit the training and test sets in Figure 5. By plotting the loss function $\mathbb{L}(\theta) = \mathbb{L}_F + \mathbb{L}_I$ against the number of iterations in Figure 6, where $\mathbb{L}_F = \frac{1}{\lambda}\sum_{\ell=1}^{\lambda}\left(\left(\hat{u}_1'(\xi_{\ell}) - \hat{u}_2(\xi_{\ell})\right)^2 + \left(\hat{u}_2'(\xi_{\ell}) - \frac{3}{2}\hat{u}_2(\xi_{\ell}) + \hat{u}_1(\xi_{\ell})\hat{u}_2(\xi_{\ell}) + \hat{u}_1(\xi_{\ell})(1 - \hat{u}_1(\xi_{\ell}))(\hat{u}_1(\xi_{\ell}) - 1)\right)^2\right)$, and $\mathbb{L}_I = \frac{1}{2}(\hat{u}_1(-5) - u(-5))^2 + \frac{1}{2}(\hat{u}_2(-5) - u'(-5))^2$, $\lambda = 100$. Some 1100 iterations later, $\mathbb{L}(\theta) = 3.042 \times 10^{-8}$.

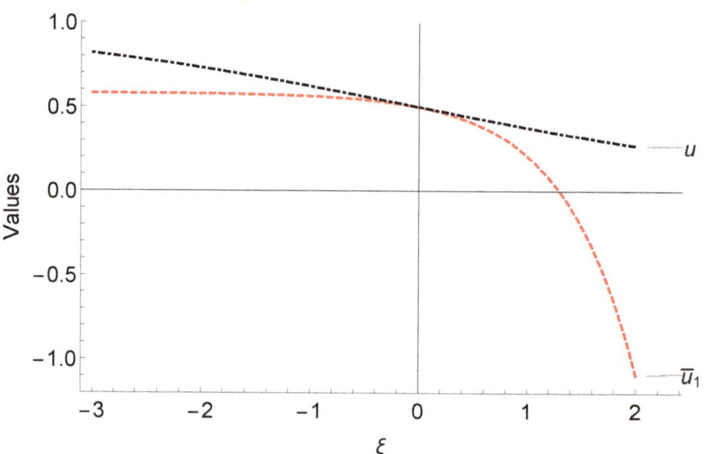

Figure 3. Comparison of the $\bar{u}_1(\xi)$ solution of the Burgers–Huxley equation with the exact solution $u(\xi)$.

We compare the solution $\hat{u}(t, x)$ containing the neural network training and the exact solution $u(t, x)$ in the interval $t \in [0, 1]$, $x \in [-5, 2]$ in the upper panel of Figure 7. Additionally, the lower panel displays the behavior of the solution at $t = 0.3, 0.5, 0.8$, demonstrating the solitary wave solution of the Burgers–Huxley equation. The contour plots for solution $\hat{u}_1(t, x)$ and the exact solution $u(t, x)$ are shown in Figure 8, further illustrating the accuracy of our proposed algorithm.

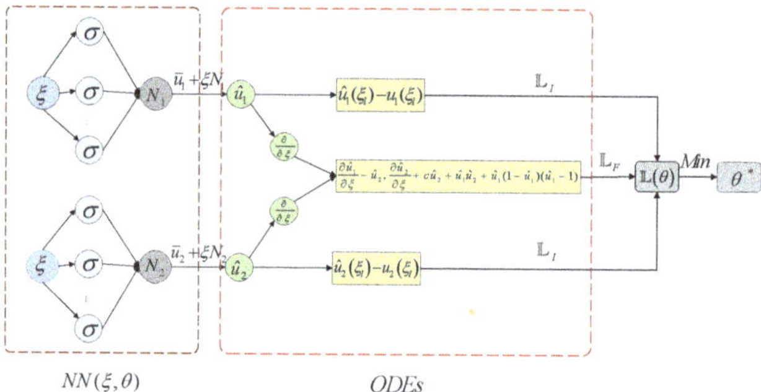

Figure 4. Schematic diagram of a Lie series-based neural network algorithm for solving Burgers–Huxley equation.

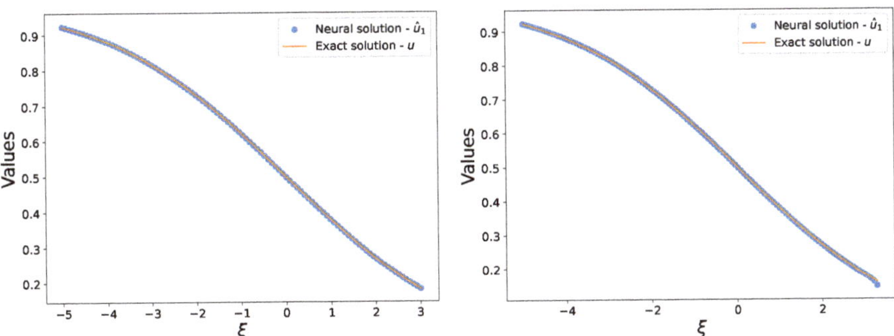

Figure 5. (**Left**) Comparison of solution $\hat{u}_1(\xi)$ with the exact solution $u(\xi) = \frac{1}{2}\left(1 - \tanh\left(\frac{\xi}{4}\right)\right)$ of (13) in the training set. (**Right**) Comparison of solution $\hat{u}_1(\xi)$ with the exact solution $u(\xi) = \frac{1}{2}\left(1 - \tanh\left(\frac{\xi}{4}\right)\right)$ of (13) in the test set.

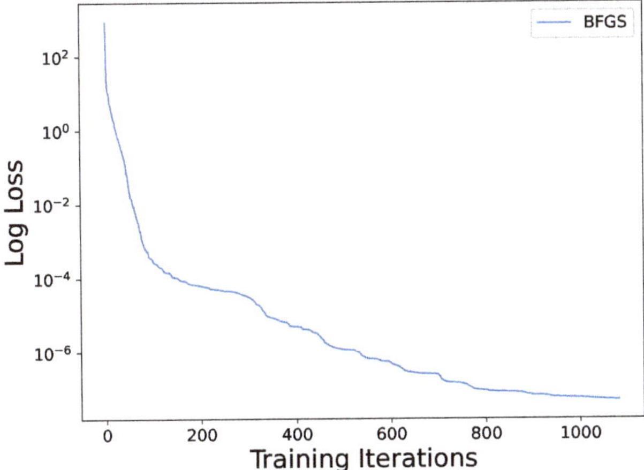

Figure 6. Curves of Loss function versus number of iterations for Burgers–Huxley equation.

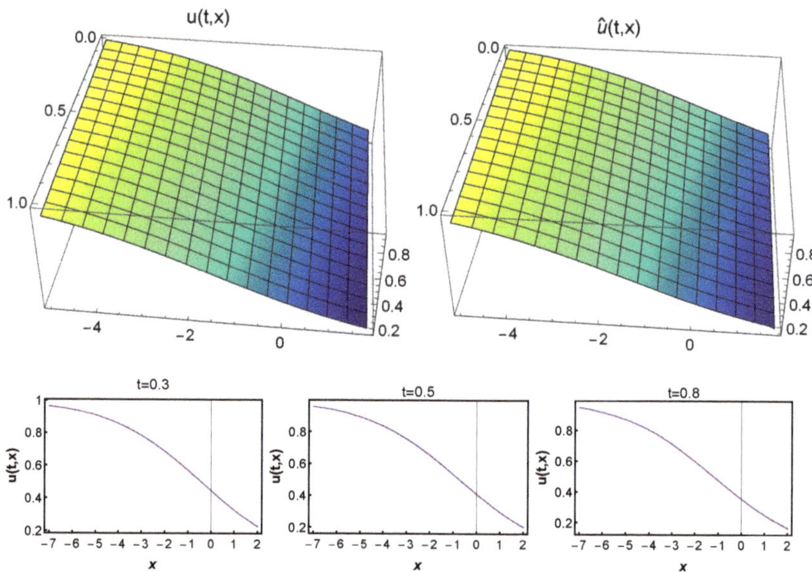

Figure 7. (**Top**) The true solution $u(t, x) = \frac{1}{2}\left(1 - \tanh\left(\frac{x}{4} + \frac{3t}{8}\right)\right)$ of the Burgers–Huxley equation is on the left, the predicted solution $\hat{u}(t, x)$ is on the right. (**Bottom**) Comparison of predicted and exact solutions at time $t = 0.3, 0.5$, and 0.8. (The dashed blue line indicates the exact solution $u(t, x)$, and the solid red line indicates the predicted solution $\hat{u}(t, x)$).

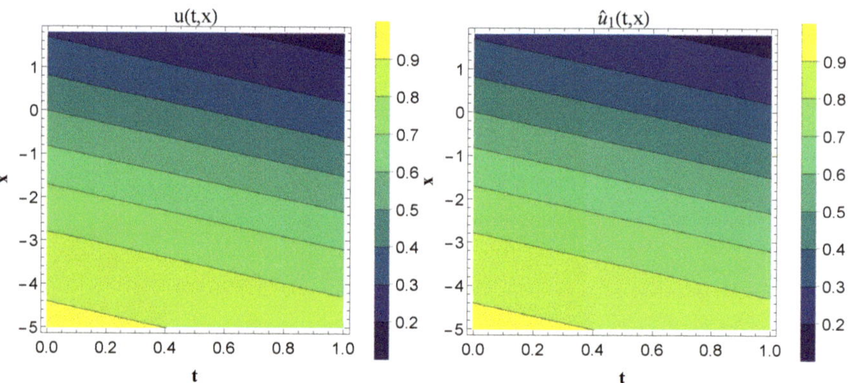

Figure 8. Contour plot of the Burgers–Huxley equation with respect to the solution $\hat{u}_1(t, x)$ and the exact solution $u(t, x)$.

To verify the validity and generality of our proposed equation, the method was applied to two classical equations, the Burgers–Fisher, and the Huxley equations. For this purpose, we performed a thorough analysis and obtained strong results that proved the validity of our method. Specifically, when $\alpha = -1, \beta = 1, \lambda = -1, \eta = 0, \delta = 1$, the Burgers–Fisher equation is as follows:

$$\frac{\partial u}{\partial t} = \frac{\partial^2 u}{\partial x^2} + u\frac{\partial u}{\partial x} + u(1 - u), \quad u(0, x) = \frac{1}{2}\left(1 + \tanh\frac{x}{4}\right) \tag{14}$$

The exact solution of (14) is $u(t, x) = \frac{1}{2}\left(1 + \tanh\left(\frac{x}{4} + \frac{5t}{8}\right)\right)$. Similarly, using the traveling wave transform $\xi = x - ct$, problem (14) is transformed into an ODE, $u'' + cu' + uu' +$

$u(1 - u) = 0$, with initial value $u(0) = \frac{1}{2}$, $u'(0) = \frac{1}{8}$. Transformation of ODEs into the form of a system of differential equations,

$$u_1' = u_2, \ u_2' = \frac{5}{2}u_2 - u_1 u_2 - u_1(1 - u_1) \tag{15}$$

where $u_1(\zeta) = u$, $c = -\frac{5}{2}$, and initial values $u_1(0) = \frac{1}{2}$, $u_2(0) = \frac{1}{8}$. The operator $D = u_2 \partial_{u_1} + (\frac{5}{2}u_2 - u_1 u_2 - u_1(1 - u_1))\partial_{u_2}$ of (15), D_1 is chosen as $u_2 \partial_{u_1} + \frac{5}{2}u_2 \partial_{u_2} - u_1 \partial_{u_2}$, the predicted solution $\hat{u}_1(\zeta_\ell) = -\frac{1}{12}e^{\zeta_\ell/2}(-7 + e^{3\zeta_\ell/2}) + \zeta_\ell N_1$, $\hat{u}_2(\zeta_\ell) = \frac{1}{24}(7e^{\zeta_\ell/2}) - \frac{1}{6}e^{2\zeta_\ell} + \zeta_\ell N_2$, where the structure of the neural network is a single hidden layer containing 30 neurons with inputs $\zeta_\ell \in [-5, 2]$ of equidistant intervals of 100 training points and test points are 120 points of the interval $[-5, 2.2]$, and the training results are shown in Figure 9. As shown in Figure 10, our method achieves an impressive performance with the loss function $\mathbb{L}(\theta)$ reaches 8.861×10^{-8} in about 700 iterations. This exceptional result again illustrates that the solution of the D_1 part of our proposed method captures the nonlinear nature of the solution, thereby reducing the computational cost associated with additional parameters which are evident from Figure 11. In addition, we provide a three-dimensional representation of the dynamics of the predicted solution $\hat{u}(t, x)$ with the exact solution $u(t, x)$ in the interval $t \in [0, 1]$ and $x \in [-5, 2]$, as shown in Figure 12.

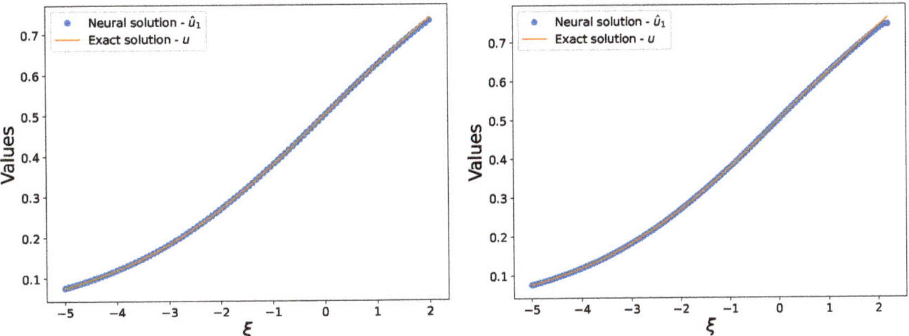

Figure 9. (**Left**) Comparison of solution $\hat{u}_1(\zeta)$ with the exact solution $u(\zeta) = \frac{1}{2}\left(1 + \tanh\left(\frac{\zeta}{4}\right)\right)$ of (15) in the training set. (**Right**) Comparison of $\hat{u}_1(\zeta)$ with the exact solution $u(\zeta) = \frac{1}{2}\left(1 + \tanh\left(\frac{\zeta}{4}\right)\right)$ of (15) in the test set.

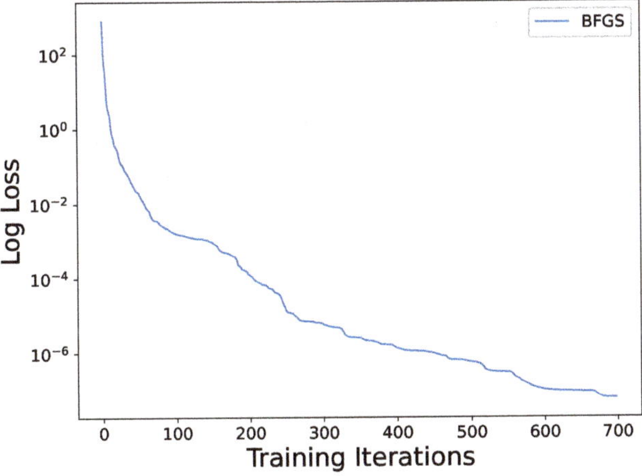

Figure 10. Curves of loss function versus number of iterations for Burgers–Fisher equation.

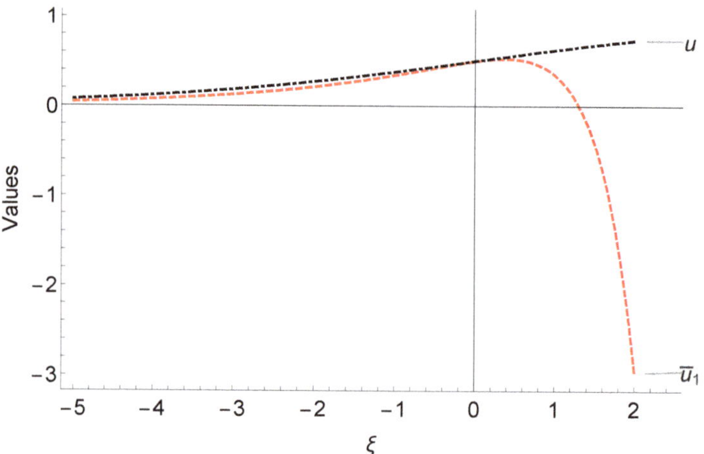

Figure 11. Comparison of the $\bar{u}_1(\xi)$ solution of the Burgers–Fisher equation with the exact solution $u(\xi)$.

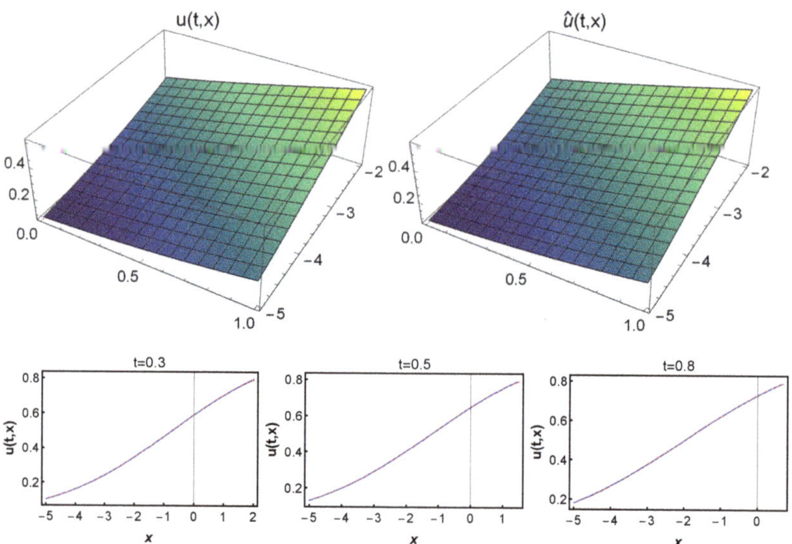

Figure 12. (**Top**) The true solution $u(t,x) = \frac{1}{2}\left(1 + \tanh\left(\frac{x}{4} + \frac{5t}{8}\right)\right)$ of the Burgers–Fisher equation is on the left, the predicted solution $\hat{u}(t,x)$ is on the right. (**Bottom**) Comparison of predicted and exact solutions at time $t = 0.3, 0.5,$ and 0.8. (The dashed blue line indicates the exact solution $u(t,x)$, and the solid red line indicates the predicted solution $\hat{u}(t,x)$).

We investigate the Huxley equation under the conditions where $\alpha = 0, \beta = 1, \lambda = 1, \eta = 1, \delta = 1$. The equations are as follows:

$$\frac{\partial u}{\partial t} = \frac{\partial^2 u}{\partial x^2} + u(1-u)(u-1), \quad u(0,x) = \frac{1}{2}\left(1 + \tanh\frac{x}{2\sqrt{2}}\right) \tag{16}$$

The exact solution of (16) is $u(t,x) = \frac{1}{2}\left(1 + \tanh\left(\frac{\sqrt{2}x}{4} - \frac{t}{4}\right)\right)$. Similarly, using the traveling wave transform $\xi = x - ct$, problem (16) is transformed into an ODE, $u'' + cu' + u(1-u)(u-1) = 0$. It is transformed into the following differential equation form

$$u_1' = u_2, \quad u_2' = -\frac{\sqrt{2}}{2}u_2 - u_1(1-u_1)(u_1-1) \tag{17}$$

where initial values $u_1(0) = \frac{1}{2}$, $u_2(0) = \frac{1}{4\sqrt{2}}$, and $c = \frac{\sqrt{2}}{2}$, it is clear that $u_1(\zeta) = u(\zeta)$, $u_2(\zeta) = u'(\zeta)$. In the case of $D_1 = u_2\partial_{u_1} - \frac{\sqrt{2}}{2}u_2\partial_{u_2}$, the system of differential equations $\bar{u}_1' = \bar{u}_2$, $\bar{u}_2' = -\frac{\sqrt{2}}{2}\bar{u}_2$, the initial values are $\bar{u}_1(0) = \frac{1}{2}$ and $\bar{u}_2(0) = \frac{1}{4\sqrt{2}}$, this time $\bar{u}_1(\zeta) = \frac{3}{4} - \frac{1}{4}e^{-\zeta/\sqrt{2}}$, $\bar{u}_2(\zeta) = \frac{1}{4\sqrt{2}}e^{-\zeta/\sqrt{2}}$.

For predicting the solution $\hat{u}_1(\zeta)$ and $\hat{u}_2(\zeta)$, the same neural network with two single hidden layers containing 30 neurons with the same structure is trained by optimization technique Broyden–Fletcher–Goldfarb–Shanno (BFGS) minimizes the Loss function $\mathbb{L}(\theta)$. The input ζ_ℓ is the interval $[-2, 7]$ equidistantly spaced by 100 points. The test set is the 150 points in the interval $[-2, 7.5]$. As shown in Figure 13, our proposed method produced excellent predictions for both the trained predicted and exact solutions. The variation of the loss function throughout the process is depicted in Figure 14, and it can be observed that the loss function decreased remarkably during training. Figure 15 shows the dynamics of $\hat{u}_1(t, x)$ with the exact solution $u(t, x)$, when $\zeta = x - ct$ is substituted into $\hat{u}_1(\zeta)$ and the predicted solution $\hat{u}_1(t, x)$ compared with the exact solution $u(t, x)$ at $t = 0.3, 0.5, 0.8$. The contour plot in Figure 16 provides a more visualization of the network solution $\hat{u}_1(t, x)$ compared to the exact solution $u(t, x)$.

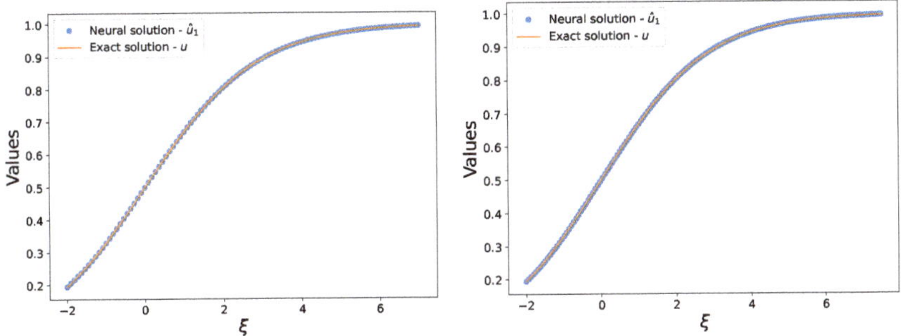

Figure 13. (**Left**) Comparison of solution $\hat{u}_1(\zeta)$ with the exact solution $u(\zeta) = \frac{1}{2}\left(1 + \tanh\left(\frac{\sqrt{2}\zeta}{4}\right)\right)$ of (17) in the training set. (**Right**) Comparison of solution $\hat{u}_1(\zeta)$ with the exact solution $u(\zeta) = \frac{1}{2}\left(1 + \tanh\left(\frac{\sqrt{2}\zeta}{4}\right)\right)$ of (17) in the test set.

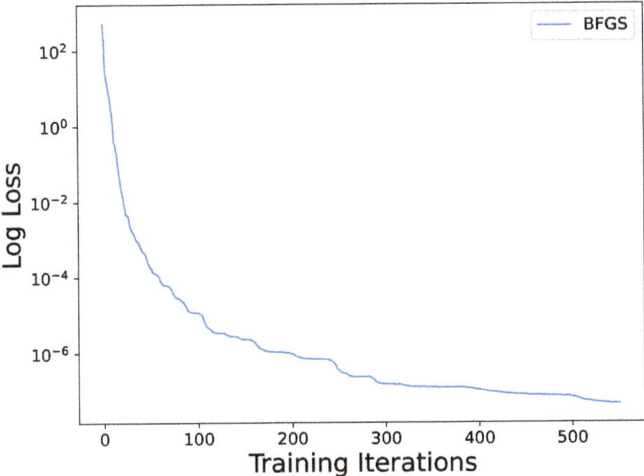

Figure 14. Curves of loss function versus number of iterations for Huxley equation.

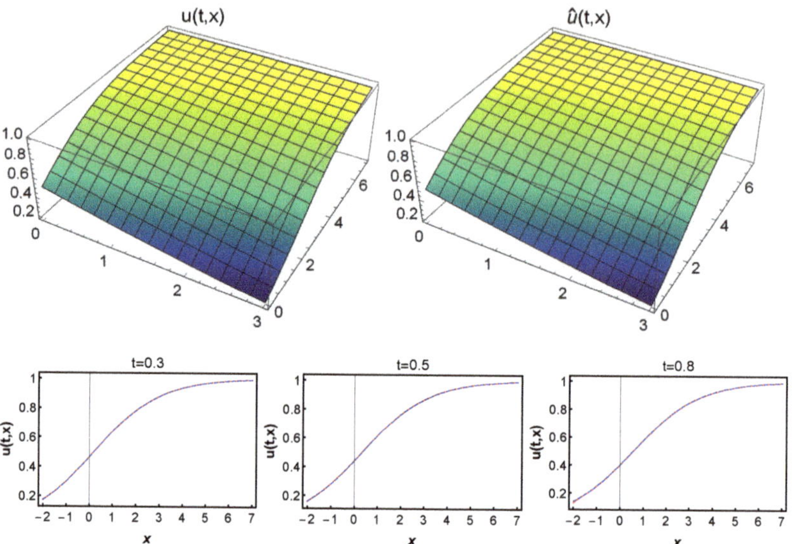

Figure 15. (**Top**) The true solution $u(t,x) = \frac{1}{2}\left(1 + \tanh\left(\frac{\sqrt{2}x}{4} - \frac{t}{4}\right)\right)$ of the Huxley equation is on the left, the predicted solution $\hat{u}(t,x)$ is on the right. (**Bottom**) Comparison of predicted and exact solutions at time $t = 0.3, 0.5$, and 0.8. (The dashed blue line indicates the exact solution $u(t,x)$, and the solid red line indicates the predicted solution $\hat{u}(t,x)$).

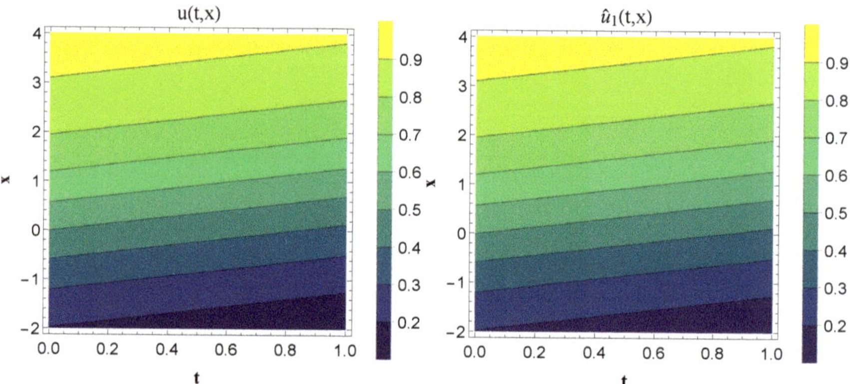

Figure 16. Contour plot of the Huxley equation with respect to the solution $\hat{u}_1(t,x)$ and the exact solution $u(t,x)$.

4. Discussion and Conclusions

The exponential growth of information data has resulted in limited data becoming a significant issue in various fields, especially in data-driven applications. Addressing this challenge has become a critical area of research in recent times. To contribute towards finding solutions to this problem, this paper proposes a novel method for resolving the Burgers-Huxley equation using a neural network based on Lie series in Lie groups of differential equations, which is an emerging field with great potential in solving complex problems. To the best of our knowledge, this study represents the first time the Burgers-Huxley equation has been solved using a Lie-series-based neural network algorithm. In physics, engineering, and biology, the Burgers–Huxley equation is a well-known mathematical model that is frequently utilized. Our novel approach offers a unique perspective on solving this equation by adding boundary or initial value items to the loss function, which leads to more accurate predictions and a better understanding of the underlying system. This research opens up new avenues for further exploration of the Lie-series-based neural network algorithm, specifically regarding its applications to other complex models beyond the Burgers–Huxley equation.

In this study, we present a novel method for obtaining a differentiable closed analytical form to provide an effective foundation for further research. The proposed approach is straightforward to use and evaluate. To verify the effectiveness of the suggested method, we applied it to two classic models of the Burgers–Fisher and Huxley equations that have well-known exact solutions. The proposed algorithm exhibits remarkable potential in capturing the nonlinear nature of equations and accelerating the computation process of neural networks. The performance of our method is demonstrated in Figures 3 and 11, which show how the proposed algorithm can capture the nonlinear behavior of the equations more effectively and speed up the computation of subsequent neural networks. To further evaluate the effectiveness of the proposed technique, we plotted the relationship between the loss function and the number of iterations in Figures 6, 10 and 14. Our results indicate that under the influence of the Lie series in Lie groups of differential equations, our algorithm can converge quickly and achieve more precise solutions with fewer data. Moreover, the accuracy of the obtained solutions is significant, and the generalization ability of the neural network is demonstrated by its ability to maintain high accuracy even outside the training domain, as shown in Figures 5, 9 and 13. We compared the performance of each neural network using small parameters (60 weight parameters and 31 bias parameters) with the exact solution to the problem. Our results highlight that the addition of the Lie series in Lie groups of differential equations algorithm remarkably enhances the ability of the neural network to solve a given equation.

Undoubtedly, the proposed method has several limitations that need to be carefully considered. Firstly, the method requires the transformation of PDEs into ODEs before applying the suggested algorithm. Although the results obtained after this transformation are preliminary, they provide useful insights for researchers. Additionally, an inverse transformation must be employed to produce the final solution $\hat{u}(t, x)$, taking into account the range of values for various variables. The choice of the operator D_1 may also influence the outcomes. Secondly, the current study only addresses nonlinear diffusion issues of the type $F(u) = \alpha u^\delta u_x + u_{xx} + \beta u(1 - u^\delta)(\eta u^\delta - \lambda)$, and the suitability of the technique was assessed via the computation of the loss function. Therefore, the applicability of the method to other types of non-linear PDEs is yet to be investigated, and it might require further adjustments to accommodate such problems. Despite some inherent challenges, our work offers a promising strategy for solving complex mathematical models using neural network algorithms based on Lie series. The computational performance of the proposed algorithm is noteworthy, achieving high solution accuracy at a relatively low time and parameter cost. In light of these findings, it is worth considering the prospect of applying this algorithm to financial modeling, where accurate predictions can have a significant impact.

Moving forward, there is ample scope for extending and improving the proposed algorithm further. Future research could explore how to optimize the performance of the algorithm by addressing its limitations and weaknesses for nonlinear PDE problems. For example, choosing a different neural network framework, CNN or recurrent neural network, etc., may improve the efficiency and accuracy of the method. Additionally, expanding the method's applicability beyond nonlinear diffusion issues may also yield valuable insights into other areas of mathematical modeling.

In summary, we believe that our work presents an exciting avenue for future research. By building upon our findings and addressing the limitations of the proposed algorithm, we can develop more sophisticated techniques for solving complex mathematical models in finance and other areas. Solving the above problems is the main goal of our next research work.

Author Contributions: Conceptualization, Y.W. and T.C.; methodology, Y.W.; software, Y.W.; validation, Y.W.; writing—original draft preparation, Y.W.; writing—review and editing, Y.W. and T.C. All authors have read and agreed to the published version of the manuscript.

Funding: This research was funded by the National Natural Science Foundation of China grant number 11571008.

Data Availability Statement: The data used to support the findings of this study are included within the article. The link to the code is https://github.com/yingWWen/Study-of-Burger-Huxley-Equation-using-neural-network-method (accessed on 14 March 2023).

Acknowledgments: The authors thank the support of the National Natural Science Foundation of China [grant number 11571008].

Conflicts of Interest: As far as we know, there are no conflict of interest or financial or other conflicts. The funders had no role in the design of the study; in the collection, analyses, or interpretation of data; in the writing of the manuscript; or in the decision to publish the results.

References

1. Ockendon, J.R.; Howison, S.; Lacey, A.; Movchan, A. *Applied Partial Differential Equations*; Oxford University Press on Demand: Oxford, UK, 2003.
2. Mattheij, R.M.; Rienstra, S.W.; Boonkkamp, J.T.T. *Partial Differential Equations: Modeling, Analysis, Computation*; SIAM: Philadelphia, PA, USA, 2005.
3. Duffy, D.J. *Finite Difference Methods in Financial Engineering: A Partial Differential Equation Approach*; John Wiley & Sons: Hoboken, NJ, USA, 2013.
4. Jordan, M.I.; Mitchell, T.M. Machine learning: Trends, perspectives, and prospects. *Science* **2015**, *349*, 255–260. [CrossRef]
5. Mahesh, B. Machine learning algorithms—A review. *Int. J. Sci. Res. (IJSR)* **2020**, *9*, 381–386.
6. Yegnanarayana, B. *Artificial Neural Networks*; PHI Learning Pvt. Ltd.: New Delhi, India, 2009.
7. Zou, J.; Han, Y.; So, S.S. Overview of artificial neural networks. In *Artificial Neural Networks: Methods and Applications*; Humana Press: Totowa, NJ, USA, 2009; pp. 14–22.
8. Hornik, K. Approximation capabilities of multilayer feedforward networks. *Neural Netw.* **1991**, *4*, 251–257. [CrossRef]
9. Lagaris, I.E.; Likas, A.; Fotiadis, D.I. Artificial neural networks for solving ordinary and partial differential equations. *IEEE Trans. Neural Netw.* **1998**, *9*, 987–1000. [CrossRef] [PubMed]
10. Chakraverty, S.; Mall, S. *Artificial Neural Networks for Engineers and Scientists: Solving Ordinary Differential Equations*; CRC Press: Boca Raton, FL, USA, 2017.
11. Yang, L.; Meng, X.; Karniadakis, G.E. B-PINNs: Bayesian physics-informed neural networks for forward and inverse PDE problems with noisy data. *J. Comput. Phys.* **2021**, *425*, 109913. [CrossRef]
12. Blechschmidt, J.; Ernst, O.G. Three ways to solve partial differential equations with neural networks–review. *GAMM-Mitteilungen* **2021**, *44*, e202100006. [CrossRef]
13. Han, J.; Jentzen, A. Deep learning-based numerical methods for high-dimensional parabolic partial differential equations and backward stochastic differential equations. *Commun. Math. Stat.* **2017**, *5*, 349–380.
14. Nabian, M.A.; Meidani, H. A deep learning solution approach for high-dimensional random differential equations. *Probabilistic Eng. Mech.* **2019**, *57*, 14–25. [CrossRef]
15. Chen, R.T.; Rubanova, Y.; Bettencourt, J.; Duvenaud, D.K. Neural ordinary differential equations. *Adv. Neural Inf. Process. Syst.* **2018**, *31*, 6572–6583.
16. Sirignano, J.; Spiliopoulos, K. DGM: A deep learning algorithm for solving partial differential equations. *J. Comput. Phys.* **2018**, *375*, 1339–1364. [CrossRef]
17. Gorikhovskii, V.; Evdokimova, T.; Poletansky, V. Neural networks in solving differential equations. *J. Phys. Conf. Ser.* **2022**, *2308*, 012008. [CrossRef]
18. Huang, Z.; Liang, M.; Lin, L. On Robust Numerical Solver for ODE via Self-Attention Mechanism. *arXiv* **2023**, arXiv:2302.10184.
19. Lu, L.; Meng, X.; Mao, Z.; Karniadakis, G.E. DeepXDE: A deep learning library for solving differential equations. *SIAM Rev.* **2021**, *63*, 208–228. [CrossRef]
20. Berg, J.; Nyström, K. A unified deep artificial neural network approach to partial differential equations in complex geometries. *Neurocomputing* **2018**, *317*, 28–41. [CrossRef]
21. Ruthotto, L.; Haber, E. Deep neural networks motivated by partial differential equations. *J. Math. Imaging Vis.* **2020**, *62*, 352–364. [CrossRef]
22. Quan, H.D.; Huynh, H.T. Solving partial differential equation based on extreme learning machine. *Math. Comput. Simul.* **2023**, *205*, 697–708. [CrossRef]
23. Tang, K.; Wan, X.; Yang, C. DAS-PINNs: A deep adaptive sampling method for solving high-dimensional partial differential equations. *J. Comput. Phys.* **2023**, *476*, 111868. [CrossRef]

24. Slavova, A.; Zecc, P. Travelling wave solution of polynomial cellular neural network model for burgers-huxley equation. *C. R. l'Acad. Bulg. Sci.* **2012**, *65*, 1335–1342.
25. Panghal, S.; Kumar, M. Approximate analytic solution of Burger Huxley equation using feed-forward artificial neural network. *Neural Process Lett.* **2021**, *53*, 2147–2163. [CrossRef]
26. Kumar, H.; Yadav, N.; Nagar, A.K. Numerical solution of Generalized Burger–Huxley & Huxley's equation using Deep Galerkin neural network method. *Eng. Appl. Artif. Intell.* **2022**, *115*, 105289.
27. Olver, P.J. *Applications of Lie Groups to Differential Equations*; Springer Science & Business Media: Berlin/Heidelberg, Germany, 1993; Volume 107.
28. Gröbner, W.; Knapp, H. *Contributions to the Method of Lie Series*; Bibliographisches Institut Mannheim: Mannheim, Germany, 1967; Volume 802.
29. Wen, Y.; Chaolu, T.; Wang, X. Solving the initial value problem of ordinary differential equations by Lie group based neural network method. *PLoS ONE* **2022**, *17*, e0265992. [CrossRef] [PubMed]
30. Wang, X.; Zhu, Z.; Lu, Y. Solitary wave solutions of the generalised Burgers-Huxley equation. *J. Phys. Math. Gen.* **1990**, *23*, 271. [CrossRef]

Article

Higher-Order Nabla Difference Equations of Arbitrary Order with Forcing, Positive and Negative Terms: Non-Oscillatory Solutions

Jehad Alzabut [1,2,*,†], Said R. Grace [3,†], Jagan Mohan Jonnalagadda [4,†], Shyam Sundar Santra [5,6,*,†] and Bahaaeldin Abdalla [1,†]

1 Department of Mathematics and Sciences, Prince Sultan University, Riyadh 11586, Saudi Arabia
2 Department of Industrial Engineering, OSTİM Technical University, Ankara 06374, Türkiye
3 Turkey Department of Engineering Mathematics, Faculty of Engineering, Cairo University, Giza 12221, Egypt
4 Department of Mathematics, Birla Institute of Technology and Science Pilani, Hyderabad 500078, Telangana, India
5 Department of Mathematics, JIS College of Engineering, Kalyani 741235, West Bengal, India
6 Department of Mathematics, Applied Science Cluster, University of Petroleum and Energy Studies, Dehradun 248007, Uttarakhand, India
* Correspondence: jalzabut@psu.edu.sa or jehad.alzabut@ostimteknik.edu.tr (J.A.); shyam01.math@gmail.com (S.S.S.)
† These authors contributed equally to this work.

Abstract: This work provides new adequate conditions for difference equations with forcing, positive and negative terms to have non-oscillatory solutions. A few mathematical inequalities and the properties of discrete fractional calculus serve as the fundamental foundation to our approach. To help establish the main results, an analogous representation for the main equation, called a Volterra-type summation equation, is constructed. Two numerical examples are provided to demonstrate the validity of the theoretical findings; no earlier publications have been able to comment on their solutions' non-oscillatory behavior.

Keywords: non-oscillatory solutions; asymptotic behavior; caputo nabla fractional difference; nabla fractional difference equations

MSC: 34K11; 34N05

Citation: Alzabut, J.; Grace, S.R.; Jonnalagadda, J.M.; Santra, S.S.; Abdalla, B. Higher-Order Nabla Difference Equations of Arbitrary Order with Forcing, Positive and Negative Terms: Non-Oscillatory Solutions. *Axioms* **2023**, *12*, 325. https://doi.org/10.3390/axioms12040325

Academic Editor: Azhar Ali Zafar and Nehad Ali Shah

Received: 30 January 2023
Revised: 8 March 2023
Accepted: 24 March 2023
Published: 27 March 2023

1. Introduction

Fractional order differential equations (FDEs) are generalized, non-integer order differential equations that can be obtained in time and space with a power law memory kernel of the nonlocal relationships; they offer an effective means of describing the memory of various substances and the characteristics of inheritance. The authors, who have shown a great deal of interest in studying the qualitative characteristics of the solution of FDEs, such as existence, uniqueness, oscillation, stability, and control, have provided details of significant findings in this area; see some of the illustrious monographs [1–3] and recent papers [4–10]. In particular, the oscillation of solutions was a subject that was taken into account for FDEs; the review paper in [11] is available to readers.

In recent years, academics have started to pay significant attention to discrete fractional calculus. The arbitrary order difference and summation features have considerably demonstrated their utility and validity due to their long memory nature and their flexible capability in carrying out mathematical computations [12]. As a result, numerous studies that investigate the qualitative traits of fractional difference equation solutions have been published, including their oscillation properties [13–16].

Let $\mathbb{N}_\chi = \{\chi, \chi + 1, \chi + 2, \ldots\}$ for any $\chi \in \mathbb{R}$. Research on the oscillation of solutions of nabla fractional difference equations was started by Alzabut et al. [15] with the following problems:

$$\begin{cases} \nabla^\eta_{\sigma+\varkappa-2}\varphi(\varpi) + \xi_1(\varpi, \varphi(\varpi)) = \zeta(\varpi) + \xi_2(\varpi, \varphi(\varpi)), & \varpi \in \mathbb{N}_{\eta+\sigma-1}, \\ \nabla^{-(1-\eta)}_{\sigma+\varkappa-2}\varphi(\varpi)\Big|_{\varpi=\sigma+\varkappa-1} = \chi, & \chi \in \mathbb{R}, \end{cases} \tag{1}$$

and

$$\begin{cases} \nabla^\eta_{\sigma+\varkappa-1*}\varphi(\varpi) + \xi_1(\varpi, \varphi(\varpi)) = \zeta(\varpi) + \xi_2(\varpi, \varphi(\varpi)), & \varpi \in \mathbb{N}_{\sigma+\varkappa-1}, \\ \nabla^m y(\sigma + \varkappa - 1) = \chi_m, & \chi_m \in \mathbb{R}, \quad m = 0,1,2,\cdots,\varkappa-1, \end{cases} \tag{2}$$

where $\eta > 0$ and $\varkappa \in \mathbb{N}_1$ such that $\varkappa - 1 < \eta < \varkappa$; $\xi_1, \xi_2 : \mathbb{N}_{\sigma+\varkappa-1} \times \mathbb{R} \to \mathbb{R}$ and $\zeta : \mathbb{N}_{\sigma+\varkappa-1} \to \mathbb{R}$.

Then, Abdalla et al. [13,14] continued to study the oscillation of solutions of different types of mixed nonlinear nabla fractional difference equations:

$$\begin{cases} \nabla^\eta_{\sigma+\varkappa-2}\varphi(\varpi) - b(\varpi)\varphi(\varpi) + \sum_{j=1}^k b_j(\varpi)|\varphi(\varpi)|^{\alpha_j-1} = \zeta(\varpi), & \varpi \in \mathbb{N}_{\sigma+\varkappa}, \\ \nabla^{-(\varkappa-\eta)}_{\sigma+\varkappa-2}\varphi(\varpi)\Big|_{\varpi=\sigma+\varkappa-1} = \chi, & \chi \in \mathbb{R}, \end{cases} \tag{3}$$

and

$$\begin{cases} \nabla^\eta_{\sigma+\varkappa-1*}\varphi(\varpi) - b(\varpi)\varphi(\varpi) + \sum_{j=1}^k b_j(\varpi)|\varphi(\varpi)|^{\alpha_j-1} = \zeta(\varpi), & \varpi \in \mathbb{N}_{\sigma+\varkappa-1}, \\ \nabla^m \varphi(\sigma + \varkappa - 1) = \chi_m, & \chi_m \in \mathbb{R}, \quad m = 0,1,2,\cdots,\varkappa-1, \end{cases} \tag{4}$$

where $b, b_j : \mathbb{N}_{\sigma+\varkappa-1} \to \mathbb{R}$, $j = 1,2,\cdots k$; $\alpha_1, \alpha_2, \cdots$, and α_k are the ratios of odd natural numbers with $\alpha_1 > \cdots > \alpha_i > 1 > \alpha_{i+1} > \cdots > \alpha_k$.

In this vein, Alzabut et al. [16] derived the conditions for the oscillation of solutions of a forced and damped nabla fractional difference equation:

$$\begin{cases} (1 - p(\varpi))\nabla\nabla^\eta_0\varphi(\varpi) + p(\varpi)\nabla^\eta_0\varphi(\varpi) + p_2(\varpi)\xi(\varphi(\varpi)) = p_1(\varpi), & \varpi \in \mathbb{N}_1, \\ \nabla^{-(1-\eta)}_0\varphi(\varpi)\Big|_{\varpi=1} = \chi, & \chi \in \mathbb{R}, \end{cases} \tag{5}$$

where $0 < \mu < 1$; $\xi : \mathbb{R} \to \mathbb{R}$; $p, p_1 : \mathbb{N}_1 \to \mathbb{R}$ and $p_2 : \mathbb{N}_1 \to \mathbb{R}^+$.

Motivated by the above studies, which concentrated on oscillation discussion, and for the sake of giving an affirmative response about the behavior of non-oscillatory solutions, in this work, we consider the higher-order forced nabla fractional difference equation with positive and negative terms of the following form:

$$\nabla^x_{c*}z(\varpi) + \phi(\varpi, y(\varpi)) = \eta(\varpi) + \zeta(\varpi)y^\beta(\varpi) + \Phi(\varpi, y(\varpi)), \quad \varpi \in \mathbb{N}_{c+1}, \tag{6}$$

where

$$z(\varpi) = \nabla^{n-1}\Big[d(\varpi)(\nabla y(\varpi))^\beta\Big], \quad \varpi \in \mathbb{N}_c, \quad n \in \mathbb{N}_1, \tag{7}$$

where $0 < x < 1$, β is the ratio of two odd natural numbers, $c \in \mathbb{N}_1$, and $\nabla^x_{c*}z$ denotes the xth Caputo nabla fractional difference of z. Throughout this work, we need the following conditions in the sequel.

(i) $\zeta, d : \mathbb{N}_c \to (0, \infty)$, $\eta : \mathbb{N}_c \to \mathbb{R}$ and $\Phi, \phi : \mathbb{N}_c \times \mathbb{R} \to \mathbb{R}$ are real valued continuous functions;

(ii)   There exist two continuous functions Θ_1 and $\Theta_2 : \mathbb{N}_c \to (0, \infty)$, and positive real numbers λ and γ, where $\lambda > \gamma$ such that

$$y\phi(\varpi, y) \geq \Theta_1(\varpi)|y|^{\lambda+1}, \quad 0 \leq y\Phi(\varpi, y) \leq \Theta_2(\varpi)|y|^{\gamma+1}$$

for $y \neq 0$ and $\omega \in \mathbb{N}_c$.

Unlike most existing results, which often discuss the oscillation of solutions, the asymptotic behavior of the Equation (6)'s non-oscillatory solutions is examined in this study. Our method is essentially based on some mathematical inequalities and the properties of discrete fractional calculus. A Volterra-type summation equation is built as an analogous representation for Equation (6) to aid in establishing the key conclusions. In order to demonstrate the validity of the theoretical findings, we offer numerical examples.

2. Essential Preliminaries

The results in this section are adopted from the two main monographs [12,17].

Definition 1 (See [12]). *For* $\omega \in \mathbb{R} \setminus \{\ldots, -2, -1, 0\}$ *and* $\theta \in \mathbb{R}$ *such that* $(\omega + \theta) \in \mathbb{R} \setminus \{\ldots, -2, -1, 0\}$, *we define the generalized rising function by*

$$\omega^{\bar{\theta}} = \frac{\Gamma(\omega + \theta)}{\Gamma(\omega)}.$$

Furthermore, if $\omega \in \{\ldots, -2, -1, 0\}$ *and* $\theta \in \mathbb{R}$ *such that* $(\omega + \theta) \in \mathbb{R} \setminus \{\ldots, -2, -1, 0\}$, *then* $\omega^{\bar{\theta}} = 0$.

Definition 2 (See [12]). *Let* κ *be a real valued function defined on* $\mathbb{N}_\chi$. *The first nabla difference of* κ *is given by*

$$\nabla \kappa(\omega) = \kappa(\omega) - \kappa(\omega - 1), \quad \omega \in \mathbb{N}_{\chi+1}.$$

Definition 3 (See [12]). *Let* κ *be a real valued function defined on* $\mathbb{N}_{\chi+1}$ *and* $x > 0$. *The xth nabla fractional sum of* κ *based at* χ *is given by*

$$\nabla_\chi^{-x} \kappa(\omega) = \frac{1}{\Gamma(x)} \sum_{\omega_1 = \chi+1}^{\omega} (\omega - \omega_1 + 1)^{\overline{x-1}} \kappa(\omega_1), \quad \omega \in \mathbb{N}_\chi,$$

where, by convention, $\nabla_\chi^{-x} \kappa(\chi) = 0$.

Definition 4 (See [3]). *Let* $0 < x < 1$ *and* κ *be a real valued function defined on* $\mathbb{N}_\chi$. *The xth Caputo nabla fractional difference of* κ *based at* χ *is given by*

$$\nabla_{\chi*}^{x} \kappa(\omega) = \nabla_\chi^{-(1-x)} \nabla \kappa(\omega), \quad \omega \in \mathbb{N}_{\chi+1}.$$

Theorem 1. *The initial value problem*

$$\begin{cases} \nabla_{a*}^{x} \kappa(\omega) = w(\omega), & \omega \in \mathbb{N}_{a+1}, \\ \kappa(a) = \kappa_0, \end{cases} \tag{8}$$

has the unique solution

$$\kappa(\omega) = \kappa_0 + \frac{1}{\Gamma(x)} \sum_{\omega_1 = a+1}^{\omega} (\omega - \omega_1 + 1)^{\overline{x-1}} w(\omega_1), \quad \omega \in \mathbb{N}_a \tag{9}$$

where $0 < x < 1$ *and* $w : \mathbb{N}_{a+1} \to \mathbb{R}$.

Lemma 1. *The following properties hold well.*

1. *If* $r_3 < \omega \leq \omega_1$, *then* $\omega_1^{\overline{-r_3}} \leq \omega^{\overline{-r_3}}$;
2. $\omega^{\overline{r_1}} (\omega + r_1)^{\overline{r_2}} = \omega^{\overline{r_1 + r_2}}$;

3. If $0 < r_3 < 1$ and $\vartheta > 1$, then

$$\left[\omega^{\overline{-r_3}}\right]^\vartheta \leq \frac{\Gamma(1+r_3\vartheta)}{[\Gamma(1+r_3)]^\vartheta}\omega^{\overline{-r_3\vartheta}}, \quad \omega > r_3\vartheta.$$

Lemma 2. *Under the assumption that b, x and p are positive constants with $b > 1$ and $p(x-1) + 1 > 0$, we obtain*

$$\sum_{\omega_1=1}^{\omega} (\omega - \omega_1 + 1)^{\overline{p(x-1)}} b^{p\omega_1} \leq Qb^{pt}, \quad \omega \in \mathbb{N}_1,$$

where

$$Q = \left(\frac{b^p}{b^p - 1}\right)^{p(x-1)+1} \Gamma(p(x-1)+1).$$

Lemma 3. *If R and S are nonnegative, $\frac{1}{\gamma} + \frac{1}{v} = 1$, and $\gamma > 1$, then*

$$RS \leq \frac{1}{\gamma}P^\gamma + \frac{1}{v}S^v, \tag{10}$$

where equality holds if and only if $S = R^{\gamma-1}$.

We denote

$$m(\omega) = \left[\frac{\Theta_2^\lambda(\omega)}{\Theta_1^\gamma(\omega)}\right]^{\left(\frac{1}{\lambda-\gamma}\right)}, \tag{11}$$

and

$$A(\omega,c) = \sum_{\omega_1=c+1}^{\omega} d^{-\frac{1}{\beta}}(\omega_1). \tag{12}$$

3. Main Results

In this section, we provide sufficient conditions for which any non-oscillatory solution of (6) satisfies

$$|y(\omega)| = O\left(\left[\omega^{\overline{n-1}}\right]^{\frac{1}{\beta}} b^{\frac{\omega}{\beta}} A(\omega,c)\right) \text{ as } \omega \to \infty.$$

Theorem 2. *Under the assumptions that (i)–(ii), $0 < x < 1$, $p(x-1)+1 > 0$ for $p > 1$ and*

$$\sum_{\omega_1=c+1}^{\infty} \zeta^q(\omega_1)\left[\omega_1^{\overline{n-1}}\right]^q A^{\beta q}(\omega_1,c) < \infty, \quad q = \frac{p}{p-1}, \tag{13}$$

$$\lim_{\omega\to\infty}\left[\frac{1}{\Gamma(x)}\sum_{\omega_1=c+1}^{\omega}(\omega-\omega_1+1)^{\overline{x-1}}|\eta(\omega_1)|\right] < \infty, \tag{14}$$

$$\lim_{\omega\to\infty}\left[\frac{1}{\Gamma(x)}\sum_{\omega_1=c+1}^{\omega}(\omega-\omega_1+1)^{\overline{x-1}}m(\omega_1)\right] < \infty, \tag{15}$$

every non-oscillatory solution of (6) satisfies

$$\limsup_{\omega\to\infty}\frac{|y(\omega)|}{\left[\omega^{\overline{n-1}}\right]^{\frac{1}{\beta}}b^{\frac{\omega}{\beta}}A(\omega,c)} < \infty. \tag{16}$$

Proof. Let y be a non-oscillatory solution of (6), say $y(\omega) > 0$ for $\omega \in \mathbb{N}_{\omega_1}$ for some $\omega_1 \in \mathbb{N}_{c+1}$. Take $z(c) = c_0$. Letting $F(\omega) = \Phi(\omega, y(\omega)) - \phi(\omega, y(\omega))$, it follows from (6) and (i)–(ii) that, for $\omega \in \mathbb{N}_c$,

$$\nabla^{n-1}\left[d(\omega)(\nabla y(\omega))^{\beta}\right]$$

$$= c_0 + \frac{1}{\Gamma(x)} \sum_{\omega_1=c+1}^{\omega} (\omega - \omega_1 + 1)^{\overline{x-1}}\left[\eta(\omega_1) + \zeta(\omega_1)y^{\beta}(\omega_1) + F(\omega_1)\right]$$

$$\leq |c_0| + \frac{1}{\Gamma(x)} \sum_{\omega_1=c+1}^{\omega_1} (\omega - \omega_1 + 1)^{\overline{x-1}}|F(\omega_1)| + \frac{1}{\Gamma(x)} \sum_{\omega_1=c+1}^{\omega} (\omega - \omega_1 + 1)^{\overline{x-1}}|\eta(\omega_1)|$$

$$+ \frac{1}{\Gamma(x)} \sum_{\omega_1=\omega_1+1}^{\omega} (\omega - \omega_1 + 1)^{\overline{x-1}}\left[\Theta_2(\omega_1)y^{\gamma}(\omega_1) - \Theta_1(\omega_1)y^{\lambda}(\omega_1)\right] \tag{17}$$

$$+ \frac{1}{\Gamma(x)} \sum_{\omega_1=c+1}^{\omega_1} (\omega - \omega_1 + 1)^{\overline{x-1}}\zeta(\omega_1)\left|y^{\beta}(\omega_1)\right|$$

$$+ \frac{1}{\Gamma(x)} \sum_{\omega_1=\omega_1+1}^{\omega} (\omega - \omega_1 + 1)^{\overline{x-1}}\zeta(\omega_1)y^{\beta}(\omega_1).$$

Applying Lemma 3 to $\left[\Theta_2(\omega)y^{\gamma}(\omega) - \Theta_1(\omega)y^{\lambda}(\omega)\right]$ with

$$\delta = \frac{\lambda}{\gamma} > 1, \quad X = y^{\gamma}(\omega), \quad Y = \frac{\gamma}{\lambda}\frac{\Theta_2(\omega)}{\Theta_1(\omega)}, \quad \eta = \frac{\lambda}{\lambda - \gamma},$$

we obtain

$$\Theta_2(\omega)y^{\gamma}(\omega) - \Theta_1(\omega)y^{\lambda}(\omega) = \frac{\lambda}{\gamma}\Theta_1(\omega)\left[y^{\gamma}(\omega)\frac{\gamma}{\lambda}\frac{\Theta_2(\omega)}{\Theta_1(\omega)} - \frac{\gamma}{\lambda}(y^{\gamma}(\omega))^{\frac{\lambda}{\gamma}}\right]$$

$$= \frac{\lambda}{\gamma}\Theta_1(\omega)\left[XY - \frac{1}{\delta}X^{\delta}\right]$$

$$\leq \frac{\lambda}{\gamma}\Theta_1(\omega)\left[\frac{1}{\eta}Y^{\eta}\right] \tag{18}$$

$$= \left(\frac{\lambda - \gamma}{\gamma}\right)\Theta_1(\omega)\left[\frac{\gamma}{\lambda}\frac{\Theta_2(\omega)}{\Theta_1(\omega)}\right]^{\frac{\lambda}{\lambda-\gamma}}$$

$$= (\lambda - \gamma)\left[\frac{\gamma^{\gamma}}{\lambda^{\lambda}}\right]^{\left(\frac{1}{\lambda-\gamma}\right)}m(\omega).$$

Substituting (18) into (17) and applying Lemma 1, for $\omega \in \mathbb{N}_c$, we obtain

$$\nabla^{n-1}\left[d(\omega)(\nabla y(\omega))^{\beta}\right]$$

$$\leq |c_0| + \frac{1}{\Gamma(x)} \sum_{\omega_1=c+1}^{\omega_1} (\omega_1 - \omega_1 + 1)^{\overline{x-1}}|F(\omega_1)| + \frac{1}{\Gamma(x)} \sum_{\omega_1=c+1}^{\omega} (\omega - \omega_1 + 1)^{\overline{x-1}}|\eta(\omega_1)|$$

$$+ \frac{1}{\Gamma(x)}(\lambda - \gamma)\left[\frac{\gamma^{\gamma}}{\lambda^{\lambda}}\right]^{\left(\frac{1}{\lambda-\gamma}\right)} \sum_{\omega_1=\omega_1+1}^{\omega} (\omega - \omega_1 + 1)^{\overline{x-1}}m(\omega_1) \tag{19}$$

$$+ \frac{1}{\Gamma(x)} \sum_{\omega_1=c+1}^{\omega_1} (\omega_1 - \omega_1 + 1)^{\overline{x-1}}\zeta(\omega_1)\left|y^{\beta}(\omega_1)\right|$$

$$+ \frac{1}{\Gamma(x)} \sum_{\omega_1=c+1}^{\omega} (\omega - \omega_1 + 1)^{\overline{x-1}}\zeta(\omega_1)y^{\beta}(\omega_1).$$

In view of (14) and (15), we see from (19) that, for $\varpi \in \mathbb{N}_c$,

$$\nabla^{n-1}\left[d(\varpi)(\nabla y(\varpi))^\beta\right] \le C_{n-1} + \frac{1}{\Gamma(x)} \sum_{\varpi_1=\varpi_1+1}^{\varpi} (\varpi - \varpi_1 + 1)^{\overline{x-1}} \zeta(\varpi_1) y^\beta(\varpi_1), \qquad (20)$$

where $C_{n-1} > 0$ is defined by

$$
\begin{aligned}
C_{n-1} = |c_0| &+ \frac{1}{\Gamma(x)} \sum_{\varpi_1=c+1}^{\varpi_1} (\varpi_1 - \varpi_1 + 1)^{\overline{x-1}} |F(\varpi_1)| + \frac{1}{\Gamma(x)} \sum_{\varpi_1=c+1}^{\varpi} (\varpi - \varpi_1 + 1)^{\overline{x-1}} |\eta(\varpi_1)| \\
&+ \frac{1}{\Gamma(x)} (\lambda - \gamma) \left[\frac{\gamma^\gamma}{\lambda^\lambda}\right]^{\left(\frac{1}{\lambda-\gamma}\right)} \sum_{\varpi_1=\varpi_1+1}^{\varpi} (\varpi - \varpi_1 + 1)^{\overline{x-1}} m(\varpi_1) \\
&+ \frac{1}{\Gamma(x)} \sum_{\varpi_1=c+1}^{\varpi_1} (\varpi - \varpi_1 + 1)^{\overline{x-1}} \zeta(\varpi_1) \left|y^\beta(\varpi_1)\right|.
\end{aligned}
$$

By the integer order variation of constants formula, it follows from (20) that

$$
\begin{aligned}
d(\varpi)&(\nabla y(\varpi))^\beta \\
&\le \sum_{k=0}^{n-2} \left(\nabla^k\left[d(\varpi)(\nabla y(\varpi))^\beta\right]\right)_{\varpi=\varpi_1-1} \frac{(\varpi - \varpi_1 + 1)^{\overline{k}}}{\Gamma(k+1)} \\
&\quad + \sum_{r=\varpi_1}^{\varpi} \frac{(\varpi - r + 1)^{\overline{n-2}}}{\Gamma(n-1)} \left[C_{n-1} + \frac{1}{\Gamma(x)} \sum_{\varpi_1=\varpi_1+1}^{r} (r - \varpi_1 + 1)^{\overline{x-1}} \zeta(\varpi_1) y^\beta(\varpi_1)\right] \\
&\le \sum_{k=0}^{n-2} \left|\left(\nabla^k\left[d(\varpi)(\nabla y(\varpi))^\beta\right]\right)_{\varpi=\varpi_1-1}\right| \frac{(\varpi - \varpi_1 + 1)^{\overline{k}}}{\Gamma(k+1)} \\
&\quad + C_{n-1} \sum_{r=\varpi_1}^{\varpi} \frac{(\varpi - r + 1)^{\overline{n-2}}}{\Gamma(n-1)} \\
&\quad + \sum_{r=\varpi_1+1}^{\varpi} \frac{(\varpi - r + 1)^{\overline{n-2}}}{\Gamma(n-1)} \left[\frac{1}{\Gamma(x)} \sum_{\varpi_1=\varpi_1+1}^{r} (r - \varpi_1 + 1)^{\overline{x-1}} \zeta(\varpi_1) y^\beta(\varpi_1)\right] \qquad (21) \\
&= \sum_{k=0}^{n-2} \left|\left(\nabla^k\left[d(\varpi)(\nabla y(\varpi))^\beta\right]\right)_{\varpi=\varpi_1-1}\right| \frac{(\varpi - \varpi_1 + 1)^{\overline{k}}}{\Gamma(k+1)} \\
&\quad + C_{n-1} \frac{(\varpi - \varpi_1 + 1)^{\overline{n-1}}}{\Gamma(n)} \\
&\quad + \sum_{\varpi_1=\varpi_1+1}^{\varpi} \left[\sum_{r=\varpi_1}^{\varpi} \frac{(\varpi - r + 1)^{\overline{n-2}}}{\Gamma(n-1)} \frac{(r - \varpi_1 + 1)^{\overline{x-1}}}{\Gamma(x)}\right] \zeta(\varpi_1) y^\beta(\varpi_1) \\
&= \sum_{k=0}^{n-1} C_k \frac{(\varpi - \varpi_1 + 1)^{\overline{k}}}{\Gamma(k+1)} + \sum_{\varpi_1=\varpi_1+1}^{\varpi} \frac{(\varpi - \varpi_1 + 1)^{\overline{x+n-2}}}{\Gamma(x+n-1)} \zeta(\varpi_1) y^\beta(\varpi_1).
\end{aligned}
$$

where

$$C_k = \left|\left(\nabla^k\left[d(\varpi)(\nabla y(\varpi))^\beta\right]\right)_{\varpi=\varpi_1-1}\right| > 0, \quad k = 0, 1, 2, \cdots, n-2.$$

Note that (21) holds for $n = 1$. Hence, (21) holds for all $n \in \mathbb{N}_1$ and for all $\varpi \in \mathbb{N}_{\varpi_1}$. Next, we proceed to estimate (21) as

$$d(\omega)(\nabla y(\omega))^{\beta} \leq \sum_{k=0}^{n-1} C_k \frac{\omega^{\overline{k}}}{\Gamma(k+1)} + \sum_{\omega_1=\varpi_1+1}^{\omega} \frac{(\omega-\omega_1)^{\overline{n-1}}(\omega-\omega_1+n)^{\overline{x-1}}}{\Gamma(x+n-1)} \zeta(\omega_1) y^{\beta}(\omega_1)$$

$$\leq \omega^{\overline{n-1}} \left[\sum_{k=0}^{n-1} \frac{C_k}{k!} + \frac{1}{\Gamma(x+n-1)} \sum_{\omega_1=\varpi_1+1}^{\omega} (\omega-\omega_1+1)^{\overline{x-1}} \zeta(\omega_1) y^{\beta}(\omega_1) \right],$$

implying that

$$d(\omega)(\nabla y(\omega))^{\beta} \leq \omega^{\overline{n-1}} \left[\Theta_1 + \Theta_2 \sum_{\omega_1=\varpi_1+1}^{\omega} (\omega-\omega_1+1)^{\overline{x-1}} \zeta(\omega_1) y^{\beta}(\omega_1) \right], \tag{22}$$

where

$$\Theta_1 = \sum_{k=0}^{n-1} \frac{C_k}{k!} > 0, \quad \Theta_2 = \frac{1}{\Gamma(x+n-1)} > 0.$$

Applying Lemmas 1 and 2, and Holder's inequality to the sum on the far right in (22), we have

$$\sum_{\omega_1=\varpi_1+1}^{\omega} (\omega-\omega_1+1)^{\overline{x-1}} \zeta(\omega_1) y^{\beta}(\omega_1)$$

$$= \sum_{\omega_1=\varpi_1+1}^{\omega} \left[(\omega-\omega_1+1)^{\overline{x-1}} b^{\omega_1} \right] \left[b^{-\omega_1} \zeta(\omega_1) y^{\beta}(\omega_1) \right]$$

$$\leq \left(\sum_{\omega_1=\varpi_1+1}^{\omega} \left[(\omega-\omega_1+1)^{\overline{x-1}} \right]^{p} b^{p\omega_1} \right)^{1/p} \left(\sum_{\omega_1=\varpi_1+1}^{\omega} b^{-q\omega_1} \zeta^{q}(\omega_1) y^{\beta q}(\omega_1) \right)^{1/q}$$

$$\leq \left(A \sum_{\omega_1=\varpi_1+1}^{\omega} (\omega-\omega_1+1)^{\overline{p(x-1)}} b^{p\omega_1} \right)^{1/p} \left(\sum_{\omega_1=\varpi_1+1}^{\omega} b^{-q\omega_1} \zeta^{q}(\omega_1) y^{\beta q}(\omega_1) \right)^{1/q} \tag{23}$$

$$\leq \left(A Q b^{p\omega} \right)^{1/p} \left(\sum_{\omega_1=\varpi_1+1}^{\omega} b^{-q\omega_1} \zeta^{q}(\omega_1) y^{\beta q}(\omega_1) \right)^{1/q}$$

$$= (AQ)^{1/p} b^{\omega} \left(\sum_{\omega_1=\varpi_1+1}^{\omega} b^{-q\omega_1} \zeta^{q}(\omega_1) y^{\beta q}(\omega_1) \right)^{1/q},$$

where

$$A = \frac{\Gamma(1+(1-x)p)}{[\Gamma(2-x)]^{p}}.$$

Using (23) in (22), we obtain from (22) that

$$d(\omega)(\nabla y(\omega))^{\beta} \leq \omega^{\overline{n-1}} b^{\omega} \omega(\omega), \tag{24}$$

where

$$\omega(\omega) = \Theta_1 + M_3 \left(\sum_{\omega_1=\varpi_1+1}^{\omega} b^{-q\omega_1} \zeta^{q}(\omega_1) y^{\beta q}(\omega_1) \right)^{1/q},$$

with

$$M_3 = \Theta_2 (AQ)^{1/p} > 0.$$

We rewrite (24) as

$$\nabla y(\omega) \leq \left(\frac{\omega^{\overline{n-1}} b^{\omega} \omega(\omega)}{d(\omega)} \right)^{\frac{1}{\beta}}, \quad \omega \in \mathbb{N}_{\varpi_1}. \tag{25}$$

Noting that $\varpi^{\overline{n-1}}$, b^{ϖ}, and $\omega(\varpi)$ are all increasing, summing (25) from $\varpi_1 + 1$ to ϖ yields that

$$
\begin{aligned}
y(\varpi) &\leq y(\varpi_1) + \sum_{\varpi_1=\varpi_1+1}^{\varpi} \left[\varpi_1^{\overline{n-1}}\right]^{\frac{1}{\beta}} b^{\frac{\varpi_1}{\beta}} \omega^{\frac{1}{\beta}}(\varpi_1) d^{-\frac{1}{\beta}}(\varpi_1) \\
&\leq y(\varpi_1) + \left[\varpi^{\overline{n-1}}\right]^{\frac{1}{\beta}} b^{\frac{\varpi}{\beta}} \omega^{\frac{1}{\beta}}(\varpi) \sum_{\varpi_1=\varpi_1+1}^{\varpi} d^{-\frac{1}{\beta}}(\varpi_1) \\
&= y(\varpi_1) + \left[\varpi^{\overline{n-1}}\right]^{\frac{1}{\beta}} b^{\frac{\varpi}{\beta}} \omega^{\frac{1}{\beta}}(\varpi) A(\varpi, \varpi_1) \\
&= \left(\frac{y(\varpi_1)}{\left[\varpi^{\overline{n-1}}\right]^{\frac{1}{\beta}} b^{\frac{\varpi}{\beta}} A(\varpi, \varpi_1)} + \omega^{\frac{1}{\beta}}(\varpi) \right) \left[\varpi^{\overline{n-1}}\right]^{\frac{1}{\beta}} b^{\frac{\varpi}{\beta}} A(\varpi, \varpi_1) \\
&\leq \left(\frac{y(\varpi_1)}{\left[\varpi_2^{\overline{n-1}}\right]^{\frac{1}{\beta}} b^{\frac{\varpi_2}{\beta}} A(\varpi_2, \varpi_1)} + \omega^{\frac{1}{\beta}}(\varpi) \right) \left[\varpi^{\overline{n-1}}\right]^{\frac{1}{\beta}} b^{\frac{\varpi}{\beta}} A(\varpi, \varpi_1),
\end{aligned}
$$

holds for $\varpi \in \mathbb{N}_{\varpi_2}$ with $\varpi_2 > \varpi_1$. Thus,

$$
\frac{y(\varpi)}{\left[\varpi^{\overline{n-1}}\right]^{\frac{1}{\beta}} b^{\frac{\varpi}{\beta}} A(\varpi, \varpi_1)} \leq M_4 + \omega^{\frac{1}{\beta}}(\varpi), \quad \varpi \in \mathbb{N}_{\varpi_2}, \tag{26}
$$

where

$$
M_4 = \frac{y(\varpi_1)}{\left[\varpi_2^{\overline{n-1}}\right]^{\frac{1}{\beta}} b^{\frac{\varpi_2}{\beta}} A(\varpi_2, \varpi_1)}.
$$

Applying one of the elementary inequalities

$$
(y+z)^q \leq \begin{cases} 2^{q-1}(y^q + z^q), & q \geq 1, \\ y^q + z^q, & 0 < q < 1, \end{cases} \tag{27}
$$

with $y, z \geq 0$, to (26) gives

$$
\left(\frac{y(\varpi)}{\left[\varpi^{\overline{n-1}}\right]^{\frac{1}{\beta}} b^{\frac{\varpi}{\beta}} A(\varpi, \varpi_1)} \right)^{\beta} \leq M_5 + M_6 \omega(\varpi), \quad \varpi \in \mathbb{N}_{\varpi_2}, \tag{28}
$$

where M_5 and $M_6 > 0$ are defined by

$$
M_5 = \begin{cases} 2^{\beta-1} M_4^{\beta}, & q \geq 1, \\ M_4^{\beta}, & 0 < q < 1, \end{cases} \tag{29}
$$

and

$$
M_6 = \begin{cases} 2^{\beta-1}, & q \geq 1, \\ 1, & 0 < q < 1. \end{cases} \tag{30}
$$

Recalling the definition of $w(\omega)$, from (28), we have that

$$\left(\frac{y(\omega)}{\left[\omega^{\overline{n-1}}\right]^{\frac{1}{\beta}}b^{\frac{\omega}{\beta}}A(\omega,\omega_1)}\right)^{\beta} \leq M_7 + M_8\left(\sum_{\omega_1=\omega_1+1}^{\omega} b^{-q\omega_1}\zeta^q(\omega_1)y^{\beta q}(\omega_1)\right)^{1/q}, \tag{31}$$

holds for $\omega \in \mathbb{N}_{\omega_2}$, where

$$M_7 = M_5 + \Theta_1 M_6 > 0, \quad M_8 = M_3 M_6 > 0.$$

Applying the inequality (27) to (31) gives that

$$\left(\frac{y(\omega)}{\left[\omega^{\overline{n-1}}\right]^{\frac{1}{\beta}}b^{\frac{\omega}{\beta}}A(\omega,\omega_1)}\right)^{\beta q} \leq M_9 + M_{10}\sum_{r=\omega_1+1}^{\omega} b^{-qr}\zeta^q(r)y^{\beta q}(r), \tag{32}$$

holds for $\omega \in \mathbb{N}_{\omega_2}$, where

$$M_9 = 2^{\beta-1}M_7^q > 0, \quad M_{10} = 2^{\beta-1}M_8^q > 0.$$

Denoting the left-hand side of (32) by $w(\omega)$, (32) yields that

$$w(\omega) \leq M_9 + M_{10}\sum_{\omega_1=\omega_1+1}^{\omega}\left[\omega_1^{\overline{n-1}}\right]^q A^{\beta q}(\omega_1,\omega_1)\zeta^q(\omega_1)w(\omega_1), \tag{33}$$

holds for $\omega \in \mathbb{N}_{\omega_2}$, and this can be rewritten as

$$w(\omega) \leq M_{11} + M_{10}\sum_{\omega_1=\omega_2+1}^{\omega}\left[\omega_1^{\overline{n-1}}\right]^q A^{\beta q}(\omega_1,\omega_1)\zeta^q(\omega_1)w(\omega_1), \tag{34}$$

which holds for $\omega \in \mathbb{N}_{\omega_2}$, where

$$M_{11} = M_9 + M_{10}\sum_{\omega_1=\omega_1+1}^{\omega_2}\left[\omega_1^{\overline{n-1}}\right]^q A^{\beta q}(\omega_1,\omega_1)\zeta^q(\omega_1)w(\omega_1) > 0.$$

Using (13) and Gronwall's inequality, we have the conclusion to the theorem. The proof for an eventually negative solution is similar. So, we omit it here. Thus, the theorem is proved. $\square$

Next, we consider $\beta = 1$ and we provide sufficient conditions for which any non-oscillatory solution of (6) is bounded.

Theorem 3. *Assume that* $(i) - (ii)$, $0 < x < 1$, $p(x-1)+1 > 0$ *for* $p > 1$ *and that (14) and (15) hold. Furthermore, assume that there exist real numbers* $S > 0$ *and* $\tau > 1$ *such that*

$$\left(\frac{\omega^{\overline{n-1}}}{d(\omega)}\right) \leq \omega_1 b^{-\tau\omega} \tag{35}$$

and

$$\sum_{\omega_1=c+1}^{\infty} b^{-q\omega_1}\zeta^q(\omega_1) < \infty, \quad q = \frac{p}{p-1}, \tag{36}$$

hold; then, all non-oscillatory solutions of (6) are bounded.

Proof. Let y be a non-oscillatory solution of (6), say $y(\omega) > 0$ for $\omega \in \mathbb{N}_{\omega_1}$ for some $\omega_1 \in \mathbb{N}_{c+1}$. Proceeding as in the proof of Theorem 2, we obtain (25) when $\beta = 1$. Since ω is increasing, summing (25) from $\omega_1 + 1$ to ω yields

$$
\begin{aligned}
y(\omega) &\leq y(\omega_1) + \sum_{\omega_1=\omega_1+1}^{\omega} \frac{\omega_1^{\overline{n-1}} b^{\omega_1} \omega(\omega_1)}{d(\omega_1)} \\
&\leq y(\omega_1) + \sum_{\omega_1=\omega_1+1}^{\omega} S b^{(1-\tau)\omega_1} \omega(\omega_1) \\
&\leq y(\omega_1) + S\omega(t) \sum_{\omega_1=\omega_1+1}^{\omega} b^{(1-\tau)\omega_1} \\
&\leq y(\omega_1) + S\omega(t) \sum_{\omega_1=\omega_1+1}^{\omega} \left(\frac{1}{b^{(\tau-1)}} \right)^s \\
&= y(\omega_1) + S\omega(t) \left(\frac{b^{(\tau-1)}}{b^{(\tau-1)} - 1} \right) \left[\left(\frac{1}{b^{(\tau-1)}} \right)^{\omega_1+1} - \left(\frac{1}{b^{(\tau-1)}} \right)^{\omega+1} \right] \\
&= y(\omega_1) + S\omega(t) \left(\frac{1}{b^{(\tau-1)} - 1} \right) \left[\left(\frac{1}{b^{(\tau-1)}} \right)^{\omega_1} - \left(\frac{1}{b^{(\tau-1)}} \right)^{\omega} \right] \\
&\leq y(\omega_1) + S\omega(t) \left(\frac{1}{b^{(\tau-1)} - 1} \right) \left(\frac{1}{b^{(\tau-1)}} \right)^{\omega_1}.
\end{aligned}
$$

Using the definition of ω, we obtain

$$
y(\omega) \leq M_{12} + M_{13} \left(\sum_{\omega_1=\omega_1+1}^{\omega} b^{-q\omega_1} \zeta^q(\omega_1) y^q(\omega_1) \right)^{1/q}, \tag{37}
$$

for $\omega \in \mathbb{N}_{\omega_2}$, where

$$
M_{12} = y(\omega_1) + \Theta_1 S \left(\frac{1}{b^{(\tau-1)} - 1} \right) \left(\frac{1}{b^{(\tau-1)}} \right)^{\omega_1} > 0,
$$

and

$$
M_{13} = M_3 S \left(\frac{1}{b^{(\tau-1)} - 1} \right) \left(\frac{1}{b^{(\tau-1)}} \right)^{\omega_1} > 0.
$$

Using the inequality (27) to (37), we have

$$
y^q(\omega) \leq M_{14} + M_{15} \sum_{\omega_1=\omega_1+1}^{\omega} b^{-q\omega_1} \zeta^q(\omega_1) y^q(\omega_1), \tag{38}
$$

for $\omega \in \mathbb{N}_{\omega_1}$, where

$$
M_{14} = 2^{q-1} M_{12}^q > 0, \quad M_{15} = 2^{q-1} M_{13}^q > 0.
$$

Now, using (36) and Gronwall's inequality, we have the conclusion to the theorem. The proof for an eventually negative solution is similar. So, we omit it here. The theorem is proved. $\square$

4. Examples

We conclude this paper with the following examples to illustrate our main results.

Example 1. *Consider the equation*

$$\nabla_{1*}^{0.75}\left(\nabla^3\left(e^{3\omega}(\nabla y(\omega))^3\right)\right) + \phi(\omega, y(\omega))$$

$$= (\omega - 1)^{\overline{-0.9}} + \frac{y(\omega)}{\omega(\omega+1)(\omega+2)e^{\omega/2}} + \Phi(\omega, y(\omega)), \quad \omega \in \mathbb{N}_2. \quad (39)$$

Here, we have $z(\omega) = \nabla^3\left(e^{3\omega}(\nabla y(\omega))^3\right)$, $n = 4$, $x = 0.75$, $c = 1$, $\beta = 3$, $d(\omega) = e^{3\omega}$, $\eta(\omega) = (\omega - 1)^{\overline{-0.9}}$, $\zeta(\omega) = \frac{1}{\omega(\omega+1)(\omega+2)e^{\omega/2}}$, and

$$A(\omega, c) = A(\omega, 1) = \sum_{\omega_1=2}^{\omega} d^{-\frac{1}{3}}(\omega_1) = \sum_{\omega_1=2}^{\omega} e^{-\omega_1} = \frac{1}{e(e-1)}\left[1 - \left(\frac{1}{e}\right)^{\omega-1}\right] \le \frac{1}{e(e-1)}.$$

Clearly, condition (i) holds. Let $b = e$ and $p = 2$. Clearly, $p(x-1)+1 > 0$. Additionally, we have $q = 2$, and

$$\sum_{\omega_1=c+1}^{\infty} \zeta^q(\omega_1)\left[\omega_1^{\overline{n-1}}\right]^q A^{\beta q}(\omega_1, c) \le \frac{1}{e^2(e-1)^2}\sum_{\omega_1=2}^{\infty} e^{-\omega_1} < \infty,$$

implying that (13) holds. Considering $\phi(\omega, y(\omega)) = \Theta_1(\omega)|y(\omega)|^{\lambda-1}y(\omega)$ and $\Phi(\omega, y(\omega)) = \Theta_2(\omega)|y(\omega)|^{\gamma-1}y(\omega)$ with $\lambda > \gamma$, $\Theta_1(\omega) = \Theta_2(\omega) = (\omega - 1)^{\overline{-0.9}}$, we see that (ii) holds. To check (14), we assume

$$\frac{1}{\Gamma(0.75)}\sum_{\omega_1=1+1}^{\omega}(\omega - \omega_1 + 1)^{\overline{0.75-1}}|\eta(\omega_1)| = \frac{1}{\Gamma(0.75)}\sum_{\omega_1=2}^{\omega}(\omega - \omega_1 + 1)^{\overline{0.75-1}}\left|(\omega_1 - 1)^{\overline{-0.9}}\right|$$

$$= \frac{1}{\Gamma(0.75)}\sum_{\omega_1=2}^{\omega}(\omega - \omega_1 + 1)^{\overline{0.75-1}}(\omega_1 - 1)^{\overline{-0.9}}$$

$$= \nabla_1^{-0.75}(\omega - 1)^{\overline{-0.9}}$$

$$= \frac{\Gamma(1 - 0.9)}{\Gamma(1 - 0.9 + 0.75)}(\omega - 1)^{\overline{-0.9+0.75}}$$

$$= \frac{\Gamma(0.1)}{\Gamma(0.85)}(\omega - 1)^{\overline{-0.15}}$$

$$\le \frac{\Gamma(0.1)}{\Gamma(0.85)}1^{\overline{-0.15}}$$

$$= \Gamma(0.1),$$

that is,

$$\lim_{\omega\to\infty}\left[\frac{1}{\Gamma(0.75)}\sum_{\omega_1=1+1}^{\omega}(\omega - \omega_1 + 1)^{\overline{0.75-1}}|e(\omega_1)|\right] < \infty.$$

Similarly, it is easy to verify that (15) holds. Therefore, all conditions of Theorem 2 are satisfied. Thus, every non-oscillatory solution of (6) satisfies

$$\limsup_{\omega\to\infty}\frac{|y(\omega)|}{\left[\omega^{\overline{3}}\right]^{\frac{1}{2}}e^{\frac{\omega}{2}}A(\omega, 1)} < \infty. \quad (40)$$

Example 2. *Consider the equation*

$$\nabla_{1*}^{0.5}\left(\nabla^2\left(\omega(\omega+1)e^{5\omega}\left(\nabla v(\omega)\right)\right)\right) + \phi(\omega,y(\omega))$$

$$= (\omega-1)^{\overline{-0.75}} + e^{2\omega/3}y(\omega) + \Phi(\omega,y(\omega)), \quad \omega \in \mathbb{N}_2. \quad (41)$$

Here, we have $z(\omega) = \nabla^2\left(\omega(\omega+1)e^{5\omega}\left(\nabla v(\omega)\right)\right)$, $c = 1$, $x = 0.5$, $n = 3$, $d(\omega) = \omega(\omega+1)e^{5\omega}$, $e(\omega) = (\omega-1)^{\overline{-0.75}}$, and $\zeta(\omega) = e^{2\omega/3}$. Hence, condition (i) holds. Assuming $b = e$, $\omega_1 = 1$, and $\tau = 5$, we find

$$\left(\frac{\omega^{\overline{2}}}{d(\omega)}\right) = e^{-5\omega}.$$

Therefore, (35) holds. Now, if we take $p = 3/2$, then we have $q = 3$, and

$$\sum_{\omega_1=c+1}^{\infty} b^{-q\omega_1}\zeta^q(\omega_1) = \sum_{\omega_1=2}^{\infty} e^{-3\omega_1}e^{2\omega_1} = \sum_{\omega_1=2}^{\infty} e^{-\omega_1} = \frac{1}{e(e-1)} < \infty,$$

that is, (36) holds. Again, if

$$\phi(\omega,y(\omega)) = \Theta_1(\omega)|y(\omega)|^{\lambda-1}y(\omega) \quad \text{and} \quad \Phi(\omega,y(\omega)) = \Theta_2(\omega)|y(\omega)|^{\gamma-1}y(\omega)$$

with $\lambda > \gamma$, $\Theta_1(\omega) = \Theta_2(\omega) = (\omega-1)^{\overline{-0.75}}$, then it is easy to verify that condition (ii) holds. To check that (14) holds, we assume

$$\frac{1}{\Gamma(0.5)} \sum_{\omega_1=1+1}^{\omega} (\omega-\omega_1+1)^{\overline{0.5-1}}|\eta(\omega_1)| = \frac{1}{\Gamma(0.5)} \sum_{\omega_1=2}^{\omega} (\omega-\omega_1+1)^{\overline{0.5-1}}\left|(\omega_1-1)^{\overline{-0.75}}\right|$$

$$= \frac{1}{\Gamma(0.5)} \sum_{\omega_1=2}^{\omega} (\omega-\omega_1+1)^{\overline{0.5-1}}(\omega_1-1)^{\overline{-0.75}}$$

$$= \nabla_1^{-0.5}(\omega-1)^{\overline{-0.75}}$$

$$= \frac{\Gamma(1-0.75)}{\Gamma(1-0.75+0.5)}(\omega-1)^{\overline{-0.75+0.5}}$$

$$= \frac{\Gamma(0.25)}{\Gamma(0.75)}(\omega-1)^{\overline{-0.25}}$$

$$\leq \frac{\Gamma(0.25)}{\Gamma(0.75)}1^{\overline{-0.25}}$$

$$= \Gamma(0.25),$$

that is,

$$\lim_{\omega\to\infty}\left[\frac{1}{\Gamma(0.5)} \sum_{\omega_1=1+1}^{\omega} (\omega-\omega_1+1)^{\overline{0.5-1}}|e(\omega_1)|\right] < \infty.$$

Similarly, it is easy to verify that (15) holds. Therefore, all conditions of Theorem 3 are satisfied. Thus, every non-oscillatory solution of (41) is bounded.

5. Concluding Remarks

Unlike most existing results in the literature that have been dedicated to oscillation criteria, we introduced a number of additional necessary conditions for non-oscillatory solutions to forced nabla difference equations with positive and negative terms. The main equation is of a general nature, and it covers many particular cases. By creating an equivalent representation of the primary equation in the form of a summation equation similar to Volterra and using some mathematical inequalities, the results are stated and proved. Some earlier findings in the literature were enhanced by the results. In fact, we give two brand-new cases, the non-oscillatory behavior of whose solutions has never been discussed in earlier studies. The existing methodology can be used in the future to produce comparable outcomes for higher order dynamic equations with forcing, positive and negative terms.

Author Contributions: Conceptualization, J.A., S.R.G., J.M.J., S.S.S. and B.A.; methodology, J.A. S.R.G., J.M.J., S.S.S. and B.A.; validation, J.A., S.R.G., J.M.J., S.S.S. and B.A.; formal analysis, J.A. S.R.G., J.M.J. and S.S.S.; investigation, J.A., S.R.G., J.M.J. and S.S.S.; resources, J.A., S.R.G., J.M.J. and S.S.S.; data curation, J.A., S.R.G., J.M.J. and S.S.S.; writing—original draft preparation, J.A., S.R.G. J.M.J. and S.S.S.; writing—review and editing, J.A., S.R.G., J.M.J., S.S.S. and B.A.; visualization, J.A., S.R.G., J.M.J. and S.S.S.; project administration, J.A. and B.A.; funding acquisition, J.A. and B.A. All authors have read and agreed to the published version of the manuscript.

Funding: This research received no external funding.

Institutional Review Board Statement: Not applicable.

Informed Consent Statement: Not applicable.

Data Availability Statement: Not applicable.

Acknowledgments: The authors would like to thank the editor and the three anonymous reviewers for their constructive comments and suggestions, which helped us to improve themanuscript considerably. J. Alzabut and B. Abdalla express their gratitude to Prince Sultan University for their unwavering support. J. Alzabut also thanks OSTIM Technical University for helping him finish this paper.

Conflicts of Interest: The authors declare no conflict of interest.

References

1. Kilbas, A.A.; Srivastava, H.M.; Trujillo, J.J. Theory and Applications of Fractional Differential Equations. In *North-Holland Mathematics Studies*; Elsevier Science B.V.: Amsterdam, The Netherlands, 2006; Volume 204.
2. Podlubny, I. Fractional differential equations. An introduction to fractional derivatives, fractional differential equations, to methods of their solution and some of their applications. In *Mathematics in Science and Engineering*; Academic Press, Inc.: San Diego, CA, USA, 1999; Volume 198.
3. Anastassiou, G.A. Nabla discrete fractional calculus and nabla inequalities. *Math. Comput. Model.* **2010**, *51*, 562–571. [CrossRef]
4. Shah, K.; Khan, R.A. Existence and uniqueness results to a coupled system of fractional order boundary value problems by topological degree theory. *Numer. Funct. Anal. Optim.* **2016**, *37*, 887–899. [CrossRef]
5. Shatanawi, W.; Boutiara, A.; Abdo, M.S.; Jeelani, M.B.; Abodayeh, K. Nonlocal and multiple-point fractional boundary value problem in the frame of a generalized Hilfer derivative. *Adv. Differ. Equ.* **2021**, 1–19. [CrossRef]
6. Wang, J.; Zhou, Y.; Wei, W. Study in fractional differential equations by means of topological degree methods. *Numer. Funct. Anal. Optim.* **2012**, *33*, 216–238. [CrossRef]
7. Khan, Z.A.; Khan, A.; Abdeljawad, T.; Khan, H. *Computational Analysis of Fractional Order Imperfect Testing Infection Disease Model*; World Scientific Publishing Co. Pte Ltd.: Singapore, 2022. [CrossRef]
8. Alzabut, J.; Grace, S.R.; Santra, S.S.; Chhatria, G.N. Asymptotic and oscillatory behaviour of third order non-linear differential equations with canonical operator and mixed neutral terms. *Qual. Theory Dyn. Syst.* **2023**, *22*, 1–15. [CrossRef]
9. Palanisamy, A.; Alzabut, J.; Muthulakshmi, V.; Santra, S.S.; Nonlaopon, K. Oscillation results for a fractional partial differential system with damping and forcing terms. *AIMS Math.* **2023**, *8*, 4261–4279. [CrossRef]
10. Altanji, M.; Chhatria, G.N.; Santra, S.S.; Scapellato, A. Oscillation criteria for sublinear and superlinear first-order difference equations of neutral type with several delays. *AIMS Math.* **2022**, *7*, 17670–17684. [CrossRef]
11. Alzabut, J.; Agarwal, R.P.; Grace, S.R.; Jonnalagadda, J.M.; Selvam, A.G.M.; Wang, C. A Survey on the Oscillation of Solutions for Fractional Difference Equations. *Mathematics* **2022**, *10*, 894. [CrossRef]
12. Goodrich, C.; Peterson, A.C. *Discrete Fractional Calculus*; Springer: Cham, Switzerland, 2015.
13. Abdalla, B.; Abodayeh, K.; Abdeljawad, T.; Alzabut, J. New oscillation criteria for forced nonlinear fractional difference equations. *Vietnam J. Math.* **2017**, *45*, 609–618. [CrossRef]
14. Abdalla, B.; Alzabut, J.; Abdeljawad, T. On the oscillation of higher order fractional difference equations with mixed nonlinearities. *Hacet. J. Math. Stat.* **2018**, *47*, 207–217. [CrossRef]
15. Alzabut, J.O.; Abdeljawad, T. Sufficient conditions for the oscillation of nonlinear fractional difference equations. *J. Fract. Calc. Appl.* **2014**, *5*, 177–187.

16. Alzabut, J.; Abdeljawad, T.; Alrabaiah, H. Oscillation criteria for forced and damped nabla fractional difference equations. *J. Comput. Anal. Appl.* **2018**, *24*, 1387–1394.
17. Hardy, G.H.; Littlewood, J.E.; Polya, G. *Inequalities*; Reprint of the 1952 Edition; Cambridge Mathematical Library, Cambridge University Press: Cambridge, UK, 1988.

MDPI AG
Grosspeteranlage 5
4052 Basel
Switzerland
Tel.: +41 61 683 77 34

Axioms Editorial Office
E-mail: axioms@mdpi.com
www.mdpi.com/journal/axioms

9 783725 823598